VOLUME 1

LIFE OF CHRIST

God's Word for the *Biblically-Inept*™ SERIES

CARTOONS BY
Reverend Fun
(Dennis "Max" Hengeveld)
Dennis is a graphic de-
signer for Gospel Films and
the author of *Has
Anybody Seen My Locust?*
His cartoons can
be seen worldwide at
www.reverendfun.com.

To schedule author appearances, write:
Author Appearances
Starburst Publishers
P.O. Box 4123
Lancaster, Pennsylvania 17604
(717) 293-0939

www.starburstpublishers.com

CREDITS:
Cover design by David Marty Design
Text design and composition by John Reinhardt Book Design
Illustrations by Melissa A. Burkhart and Bruce Burkhart
Cartoons by Dennis "Max" Hengeveld

Unless otherwise noted, or paraphrased by the author, all Scripture quotations are from the New International Version of The Holy Bible.

First Printing, March 2000

ISBN: 1-892016-23-0
Library of Congress Number 99-67256

Printed in the United States of America

Life of Christ, Volume 2
God's Word for the Biblically-Inept™

Robert C. Girard

TITLE CODE: GWLC2

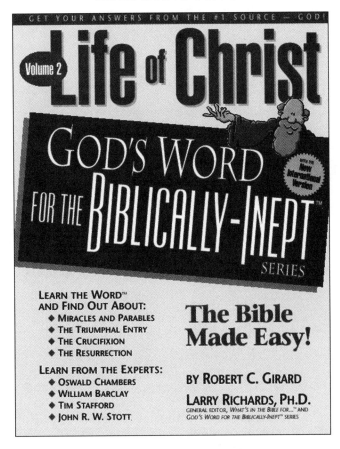

Life of Christ, Volume 2, begins with events recorded in Matthew 16. Read about Jesus' transfiguration, his miracles and parables, triumphal ride through Jerusalem, capture in the Garden of Gethsemane, and his trial, crucifixion, resurrection, and ascension.

The eleventh release in the popular *God's Word for the Biblically-Inept™* series covers how to be great in the kingdom of God, what Jesus meant when he called himself the light of the world, and what makes up real worship.

(trade paper) ISBN 1892016397 $16.95 Available Fall 2000

● **Learn more at www.biblicallyinept.com** ●

READ THIS PAGE BEFORE YOU READ THIS BOOK . . .

Welcome to the *God's Word for the Biblically-Inept™* series. If you find reading the Bible over whelming, baffling, and frustrating, then this Revolutionary Commentary™ is for you!

Each page of the series is organized for easy reading with icons, sidebars, and bullets to make the Bible's message easy to understand. *God's Word for the Biblically-Inept™* series includes opinions and insights from Bible experts of all kinds, so you get various opinions on Bible teachings—not just one!

There are more *God's Word for the Biblically-Inept™* titles on the way. The following is a list of available books. (See page v for ordering information.) We have assigned each title an abbreviated **title code**. This code along with page numbers is incorporated in the text **throughout the series**, allowing easy reference from one title to another.

God's Word for the Biblically-Inept™ Series

Announcing Our New Series!!!

What's in the Bible for . . .™

From the creators of the *God's Word for the Biblically-Inept*™ series comes the innovative *What's in the Bible for . . .*™ series. Scripture has certain things to say to certain people, but without a guide, hunting down *all* of what the Bible has to say to you can be overwhelming. Borrowing the user-friendly format of the *God's Word for the Biblically-Inept*™ series, this new series spotlights those passages and themes of Scripture that are relevant to particular groups of people. Whether you're young or old, married or single, male or female, this series will simplify the very important process of applying the Bible to your life.

What's in the Bible for . . .™ Women—*Georgia Curtis Ling*　　**WBFW**
(trade paper) ISBN 1892016109 **$16.95**

What's in the Bible for . . . ™ Mothers—*Judy Bodmer*　　**WBFM**
(trade paper) ISBN 1892016265 **$16.95**

What's in the Bible for . . . ™ Teens—*Mark and Jeanette Littleton*　　**WBFT**
(trade paper) ISBN 1892016052 **$16.95** (Available Fall 2000)

●　**Learn more at www.biblicallyinept.com**　●

Purchasing Information

www.starburstpublishers.com

Books are available from your favorite bookstore, either from current stock or special order. To assist bookstores in locating your selection, be sure to give title, author, and ISBN. If unable to purchase from a bookstore, you may order direct from STARBURST PUBLISHERS. When ordering please enclose full payment plus shipping and handling as follows:

Post Office (4th class)
$3.00 with a purchase of up to $20.00
$4.00 ($20.01–$50.00)
5% of purchase price for purchases of $50.01 and up

United Parcel Service (UPS)
$4.50 (up to $20.00)
$6.00 ($20.01–$50.00)
7% ($50.01 and up)

Canada
$5.00 (up to $35.00)
%15 ($35.01 and up)

Overseas
$5.00 (up to $25.00)
20% ($25.01 and up)

Payment in U.S. funds only. Please allow two to three weeks minimum (longer overseas) for delivery. Make checks payable to and mail to:

Starburst Publishers®
P.O. Box 4123
Lancaster, PA 17604

Credit card orders may be placed by calling 1-800-441-1456, Mon–Fri, 8:30 A.M. to 5:30 P.M. Eastern Standard Time. Prices are subject to change without notice. Catalogs are available for a 9 x 12 self-addressed envelope with four first-class stamps.

CHAPTERS AT A GLANCE

PART III: Galilee: Battle for Home Turf

ILLUSTRATIONS

INTRODUCTION

Welcome to *Life of Christ, Volume 1—God's Word for the Biblically-Inept*™. This is a REVOLUTIONARY COMMENTARY™ designed to uncomplicate the Bible. We have done our best to make it easy and fun to discover what's in this amazing book that has had such an enormous influence on the culture in which we live. We intend to change your outlook on the Bible forever. You *will* Learn the Word™.

To Gain Your Confidence

Life of Christ, Volume 1—God's Word for the Biblically-Inept is designed to make the Bible user-friendly. You can be sure I have tried to take a sound educational approach. I've also put a lot of effort into keeping things simple, yet allowing you to participate in an exciting adventure of enlightenment and joy when you discover what the Bible is all about (see John 15:11). In trying to explain, writers sometimes make it complicated. I have tried to make it uncomplicated.

Working with me to keep my writing clear and understandable, as "first responder" on the scene to rescue me from being **obtuse**, and doing valuable research, has been my best friend and most honest critic, my wife, Audrey.

Audrey and I sat beside a young Jewish woman on a flight from Phoenix to Los Angeles. When she asked what I did for a living, I answered that I wrote commentary on the Bible. She asked what I meant by "commentary." I told her I write to explain the meaning of the Bible. Her response startled me and, ever since, has been a burr under my saddle whenever I sit down to write. She asked, "What's wrong with the *real* thing?"

The best source of information needed to understand the Bible is the Bible itself—"the *real* thing." That's why I often use other Bible references to shed light on Bible statements I'm trying to explain. The Bible is its own best commentary.

Let's Get Started

(Let's Get Started)

> **Matthew 1:1** A record of the genealogy of Jesus Christ . . .

(Verse of Scripture)

obtuse: *difficult to understand*

(What?)

Remember This . . .

(Remember This)

What Others are Saying:

(What Others Are Saying)

THE BIG PICTURE

Matthew 1:1–17
Matthew lists the generations from Abraham to Christ

(The Big Picture)

b.c.: *Before Christ*

a.d.: *Latin phrase* anno domini, *meaning "in the year of our Lord"*

EARLY CHURCH LIFE:

(Early Church Life)

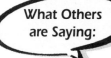

What Others are Saying:

KEY POINT

When we acknowledge our guilt and trust Jesus as Savior, God forgives our sins freely and completely.

(Key Point)

Madeleine L'Engle: I'm particularly grateful that I was allowed to read my Bible as I read my other books, to read it as story, that story which is a revelation of truth. People are sometimes kept from reading the Bible itself by what they are taught about it.[1]

What Is The Bible?

In the front pages of most Bibles you will find a table of contents listing the 66 books that form the Bible, with page numbers. The list will be in two sections—an "Old" Testament list of 39 books and a "New" Testament list of 27 books. The Old Testament was written by different authors and poets, mostly of Hebrew heritage, between 1400 and 400 b.c. The New Testament was written in 60 years between 40 and 100 a.d.

Centuries later, scholars divided the books of the Bible into chapters and verses to make it easier to locate its stories and teachings. Thus John 3:16 indicates the third chapter of the book written by John and the 16th verse of that chapter.

Old Testament And New Testament— What's The Difference?

The Old Testament deals with events before the birth of Jesus Christ that mostly center on the nation of Israel. The New Testament tells about the birth, life, teachings, death, and resurrection of a historical person named Jesus, and about the movement begun by the people who believed Jesus was the Son of God.

Henry H. Halley: The Old Testament is an account of a Nation. The New Testament is an account of a Man. The nation was founded and nurtured by God to bring the Man into the world.[2]

The Life Of Jesus Christ

The person whose story is told in the New Testament is Jesus, also known as "Christ," "Jesus Christ," "the Lord Jesus Christ," and "Jesus of Nazareth." If the stories and teachings of Jesus recorded in the New Testament are true (and millions of Christians worldwide stake their lives on the belief that they are!) then Jesus was the most unusual person who ever lived. The study of his life and accomplishments is one of the most important pursuits in which anyone can engage.

Life of Christ, Volume 1 begins before Jesus is born, describes what we know about his childhood, and details his ministry and teachings, including many of his parables. *Life of Christ, Volume 2*

---

begins with the events described in Matthew 16 and discusses Jesus' final teachings, his crucifixion, and resurrection.

The Search For The Historical Jesus

Dozens of scholars, writers, and artists have set about to compose their own interpretations of the life of Jesus Christ. They have based their writings on available evidence not only from the New Testament but also from **archaeological** research, visits to the Holy Land (Israel), study of early Christian writings and those of other Middle Eastern religions, along with ample doses of personal intuition and imagination. In 1906 in a book titled *The Quest of the Historical Jesus,* missionary-statesman Albert Schweitzer reviewed the history of those scholarly attempts to "discover" Jesus. He concluded that while the last 200 years of investigation and scholarship had produced a wide range of descriptions of Jesus' life and personality, almost all of these descriptions bore "a suspicious resemblance" to the person who wrote the story rather than to the real Christ whose story is told in the Bible![3]

archaeological: scientific study of material remains of past human life and activities

---

John G. Stackhouse Jr.: Skeptics dismiss Jesus as a lunatic, a charlatan, a troubled poet, or an impotent revolutionary—or embrace him as an ironical, detached, innocuous fellow such as they see themselves to be. Rationalists who do not discard him discover him to be logical, sensible, and practical. Liberals admire him as idealistic, brave, kind, and wise. Romantics extol him as passionate, vital, and free. Reformers revere him as bold, visionary, impatient, and forceful.[4]

What Others are Saying:

Just The Facts, Ma'am

The approach taken in this commentary is to present the facts of Jesus' story as the New Testament writers recorded them and to provide a simple explanation of those facts where necessary. When facts from the culture and history of Jesus' times can help us understand more clearly the significance of some event or report or teaching, I will share those facts too. My goal is to present a picture of Jesus accurately and simply, consistent with the way the New Testament pictures him.

KEY Outline:

Christ's Revolution
Spiritual
Social
Economic

(Key Outline)

Not everything Jesus did or said is recorded in the Bible. One New Testament writer insists that if everything were told, *"the whole world would not have room for the books that would have to be written"* (John 21:25). So many thousands were touched and changed by his life, and his was a life Bible

Something to Ponder

(Something to Ponder)

Dig Deeper

(Dig Deeper)

gospels: *biblical stories of good news*

Who's Who

(Who's Who)

the 12: *original group of disciples who became apostles*

apostle: *ambassador, one sent on a mission*

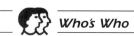

☞ GO TO:

Luke 5:27–28 (tax collector)

Matthew 10:3 (the 12)

1 Corinthians 15:3–8; Acts 1:8; 2:32; 5:32; 10:39 (eyewitness)

(Go To)

writers insist began before time (John 1:1) and will continue forever (Isaiah 9:6–7).

The Four Gospels—Why Four "Lives Of Christ"?

My daughter, Christine, joined a "Reconciliation Walk" team for two weeks on its way through central Turkey. In most towns the reconciliation walkers were welcomed with typical generous Mid-Eastern hospitality. As they shared tea with a Muslim pastor in one city, he posed a question Muslims often ask: "We have only one holy book, the Koran. Why do you Christians have four different stories of the life of Christ?" He was referring to the four **gospels**—Matthew, Mark, Luke, and John.

The language barrier made answering the question challenging. Christi spoke very little Turkish, and the Muslim spoke very little English. In a flash of insight, she held up her camera and proceeded to pantomime taking four photographs of the pastor, each from a different angle around the room. The Muslim leader got the point: The four gospels represent four pictures (angles, perspectives) of the same person—Jesus Christ.

Author, Author!

The four New Testament versions of the life of Christ were written by three Jewish men and one Greek. None includes a byline identifying the author. But from earliest times, the church has attributed the four to Matthew, Mark, Luke, and John. These accounts do not pretend to be objective. These men are convinced that the Jesus about whom they write is exactly what he claimed— Son of God, Savior, Messiah, King. They are not writing to encourage speculation and further research about who Jesus is. They know who he is. And each aims to help readers know Jesus of Nazareth. The contents of their books are not inventions to spark a Christ-legend. Each is carefully composed from eyewitness testimony and well-researched fact.

Matthew's Life Of Christ

AUTHOR: MATTHEW: Also known as Levi. A <u>tax collector</u> who worked for the Roman government before Jesus invited him to join his team. As one of **the 12** he spent three years with Jesus and was appointed by him as his first **apostle**. He was an <u>eyewitness</u> to most of the events of which he writes.

TARGET: The Jewish people. To prove Jesus was the promised **Messiah**, Matthew carefully documents Jesus' fulfillment of Old Testament prophecies.

DATE: Written between 50–70 A.D., no way to tell exactly. Early Christians considered Matthew's to be the first of the four authoritative accounts of Jesus' life.

Messiah: Hebrew for Christ, God-sent deliverer

Papias: Matthew collected the sayings of Jesus in the Hebrew tongue.[5]

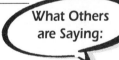
What Others are Saying:

Mark's Life Of Christ

☞ GO TO:

AUTHOR: JOHN MARK: Also called "John" or "Mark." Companion to Paul, Barnabas, and Peter. Mark was an eyewitness in a limited sense. He was personally acquainted with Jesus and present at key points in the story he tells (see Mark 14:51–52). Peter was Mark's major source of information.

Acts 12:25; Philemon 24 (Companion to Paul)

Acts 15:39 (Barnabas)

TARGET: Primarily Romans and others unfamiliar with the Old Testament or biblical **theology**. Pictures Jesus as a man of action and authority—the kind of man who would appeal to the pragmatic, militaristic Romans.

1 Peter 5:13 (Peter)

theology: study of God

DATE: Probably written near the time of Peter's **martyrdom** in Rome, 68 A.D.

martyrdom: killed for being a Christian

Papias: Mark, having become the interpreter of Peter, wrote down accurately, though not indeed in order, whatever he remembered of the things said or done by Christ.[6]

What Others are Saying:

Luke's Life Of Christ

☞ GO TO:

AUTHOR: LUKE: A well-educated Greek that Paul calls *"our dear friend Luke, the doctor"* (Colossians 4:14). Authored both the third gospel and Acts. His use of medical language indicates the writing of a physician (and his writing was readable!). He was Paul's companion, even in jail. Luke was not an eyewitness. He probably first heard the story from Paul and his missionary team. He wrote his Life of Christ after thorough research, mostly done in Caesarea where Paul was imprisoned for two years.

Acts 13:2–3, 5; 15:40–16:2, 10 (missionary team)

Luke 1:3 (thorough research)

Acts 23:23–24; 24:27 (Caesarea)

☞ **GO TO:**

Acts 28:30–31
(house arrest)

TARGET: Greeks and other Gentiles, like himself. His Life of Christ focuses on Jesus' relationships with all sorts of people—especially women, the poor, and oppressed.

DATE: Written between 58 A.D., while Paul was in jail in Caesarea, and 63 A.D., when Paul was under house arrest in Rome.

What Others are Saying:

William Barclay: The gospel according to St. Luke has been called the loveliest book in the world. . . . It would not be far wrong to say that the third Gospel is the best Life of Christ ever written.[7]

John's Life Of Christ

AUTHOR: JOHN: An "insider"—one of the 12 who was with Jesus for three years. When Jesus called him, John was a partner in a fishing business on the Sea of Galilee with his brother James and their father, Zebedee. Like the other Life-of-Christ authors in the New Testament, John never identifies himself by name. He calls himself *"the disciple whom Jesus loved"* (John 21:20–24).

☞ **GO TO:**

Matthew 4:21–22
(fishing business)

☞ **Check It Out:**

John 2:12–22

(Check It Out)

TARGET: The whole world. The heartbeat of his writing may be summed up in a sentence called "the golden text of the Bible"—John 3:16: Because God loves the world of human beings, he gave his Son so that whoever puts their faith in him might escape spiritual disaster and live forever!

DATE: John was the last of the original apostles to write—between 75–100 A.D.

What Others are Saying:

synoptic: summary, tell the story in similar fashion

Clement of Alexandria: John . . . being urged by friends and inspired by the Spirit, composed a spiritual gospel.[8]

The Gospel Quartet In Harmony

This commentary will use all four gospels—Matthew, Mark, Luke, and John—to tell the story. The first three are called **synoptic** gospels. That is, while each author has distinctive purposes in mind, all three take the same basic approach to telling the story. John marches to a slightly different drumbeat. He focuses more on Christ as a person and the teachings and signs that prove Jesus is the Son of God. The first three report many of the same incidents. A few are reported by all four. My approach will be to collect the facts from all four and focus on the events of Jesus' life in chronological order (which is not always easy to figure out). Watch for the Gospel Quartet in Harmony icon, which tells when and where an event is reported by more than one writer.

The Original Language Of The Good News

Archaeological discoveries and evidence from the New Testament show the **Jews** were trilingual:

1. Aramaic had once been the language of the aristocracy, but by Jesus' time it had filtered down to the lower classes and was used in daily conversation.

2. Hebrew was the language of religious life at synagogues and the Temple and was also used in daily conversation.

3. Greek, like English today, was the universal language spoken all over the world. Alexander the Great (who preceded the Romans in conquest of the area) had invented a language called *koine* (koy-nay) or "common" Greek. As his empire spread, Alexander instituted the use of koine Greek from Europe to Asia. Most Jews were fluent in it. It was the language for interaction with Roman authorities and trade with foreigners. Palestinian Jews also spoke and wrote Greek in their communication with each other.

There is evidence Jesus was fluent in all three languages. The New Testament was originally written in common Greek so as to be read and understood by people all over the **Roman Empire**. By Jesus' time scholars believe much of the Old Testament had been copied onto papyrus scrolls. It is likely the gospel writers used papyrus as well.

Why Use The New International Version (NIV)?

Today English-speaking people have a wide range of Bible translations and paraphrases from which to choose. I used several in preparation of this book. In addition, I often looked at verses in the original language. At the same time I tried to write for the person who is new at finding his or her way around the Bible. That's why we use the New International Version (NIV) of the Bible. It is a scholarly translation that accurately expresses the original Scriptures in clear and contemporary English and, at the same time, faithfully communicates the thoughts of the original writers.

How To Use *The Life of Christ—God's Word For The Biblically-Inept*™

Study Questions

(Study Questions)

CHAPTER WRAP-UP

(Chapter Summary)

Sit down with this book and your Bible.

- Start the book at chapter 1.
- As you work through each chapter, read the accompanying verses, or the CHECK IT OUT passages in your Bible.
- Use the sidebars loaded with icons and helpful information to give you a knowledge boost.
- Answer the Study Questions and review with the Chapter Wrap-Up.
- Then go on to the next chapter. It's simple!

This book contains a variety of special features that will help you learn. Here they are, with a brief explanation of each.

Sections and Icons	What's It For?
CHAPTER HIGHLIGHTS	the most prominent points of the chapter
GOSPEL QUARTET	all the places where this story is reported
Let's Get Started	a chapter warm-up
Verse of Scripture	what you came for—the Bible
THE BIG PICTURE	summarizes long passages
Commentary	my thoughts on what the verses mean
CHECK IT OUT:	Bible passages to look up
GO TO:	other Bible verses to help you better understand (underlined in text)
What?	the meaning of a word (bold in text)
KEY POINT	major point of the chapter
Key Outline	mini-outline of information
What Others are Saying:	if you don't believe me, listen to the experts
Illustrations	a picture is worth a thousand words
Time Lines	shows how events fit in history
Act of the Holy Spirit	indicates God's personal intervention in people's lives identified as the work of the Holy Spirit
Who's Who	identifies key people
Something to Ponder	interesting points to get you thinking
Remember This . . .	don't forget this
Dig Deeper	find out more from the Bible
Kingdom of God	a taste of the kingdom; facts and teachings related to God's reign in persons and the community of faith
Early Church Life	practices and principles of the church in the first century
Study Questions	questions to get you discussing, studying, and digging deeper
CHAPTER WRAP-UP	the most prominent points revisited

Jesus said the Spirit will *"guide"* us in discovery of *"all truth"* (John 16:13). It helps to read and study the Bible with an open heart, expecting God to light up your life in some surprising and enriching ways.

Remember This . . .

A Word About Words

There are several interchangeable terms: Scripture, Scriptures, Holy Scriptures, Word, Word of God, God's Word, Gospel. All these mean the same thing and come under the broad heading called the Bible. I may use each of these terms at various times.

The word "Lord" in the Old Testament refers to Yahweh, the God of Israel. In the New Testament it refers to Jesus Christ, God's Son.

The Ultimate Purpose Of A "Life Of Christ"

ACT OF THE HOLY SPIRIT

Real faith is a miracle from the Holy Spirit

(Act of the Holy Spirit)

The Bible was never given by God as an end in itself. And knowing what the Bible says and means is not all there is to being an authentic God-worshiper. The Bible is a means to an end. The end and goal of learning God's Word is to know God. The reason for learning about Jesus Christ is that by knowing him we can know his Father, God.

When we maintain an openness about Jesus of Nazareth, God rewards us with understanding. Many types of people can profit from reading about Jesus:

- New believers just beginning in their new way of life
- Untaught or untrained **believers**—new and old
- Seekers of God and truth who have not fully embraced him
- Respected **unbelievers**—friends, neighbors, relatives, business associates

believers: *Christians, followers of Christ*

unbelievers: *don't yet trust Christ as Savior*

Both volumes of *Life of Christ—God's Word for the Biblically-Inept*™ speak to such people.

Expect to be surprised and excited about the knowledge you are about to gain. No one who ever lived is as surprising and exciting as Jesus Christ.

Here's a Sample Page!

Bible Quote: This is where you'll read a quote from the Bible.

> **James 1:5** If any of you lacks wisdom, he should ask God, who gives generously to all without finding fault and it will be given to him.

Decisions, Decisions: In Or Out?

James, the brother of Jesus, is writing to the new believers who were scattered about the Roman world (see GWBI, pages 213–214) when they fled from persecution. James knows that godly wisdom is a great gift. He gives a simple plan to get it: if you need wisdom, ask for it. God will give it to us.

Up 'til now we've concentrated on finding the wind for the sails of your drifting marriage and overcoming marital problems. But you may be the reader who is shaking her head, thinking that I just don't understand what you're going through. You can't take the abuse any longer; you've forgiven the **infidelity** time after time; and in order for you and your children to survive, you see no alternative but divorce.

So let me urge you to reconsider. You believe your husband could... get out a... abuse sec... ...nues, ...ep the ...ing to you; they are also harmful to your children's physical and emotional state.

When you feel you've depleted all of your options, continue to ask God for wisdom in order to have the knowledge to make the right decisions. Wise women seek God. God is the source of wisdom and wisdom is found in Christ and the Word.

Gary Chapman, Ph.D.: Is there hope for women who suffer physical abuse from their husbands? Does reality living offer any genuine hope? I believe the answer to those questions is yes.[6]

Give It Away

You don't have to be a farmer to understand what the Apostle Paul wrote to the Corinthian church (see illustration, page 143). A picture is worth a thousand words, and Paul is painting a masterpiece. He reminds us of what any smart farmer knows: in order to produce a bountiful harvest, he has to plan for it,

Commentary: This is where you'll read commentary about the biblical quote.

"What?": When you see a word in bold, go to the sidebar for a definition.

Go To: When you see a word or phrase that's underlined, go to the sidebar for a biblical cross-reference.

infidelity: sexual unfaithfulness of a spouse

☞ **GO TO:**

Psalm 111:10 (source)

Remember This . . .

What Others are Saying:

What Others Are Saying: This is where you'll read what an expert has to say about the subject at hand.

MEN OF POWER LESSONS IN MIGHT AND MISSTEPS 9

127

Feature with icon in the sidebar: Thoughout the book you will see sections of text with corresponding icons in the sidebar. See the chart on page xviii for a description of all the features in this book.

Part One

GIFT CHILD

"Why can't you just be like that Jesus boy in your class?
He always behaves and has his homework done on time."

1 BREAKING NEWS

CHAPTER HIGHLIGHTS

- The Long Wait
- Advance Man
- Mission Possible
- No Impossibilities
- Baby Baptist

Let's Get Started

In **5 B.C.** two special baby boys were born in the land of Israel. They were <u>cousins</u>. One was born into the priestly clan of Aaron. The other, though born into poverty, was from the royal line of David. They were born six months apart. An angel sent from God predicted both births. Each set of parents was told that, in the plan of Almighty God, their son was slated to be a man of destiny.

Although each would have a very short time to minister, these two men were part of a strategy to bring the grace of God to all people. The lives of both would end violently in their early 30s. The first would be beheaded. The second would be crucified. The first would be known as the greatest prophet ever born. The second would be known as the Son of God—"the One and Only." The first would introduce the second to the world, then fade from the scene. The second would sit on the throne of a never-ending kingdom. In the Bible, the life of Christ begins with the birth stories of these two men whose lives and destinies were so intertwined.

> **John 1:14** We have seen his glory, the glory of the One and Only, who came from the Father, full of grace and truth.

Israel's Long Wait

When *"the One and Only"* was born into the human family in the person of Jesus of Nazareth, Israel was under the thumb of another in the long series of foreign armies that oppressed its citi-

☞ **Check It Out:**

Luke 1:5–80

5 B.C.: Dyonysius Exiguus, author of our calendar, goofed slightly in his calculations

☞ **GO TO:**

Luke 1:36 (cousins)

zens for seven centuries (see chart below). The Romans ruled with a fist of iron. They brought with them such big-government "blessings" as heavy taxation, poverty, and martial law. Of all the Roman Empire's conquered peoples, the Jews were the most zealous for freedom. They were programmed by the promises of God to consider only national sovereignty and personal liberty the norm. Centuries of oppression had failed to take the edge off their yearning to be free.

700 Years of Conquest and Occupation

Empire	Leader	Date	Results for Jews	Scripture
Assyrian	Shalmaneser V	722 B.C.	**Israel** conquered, exiled to Assyria or **mixed** with foreigners	2 Kings 17
Babylonian	Nebuchadnezzar	586 B.C.	**Judah** conquered, exiled to Babylon, Jerusalem destroyed	2 Kings 24–25; 2 Chronicles 36
Persian	Cyrus	539 B.C.	Three groups return home, begin rebuilding	Daniel 5:30; 2 Chronicles 36: 22–23
Greek	Alexander	332 B.C.	Occupation, learned Greek language; **Hellenization**	Daniel 8:8–12; 11:2–4; Ezekiel 26:12–14 (prophecies)
Roman	Julius Caesar	49 B.C.	Occupation, oppression, cruelty	Daniel 2:33, 40 (prophecy)

Please, Mr. Caesar, I Don't Want To Go!

Of all the places a Roman soldier could be assigned, Israel was the least desirable. It was the one place in Caesar's world where revolt or insurrection was ready to boil over in open violence at the least expected moment. It was wisest for the occupation army to expect riot or terrorism at any time—especially on feast days.

Come, O Come, Immanuel!

Israel's obsession with national sovereignty rose from the belief that God would send a deliverer from the King David's royal family to drive the conquerors into the sea and establish an eternal government that would end slavery, poverty, and oppression forever and bring Israel to prominence among the nations. Ancient prophecies, messages from God about the present and future, fanned the fire of hope. God himself created the yearning for freedom and national sovereignty by promising the Messiah! In Hebrew *Messiah* means "Anointed One." In Greek the word is translated "Christ."

Samples of Old Testament Promises of the Coming King

Genesis 49:10—The nations will obey the scepter-bearer ("**Shiloh**," KJV) a member of **Judah**'s clan.

Deuteronomy 18:18—God will give Israel a prophet like Moses (see GWMB, pages 71–90) who will speak God's Words.

2 Samuel 17:12–16—One of King David's offspring will reign forever. (Read about David in GWMB, pages 91–106.)

Isaiah 7:14—A young woman will bear a son who will be called **Immanuel**.

Isaiah 9:6–7—A native son of Israel will establish an eternal kingdom of peace, justice, and righteousness.

Isaiah 61:1–4—**Anointed** One will end oppression, mend heartbreak, free captives, proclaim God's **favor**.

Ezekiel 37:21–28—Israel will be restored to its homeland and a king called **David** will rule forever.

God's Silence Takes Its Toll

It had been 400 years since God had sent a prophet to Israel with a message. During the wait, some **Israelites** gave up hope and lived in disillusioned depression. The Pharisees, a vocal religious party committed to the traditions of the Jewish religion, settled for strict rule keeping and boring discussion of religious traditions and regulations. An arrogant and corrupt class of high priests ran the Temple. They were consumed with maintaining their positions of wealth and political influence by collaborating with the Roman occupation government. Seven centuries under the boots of the conquerors had made political maneuvering and intrigue a way of life. Violent gangs of **Zealots** conducted guerilla warfare against the occupation forces and sometimes against the high priests, believing they could bring the changes God promised without God's help.

A minority of priests and ordinary citizens still hung on to the ancient promises, followed the rituals, and attended the festivals because these things were part of a **covenant** with God they considered absolutely essential to meaningful living. These people lived daily in anticipation of the coming Deliverer. Every child conceived was prized as a potential Messiah. (Even in our day, Jewish families often name their first son David in hopes he might be the Messiah.)

Dig Deeper

Shiloh: One to whom tribute/obedience belongs

Judah: descended from third son of Jacob, father of Israel's leading tribe

Immanuel: God with us

Anointed: chosen for kingly, priestly, or prophetic authority

favor: grace, loving-kindness, mercy

David: figurative title for Messiah-King

KEY POINT

Israel's intense yearning for sovereignty was fueled by God's promise of the Messiah-Deliverer.

Israelites: Jews descended from Israel (also known as Jacob)

Zealots: party committed to violent overthrow of Romans

covenant: agreement or contract

Oswald Chambers: Hope without faith loses itself in vague speculation, but the hope of the saints transfigured by faith grows not faint, but endures "as seeing him who is invisible."[1]

> **Luke 1:5–7** In the time of Herod king of Judea there was a priest named Zechariah, who belonged to the priestly division of Abijah; his wife Elizabeth was also a descendant of Aaron. Both of them were upright in the sight of God, observing all the Lord's commandments and regulations blamelessly. But they had no children, because Elizabeth was barren; and they were both well along in years.

well along in years: no retirement from priesthood—Zechariah may have been very old

upright/blamelessly: faithful, not sinless

major festivals: Passover, Unleavened Bread, Pentecost, Trumpets (Rosh Hashanah), Atonement (Yom Kippur), Tabernacles. Others added later: Lights (Hanukkah), Esther (Purim).

The Advance Man Cometh . . . But When?

A Jewish man named Zechariah and his wife Elizabeth were childless and *"**well along in years**."* They had given up hope of conceiving. Because they and the people around them believed faithful servants of God would be blessed with children, this was hard to understand. They had been faithful. To face the "declining years" without children and grandchildren to care for them was disappointing and cause for anxiety.

Still, they were two of the "good guys" who kept the hope of the promised Messiah alive in their hearts. Luke 1:6 reports:

- They were **upright** in God's sight.
- They observed all God's commandments and all the ceremonial regulations **blamelessly.**

 Who's Who

ZECHARIAH: Zechariah was a priest. He was a member of the priestly clan (see Exodus 28:1) that led worship at the Temple in Jerusalem. There were too many for them all to serve at one time (except at the **major festivals** described in Leviticus 23), so they served on a roster system (2 Chronicles 24:1–6). Priests were divided into 24 divisions. Each division served at the Temple for one week twice a year. The division of Abijah was the eighth division (1 Chronicles 24:10). Zechariah was part of team Abijah.

Who's Who

ELIZABETH: Elizabeth was Zechariah's wife. She too was a descendant of Aaron, the priestly clan. As a priest Zechariah was required by law to marry an Israelite virgin (see Leviticus 21:13–14). For her also to be from priestly stock was considered, for the priest, a special spiritual benefit.

Year of the Rat

Luke carefully documents his Life of Christ by telling us who was in charge of what when it happened—emperors, kings, governors, high priests, and so on. The incidents in Luke 1 took place during the reign of **Herod** king of Judah (see illustration, page 40). Herod was not a nice man. He was an unmitigated rat!

His personal crimes look like the criminal record of a felon on the FBI's Ten Most Wanted list! He was guilty of these dastardly deeds:

- Count 1: Personally drowning his brother-in-law, the Jewish High Priest
- Count 2: Ordering the murder of his mother-in-law
- Count 3: Ordering the murder of his favorite wife, Miriamne
- Count 4: Ordering the murder of two of his sons while on his deathbed
- Count 5: Ordering the slaughter of the baby boys of Bethlehem

In addition to his crimes, Herod built a palace for himself adjacent to the **Temple Mount** in Jerusalem and an amphitheater outside the city where athletes competed in sports events stark naked. Most Jews hated him.

But Herod did one thing that pleased the Jews: He tore down the meager temple built 500 years earlier by Hebrew refugees returning from exile in Babylon and replaced it with a temple twice as big and more splendid than the one originally built by King Solomon in Israel's glory days (970–931 B.C.). Herod's temple took 40 years to build, and the project wasn't finished until 24 years after his death. The rebuilt temple is the site of many incidents reported in the four New Testament gospels, including the incident which begins in Luke 1:5.

HEROD: Alias: Herod the Great (see illustration, page 40). In 37 B.C. the Roman Senate crowned him king of Judea, Samaria, and Idumea, at the urging of **Caesar Augustus**. Herod, who was not a Jew but an **Idumean**, took control of Jerusalem by laying siege to it. He was a cruel and ruthless tyrant.

Remember This . . .

Herod: *"the Great," first of NT Herods*

Temple Mount: *Mount Zion, site of all Jewish temples*

Who's Who

Caesar Augustus: *also known as Octavian*

Idumean: *person from region south of Judea*

☞ **GO TO:**

Proverbs 16:33; 18:18
(lot)

Revelation 5:8
(prayers rising)

lot: *drawing straws or throwing dice to settle an issue*

holy place: *second most sacred room in the Temple*

altar of incense: *stand for burning incense*

veil: *thick curtain barring the way into the Holy of Holies*

Holy of Holies: *most sacred room, housing the Ark of the Covenant*

☞ **GO TO:**

Numbers 6:1–21
(teetotaler)

Luke 1:39–44
(from birth)

Matthew 5:9;
2 Corinthians 5:20
(peacemaker)

teetotaler: *person who abstains from alcohol*

from birth: *only person in the NT filled with the Spirit from birth*

evangelist: *proclaimer of good news*

Sweet-Smelling Serendipity

During a priestly division's period of service at the Temple, specific tasks were assigned by **lot** (Luke 1:9). One of the most honored jobs was burning incense, which represented <u>prayers rising</u> to God. Zechariah won the coveted assignment. When it came time to burn incense, the old priest was left alone inside the **holy place** in the Temple. All the others were outside, with the other worshipers, praying. At the signal, Zechariah burned the sweet-smelling stuff on the **altar of incense** just outside the **veil** that covered the **Holy of Holies** from view. To Zechariah, this was probably the mountaintop experience of his life. But he had no idea just how high the mountaintop was going to be!

Angel At The Altar

As the sweet-smelling smoke wafted heavenward, a being straight out of heaven suddenly stood right there beside the incense altar. A bolt of terror shot through Zechariah's old frame. Nobody sees an angel without dying! (So went a popular-but-bogus maxim of the time.) Zechariah braced himself for death. But the angel's first words disarmed his fears: *"Don't be afraid, Zechariah"* (Luke 1:13). The angel wasn't there to terminate the faithful priest, but to deliver some incredible news. Imagine reading the headlines below in your newspaper:

Angelic Headlines for Zech and Liz

Prayers Answered!
  You've been praying for a child. Well, you're about to have one (Luke 1:13)!

Elizabeth to Get Pregnant!
  Imagine it! At her age (verse 13)!

It's a Boy!
  Name him *John* (verse 13).

Your Pride and Joy!
  The neighbors will celebrate with you (verse 14).

Boy Destined for Greatness!
  He'll be Billy Graham and Mother Teresa rolled into one!

  • Great in God's eyes (verse 15)

  • A **teetotaler** (verse 15)

  • A spiritual man—filled with the Holy Spirit **from birth** (verse 15)

  • A great **evangelist**—bringing people to the Lord (verse 16)

- A <u>peacemaker</u>—reconciling families (verse 17)
- A powerful prophet—<u>like Elijah</u> (verse 17)
- A guide—<u>preparing a people</u> to welcome the Lord (verse 17)

Silent Witness

To Zechariah's practical mind, this news was just too good to be true! There were limits even to what a believer like him could believe—especially considering he was an old man and his wife was no spring chicken! Zechariah's faith needed proof—so the angel gave him proof: Zechariah emerged from the Temple, speechless. Usually the incense offering was followed by a benediction for waiting worshipers. The old priest could only gesture. They concluded he'd seen a vision (Luke 1:22).

Five Faith-Enhancers for Doubting Zechariah (Luke 1:19–20)

1. The angel's name: *Gabriel*, which means "man of God."
2. The angel's position: *"I stand before God"*—he was a top angel close to God. Would an angel close to God lie?
3. The angel's authority: He was *"sent"* from God with *"this good news."*
4. The unwanted sign of the zipped lip: To keep Zechariah from questioning God's word out loud, he'd be unable to speak till baby John was born.
5. The ultimate proof: *"My words . . . will come true"* at the *"proper time."*

Honey, I'm Home!

Zechariah completed his week of Temple duties, then went home to his wife in the hills of Judea (Luke 1:39). Although speechless, Zechariah could write (verse 63). He probably wrote every detail of his experience for Elizabeth to read, including the child's name.

Surprise! Surprise! Elizabeth became pregnant. Upon discovery she was "PG," she went into five months of seclusion—not because there was any shame in pregnancy. Exactly the opposite. Among Jews childbearing was cause for celebration. To be childless was a tragedy. Some considered it punishment by God. Elizabeth had put up with put-downs from people who failed to recognize what a godly person she was. Maybe she wanted to be sure that when she told the neighbors she was pregnant, it showed!

KEY Outline:

Zechariah
Good guy

Elizabeth
Good guy's good wife

Herod
Bad guy

Gabriel
God's angel

John
Good guy and wife's good kid

John the Baptist
Good kid grown up

Remember This . . .

☞ **GO TO:**

Malachi 4:5–6; Matthew 11:13–14 (like Elijah)

Isaiah 40:3–11 (preparing a people)

Daniel 8:15–18; Luke 1:26 (Gabriel)

Isaiah 55:10–11 (will come true)

Mark 1:15; Galatians 4:4; Ephesians 1:10 (proper time)

☞ **Check It Out:**

Luke 1:26–45

KEY Outline:

Gabriel
Angel
Man of God
Top angel
Sent from God

Who's Who

highly favored: *object of God's grace (forgiveness, acceptance, giftedness)*

virgin: *no sexual contact with a man*

Remember This . . .

What Others are Saying:

Mission Possible

In the sixth month of Elizabeth's pregnancy the same angel who met Zechariah in the Temple visited the town of Nazareth in Galilee. Once again, we overhear a private conversation—this time between the angel Gabriel and a young woman named Mary (see GWWB, pages 87–101). Gabriel's greeting indicates Mary had a relationship with God that was alive and well:

- *"You . . . are **highly favored**."*
- *"The Lord is with you."*

MARY: Mary was probably in her early to mid teens. First century Jewish girls were marriageable when they reached the ripe old age of 12 years and one day. Mary was a **virgin**, unmarried, and engaged to a Nazarene named Joseph, a descendant of David, Israel's most illustrious king from whose family Christ was expected to be born.

Real Mary, Full of Grace

Disregard religious paintings picturing Mary with a halo or special glow. There is no indication she was other than an ordinary Jewish teenager who had done her spiritual homework and kept her faith alive. Nothing in the Bible suggests she was sinless.

Francis Schaeffer: When in the Renaissance Mary was painted as a real person, this was an advance over the representations of Mary in the earlier age, because the Bible tells us that Mary was a real girl and that the baby Jesus was a real baby.[2]

Get The Nursery Ready!

If the angel's greeting disturbed and amazed Mary (verse 29), she must have felt the wind knocked out of her when he got to the main message he'd come to deliver. It was enough to send any teenage girl into panic. But God's man Gabriel wisely paved the way with the encouraging word that she need not be afraid because God was on her side and was about to do her a *"high favor."* The news that changed Mary's life forever was that she was about to become pregnant and give birth to a boy to whom she was to give the name *Jesus*, meaning "Savior."

 Mary's son would be unique among all sons ever born in this world in five ways:

1. He would be *"great"*—meaning great in rank, importance, and length of life.

2. He would be known as *"the Son of the Most High"*—*"Son of"* is a Jewish idiom indicating Mary's child would be a carbon copy of his Father who is none other than *"the Most High"*—the English equivalent of *Elyon*, a Hebrew name for God.

3. God would give him the *"throne of his father David"*—his human heritage would be the royal bloodline of King David. *Father*, in this statement, means "ancestor."

4. He would be king of *"the house of Jacob"*—Israel, the Jewish nation.

5. His *"kingdom would never end"* (see GWDN, page 65).

> **Luke 1:34** "How will this be," Mary asked the angel, "since I am a virgin?"

"How Will This Be?"

Good question (Luke 1:34). Mary knows the facts of life. It will be a while before she and Joseph complete their engagement period and consummate their marriage. She has never had sex with him or any other man. Without that, how can she conceive the promised child? Mary seems to understand that conception of her special baby will take place immediately and that no man will be involved. Unlike Zechariah, who couldn't believe without further certification of the angel's prophecy (verse 18), Mary is simply puzzled about how what is about to happen is about to happen.

No problem. Gabriel answers her question with delicate reserve.

Science Of The Incarnation

Here's how the angel describes the process by which the Son of God would come into the world as a human boy-child:

1. *"The Holy Spirit will come upon you."* It is a mistake to imagine some sort of "mating" between the Holy Spirit and Mary. Jesus uses these same words to describe the entrance of the Holy Spirit into the lives of his disciples on the Day of <u>Pentecost</u> (see GWBI, page 216). It is a way of saying the conception of Jesus in the womb of the virgin was an act of God—a miracle.

2. *"The power of the Most High will overshadow you."* In Scripture, God's presence is often indicated by the appearance of an <u>overshadowing cloud</u>. The presence and power of God himself would perform a totally new act of creation in her womb to produce a *"holy"* child—free from sin of any kind.

No Impossibilities With God!

"Nothing is impossible with God," the angel said. Mary's body would be the site of a miracle. Her willingness to go along with the plan would be her greatest act of faith. She knew the risks. In the minds of neighbors and relatives pregnancy without marriage proved only one thing—adultery. Adultery was a capital offense (Deuteronomy 22:22–24). Although this punishment was seldom carried out, the law was reflected in the attitudes of the people. When Joseph found out he would try to divorce her (Matthew 1:19). Any explanation she would try to give was sure to be doubted.

In the face of seeming impossibilities and anticipated difficulties, Mary's response is a model for all who seek to know and do the will of God: *"I am the Lord's servant . . . May it be to me as you have said"* (Luke 1:38).

 GO TO:

Acts 1:8 (Pentecost)

Exodus 13:21; 14:19–20; 1 Kings 8:10–12; Isaiah 6:4 (overshadowing cloud)

ACT OF THE HOLY SPIRIT

Christ child is conceived in the womb of the virgin

KEY POINT

Nothing is impossible with God!

Remember This . . .

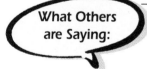
What Others are Saying:

William Barclay: Mary had learned to forget the world's commonest prayer—"Thy will be *changed*"—and to pray the world's greatest prayer—"Thy will be *done*."[3]

KINGDOM OF GOD

The Mystery of the Virgin Birth

The idea that Christ was conceived in the womb of a young woman without a man's participation drives some people crazy. They simply can't believe it. The Bible doesn't argue. It states simply that Christ's mother was a *virgin*. The word means not merely that she was unmarried but that she had never had sex with a man. Jesus of Nazareth did not have an earthly biological father (Joseph became his adoptive father). Jesus' "biological" Father was God.

The virgin birth of Jesus Christ is the root from which everything the New Testament says about him grows. Theologians and ordinary men struggle with it. But to the mind willing to believe *"nothing is impossible with God,"* it is not at all hard to accept. Both Luke and Matthew state it up front as a fact, which they are convinced explains the unusual nature of the man, Jesus, and the amazing things he said and did.

Something to Ponder

Eugene H. Peterson: This profound mystery is presented to us very simply. God comes to us in Jesus, in the simplest form, as an infant.[4]

What Others are Saying:

Terms to Help Us Understand the Significance of the Virgin Birth of Jesus

Incarnation: God wrapped himself in humanness (flesh) in the person of Jesus Christ (John 1:14).

Virgin birth: Without a human father, Jesus began his earthly life in the womb of the virgin Mary, was carried through the normal human gestation period, and was born a human baby (Luke 1:27, 34).

Theanthropic person: Term based on two Greek words—*theos*, "*God*," and *anthropos*, "man"—used to describe the uniqueness of Christ's personality, in which deity and humanity are united in a single individual (Hebrews 2:11–18).

Kenosis: From the Greek word *kenosen*, meaning "emptied." It describes the process through which the preexisting Son of God voluntarily laid aside or restricted the independent use of his divine abilities so he could be born, live, and die as a human being dependent on God (Philippians 2:5–8).

Dig Deeper

EARLY CHURCH LIFE: Early Christian thinkers struggled to put into words the realities of the faith.

KEY POINT

The virgin birth of Jesus Christ is the root from which everything the New Testament says about him grows.

The Athanasian Creed (mid-fifth century A.D.): Our Lord Jesus Christ, the Son of God, is God and man; . . . perfect God, and perfect man: . . . who although he be God and man: yet he is not two, but one Christ; one, not by conversion of the Godhead into flesh: but by taking of the manhood into God.

John F. MacArthur Jr.: The virgin birth is an underlying assumption of everything the Bible says about Jesus. To throw out the virgin birth is to reject Christ's deity, the accuracy and authority of Scripture, and a host of other related doctrines that are the heart of the Christian faith. No issue is more important than the virgin birth to our understanding of who Jesus is. If we deny Jesus is God, we have denied the very essence of Christianity.[5]

J. I. Packer: How are we to think of the incarnation? The New Testament does not encourage us to puzzle our heads over the physical and psychological problems that it raises, but to worship God for the love that was shown in it.[6]

A Visit With Cousin Liz

After her unconditional surrender to the will of God (Luke 1:38) Mary needs time to process all she has been told and to prepare for the months ahead. So she hurries from the well-watered grassy hills of Galilee to the desert-dry hills of Judea for a visit with her relative, Elizabeth (verses 39–45). The angel Gabriel had cited Elizabeth's pregnancy as proof to Mary that *"nothing is impossible with God"* (verses 36–37). Elizabeth would understand. Aside from Elizabeth's husband Zechariah, Mary may have been the first to see the older woman since she became pregnant six months earlier and entered her self-imposed seclusion. The exchange that took place upon Mary's arrival was astonishing.

1. The baby in Elizabeth's womb jumped at the sound of Mary's greeting. Elizabeth interpreted the fetal leap as the unborn prophet's joyful recognition of the mother of the unborn Christ (as if he couldn't wait to dive into his work as the **forerunner**!)

2. The Holy Spirit gave Elizabeth exactly the words Mary needed to hear, reassuring her that what was happening to her was a result of God's grace and blessing, and that her faith would be rewarded.

3. Elizabeth acknowledged the divine origin of Mary's unborn child, calling him *"my Lord."*

KEY Outline:

Young Cousin Mary
Jesus' mom

Old Cousin Elizabeth
John the Baptist's mom

☞ **GO TO:**

Isaiah 40:3–5; Matthew 3:1–3; Luke 1:17, 3:15–17 (forerunner)

forerunner: advance man, introducer

> **Luke 1:46–48** And Mary said: "My soul glorifies the Lord and my spirit rejoices in God my Savior, for he has been mindful of the humble state of his servant."

ACT OF THE HOLY SPIRIT

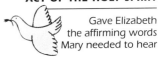
Gave Elizabeth the affirming words Mary needed to hear

Battle Hymn

Mary's heart was bustin' to express her thoughts and feelings. Elizabeth's greeting gave her the chance she'd been waiting for all the way from Nazareth. She broke into a joyful poem of worship. Christians call it "The Magnificat." It has been set to music. The song magnifies the Saviorhood of God and puts the arrival of the Messiah in a revolution perspective. The *"arm"* of the Lord (verse 51) is an Old Testament reference to the promised Messiah—the Christ child she was carrying. She credits God's arm with the performance of *"mighty deeds"* in the past. She sees his arrival as continuing God's program in the present and future. The specific *"mighty deeds"* she mentions fulfill the revolutionary longings of the Jewish people (and, for that matter, all oppressed people). Mary's boy will ignite the fires of a most unusual revolution!

☞ **Check It Out:**

Luke 1:46–55

KEY POINT

Mary believed the birth of Christ was God's answer to the cry of the poor and oppressed for justice.

KINGDOM OF GOD

Three Types of Revolution

1. Spiritual revolution: *"He has scattered those who are proud in their inmost thoughts"* (verse 51). Pride is the basis of human sin. Surrender to Christ kills pride and opens the way for spiritual renovation and renewal.

2. Social revolution: *"He has brought down rulers from their thrones but has lifted up the humble"* (verse 52). With the death of arrogance comes the end of pride-driven injustice and oppression, which crushes the weak under the feet of the strong and uses the powerless to further the selfish goals of the powerful.

3. Economic revolution: *"He has filled the hungry with good things but has sent the rich away empty"* (verse 53). Christ changes people's attitudes toward each other. Love replaces indifference to the needs of others. Care for one another replaces greed. Wealth becomes a means to serve not merely to satisfy self.

☞ **GO TO:**

Isaiah 52:10; 53:1; John 12:37–38 (God's arm)

Romans 12:1–2 (renewal)

James 5:1–6 (injustice)

Romans 12:9–13 (replaces indifference)

Acts 2:44–46 (care)

2 Corinthians 9:10 (means to serve)

Leon Morris: In the ancient world it was accepted that the rich would be well cared for. Poor people must expect to be hungry. But Mary sings of a God who is not bound by what people do. He turns human attitudes and orders of society upside down.[7]

What Others are Saying:

> **Luke 1:57–58** When it was time for Elizabeth to have her baby, she gave birth to a son. Her neighbors and relatives heard that the Lord had shown her great mercy, and they shared the joy.

Baby Baptist

After three months with Elizabeth, Mary returned to Nazareth. She apparently left before baby John's birth. When Elizabeth had her baby, neighbors and relatives converged on the scene in celebration. Single and pregnant, perhaps experiencing morning sickness, Mary may have wanted to avoid the questions and hubbub.

Jewish law prescribed that baby boys should be circumcised the <u>eighth day</u> after birth. Among first century Jews the child was also <u>named</u> on that day. Without consulting the parents, presumptive relatives picked a family name (why bother trying to talk to old Zechariah about anything? He was deaf and dumb as a post! (See Luke 1:20.) The boy should, they decided, be named after his father who was named after his father who was named after his father who was named . . . (you get the picture).

"His Name Is John"

"No!" shouted Elizabeth over the cacophony of noisy kinfolk. "*He is to be called John*" (the name the angel gave him—Luke 1:13).

Unheard of! He should be named for his father, they insisted. They went to Zechariah and, with a lot of arm waving, asked him for the final word. His handwritten answer was more emphatic than his wife's: "*His name is John.*"

Obedience to the angel's instructions demonstrated the old priest's faith. The last shred of doubt (verse 18) disappeared, along with his inability to speak. Once he had his faith and tongue back, Zechariah

- praised the Lord for keeping his promises (verses 68–75)
- prophesied about his son's place in God's redemptive plan (verses 76–79)

Like Mary's Magnificat, Zechariah's song has been set to music. It's called "Benedictus."

Desert Prep School

Zech and Liz's boy grew up in the desert (verse 80), where he spent <u>30 years</u> preparing for the strategic task of introducing his cousin Jesus to Israel when it was time for Jesus to begin his mes-

☞ **Check It Out:**

Luke 1:56–80

☞ **GO TO:**

Genesis 17:12; Leviticus 12:3 (eighth day)

Luke 2:21 (named)

KEY Outline:

Christ's Revolution
  Spiritual
  Social
  Economic

KEY POINT

Zechariah's speech returned when he named the child "John" according to the angel's instructions.

☞ **GO TO:**

Luke 3:23 (30 years)

sianic ministry. Jesus would one day say of John: *"Among those born of women there is no greater than John!"* (Luke 7:24).

Study Questions

1. What great world power was oppressing the Jews at the time of John's and Jesus' conception and birth?
2. Identify three Old Testament promises upon which the Jewish expectations of Christ's birth were based.
3. List at least four of the angel's predictions concerning John's ministry?
4. What "miracle" kept Zechariah from expressing his doubts?
5. Speaking personally, which of Gabriel's five predictions concerning Mary's baby most amazes or impresses you? Why?
6. Identify the three "revolutions" Mary's song (Luke 1:46–55) says the *"arm"* of the Lord (Christ) has accomplished?

KEY Outline:

Incarnation Songs
Mary's Magnificat
Zechariah's Benedictus

CHAPTER WRAP-UP

- Seven hundred years of oppression and 400 years of prophetic silence—without a fresh message from God—left Israelites either hungry for the Messiah or settling for a hopeless existence.

- The angel Gabriel announced to a childless old priest named Zechariah that he and his wife Elizabeth would soon be parents of a son who would grow up to be the great prophet (John the Baptist) who would prepare Israel for the arrival of the Christ. (Luke 1:5–25)

- Six months later the same angel appeared to the virgin Mary and revealed God's plan for her to be mother of the Messiah, the Son of God. Virgin birth was possible because conception took place through the overshadowing of the Holy Spirit. (Luke 1:26–38)

- On a visit to Elizabeth in Judea, Mary's faith was affirmed. Mary composed a song of worship that Christians call "The Magnificat." It was a song magnifying God for the spiritual and social revolution the birth of her baby would bring to Israel. (Luke 1:39–45)

- Elizabeth and Zechariah's baby was born and named "John." He grew up in the Judean desert until the time his ministry as Christ's forerunner began. (Luke 1:56–80)

2 MARY'S LITTLE LAMB

Let's Get Started

How would you like to have to tell the man to whom you are engaged that you are pregnant by someone else? That was the dilemma facing young Mary of Nazareth when she returned home from a <u>three-month</u> hiatus in Judea. The baby in her womb was entering its second trimester. She might be able to hide her condition a little more but not for long. The good man to whom she was <u>pledged</u> must be told the wonderful secret she was carrying.

> **Matthew 1:18** This is how the birth of Jesus Christ came about: His mother Mary was pledged to be married to Joseph, but before they came together, she was found to be with child through the Holy Spirit.

The Scandal Of God With Us

How soon after Mary's return to Nazareth she broke the news to Joseph we are not told. We're told he knew the truth *"before they came together"* (Matthew 1:18). She told him

- she was pregnant;
- her pregnancy was an act of the Holy Spirit.

Joseph took it hard. The idea that his bride-to-be's pregnancy was the work of the Holy Spirit was just too incredible.

GOSPEL QUARTET IN HARMONY

Matthew 1:18–2:12
Luke 2:1–39

☞ **GO TO:**

Luke 1:56 (three-month)

Matthew 1:18;
   Luke 1:27 (pledged)

came together:
consummated marriage
by sexual union

ACT OF THE HOLY SPIRIT

Mary's pregnancy;
conception of Jesus

Betrothal And Marriage—First Century Jewish Style

Jewish betrothal was as legally and morally binding as marriage itself. Marriage involved the following three stages:

1. Engagement, which was often arranged when the couple were children.

2. Betrothal came when the engaged children reached marriageable age—12 years and one day, for girls; most men were married by the time they reached 20. At this point, the girl had a choice; if she consented the couple pledged themselves to each other, and this pledge was absolutely binding. Betrothal lasted about a year. The betrothed couple was known as husband and wife, even though they did not live together or engage in sex. If the husband died during the betrothal year, she was considered "a virgin who is a widow." The only way to <u>terminate a betrothal</u> was either for the man to die or to give his wife a written certificate of divorce.

3. The wedding ceremony took place at the end of the betrothal period. The marriage was consummated only after the wedding.

The Quiet Little Divorce That Never Happened

Mary's Joseph was a good Joe. He found her story unbelievable, but he did not want to make a spectacle of breaking off the relationship. He was leaning toward a quiet little divorce—a private transaction between himself and the synagogue leaders (Matthew 1:19). As he made plans to do this he dreamed *"an angel of the Lord appeared to him"*—most likely a repeat performance by the angel <u>Gabriel</u>. The angel in the dream verified Mary's story—the child she carried was *"from the Holy Spirit."* The dream-angel went on to reaffirm what Mary herself must have told him:

1. The baby is a *"son"* (Matthew 1:21).

2. His name is *"Jesus"*—Greek for *Joshua* which means "Yahweh is salvation"—*"because he will save his people from their sins"* (Matthew 1:21).

3. The conception in the womb of a virgin fulfills Old Testament prophecy (Matthew 1:22–23; Isaiah 7:14).

4. Mary's son will be *"Immanuel"*—no ordinary child—*"<u>God with us</u>"* (Matthew 1:23).

Joseph woke up convinced. Fear that Mary had been unfaithful vanished. He immediately changed his plans. He ended their be-

---

☞ GO TO:

Deuteronomy 20:7; 24:1 (terminate a betrothal)

KEY Outline:

Three Steps to Marriage

Engagement
- arranged by parents

Betrothal
- binding as marriage

Marriage
- after betrothal

☞ GO TO:

Luke 1:19, 26 (Gabriel)

Luke 1:32, 35; Isaiah 7:14 (God with us)

KEY Outline:

Jesus
"Yahweh is salvation"

Immanuel
"God with us"

---

trothal, but not with a divorce. Instead, he married the girl! He *"took Mary home as his wife"* (verse 24). Joseph and Mary did not share physical intimacy until the miracle child was born.

> **Luke 2:1–3** In those days Caesar Augustus issued a decree that a census should be taken of the entire Roman world. (This was the first census that took place while Quirinius was governor of Syria.) And everyone went to his own town to register.

Joy Fest!

The whole parade of Christmas characters—Mary, Joseph, the shepherds, Simeon, Anna, the wise men, even the angels who announced his birth—erupted with expressions of joy when they laid eyes on the Christ child. In many of their lives there was pain, so his presence gave them hope.

But first God called, "Places, everyone!" All the participants in this divine drama had to travel to their appointed spot.

Senseless Census

Hundreds of years earlier the prophet Micah had predicted Christ would be born in the little town of Bethlehem, Judea—King <u>David's hometown</u>—about five miles south of Jerusalem (Micah 5:2). Mary and Joseph lived in Nazareth, Galilee, about 80 or 90 miles north of Bethlehem (see appendix A). Without being aware of its participation in God's redemptive plan, the mighty Roman Imperial government made the arrangements for fulfillment of Micah's prophecy. They decreed a census for the purpose of increasing taxes. That census brought Joseph and Mary to Bethlehem in time for Jesus to be born there.

The notice of a later census in Egypt illustrates Rome's head-counting technique:

"Gaius Vibius Maximus, Prefect of Egypt, orders: 'Seeing that the time has come for the house to house census, it is necessary to compel all those, who for any cause whatsoever are residing outside their districts, to return to their own homes, that they may both carry out the regular order of the census, and may also diligently attend to the cultivation of their allotments.'"

The census of Luke 2:1–2 was especially disruptive for Jewish men and their families. They were forced to leave home and travel to their ancestral headquarters just for the privilege of being socked with higher taxes.

☞ **Check It Out:**

Luke 2:1–38

☞ **GO TO:**

1 Samuel 16:1–13 (David's hometown)

KEY POINT

God controls secular governments to fulfill his purposes.

Remember This . . .

The authors of the New Testament gospels (especially Luke) are careful to set the events of Jesus' life in the context of the times in which they happened (see illustration this page). Luke, a doctor, wrote his gospel to give an *"orderly account"* of the facts about Jesus' life, so providing an accurate historical setting for Jesus' birth was important to him.

Who's Who

CAESAR AUGUSTUS (Luke 2:1): Ruler of the Roman Empire—31 B.C. to 14 A.D.

Who's Who

QUIRINIUS (Luke 2:2): Twice served the Roman Empire in Syria: (1) as a military commander from 7–5 B.C., and (2) later, after Jesus' birth, as governor. The census mentioned began in 8 B.C. and took 14 years to complete. It was completed during Quirinius' governorship.

Who's Who

HEROD (Matthew 2:1): Appointed "King" of Judea and Samaria by Caesar Augustus in 30 B.C. (See chapter 1, page 7, for details of the reign of this ruthless "rat.")

What Others are Saying:

Charles R. Swindoll: Without realizing it, mighty Augustus was only an errand boy for the fulfillment of Micah's prediction . . . a pawn in the hand of Jehovah . . . a piece of lint on the pages of prophecy. While Rome was busy making history, God arrived. . . . The world didn't even notice. Reeling from the wake of Alexander the Great . . . Herod the Great . . . Augustus the Great, the world overlooked Mary's little Lamb. It still does.[1]

Historical Events Surrounding Christ's Birth

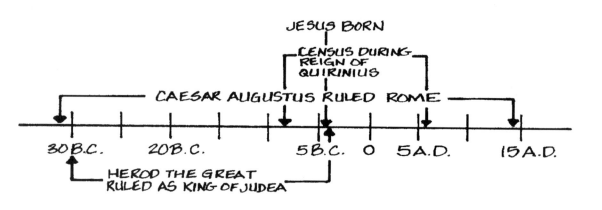

Hiking to Bethlehem

Joseph was a descendant of David (verse 4). Mary too (Luke 1:32; Romans 1:3). The Roman decree meant an 80-mile, six-day trek through the Palestinian countryside (probably camping each night along the way) from Nazareth to Bethlehem (farther if they avoided traveling through hostile Samaritan territory, as some Jews did). It was a hard trip. Travelers could face attack by bandits or wild animals, including lions and Syrian bears along the Jordan Valley. To complicate things, Mary was in the ninth month of pregnancy.

Even though Matthew reports that Joseph had taken Mary home as his wife, Luke describes her, on the way to Bethlehem, as *"pledged to be married to"* Joseph (Luke 2:5). This emphasizes the fact that the marriage was not consummated sexually until after her child was born (Matthew 1:24–25). Christ must be virgin-born (Isaiah 7:14).

KEY Outline:

Bethlehem
David's hometown
Joseph's family's town

Remember This . . .

Travel Distances on First-Century Roads*

From Nazareth to:

• Jerusalem (via Jericho)	97 miles
• Jerusalem (via Samaria)	75 miles
• Capernaum	20 miles
• Cana	9.5 miles
• Nain	8 miles

From Bethlehem to:

• Jerusalem	5.5 miles

From Capernaum to:

• Jerusalem	106 miles
• Caesarea Philippi	34 miles
• Magdala	7 miles by land, 3 by boat
• Gergesa	6 miles by boat
• Bethsaida	4 miles
• Korazin	2 miles

From Shechem (Jacob's Well) to:

• Jerusalem	39 miles

From Jericho to:

• Bethany	14 miles

*For a map showing the location of these places, see appendix A.

> **Luke 2:4–7** So Joseph also went up from the town of Nazareth in Galilee to Judea, to Bethlehem the town of David, because he belonged to the house and line of David. He went there to register with Mary, who was pledged to be married to him and was expecting a child. When they were there, the time came for the baby to be born, and she gave birth to her firstborn, a son. She wrapped him in cloths and placed him in a manger, because there was no room for them in the inn.

No Holiday Inn

Those days, the typical inn (caravansary) was a series of stalls surrounding a common courtyard. There was no such thing as "fine dining" in the hotel restaurant—travelers brought their own food. For the price of a night's lodging, the innkeeper provided a stall, fodder for the horses or camels, and a fire for cooking. When Joseph and Mary arrived the only inn in tiny Bethlehem was already jammed with stressed descendants of David forced to return home for registration. There was *"no room for them in the inn."* They apparently spent the night (perhaps several nights) in a stable—a cave in the side of a hill (see illustration this page) or a rough shed where animals were sheltered and fed.

Cave with Manger

In the area of Jesus' birth natural caves were often used for animal shelters. Animal feed boxes, or mangers, were often formed out of stone ledges.

The Hope Of The World—Cradled In Straw

The Bible doesn't actually say the birth of Jesus took place in a stable. Here are the facts:

- There was no room in the inn.
- Mary wrapped the baby in cloths (clean rags).
- She laid him in a manger.

The traditional conclusion based on those facts is that a stable was the birthplace. Other possibilities are as follows:

- A very poor home where the family and animals sheltered under the same roof
- The courtyard of the inn where there might be a manger
- Outdoors where Joseph and Mary camped for the night

After settling into such fine accommodations and sharing shelter with beasts of burden, Mary went into labor. The child—the focus of centuries of expressed Jewish hopes and the secret longings of a whole world languishing in sin's disastrous consequences—was born. According to custom, Mary bathed the baby, rubbed salt over his body to prevent infection, and wrapped him tightly in strips of linen cloth from head to toe (see illustration this page). After nursing him, she used a nearby feed trough for his first crib.

Ronald B. Allen: He is the one whose goings forth have been from everlasting, but he was also a human baby born in the normal manner, needing the care of his blessed mother. He created the universe; but helpless, he needed a diaper change. He placed

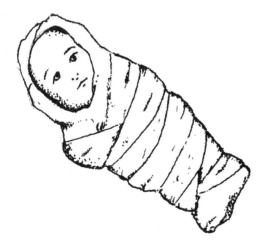

KEY POINT

Although Jesus had an ordinary birth, he was an extraordinary child.

What Others are Saying:

Swaddling Clothes

Mary wrapped newborn Jesus in strips of cloth. The King James Version calls these strips "swaddling clothes."

the stars and stretched the expanse, but was now subject to colds and colic, to rash and runny nose. The omnipotent God became vulnerable; the eternal One had a new beginning. There is no mystery in all the universe to be compared with the mystery of the Incarnation.[2]

What Others
are Saying:

Michael Card: We know from Scripture that Jesus wept as a man. It is naïve to think he did not cry as a baby. Tears are a basic part of what it means to be human. It is one of the sad signs of our fallen world that the first sign we give to show that we're alive is a cry. It is to this fallen world that Jesus came, not an imaginary one without tears.[3]

Sheepherders Hear The Good News

The scene shifts to the hills near Bethlehem. Mary and Joseph are not the only ones spending the night without decent shelter. There are shepherds nearby living outdoors to protect flocks of sheep assigned to their care. They are the first to be told Christ has been born in Bethlehem. Their part in the story helps fill in some blanks. Without the report of the announcement to the shepherds, we would not know the following:

1. Jesus was born in the middle of the night (Luke 2:8).
2. What time of year it was (or wasn't). Most of the year Bethlehem's climate is mild and lends itself to keeping flocks in the hills all night. But in winter in that mountainous area nights are cold, so most flocks are in the sheepfold, protected against winter storms. This may rule out December as the logical time of Christ's birth. (Not to worry: The Bible gives no command to celebrate Christmas on a specific day—December 25 is probably as good a day as any!)

What Others
are Saying:

Albert Barnes: It is probable from this that our Savior was born before the 25th of December, or before what we call Christmas.[4]

Michael Card: The Bible says nothing about the season, apart from a reference to the fact that the shepherds were "keeping watch" in the fields all through the night, which might mean it was the season when lambs were being born, the only time shepherds stay in the fields all night. If that is so, Jesus was probably born in the spring. I'd like to think it was April, since that is the month of my own birthday![5]

Sacrificial Lamb Keepers

Flocks of sheep were kept out in the fields near Bethlehem and watched over by shepherds 24 hours a day in preparation for the Feast of Passover (see GWBI, page 28) and other festivals at the Temple in Jerusalem, less than five miles away. Temple rituals—<u>especially Passover</u>—required thousands of sacrificial animals. A respected Jewish rabbi writing in the first century A.D. tells of huge flocks of sacrificial sheep near Bethlehem "thirty days before the feast" (meaning the Passover, held in March or early April each year).[6] For sure, shepherds and sheep were in the fields in February. Some may have drawn this rugged duty all winter long—even December. (Oops! December 25 may not be ruled out after all.)

Angelic Cheerleaders

Angels appear, disappear, and reappear all through the story of Christ's birth. Hebrews 1:14 describes angels as *"ministering spirits sent to serve those who will inherit salvation."* The angels who exploded into the shepherds' skyscape were bustin' with exciting news they served up in spectacular fashion—news inseparably tied to that rag-bundled babe resting in Bethlehem's hay (Luke 2:9–14):

- No fear!
- Great joy for all people!
- A Savior, Christ the Lord, has been born!
- Glory to God!
- Peace on earth!
- God favors (is positively, graciously inclined toward) people!

Stuart and Jill Briscoe: At Christmas time God cups his hands over his mouth, as it were, and shouts at the top of his voice, so that with all the din going on around them, human beings might hear what he has to say: "Listen! I've got great news that will bring you glorious joy!"[7]

The first people to hear, see, believe, and share the good news of the arrival of Christ, the <u>Lamb of God</u>, were men caring for sacrificial lambs. The sacrifice of the lambs was the Old Testament's <u>shadowy picture</u> of Christ's most important work, to *"save his people from their sins"* (Matthew 1:21).

Something to Ponder

Remember This . . .

☞ **GO TO:**

Deuteronomy 16:1–8 (especially Passover)

☞ **GO TO:**

John 1:29, 35 (Lamb of God)

Hebrews 10:1 (shadowy picture)

What Others are Saying:

Something to Ponder

☞ **GO TO:**

Hebrews 10:9–14
(end all sacrifices)

Luke 2:17–18 (shep-
herds would tell)

KEY Outline:

Poor People
Give 'em good news!

Powerful People
Let 'em sleep!

Something
to Ponder

What Others
are Saying:

☞ **GO TO:**

Luke 18:24–25 (wealth,
power, and pride)

KEY POINT

Sacrificial lamb keepers
were first to see the
Lamb of God.

☞ **Check It Out:**

Luke 2:21–38

The Temple lamb keepers were witnesses to the birth of the Sacrifice to <u>end all sacrifices</u>. In a few days, these same shepherds would be in the Temple delivering sheep for the daily sacrifices. In the course of their work they would meet priests and worshipers. As Templegoers selected their sacrificial animals, the <u>shepherds would tell</u> how they had seen with their own eyes the reality toward which the sacrifices pointed.

The Rich And Powerful—The Last To Know

While angels were telling raggedy sheepherders the news of Christ's birth, the rich and powerful slept on, oblivious of the most exciting event in history. God deliberately bypassed the political and religious leadership. Theological and political intelligentsia, clergy, and government officials are not most likely to welcome God's Word.

<u>Wealth, power, and pride</u> often hinder the simple exuberance that gives Christian witness its impact. The first to hear from God are often ordinary people looking for him in the midst of their ordinary lives.

The shepherds hurried to see the baby Christ. They told everybody what they had seen and heard. You could hear them praising God a mile away (Luke 2:20)!

William Barclay: It is a wonderful thing that . . . the first announcement of God came to some shepherds. Shepherds were despised by orthodox good people of the day. They were quite unable to keep the details of the ceremonial law; they could not observe the meticulous hand-washings and rules and regulations. Their flocks made far too constant demands on them; and so the orthodox looked down on them. It was to simple men of the fields that God's message first came.[8]

> **Luke 2:21** On the eighth day, when it was time to circumcise him, he was named Jesus, the name the angel had given him before he had been conceived.

The Rite Stuff

Old Testament Law called for three ceremonies to get a baby boy off to a good start:

1. Circumcision (Luke 2:21; Leviticus 12:3). The eighth day after birth, the ceremonial surgery took place that set a

male child apart as a son of Israel. The procedure was usually performed by the father (although Exodus 4:25 provides that another could do it if necessary). Even if the eighth day fell on the **Sabbath**, when work of any kind was forbidden, this act could be done. The coupling of the day of circumcision with the naming of the child was not prescribed by law, but over the years it became a custom among the Jews (Luke 1:59; 2:21). Mary's baby was called *Jesus* the same day he was set apart as a Jew. This took place in Bethlehem.

2. Redemption of the firstborn (Luke 2:23; Numbers 18:15–16). A firstborn son was to be considered especially set apart for and belonging to the Lord. Soon after he was a month old he was to be taken to the Temple and a **redemption price** of **five shekels** was to be paid to the priest in the child's behalf.

3. Purification after childbirth (Luke 2:22, 24; Leviticus 12). For 40 days after the birth of a son, a Jewish woman was required to avoid the Temple and all religious ceremonies (for a daughter, 80 days). This was considered her time of "purification." On the 41st day, she could be declared **ceremonially clean** if she went to the Temple and made two offerings—a lamb for a **burnt offering** and a dove for a **sin offering.**

The trip from Bethlehem to the Temple in Jerusalem, for these last two ceremonies, was made when Jesus was about six weeks old.

The fact that Mary offered a couple of pigeons for her purification offerings (Luke 2:24) indicates the family was poor—too poor to afford a lamb (Leviticus 12:8). The pigeon-offering was known among Jews as "the Offering of the Poor."

Matthew Henry: [about Mary's sin offering] Christ was not conceived or born in sin, as others are, yet, because he was made under the law, he complied with it.[10]

William Barclay: Of all God's gifts there is none for which we shall be so answerable as the gift of a child.[11]

Sabbath: *seventh day, Jewish day of rest*

redemption price: *to "buy back" firstborn son who, by Law, belongs to the Lord*

five shekels: *Jewish coins equaling two ounces of silver*

ceremonially clean: *fulfilled rituals[9] required to renew commitment to the Lord*

burnt offering: *sacrificial animal burned, signifying surrender to God*

sin offering: *sacrifice to atone for sin or ceremonial uncleanness*

Remember This . . .

What Others are Saying:

Audrey I. Girard: When we stand before the Lord, the first question we will be asked is, "What did you do with Jesus?" The second question will be, "What did you do with your children?"[12]

Behind the three ceremonies Jesus and Mary went through after his birth lies the deep conviction running through both Jewish and Christian beliefs: A child is a gift from God.

> **Luke 2:28–30** Simeon took [Jesus] in his arms and praised God, saying: "Sovereign Lord, as you have promised, you now dismiss your servant in peace. For my eyes have seen your salvation."

The Messiah Watchers

In a society becoming more and more cynical and legalistic, with increasing numbers pinning their hopes of freedom on the politics of violence, faithful Jews stuck like flypaper to the ancient promises about a Redeemer-King who would come and deliver Israel from her enemies (see GWDN, pages 251–252; GWGN, page 45). Some of these dreamers were called the "Quiet in the Land."[13] They spent their lives quietly waiting for God. They served him in the Temple, in prayer, in worship, in quiet expectation of Messiah's coming. Among them were a man named Simeon (Luke 2:25) and an 84-year-old woman named Anna (verses 36–37).

Simeon, *"moved by the Spirit,"* recognized the baby in Joseph's arms as the One for whom he had been waiting. The words Simeon spoke as he held the child became a hymn sung in early church gatherings and known as *Nunc Dimittis* ("Now Let Me Depart"). In six-week-old Jesus, Simeon believed he was seeing God's salvation in personal form—the light by which the Lord would disclose himself not only to Israel but to *"all people"* (Luke 2:31). After blessing the special little family, Simeon issued four prophetic predictions concerning the child Jesus (verses 34–35):

1. He will cause many people to fall (John 3:16–17).
2. He will cause many people to rise (John 5:21; 11:25–26).
3. He will be opposed and rejected (John 1:10–11).
4. He will expose the thoughts of people's hearts (John 3:19–21).

As Simeon wrapped up his prophecy, Anna approached, thanking God. She too recognized the child as *"the **redemption of Jerusa-***

🔑 **KEY Outline:**

Start for Jewish Messiah
Circumcision
- named Jesus

Redemption
- firstborn son

Purification
- Mary's ceremony

KEY POINT

The Quiet in the Land were waiting for Messiah.

redemption of Jerusalem: *Israel's deliverance from oppression*

lem." She shared news about him with others of the "Quiet in the Land," whom she knew were eager to hear the news.

SIMEON (Simon): Luke 2:25–27 describes him as *"righteous"* (just) *"and devout"* (committed to God), *"waiting for"* (desiring, hoping, expecting) *"the consolation"* (comfort) *"of Israel,"* *"the Holy Spirit was upon him"* (controlled and empowered by the Holy Spirit), *"moved"* (led, prompted) *"by the Spirit."* The Holy Spirit had revealed (an inner conviction) that he would live to see *"the Lord's Christ."*

Outside the New Testament, Jewish writers mention a deeply spiritual man named Simeon living in Jerusalem at this time. He was the son of Rabbi **Hillel** and father of the famous **Pharisee**, Gamaliel. He had a prophetic gift, the ability to speak messages from God. This may have been the man who met Joseph, Mary, and baby Jesus in the Temple.

ANNA: Her name means "gracious." She was a prophetess (a woman gifted to speak God's message). She was a regular "fixture" at the Temple where she *"worshiped night and day, fasting and praying."* Her family roots were in the Israelite tribe of Asher, who mostly lived in Galilee. As a young woman she had been married for seven years. After her husband died she remained single. At the time of Jesus' birth she was 84. (For more information, see GWWB, pages 294–295.)

> **Matthew 2:1–2** After Jesus was born in Bethlehem in Judea, during the time of King Herod, Magi from the east came to Jerusalem and asked, "Where is the one who has been born king of the Jews? We saw his star in the east and have come to worship him."

"Magic" Visitors

It is probable the Eastern visitors seeking Jesus were influenced by Daniel's writings. Additional influence came from the large Jewish population residing in Babylon and other Eastern cities—people who had not returned to Israel after the Babylonian **exile**. The entire Hebrew Bible was available, along with extensive Jewish commentaries known as the Babylonian Talmud. The Magi may even have been aware of messianic prophecies, or Old Testament predictions about the expected Deliverer from God. One such proph-

Who's Who

ACT OF THE HOLY SPIRIT

Simeon, filled, led, and enlightened, recognized baby Messiah

Something to Ponder

Who's Who

☞ **GO TO:**

Acts 5:34–40 (Gamaliel)

1 Corinthians 14; Ephesians 4:11 (prophetic gift)

2 Kings 25:11; 2 Chronicles 24:14 (exile)

Hillel: *influential Jewish teacher*

Pharisee: *"separated one," teacher of Jewish law and religious tradition*

fasting: *going without food to concentrate on prayer*

exile: *After Babylonian conquest, thousands of Jews deported to Babylon*

ecy said, *"A star will come out of Jacob; a scepter will rise out of Israel"* (Numbers 24:17).

MAGI: An elite class of Eastern scholar-priests. Some Magi (also known as "magicians" and "astrologers") had been advisers to Babylonian and Persian kings. **Daniel**, a Hebrew prophet-in-exile (see GWDN, pages 15–16), was considered <u>one of the Magi</u> in the Babylonian and Persian empires. In fact, Babylon's King Nebuchadnezzar appointed him <u>chief magician</u>, even though Daniel never depended on magic arts or astrology for his wisdom—he always <u>sought God's wisdom</u>.

Who's Who

Daniel: prophet, writer of the Bible book of Daniel

☞ **GO TO:**

Daniel 1:19–21; 2:2–18 (one of the Magi)

Daniel 4:8–9; 5:11–12 (chief magician)

Daniel 2:17–23, 27–28 (sought God's wisdom)

KINGDOM OF GOD | ### Star Trek

The Eastern custom of paying homage to the rulers of other nations on special occasions was well known. In keeping with this protocol the illustrious Magi traveled to Jerusalem—if from Babylon, it was a thousand-mile, six-month journey—to honor the newborn king. The inference is drawn from the three kinds of gifts mentioned in Matthew 2:11 that there were three travelers. Matthew nowhere states how many there were. Given the distance and wildness of the country through which they had to travel, it is likely they traveled in a caravan, including not only the distinguished visitors but their servants and bodyguards.

They were led by an unusual star, which first appeared in the sky when the child was born (verse 7). Many natural explanations have been suggested for the star (alignment of planets, comets, etc.). Whatever natural phenomena might have been involved, the timing was clearly supernatural. And it led them to Jesus.

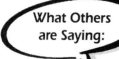

What Others are Saying:

Lawrence O. Richards: In desert countries of the East nomads find their way over the sands by following the stars. "Take that star in your hand" is a common way of giving directions. It would not be unusual at all for God to guide the Magi to the Christ Child by, in essence, telling them "Take that star in your hand and follow it until you come to the One born King of the Jews."[14]

KEY Outline:

Magi Sources
  Stars
  Daniel
  Exiles

> **Matthew 2:7** Then Herod called the Magi secretly and found out from them the exact time the star had appeared.

Herod The Great . . . Con Man

It's not surprising, knowing the monstrous paranoia of King Herod, that he would be *"disturbed"* to hear that a new king of the Jews was in the wings, waiting, he suspected, to take his throne. Herod seemed to understand immediately his new rival was *"the Christ"* (verse 4)! The arrogance and unmitigated gall of that man! You'd think the people of the city (who considered themselves closer to God because they lived down the street from the Temple), the Bible scholars (who knew the messianic prophecies by heart—verse 5), and the religious leaders (*"chief priests"*), would have been delighted at the news. They weren't. *"All Jerusalem"* went into a tizzy.

KEY POINT

Jesus fulfilled Old Testament prophecies.

The interaction between the Magi, Herod, and Jerusalem's religious intelligentsia went like this (Matthew 2:2–8, paraphrased):

> Magi: "Where is the newborn king of the Jews? We want to worship him."
> Herod (to Bible scholars): "Where was Christ supposed to be born?"
> Bible scholars: "Bethlehem." They quoted <u>Micah's prophecy</u> to prove it.
> Herod (to Magi): "When did you first see the star?"
> Magi: (They told him. Their precise answer is not recorded, but verse 16 infers the first sighting may have been as much as two years earlier.)
> Herod: "Go to Bethlehem. When you find the child report back to me. I want to worship him too!" (What a liar!)

☞ **GO TO:**

Micah 5:2
(Micah's prophecy)

Matthew is careful to record how Christ fulfilled Old Testament prophecies. Here he cites Micah 5:2. In the course of his Life of Christ he will quote the Old Testament 53 times.

Wise Men Worship Christ

Contrary to the impression given in ten million "manger scenes," the distinguished visitors did not arrive at the manger along with the shepherds the night Jesus was born. By the time they came, Joseph had moved his family into a *house* (Matthew 2:11). Jesus was probably a toddler between six months (the travel time from Babylon) and *"two years"* (the upper age of infants Herod murdered—verse 16). When the Magi entered the house they did three things that must have astounded his parents (verse 11):

Remember
This . . .

Something to Ponder

1. *"They bowed down"*—protocol for coming into the presence of a king required them to fall to their knees, lean forward, and press their foreheads to the floor.

2. They *"worshiped him"*—the Greek word for worship literally means to "kiss the hand"—a show of reverence for royalty or deity.

3. They presented him with gifts—each one symbolized something significant:

   - *"gold"*—recognition of Jesus' kingship

   - *"incense"* for burning in worship—recognition of Jesus' priesthood

   - *"myrrh,"* an embalming spice—recognition of the importance of Jesus' death, his Saviorhood

KEY Outline:

Magi Gifts
Gold: king
Incense: priest
Myrrh: savior

A Different Way Home

The Magi disobeyed King Herod's orders to report back to him. One of them had a dream that convinced them to return to their own country by an alternate route—avoiding Jerusalem and the murderous old king altogether (Matthew 2:12).

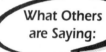

What Others are Saying:

John F. MacArthur Jr.: The magi, "having been warned by God in a dream not to return to Herod . . . departed for their own country by another way." . . . There almost seems to be a double meaning in that statement. They returned to their own country by a different geographical route, to be sure. But they also were now followers of another way in the spiritual sense. That's true of everyone who turns to Christ and becomes one of his worshipers in spirit and truth.[15]

Study Questions

1. Describe the dilemma Joseph faced when he learned of Mary's pregnancy. How was the problem resolved?
2. How did God move national and international governments to arrange for Christ to be born in Bethlehem? How does knowing that change your view of today's current events?
3. At what time of year were shepherds most likely to be out in the fields watching over their sheep at night? What was special about the sheep they were likely guarding?
4. Identify the three ceremonies required by Jewish law when a first baby boy was born.

5. What or who were the Magi? And how can we learn from their actions?
6. What is significant about each of the following prophetic statements: (a) *"They will call him Immanuel"* (Matthew 1:23) and (b) *"You Bethlehem . . . out of you will come a ruler"* (Matthew 2:6)?

CHAPTER WRAP-UP

- When Joseph learned Mary, the woman to whom he was pledged to be married, was pregnant by the Holy Spirit, he found it too incredible to believe. He decided to divorce her quietly. Before he could do so, an angel in a dream convinced him to believe Mary's story and to marry her. He did. (Matthew 1:18–25)

- Though the baby Christ was born in circumstances of extreme poverty, his arrival brought great joy to Mary and Joseph, the watching angels, some shepherds who were first told the news, and Simeon and Anna who met them in the Temple. His arrival also brought predictions from Simeon of opposition from his countrymen and suffering. (Luke 2:1–38)

- After his dedication at the Temple, a group of Eastern wise men followed an unusual star to Jerusalem and then on to Bethlehem where they bowed before the Christ child and gave him gifts. (Matthew 2:1–12)

3 AND GOD SAID, "TODAY I AM A MAN !"

CHAPTER HIGHLIGHTS

- Midnight Escape
- Boy from Nowhere
- Christ Must Be a Man

Let's Get Started

Jesus was not everyone's "fair-haired boy." His mother Mary rejoiced in his birth. His adoptive father Joseph did too. Two old saints at the Temple saw him as their salvation. A delegation of foreign stargazers brought him rich gifts. But in the halls of political and religious power, the response ranged from cool to downright terrifying. By the time the little boy Jesus took his first steps, he found himself running for his life from people obsessed with ending it all before it had barely started!

☞ **Check It Out:**

Matthew 1:1–17; 2:13–23

Luke 2:39–52; 3:23–38

> **Matthew 2:13** An angel of the Lord appeared to Joseph in a dream. "Get up," he said, "take the child and his mother and escape to Egypt. Stay there until I tell you, for Herod is going to search for the child to kill him."

Midnight Escape

It was the middle of the night after the Magi had left for home. The *"angel of the Lord"* in Joseph's dream spoke with urgency. Joseph was unaware of the threat to his family's safety looming huge and gaining terrifying intensity while he slept. The threat pulsed in the murderous heart of that insanely jealous old potentate, Herod.

The Magi had not returned to report baby Jesus' location (Matthew 2:8), and Herod was in a towering rage. Determined to do

☞ **Check It Out:**

Matthew 2:13–18

whatever it took to destroy the new rival, that very night, he had ordered a regiment of his soldiers to go to Bethlehem in the morning to break into every home and to kill every male child two years old and younger!

The Mad, Mad Baby Killer

The twisted Idumean puppet king of Judea and Samaria, Herod, was near death with a painful, incurable disease. In the ultimate act of denial, he spent his last days in a maniacal crusade to cling to the throne that death would soon tear from him. His rage at the Magi's snub and the plot he hatched to destroy the newborn king they'd come to worship were part of a series of murderous insanities near the end of his almost indescribably wicked life. Besides slaughtering the innocents of Bethlehem, in his last days of life Herod

- tortured his sons' friends to discover plots against him,
- crucified his son, Antipater, for trying to poison him, and
- imprisoned leading Jews, with instructions that they all be killed the moment he died, to ensure his death would not be a time of national rejoicing, but mourning.

Before dawn (before the grief-stricken screams of Bethlehem's mothers pierced the air around David's town) Joseph and his little family were well on their way, southward to Egypt.

Something to Ponder

expatriates: people who leave their native country

The trip from Bethlehem into Egypt (see illustration, page 39) would have been more than 150 miles, depending on where they stopped. Thousands of Jewish **expatriates**, perhaps some relatives of Joseph or Mary, lived in a number of Egyptian cities. A million Jews lived in Alexandria alone (about 300 miles from Bethlehem), but Mary and Joseph would not have needed to go that far to find a place to stay.

> **Luke 2:39–40** When Joseph and Mary had done everything required by the Law of the Lord, they returned to Galilee to their own town of Nazareth. And the child grew and became strong; he was filled with wisdom, and the grace of God was upon him.

GOSPEL QUARTET IN HARMONY

Matthew 2:19–23
Luke 2:39–52

The Boy From Nowhere

Joseph, Mary, and Jesus stayed in Egypt until an angel brought word of Herod's death (Matthew 2:19–20). The gifts of the Magi were used to pay the expenses of their impromptu Egyptian "holiday."

Upon returning to Israel, Joseph may have briefly considered establishing a home in Bethlehem (verse 22). But when he heard that Archelaus, a more brutal tyrant than his father, Herod, was on the throne of Judea, Joseph quickly decided not to "pass go or collect $200," but to proceed directly to Galilee, to the safer, familiar community of Nazareth where he and Mary knew everyone.

ARCHELAUS: Son of Herod the Great by his wife, Malthace. When his father died in 4 B.C., his kingdom was divided between three of his sons (see illustration, page 40): Herod Antipas ruled Galilee and Perea; Herod Philip ruled Iturea and Trachonitis; and Herod Archelaus ruled Judea, Samaria, and Idumea. Archelaus' reign was cruel and turbulent. In 6 A.D. the Judeans convinced Rome to replace Archelaus with a Roman governor.

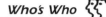 *Who's Who*

Flight to Egypt

The holy family's probable route from Bethlehem to Egypt is shown by the dashed line.

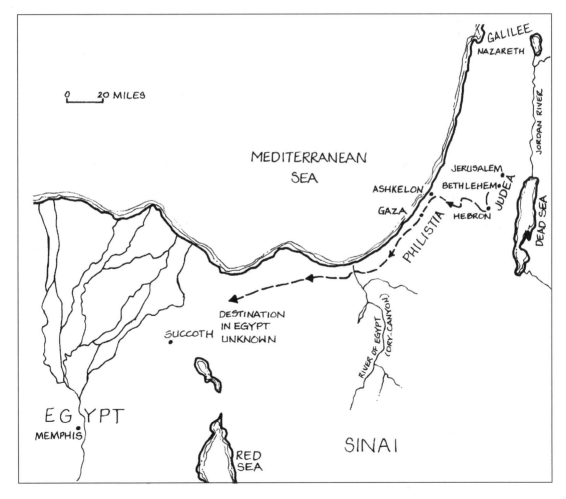

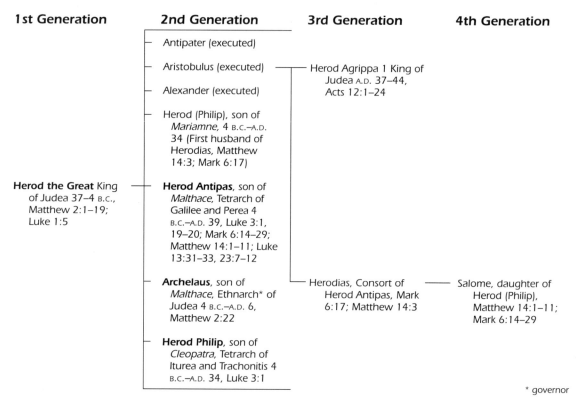

1st Generation	2nd Generation	3rd Generation	4th Generation
	Antipater (executed)		
	Aristobulus (executed)	Herod Agrippa 1 King of Judea A.D. 37–44, Acts 12:1–24	
	Alexander (executed)		
	Herod (Philip), son of *Mariamne*, 4 B.C.–A.D. 34 (First husband of Herodias, Matthew 14:3; Mark 6:17)		
Herod the Great King of Judea 37–4 B.C., Matthew 2:1–19; Luke 1:5	**Herod Antipas**, son of *Malthace*, Tetrarch of Galilee and Perea 4 B.C.–A.D. 39, Luke 3:1, 19–20; Mark 6:14–29; Matthew 14:1–11; Luke 13:31–33, 23:7–12		
	Archelaus, son of *Malthace*, Ethnarch* of Judea 4 B.C.–A.D. 6, Matthew 2:22	Herodias, Consort of Herod Antipas, Mark 6:17; Matthew 14:3	Salome, daughter of Herod (Philip), Matthew 14:1–11; Mark 6:14–29
	Herod Philip, son of *Cleopatra*, Tetrarch of Iturea and Trachonitis 4 B.C.–A.D. 34, Luke 3:1		

* governor

Herod's Family Tree

The Herod family tree shows all the Herods mentioned in the Gospels and how they were related to one another. Major leaders during Jesus' life are in bold. Wives of rulers are in italics.

☞ **GO TO:**

Matthew 2:15, 18, 23; Hosea 11:1; Jeremiah 31:15 (prophecy)

 **KEY Outline:**

Angels

Guide Joseph
- announce Jesus' birth
- warn to go to Egypt
- say when to return home

Your Basic Nobody

Matthew carefully reports how God led each movement of the family, and how each step they took fulfilled messianic prophecy. One statement Matthew attributes to the prophets—"He will be called a Nazarene" (2:23)—puzzles Bible students because it's not found in any of the prophets' writings. However, the statement is completely consistent with the spirit of all the messianic prophecies. For example, Isaiah 53:1–3 describes God's special Servant (Christ) as without beauty or majesty, despised, rejected, and not esteemed. Nazareth was decidedly not on Israel's list of "most desirable places to live." It was a little "nowhere town." To be called a "Nazarene" was to be called a "good-for-nothing." Nobody expected anybody who was somebody to come from Nazareth. The attitude expressed by Nathaniel was typical. When Philip told him the man he believed was the Christ came from Nazareth, Nathanael retorted: "Nazareth! Can anything good come from there?" (John 1:46).

Growing Up In Nazareth

In Nazareth the child Jesus grew to manhood. Jesus' four brothers and at least two sisters were born there (Mark 6:3). At Joseph's side, he learned the carpenter's trade—working in wood, metal, and stone; building furniture, farming equipment, and houses.

Education for a Jewish child began when he was still at his mother's breast. The nursing mother sang the Psalms to her babies and told them stories of Abraham, Isaac, Joseph, Moses, and David. Beginning at age five, boys were taught to read and write the Scriptures in the synagogue school. Both father and mother were responsible to teach the biblical truths to their children in the context of daily life and work. Scriptures were <u>posted</u> about the house. Jesus' family regularly attended the synagogue and the feasts at Jerusalem. Jesus had no formal education beyond these influences, yet his knowledge of the Bible continually <u>amazed</u> enemies and friends.

Jesus As A Teen

The only extended personal glimpse we have of the boy Jesus is just as he enters puberty, at 12 years of age when a Jewish boy became a "**son of the commandment**," a member of the congregation, and personally accountable for the responsibilities of the Law of Moses. On that day, at his bar mitzvah, the boy stood before parents, elders, and friends and declared: "Today, I am a man!"

According to custom, his parents then took the young man to Jerusalem for Passover (Luke 2:41). When the festival was over, they headed home, along with the group of relatives and friends who had traveled from Nazareth together. The women usually started out several hours before the men, because the men traveled faster. Evidently, Joseph thought Jesus had left with Mary and the women, and Mary thought Jesus had stayed behind to walk with the men. At day's end, when the men caught up and camp was set up for the night, they discovered that Jesus was not in either group!

Anxiously, Mary and Joseph returned to Jerusalem to look for him. After three days of searching, they found him at the Temple with the teachers.

At feast times, the practice of the members of the Jewish **Sanhedrin** (elders) was to sit in the Temple courtyard and discuss theological questions raised by anyone who cared to listen. All the time his parents hunted for him, Jesus was there. Starting out for Galilee alone would have been too dangerous for the 12 year old. So, knowing his parents would return and find him, he spent the days *"sitting among the teachers, listening to them and*

KEY POINT

Being from Nazareth was Jesus' I.D. badge to join the "nobodies."

☞ **GO TO:**

Deuteronomy 6:6–9 (posted)

John 7:15; Luke 2:47; Matthew 7:28 (amazed)

son of the commandment: *English for* bar mitzvah

KEY Outline:

Jewish Education
Parents
- tell stories
- sing Psalms
- post Scriptures
- answer questions

Sanhedrin: *70 leaders who served as High Council and Supreme Court in Hebrew law*

asking them questions" (verse 46). Those words were used to describe the process of a student learning from his teachers. This process—asking questions and listening to the teachers—is how young rabbis were trained. It's the method Jesus would later use in training his own disciples.

My Father's House

The exchange between Jesus and his mother when they found him is revealing (verses 48–49, paraphrased):

"Your *father* and I have been worried and searching for you for three days!" said Mary, with no small hint of frustration.

"Why did you spend three days searching for me?" the 12 year old answered, "Surely you knew I would be in my *Father's* **house**?"

Between the lines is an important revelation: At age 12, Jesus knew who he was. He was conscious he was the Son, not of Joseph, but of God.

Audrey I. Girard: Jesus to his mother: "I thought you'd know where I was—you know me so well—I never gave it a thought, and I lost track of time. I was so excited to find those who could answer my questions." Jesus trusted his mother and that day she grew to a new level of that trust—she hid it in her heart.[1]

> **Hebrews 2:17–18** He had to be made like his brothers in every way, in order that he might become a merciful and faithful high **priest** in service to God, and that he might make **atonement** for the sins of the people. Because he himself suffered when he was tempted, he is able to help those who are being tempted.

"Today I Am A Man"

Even though he knew he was God's Son, Jesus returned to Nazareth with Joseph and Mary and, for another 18 years, voluntarily submitted to their parental authority and to the protocols of the human community. He experienced all the stages of normal human life—fetus in his mother's womb, helpless newborn infant, toddler, growing boy, teenager, young man, and finally mature adult.

The book of Hebrews says he experienced all the temptations that go with being human, but he never sinned. In the normal course of human suffering, he *"learned obedience"* (Hebrews 5:8) to his parents and to God.

Robert L. Thomas and Stanley N. Gundry: Jesus grew up as the oldest of the children in a rather large family. Joseph supported the family through carpentry in which Jesus assisted. Joseph apparently died during the period before Jesus' public appearance and, by implications in the gospels and early church fathers, we can presume Jesus became the provider for his mother and younger brothers and sisters (Mark 6:3). He therefore seemingly continued to work at carpentry until the beginning of his public ministry. His frequent mention of articles of furniture, houses, plows, yokes, and the like in his teaching reflects an intimate acquaintance with items built by carpenters.[2]

KINGDOM OF GOD

Roots: Jesus' Family Heritage

When Jesus spoke the words of the bar mitzvah, the 12-year-old human voice was also speaking for God, making the astounding assertion: "Today, I am a man!"

Two New Testament writers list Jesus' human heritage. Many people, starting to read the New Testament at the beginning, find their heads swimming with an unfamiliar list of difficult-to-pronounce names with which Matthew fills his first 17 verses. Bo-o-or-ing! However, Jewish readers, for whom Matthew is writing, would have seen the relevance of the list immediately because it establishes Jesus' credentials as the Messiah. To Jewish readers <u>genealogies</u> were extremely important to identify who was and who was not to be counted among "God's chosen people."

Luke traces Jesus' roots back to Adam, the first human (Luke 3:38). Matthew starts with Abraham, the first Jew (Matthew 1:1–2). From Abraham to David the two lists are the same. From David to Joseph they are quite different. Bible scholars give a variety of reasons for the difference.

1. Matthew gives the royal descent of Jesus, establishing his right to <u>David's throne</u>.
2. Matthew gives Joseph's family tree, while Luke gives Mary's.
3. The differences may be explained by the fact that many Jewish men were known by <u>more than one name.</u>
4. The differences may be due to the fact that in Jewish culture it was common practice, when a man died, for his brother to <u>marry the widow</u> and raise children in his own name or in the name of the deceased.

Something to Ponder

We don't have enough data to know for sure which explanation is correct. These things we know:

- Luke's list shows the humanity of Christ and his identification with, not just the Jews, but with all mankind. Christ's roots go deeper in the human family than any single nation or race—he came from and for all people!
- Matthew's list shows that Jesus was legally Joseph's son. Under Jewish law that established his right to claim David's throne.

Good Guys, Bad Guys In Jesus' Roots

Take another quick squint at Matthew's list (Matthew 1). Yes, I admit: Reading this list of Hebrew names is only slightly more inspiring than reading the telephone directory. But if you take time to cross-reference some of the names, intriguing stuff oozes out between the lines.

Abraham, father of the Hebrew nation, "God's friend," heads the list. The best and worst of Israel's kings are listed.

☞ **GO TO:**

2 Chronicles 20:7 (God's friend)

1 Samuel 13:14 (David)

2 Kings 22–23 (Josiah)

2 Kings 21; 2 Chronicles 33 (Manasseh)

2 Chronicles 33:10–17 (back to God)

THE BEST

David (verse 6), *"a man after [God's] own heart"*
Josiah (verse 11), *"He did what was right in the eyes of the Lord . . . not turning aside to the right or to the left."*

THE WORST

Manasseh (verse 10), *"led Judah and the people of Jerusalem astray, so that they did more evil than the nations the Lord had destroyed before the Israelites"* (2 Chronicles 33:9). No king of Judah ever did more dirt than Manasseh. Yet even this old reprobate turned back to God late in his miserable life and was accepted. (Amazing grace! There's a steady stream of it running through the generations represented in Jesus' genealogy.)

Christians take great comfort in knowing Jesus comes from a long line of flawed human beings. The genes of saints and sinners combine in the humanity of the Savior of saints and sinners.

Leading Ladies

Another difference between Matthew's and Luke's genealogies is that Matthew lists several women in the ancestral register. Sticking out like sore thumbs in Jesus' family tree are some of the Bible's notorious women.

KEY POINT

Jesus' family tree represents a cross section of good guys and bad guys—he came for all.

Notorious Women in Jesus' Family Tree

Notorious Woman	Claim to Fame	Find Her Story in . . .
Tamar (verse 3)	Got pregnant in incestuous relationship with father-in-law	Genesis 38 and GWWB, pages 212–214
Rahab (verse 5)	Prostitute of Jericho who helped Israeli spies	Joshua 2:1–21; 6:25 and GWWB, page 125
Ruth (verse 5)	Pagan woman from Moab	Ruth 1 and GWWB, pages 194–205
Bathsheba (verse 6)	Adulterous affair with King David produced illegitimate child and got her husband, Uriah, killed	2 Samuel 11, 12 and GWWB, pages 214–218

Revell Bible Encyclopedia: God's grace not only reached out to save these women, but also placed them in the line of Redeemer.[3]

> **What Others are Saying:**

> **Philippians 2:8** And being found in appearance as a man, [Christ] humbled himself and became obedient to death—even the death of the cross.

Why Was It Necessary For Christ To Be A Man?

The claim of all the New Testament writers is that the child in the manger was God. But the New Testament never lets us forget Jesus was as much man as he was God. The plan of God could only be accomplished through a Redeemer who was an authentic man. In his Philippians 2 declaration above, Paul (GWBI, pages 219–224; GWMB, pages 227–235) reveals the major reason Christ must be human.

The Son of God had to become a son of man to make it possible for him to die. As God he was immortal and indestructible. As man he was **mortal**—he could die. To pay the penalty human sin deserved so human sinners could be forgiven it was necessary for Christ to be authentic man.

KEY POINT

Christ became mortal so he could die for our sins.

mortal: able to die

Ronald B. Allen: We know that the real issue of the Incarnation is that it was only as Man that God could die. The Christmas cliché—here is One who was born to die—is a vivid reality. . . . It is only the cross and the empty tomb that give Christmas its full meaning.[4]

> **What Others are Saying:**

Christ Must Be a Man

Dig Deeper

Scripture	Reasons for Christ to Become a Man
John 1:14, 18	So people can see what God is really like
Hebrews 2:6–9	So people can see a life-sized, three-dimensional picture of an authentic human being
1 Peter 2:21; 1 John 2:6	So people can observe an authentic human living by faith and in the Spirit's energy
Hebrews 2:9–13; Philippians 2:5–7	So Christ could be mortal, able to die as a substitute sacrifice for human sins
Hebrews 2:14–16	So Christ can assume his role as High Priest/Mediator between people and God

What Others are Saying:

Robert E. Coleman: In the fullness of time, God's plan to take upon himself the experience of man assumed material form in the incarnation of Christ. . . . The new Being was not a man who became God; he is God who became man, coming into history from the outside.[5]

Ronald B. Allen: So long as Christians have difficulty giving assent to the genuine humanity of the Savior, Christians are likely to have difficulty coming to terms with their own humanity.[6]

Study Questions

1. What is significant about each of the following statements: (a) *"Out of Egypt I called my son"* (Matthew 2:15) and (b) *"He will be called a Nazarene"* (Matthew 2:23)?
2. When did religious education of a Jewish child begin?
3. What does bar mitzvah mean? When was it celebrated? What did it signify?
4. How can the differences between the two genealogies of Jesus (Matthew 1; Luke 3) be explained?
5. What is the significance of including four notorious women in Jesus' family tree (Matthew 1:1–17)? How does that make you feel about your heritage?
6. Identify three of the four reasons Christ had to be a real human being.

- To save the baby Jesus from Herod's murderous intentions, an angel warned Joseph to get out of Bethlehem posthaste! He took Mary and the baby to Egypt until after Herod's death. Then another angel told him when it was safe to return to Israel. (Matthew 2:13–23)

- After returning from Egypt, Jesus grew up in Nazareth, among relatives and neighbors. After his bar mitzvah, on a trip to the Passover Feast in Jerusalem, Jesus disclosed his understanding of his special relationship to his Father in heaven. (Matthew 2:39–52)

- Both Matthew and Luke give genealogies of Jesus that demonstrate his human roots. Matthew traces his legal heritage and rightful claim to David's throne through his adoptive father, Joseph. Luke shows his natural human heritage through Mary, tracing Jesus' roots back to Adam, the first man, and to God, the Creator. (Matthew 1:1–17, Luke 3:23–38)

Part Two

THE REVOLUTION BEGINS

With only two menu items, John the Baptist's fast-food chain failed to last long.

4 SHOUT IN THE DESERT

Let's Get Started

Two boys were born six months apart. Though the boys were cousins there is no evidence they ever met until they were adults, yet their lives and destinies were inseparably bound with each other. One grew up in the **Desert** of Judea, the other in a little crossroads town in Galilee.

The first boy, John, was born to parents too old to have children. Amid celebration of his birth, the father, in a Spirit-filled song, expressed high hopes for the boy (Luke 1:67–79). Then, for 30 years nothing was heard from or about him.

The second boy, Jesus, was also raised in relative anonymity. Glowing words were spoken about him by strangers at his baby dedication. An insane tyrant tried to kill him when he was two. At age 12 on a family trip to Jerusalem, Jesus debated with fascinated scholars who were *"amazed at his understanding and his answers"* (Luke 2:47). He went home with his parents and was obedient to them for the next 18 years (Luke 2:51–52). Those 18 years of obscurity are called "the hidden years" of Jesus' life. A few highly questionable legends have circulated about those years, but nothing that can really be called "authoritative."

> **Mark 1:1** The beginning of the gospel about Jesus Christ, the Son of God.

Front-Page News

Mark's Life of Christ skipped the angels, the virgin birth, the marriage of Joseph and Mary, the visit of the Magi—Jesus' entire

CHAPTER HIGHLIGHTS

- Front-Page News
- Desert Crier
- Bulldozer Named Repentance
- John Said about Jesus
- Water Fellowship
- Spirit-Dove

GOSPEL QUARTET IN HARMONY

Matthew 3:1–17

Mark 1:1–11

Luke 3:1–22

Desert: rocky, mountainous, thinly settled country east of Jerusalem along the Jordan River and Dead Sea, better suited for pasture than tilling

☞ **GO TO:**

Joshua 15:61–62; 1 Samuel 25:1–2 (Desert of Judea)

good news: the Gospel,
the story of Christ

early life. To Mark, the **good news** began, not with a baby Jesus, but with an adult Jesus, being introduced by an adult John the Baptist.

> **Luke 3:1–2** In the fifteenth year of the reign of Tiberius Caesar—when Pontius Pilate was governor of Judea, Herod tetrarch of Galilee, his brother Philip tetrarch of Iturea and Traconitis, and Lysanias tetrarch of Abilene—during the high priesthood of Annas and Caiaphas, word of God came to John son of Zechariah in the desert.

Dateline

The "when" of this front-page news was supplied by the most finicky of the New Testament historians, Luke. He wanted readers to know the time, and to understand that the story of John the Baptist and Jesus of Nazareth was no "once upon a time" invention. It was thoroughly factual and set solidly in the history of that time. Knowing the names of five political leaders and two religious leaders who were running things, we can calculate that John began to preach sometime in late 28 or early 29 A.D.

Who's Who

TIBERIUS CAESAR: The Roman emperor, in the 15th year of his reign (between August, 28 A.D. and August, 29 A.D.). Caesar, the title of Roman emperors, was derived from Julius Caesar.

Who's Who

Herod the Great: baby killer of Bethlehem (Matthew 2:16), died 4 B.C.

tetrarch: "fourth"—ruler of a small province

PONTIUS PILATE: The governor of Judea, "Prefect" was his official Roman title. Technically, Judea was Herod's territory, which, after Herod's death was at first assigned to his son Archelaus. But hatred for Herod and his son was so intense, the Jews petitioned Rome for another governor. Pilate was one of Rome's appointees to the post.

Who's Who

HEROD: Antipas, son of the late **Herod the Great**, tetrarch of Galilee and Perea after his father's death (see illustration, page 40).

Who's Who

PHILIP: Also called "Herod Philip," another of Herod's sons, **tetrarch** of Iturea and Trachonitis, territories north of the Sea of Galilee, near Mt. Hermon.

LYSANIAS: Tetrarch of Abilene. Other than a passing mention in the writings of first century Jewish historian Josephus, nothing more is known of him beyond what Luke says.

Who's Who __

ANNAS and CAIAPHAS: The father-son combo running Jewish religious life. Annas was the former High Priest who still wielded the power and was considered by the Jews the legitimate High Priest even though the Romans had deposed him. Caiaphas, his son, officially held the office.

Who's Who __

The Late, Great, Unforgettable What's-His-Name?

All the men Luke names were men of worldly power who were well known in their heyday for wickedness and abuse of power. By contrast, John was an unknown desert preacher speaking out courageously for truth and righteousness. Today, those powerful and terrifying historical figures are all but forgotten. But the name of John the Baptist is still a household word.

Something to Ponder

> **Luke 3:3–4** He went into all the country around the Jordan, preaching a baptism of repentance for the forgiveness of sins. As is written in the book of the words of Isaiah the prophet: "A voice of one calling in the desert, 'Prepare the way for the Lord, make straight paths for him.'"

Desert Crier

John was the son of Zechariah the priest and Elizabeth his wife who had been unable to have children until baby John came along. Along with his surprising birth came <u>prophecies</u> that he would prepare Israel for Christ's arrival. Thirty years later, at the right moment on God's timetable, John emerged from seclusion and began to broadcast what was about to happen and how to prepare for it. Matthew, Mark, and Luke agree—John's ministry was the fulfillment of <u>Isaiah's prophecy</u> of a desert *"voice"* calling Israel to prepare for arrival of the Messiah-King (Isaiah 40:3–5).

GOSPEL QUARTET IN HARMONY

Matthew 3:1–6
Mark 1:2–6
Luke 3:2b–6

☞ **GO TO:**

Luke 1:14–17
(prophecies)

Isaiah 40:3–5
(Isaiah's prophecy)

Why Send An Advance Man Ahead Of Jesus?

Why does Billy Graham send an advance team ahead to make arrangements for his Crusades? So the most people possible will know he's coming and the largest crowd possible will come to hear him preach and the greatest response will be assured for the

Jeremiah 1:1; Ezekiel 6:1; 7:1
(word of God)

Isaiah 7:14; Luke 2:12, 34 (sign)

Luke 1:13
(messenger's birth)

word of God:
terminology for a prophet's commission by God

sign: proof

short time the evangelist is on the scene (usually just a few days).

About six months before Jesus' ministry began, *"the **word of God** came to John,"* commissioning him to speak out as Christ's advance messenger (Luke 3:2). John's emergence was a **sign** Israel had been taught to look for that Messiah was about to arrive.

Why should God go to all the trouble to tell the nation hundreds of years ahead of time to watch for a special advance messenger? Why, 30 years in advance, should God send an angel to announce the messenger's birth? And why, finally, should God personally tell the messenger when it was time to start announcing the approach of *"the Lord"* (Matthew 3:3; Mark 1:3)? All this attention given to the advance man and his work indicates that the one for whom Israel is preparing is a person of unusual importance in the plan of God. Jesus of Nazareth, we shall discover, is no ordinary man. It is completely appropriate that a prophet from God should introduce him.

Old Testament Prophecies Fulfilled by John's Ministry

Where Predicted	What Is Predicted	Where Fulfilled
Malachi 3:1	God would send his messenger ahead to prepare the way for Christ	Mark 1:2
Isaiah 40:3	Christ's arrival would be preceded by a shouting *"voice"* in the desert	Matthew 3:3; Mark 1:3; Luke 3:4
Isaiah 40:4–5	The ministry of the messenger would be spiritually comparable to a road-building project to prepare for arrival of a King	Luke 3:5–6

What Others are Saying:

KEY Outline:

John the Baptist
Got message from God
Fulfilled prophecies
Signaled the Messiah
Called for repentance

William Barclay: When a king proposed to tour a part of his dominions in the east, he sent a courier before him to tell the people to prepare the roads. So John is regarded as the courier of the King. But the preparation on which he insisted was a preparation of heart and of life. "The king is coming," he said. "Mend, not your roads, but your lives."[1]

KINGDOM OF GOD

John the Baptist called on all Israel to *"repent"* (Matthew 3:2). He proclaimed a new government (*"the kingdom"*) and yet he did not, as might be expected, make his revolutionary announcement in Jerusalem, the nation's governmental center. Instead he preached first to a handful of country folk living along the Jordan River, 20 miles to the east of the capital city. His first audiences may have been outnumbered by lizards and scorpions.

A Burr Under The Saddle Of The Status Quo

News of the desert crier spread like a prairie fire, and soon hundreds were coming out of the cities and towns of Israel just to see and hear the radical desert revivalist. He touched in them a deep, unsatisfied hunger for some word from God to make the tinder-dry desert of their spirits blossom <u>like a rose</u>.

Winner Of The Elijah Look-Alike Contest

John was everything a prophetic "burr under the saddle" should be. His skin was blackened by the desert sun. His eyes blazed from behind a face full of disorderly beard. (At least that's how I imagine him.) Matthew and Mark give us the authorized portrait (Matthew 3:4; Mark 1:6): John the Baptist wore a homespun camel's hair shirt (irritating enough to make a man surly!), which he kept wrapped around himself with a wide leather belt. If invited to brunch with him, don't go! John's menu was always a tasty selection of crunchy insects—*"locusts"*—made palatable by the strong, sweet taste of *"wild honey"* (see GWHN, page 136).

The New Testament nowhere else publishes descriptions of its characters—not even Jesus. Why tell how John dressed and what he ate?

It all had special meaning for people looking for the Messiah. The prophets predicted that Christ's arrival would be preceded by the <u>appearance of Elijah</u>, most <u>heroic</u> of Old Testament prophets (see GWBI, pages 86–87). Near the end of his ministry, Elijah sent word to the king of Israel that because the king had consulted with an idol instead of God he would never recover from injuries he had suffered in a fall. When the king asked for a description of the man who had the audacity to send such a message, he was told, *"He was a man with a garment of hair and with a leather belt around his waist."* From this description, the king recognized his prophet of doom as Elijah (2 Kings 1:2–8).

John the Baptist emerged from the same desert where Elijah spent most of his life. He preached with the same fireball fervor as Elijah. He dressed like Elijah. As the angel predicted before his birth, he came in Elijah's *"<u>spirit</u> and power."*

Henry H. Halley: Knowing he was to be the Elijah of prophecy . . . intentionally, perhaps, he copied the habits and dress of Elijah. He lived on locusts and wild honey. Locusts had been used for food from earliest times. They were roasted, or sun dried, and eaten like parched grain. Are said to taste like shrimps.[2]

ACT OF THE HOLY SPIRIT

Gifted John as a prophet

☞ **GO TO:**

Isaiah 35:1 (like a rose)

KEY Outline:

Similarities between John the Baptist and Elijah

Out of the desert
Fiery preacher
Hair shirt
Bugs and honey
Courageous

☞ **GO TO:**

Malachi 4:5; Matthew 11:14; 17:10–13 (appearance of Elijah)

1 Kings 18 (heroic)

Luke 1:17 (spirit)

What Others are Saying:

KEY POINT

Preparation for God's
kingdom requires
repentance, personal
change, forsaking sin,
repairing injustices,
holy living.

☞ **GO TO:**

Isaiah 40:3–5; Luke
3:4–6 (road-building)

☞ **GO TO:**

Isaiah 35:8–10 (high-
way of holiness)

☞ **Check It Out:**

Matthew 3:7–10

Luke 3:7–14

Stephen M. Miller: Some scholars have suggested that John had once been a member of the Essene sect in Qumran, the community famous for preserving the Dead Sea Scrolls. Like John, these Jews lived in the Judean wilderness and even had rules on how to eat honey and locusts. They also performed daily ritual cleansing similar to baptism, and their documents confirm that they eagerly anticipated the arrival of a Messiah promised by the prophets.[3]

Building The King's Highway

The nation of Israel at the time John began to preach may have been as "wicked and corrupt"[4] as at any time in its history. John's ministry as Christ's forerunner necessarily revolved around a spiritual transaction called *"repentance"* (Luke 3:3, 8). The Old Testament prophecies about John defined repentance in terms that took it beyond mere religious ritual (Luke 3:4–6). Fire up the bulldozer! Clearing the way for Christ is a major <u>road-building</u> project: filling ravines, leveling hills, straightening crooked roads, smoothing rough places (Luke 3:4–6; Isaiah 40:4–5).

Most roads in Bible times were little more than rugged, unsurfaced tracks worn into the land by oxen, mules, and carts. Jewish historian Josephus tells how King Solomon, to show off the splendor and wealth of his government, built and surfaced the roads leading into Jerusalem. These roads, called "the king's highway," were built especially for the king's use and were repaired whenever it was announced that the king would be traveling on them.

KINGDOM
OF GOD

John's call was not for people to make minor repairs on the roadway, but to construct a totally new, broad, easy access for Christ—a new *highway of holiness* into their lives.

> **Matthew 3:8** Produce fruit in keeping with repentance.

A Bulldozer Named Repentance

The New Testament Greek word for repentance is *metanoia*—a change in mind and attitude. As John (and later Jesus) spells out its meaning, it calls for change in basic personal values and lifestyle. The meaning of repentance can be seen in what John told people who came to hear him.

1. Pharisees and **Sadducees** (religious leaders) were corrupt, hypocritical, and pompous. When they came for baptism, John compared them to snakes fleeing before a desert brushfire (Matthew 3:7; Luke 3:7). He told them their days of authority were numbered if they didn't change their stingy, self-centered ways and start sharing what they had with others (Matthew 3:8–10; Luke 3:8–11).

2. He told **tax collectors** to be honest and to collect only what the law demanded, instead of cheating the public (Luke 3:12–13).

3. **Soldiers** came, under orders to see what kind of message the people were hearing. When they asked what he thought they should do to prepare for Christ's coming, he told them to stop falsely accusing people and extorting money by threats of violence (Luke 3:14).

When John's audience asked what they should do to prepare the way for the king, they expected to hear a call to arm themselves and fight the Roman government. They might also have expected to hear a plea to open their wallets and give to the cause. Instead, John said, "Share!" What kind of strange, new revolution is this, that people prepare for it by getting honest, refusing to take advantage of others, and sharing their possessions?

John Killinger: It is interesting that [John's] answer is couched in terms of simple justice. People who have more property than they need are to divide with those who have none. Those who have food are to share with those who are hungry. Tax collectors are to do their duty but forego the often-exorbitant fees they have been accustomed to extracting for personal use. Soldiers are to live simply and honestly, not using their positions to rob or to falsely accuse people of crimes and confiscate their property. . . . They imply a new orientation in life, a new spirit, so that God, not personal profit, becomes the center of the person's life.[5]

Micah: And what does the Lord require of you? To act justly and to love mercy and to walk humbly with your God (Micah 6:8).

Something to Ponder

What Others are Saying:

KEY Outline:

Repentance
Leaders: share
Tax collectors: don't cheat
Soldiers: don't threaten

Remember This . . .

A Process of Change

The concept of repentance, so fundamental to the preaching of John and Jesus, reminds us that following Christ involves a person in a <u>process of change</u>. The changes needed in the basic structures of our lives are so extensive that initial change (that moment of turning to Christ) can only be considered the beginning. Every new ray of spiritual light calls for more change. Repentance involves both decisive moments and life-long growth.

What Others are Saying:

Richard J. Foster: One more thing is needed, namely, our response of repentance—not just once but again and again. Martin Luther declares that the life of the Christian should be one of daily repentance. Daily we confess, daily we repent, daily we "turn, turn, 'til we turn 'round right."[6]

☞ **GO TO:**

2 Corinthians 3:18 (process of change)

The Shocking Baptism Of John

John urged his listeners to publicly dramatize their willingness to change by joining him for a soaking in the Jordan River. Gentiles in the process of converting to Judaism were baptized in special baptismal pools (see illustration, page 59) to symbolize giving up of idol worship, cleansing from idolatry and pagan sins. But life-long Jews did not need baptism. They were already God's special people.

John insisted that people who all their lives thought of themselves that way—as "God's people"—be baptized as if they were just emerging from darkest paganism! In **confrontational** conversation with the religious leaders he argued that being born into the privileged Hebrew bloodline, the right nation, and the correct religion was insufficient preparation for receiving the Lord (Matthew 3:9; Luke 3:8).

confrontational: face-to-face challenge, a clash of ideas

The Kindergarten of the Kingdom

John's baptism raises an important point for our generation of Christians and churches: Over the centuries interpretations and religious traditions have developed around the original teachings of the New Testament that seem to conflict with those original teachings. What would happen if Christians today dared to read the Bible and listen to its truths as if we were hearing them for the first time? What if we approached the stories of Christ like wide-eyed kindergartners instead of sophisticated grown-up religionists? Would we avoid being changed just like the religious leaders of Jesus' day?

Something to Ponder

KEY POINT

We must approach the kingdom of God as kindergartners, not as experts.

Ritual Bath

Jews used baptismal pools such as these in which to perform ritual cleansings and to baptize converts to Judaism. Among other revolutionary things he did, John the Baptist used rivers in which to baptize converts to the kingdom of God.

Dig Deeper

The Changing Meaning of Water Baptism

Historical Reference	Form of Baptism	Significance
Exodus 13:21–22; 14:21–22; 1 Corinthians 10:1–2	Pillar of cloud and crossing the Red Sea	Induction *"into Moses"*—OT Law, Old Covenant relationship with God
After Babylonian exile	Ceremonial baths for Gentile proselytes converting to Judaism	Rejection of false gods, commitment to the faith of Yahweh, Israel's God
Matthew 3:6, 11; Mark 1:5; Luke 3:3	John the Baptist dipping Jews in the Jordan River	Willingness to prepare for Messiah by forsaking their sins
Matthew 28:19; Acts 2:41; Acts 8:35–39	Early Christians using water to initiate converts to Christ	Identification with Christ; death to old way of life, rising to new life in Christ

KEY Outline:

John, on Christ:
*He is more powerful
I am unfit to untie his
shoes*

**GOSPEL QUARTET
IN HARMONY**

Matthew 3:11–12
Mark 1:7–8
Luke 3:15–18

*rabbinic: relating to
rabbis or their writings*

**Something
to Ponder**

☞ **GO TO:**

Acts 1:5; 2:4 (baptizes
with the Holy Spirit)

Mark 10:38–39; 1 Peter
4:12–19
(baptizes with fire)

*baptizes: dips or places
into, soaks, saturates,
dyes (as cloth)*

> **Luke 3:15–18** The people were waiting expectantly and were all wondering in their hearts if John might possibly be the Christ. John answered them all, "I baptize you with water. But one more powerful than I will come, the thongs of whose sandals I am not worthy to untie. He will baptize you with the Holy Spirit and with fire. His winnowing fork is in his hand to clear his threshing floor and to gather the wheat into his barn, but he will burn up the chaff with unquenchable fire." And with many other words John exhorted the people and preached the good news to them.

What John Said About Jesus

Messianic expectations were in the air. As Messiah-minded Jews observed John's Elijah-like preaching and appearance it was inevitable that some would begin to wonder if he might be the Christ. John never encouraged this idea, but faithfully pointed his listeners to the One who was approaching on his heels.

Christ Is Greater

John insisted Christ was more powerful than he was. He said Christ's greatness so far surpasses his that he was not even worthy enough to untie Christ's shoelaces!

> According to Jewish custom, a rabbi, though unpaid for his teaching, could expect his students to express their appreciation by a variety of personal services. A **rabbinic** saying excluded only one task that was thought too menial, too slavelike for a disciple to stoop to—the loosing of the rabbi's sandal-thongs.[7]

Christ's Baptism Is Greater

John insisted he could take people no further spiritually than to baptize them in water as a symbol of their repentance. Only Christ would do the work in their hearts that was necessary if they were to live in the kingdom of God (Luke 3:16–17).

- Only Christ **baptizes** *"with the Holy Spirit."*
- Only Christ baptizes with *"fire,"* meaning judgment, discipline, or the process of cleansing from sin.
- Only Christ can cleanse away the useless *"chaff"* from a person's life. By "chaff" John meant a person's sinful habits and actions.

KINGDOM OF GOD

John could announce the nearness of the kingdom of heaven, but only Christ can make the **new society** happen. He is a King whose Spirit personally <u>lives in</u> the citizens of his kingdom, <u>enabling</u> them to live by the principles he spells out in his teachings.

> **Matthew 3:13–17** Then Jesus came from Galilee to the Jordan to be baptized by John. But John tried to deter him, saying, "I need to be baptized by you, and do you come to me?" Jesus replied, "Let it be so now; it is proper for us to do this to fulfill all righteousness." Then John consented. As soon as Jesus was baptized, he went up out of the water. At that moment heaven was opened, and he saw the Spirit of God descending like a dove and lighting on him. And a voice from heaven said, "This is my Son, whom I love; with him I am well pleased."

Water Fellowship, Water Joy Divine

One fine day as kingdom seekers responded to John's preaching by coming down to the Jordan to be baptized, a young stranger moved toward the water with the other seekers. John recognized him as the One about whom he had been speaking.

"I need to be baptized," Jesus said—just like any repenting sinner (that is what John's baptism signified).

John **instinctively knew** this man was no sinner. He protested. Jesus insisted, saying that it was appropriate for he and John to do the right thing, whatever it might be.

The Bible agrees with John's assessment: Jesus had <u>no sins</u> of his own over which to repent. Why then did he need to be baptized, which for all others was a sign of repentance for forgiveness of sins?

Why Did Jesus Need To Be Baptized?

John's baptism involved three factors:

1. Public identification with John's message
2. Public commitment to live by God's standards of righteousness
3. Public expression of eagerness to welcome the Messiah[8]

new society: *kingdom of God, community of faith*

☞ **GO TO:**

Galatians 2:20 (lives in)

John 15:5; Acts 1:8; Galatians 5:22–23; Philippians 4:13 (enabling)

GOSPEL QUARTET IN HARMONY

Matthew 3:13–17
Mark 1:9–11
Luke 3:21–22

instinctively knew: *the Holy Spirit revealed it to him*

☞ **GO TO:**

2 Corinthians 5:21; Hebrews 4:15 (no sins)

ACT OF THE HOLY SPIRIT

Revealed Messiah's identity to John the Baptist

Baptism identified
Jesus with sinners.
That identification
became most visible
when he died on the
cross between two
thieves.

☞ **GO TO:**

Luke 5:29–32; 15:1–2
(friend of sinners)

Matthew 27:46
(cut him off)

☞ **GO TO:**

2 Corinthians 5:21 (sin
to righteousness)

Remember
This . . .

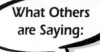

What Others
are Saying:

☞ **Check It Out:**

Luke 3:23–38

Baptism launched Jesus' career with a public declaration that he was one of us—a human being. The task the Father in heaven had dispatched him to earth to do required him to be human. When people watched him go down into the Jordan River, they had no doubt they were observing the actions of a man, not some sort of special semi-man or semi-god with whom it would be impossible for them to identify. After his baptism gossips would slander him as a liar, a blasphemer, a <u>friend of sinners</u>, and a drunk. No surprise then for Jesus to show up at the Jordan River in a crowd of repentant sinners, to file down into the water at the preacher's invitation and declare he was forsaking sin and committing himself to righteousness—just like the others.

Eventually Jesus' identification with sinners would be so complete that he would die a death reserved only for criminals and other public enemies. As he died he would experience the terrifying feeling God had <u>cut him off</u>! His identification with humans did not stop until he had experienced what human sinners experience—suffering, death, separation from God, and judgment.

KINGDOM OF GOD

By presenting himself for baptism, Jesus was not confessing that he was a sinner. He was saying,

1. "I'm with John."
2. "I'm committed to live a righteous life."
3. "I want to live under God's reign."
4. "I'm one of you."

Jesus did not need baptism, and he did not deserve the cross. The New Testament insists he willingly yielded to both to make it possible for the rest of us to be raised from <u>sin to righteousness</u> through faith in him.

Clark Peddicord: Jesus' identification with the sinful people of Israel was similar to what Moses did in the wilderness after the Israelites had sinned by making themselves a gold calf as an idol (Exodus 32:30–32). God accepted Jesus' perfect repentance for his people just as he had that of Moses. This is shown by the heavens tearing open and the Holy Spirit descending on Jesus.[9]

Descent Of The Spirit-Dove

As Jesus came out of the water after John baptized him, a white form fluttered down from the sky. It looked like a dove. It was the

Spirit of God coming to rest upon him. The Spirit of God would provide the power and direction he needed for going where he must go and doing what he must do during the next three-and-one-half years. As the Spirit's presence settled on him he heard a voice: *"This is my Son, whom I love; with him I am well pleased"* (Matthew 3:17).

Henry Alford: Two circumstances may be noticed respecting the manner of the descent of the Spirit: It was *as a dove*—the Spirit as manifested in our Lord was gentle and benign. This was not a sudden and temporary descent of the Spirit, but a permanent though special **anointing** of the Savior for his holy office. . . . And from this moment his ministry and **mediatorial** work (in the active official sense) begins.[10]

Audrey I. Girard: Perhaps the coming of the Spirit in dove-like form signified yet again God's concern for the poorest of poor; identifying to the humble the realization that Jesus came for them. They often could only afford a dove for sacrifice at the door of the tabernacle.[11]

Son Of God—Son Of Adam

It is at this point—after the voice at Jesus' baptism had affirmed his relationship to God as *"my Son, whom I love"*—Luke inserts Jesus' human genealogy. Luke traces Jesus' roots back to Adam as if to emphasize that as God's unique One and Only Son, Jesus is no less a full–fledged member of the human race.

Study Questions

1. What made the people of Israel think that a special prophet would signal the coming of Christ? What sort of prophet were they looking for?
2. What one word describes the essence of John the Baptist's message? What does it mean, and how does that word relate to your life?
3. What specific changes did John call for in the following groups of people: Pharisees and Sadducees? Tax collectors? Soldiers?
4. What was there about John's baptism that was so shocking and humbling?
5. What is the difference between the meaning of John's baptism and the baptism practiced by the early Christians?
6. List the three ways Christ's baptism is greater than John's?
7. Jesus was given two things to get him going on his life's

☞ **GO TO:**

Isaiah 11:1–2; 42:1 (Spirit of God)

What Others are Saying:

☞ **GO TO:**

Psalm 2:7 (my Son)

Isaiah 42:1 (well pleased)

Spirit of God: *the Holy Spirit*

anointing: *to confer on someone authority to fulfill his/her calling*

mediatorial: *go between God and sinners*

work—the Spirit came on him like a dove, and a heavenly voice assured him of his relationship with and approval by God. How has God affirmed you as his child in Christ?

CHAPTER WRAP-UP

- The Gospel (good news) centers in Jesus of Nazareth. By carefully documenting the timing of his story, the New Testament writers make it clear that Jesus is a real person who lived a real life at a specific time in history, which they carefully document. (Luke 3:1–2)

- The importance of Jesus of Nazareth was highlighted by the commission of John the Baptist to urge the Jews to turn from their sins in preparation to receive the Messiah. (Matthew 3:1–6)

- Preparing to receive Christ is compared to building a roadway for a king. The "earth-moving" machinery is a spiritual transaction called "repentance"—willingness to change in the basic structures of one's life. (Matthew 3:7–10)

- John invited his hearers to present themselves for a special kind of baptism, which symbolized a humiliating acknowledgment that, though they were lifelong Jews, they needed to be taught how to live in the kingdom of God from the ground up. (Luke 3:7–14)

- John insisted he was not the Christ, but that a person was coming after him who surpassed John in greatness and power to bring real change into people's lives. This Christ would baptize believers with the Holy Spirit and with fire (discipline, suffering, and judgment of sin in their lives). (Matthew 3:11–12; Luke 3:16–17)

- Jesus asked John to baptize him, in order to complete his identification with human beings, to announce his agreement with John's ministry and message, and to publicly commit himself to live a righteous life under the reign of God. (Matthew 3:13–17)

- At his baptism, the Holy Spirit was seen descending on Jesus in dove-like form, anointing him with authority for his ministry. A heavenly voice announced that Jesus was the Son of God and that God was pleased with him. (John 1:32–34)

GOD'S WORD FOR THE BIBLICALLY-INEPT

5 FIRST BLOOD

Let's Get Started

Following his baptism by John the Baptist, Jesus was purposely led by the Holy Spirit into the wild country surrounding the Jordan River and the Dead Sea. There God's <u>archenemy</u>, the devil, would test the young Messiah's grasp of his mission and what would be necessary to accomplish it. The original Greek word translated *"tempted"* is used three ways in the Bible:

- It primarily means "to be tested."
- It is also used for *"<u>trials</u>"*—external troubles that test one's faith.
- It also refers to *"<u>temptation</u>"* as we usually understand it: enticement away from God toward sin.

> **Matthew 4:1–2** Then Jesus was led up by the Spirit into the desert to be tempted by the devil. After fasting forty days and forty nights, he was hungry.

Testing, Testing

Count on it! If you are human, you will be tempted. You will experience pressures that force you to make moral choices. Trials by fire and pressure are permitted not for God to determine the state of our faith and relationship with him. <u>He knows</u>. We face temptation, trial, and testing to demonstrate to ourselves the truth about our readiness (or lack of it) to do God's will. When we make the right choice, the tempter is defeated.

CHAPTER HIGHLIGHTS

- Testing, Testing
- Invisible Peril
- Three Propositions
- Test Passed

GOSPEL QUARTET IN HARMONY

Matthew 4:1–11

Mark 1:12–13

Luke 4:1–13

☞ **GO TO:**

Luke 10:18–19; 1 Peter 5:8–9 (archenemy)

James 1:2, 12 (trials)

James 1:13–14 (temptation)

GOSPEL QUARTET IN HARMONY

Matthew 4:1–3

Mark 1:12–13

Luke 4:1–3

☞ **GO TO:**

Psalm 44:20–21; 94:11;
Luke 16:15
(He knows)

Ephesians 6:10–18
(Holy War)

Ephesians 1:21; 1 John
5:19 (evil forces)

devil: *evil being also
known as Satan*

world order: *human
society in opposition to
God*

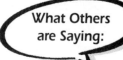

**What Others
are Saying:**

KEY Outline:

Jesus' 40-Day Test
*Fasting (physical)
Temptation (spiritual)*

KEY Outline:

Purposes of Testing
A check-up
- is faith real?
- are we growing?

A demonstration
- to angels
- to devils

Jesus' testing came in the form of (1) 40 days and nights in a desert environment without food, and (2) pressure from the **devil** to sidestep the plan of God. This would be the first face-to-face skirmish in the <u>Holy War</u> Jesus had been sent to fight against the <u>evil forces</u> that mastermind the present **world order**.

Jesus believed in not merely the concept but the reality of a personal devil. The term "personal devil" means that he is not an impersonal evil force pervading the universe, but an actual individual with intelligence, emotions, and will.

Why Are Christians Tested?

The Bible mentions several reasons why Christians are tested:

- So we can know for certain our faith is genuine (1 Peter 1:7)
- So we can be changed into Christ's likeness (Romans 8:28–29)
- So the spirit world (angels and devils) can see a visible demonstration of God's wisdom worked out in believing humanity (Ephesians 3:10–13)

William Barclay: What we call temptation is not meant to make us sin; it is meant to enable us to conquer sin. It is not meant to make us bad, it is meant to make us good. It is not meant to weaken us, it is meant to make us emerge stronger and finer and purer from the ordeal. Temptation is not the penalty of being a man, temptation is the glory of being a man.[1]

Revell Bible Dictionary: Theologically, the temptation of Jesus served to establish both his humanity and his complete commitment to God. This, in turn, established Jesus' qualifications to teach others how to live in intimate union with God.[2]

The Invisible Peril

Jeshimmon was the Hebrew name for the wild country west of the Dead Sea into which the Holy Spirit led Jesus for the specific purpose of being tempted. The name means "Devastation." It is an untamed area of sand and crumbling limestone. The hills are heaps of dust. Rocks are bare and jagged. Beneath a man's steps the ground sometimes sounds hollow. It all shimmers with heat like a furnace. It runs out to the Dead Sea where it suddenly cuts off in a drop of 1,200 feet of limestone, flint, and marl, through crags and potholes and precipices down to the sea.[3]

The ruggedness of the land, the risk from lion, bear, and other dangerous animals who inhabited it, coupled with the rigors of going 40 days and nights without food, do not suggest "the Jesus portrayed in many paintings—a fair-skinned, scrawny wimp."[4] This Jesus must have been brawny—a man who could endure the challenges involved in his temptation.

Jesus went into this rugged desert accompanied only by the Spirit of God. God's affirming voice heard at his baptism still rang in his ears: *"This is my Son, whom I love; with him I am well pleased"* (Matthew 3:17). The call to Saviorhood burned in his <u>young</u> heart. He had questions, issues to be sorted out. He knew he was God's Son. And he knew he was a man. Awareness of his human limitations and the awesomeness of his task set the tone of his thoughts and prayers.

For 40 days and nights, he hiked the wilds, fasting. Both Mark and Luke indicate that temptation dogged Jesus' tracks the entire <u>six weeks</u>.

☞ **GO TO:**

Luke 3:23 (young)

Mark 1:13; Luke 4:2 (six weeks)

Ted Olsen: After his baptism in the Jordan River just north of the Dead Sea, Jesus wandered in the barren Wilderness of Judea. Only a few miles north of Jericho, it is as barren and uninhabited as the badlands of North Dakota.[5]

What Others are Saying:

John Chrysostom: You see how the Spirit led him, not into a city or public arena, but into a wilderness. In this desolate place, the Spirit extended the devil an occasion to test him, not only by hunger, but also by loneliness, for it is there most especially that the devil assails us, when he sees us left alone and by ourselves.[6]

THE DEVIL: By his own choice the devil is the epitome of evil and the captain of everything that stands in opposition to God and righteousness. His name, *devil*, literally means "slanderer." The Bible indicates the devil is <u>an angel</u>, created to serve God, whose pride led him to rebel against God. In the Bible he is identified by many names, three of which are used in Matthew's story of Jesus' temptation: tempter, devil, and Satan.

Who's Who

☞ **GO TO:**

Job 1:6; 2:1; Matthew 25:41; 2 Corinthians 11:14; Revelation 12:7–9 (an angel)

☞ **GO TO:**

Isaiah 16:14; 27:1;
Matthew 12:24, 43;
13:19, 38; John 8:44
(titles and epithets)

Dig Deeper

What Others are Saying:

Descriptive *Titles and Epithets* for Satan

- *Devil, slanderer, accuser* (Matthew 4:1, 5, 8, 11; Revelation 20:2)
- *Tempter* (Matthew 4:3; 1 Thessalonians 3:5)
- *Satan, adversary, enemy* (Matthew 4:10; Job 1:6, 12; Acts 26:18)
- *Serpent* (Genesis 3:4, 14; Isaiah 27:1; 2 Corinthians 11:3; Revelation 12:9)
- *Dragon* (Isaiah 27:1; Revelation 12:3; 20:2)
- *Abaddon, ruin* (Job 31:12)
- *Apollyon* (Revelation 9:11)
- *Beelzebub, prince of devils, lord of flies* (Matthew 12:24; Mark 3:22; Luke 11:15)
- *Belial, worthlessness, lawlessness* (Luke 4:2–6; Revelation 20:2)
- *Lucifer, shining one, light being* (Isaiah 14:12)
- *Enemy* (Matthew 13:39)

Baudelaire: The devil's cleverest ruse is to make men believe that he does not exist.[7]

Denis de Rougemont: Recognize immediately that this stratagem of spreading the idea of his own non-existence has never been more successful than at the present time. . . . The first trick of the devil is his *incognito*.[8]

Charles C. Ryrie: If one accepts the Scriptures as revelation from God, rather than merely a record of man's thoughts about God, then the reality of Satan cannot be denied.[9]

W. Robert Cook: Contrary to much thinking, however, the Bible does not advance a dualism of good (God) and evil (the devil) with God and Satan as equals. . . . While he is a powerful spirit, the terror of good, a ravenous, roaring lion who is the enemy of God and God's people, (Satan) is nonetheless a creature accountable to his Creator and within the governing control of divine providence.[10]

Sneak Attack

Paintings, movies, and other portrayals of Jesus' desert temptations picture the devil approaching in visible humanoid, animal, or reptilian form. One movie depicts him as a beast, something like a wild boar on two legs. But nowhere in the three New Testament accounts is the tempter said to have appeared in visible form. He may have. There is no reason why he could not have done so. But I wonder.

Matthew 4:3 says the tempter *"came"* and spoke to Jesus. It doesn't say if his coming was visible. Luke 4:3 says the devil spoke to him. It doesn't say Jesus could see him.

Hebrews 4:15 says Jesus was tempted *"in every way, just as we are."* I don't know about you, but never in all my checkered temptation history has a sinister-looking personage with horns and a tail appeared, belching yellow brimstone smoke, wearing red long johns, and displaying a convention nametag announcing, "Hi! My name is Satan." If Jesus was tempted *"in every way, just as we are,"* the temptations he experienced in Judea's wild lands must have come to him like they do to us—not as outward struggles with an easily recognized enemy, but as confusing battles in the mind.

The biblical reports of Jesus' temptations use language that suggests the battle took place in the sphere of the imagination. Consider:

- There is no physical mountain high enough to be able to see all the world's kingdoms from its summit (Matthew 3:8). The mountain of the third temptation is most likely a picture triggered by the tempter in Jesus' imagination.

- It was not necessary for Jesus to physically go to the pinnacle of the Temple in order to be tempted by the devil's second suggestion (Matthew 3:5). He needed only to go there in his imagination.

It is a lot more difficult to recognize the enemy when he camouflages himself in our own imagination. That's where most of us experience our temptations.

Again, there is no reason to assume that Satan did not visibly appear to Jesus or that some supernatural transportation to the Temple pinnacle did not take place. Nothing in the text demands that we reject the literal view. But so often we fail to consider that Jesus did experience temptation in the realm of his mind.

KEY POINT

Most of our temptations take place in the theater of our imaginations.

Thomas á Kempis: At first [temptation] is a mere thought confronting the mind; then imagination paints it in stronger colors; only after that do we take pleasure in it, and the will makes a false move, and we give our assent.[11]

Roger Elwood: People aid his awful designs—the Mafia with its drug and pornography and prostitution businesses, for example. As you can see, so much of what we have around us is inspired by Satan, but he hardly needs to be on call 24 hours a day. Advertisers spend billions of dollars to promote so many sinful desires in order to sell their products. . . . Satan created this kind of atmosphere, the amoral, unspiritual atmosphere which we breathe today. A brilliant chap, this Satan, this Devil, this Lucifer, his handiwork saves him a great deal of legwork.[12]

☞ **GO TO:**

2 Corinthians 5:21;
   Hebrews 4:15
   (never yielded)

1 John 2:18–27;
   Hebrews 5:12–14
   (discerning)

Matthew 16:21–23
   (other voices)

Matthew 4:4, 7, 10
   (equipped by Scripture)

Martin Luther: I cannot keep the birds from flying over my head, but I can keep them from building a nest in my hair.

Debunking Deception

In all his 30 growing-up years, Jesus had <u>never yielded</u> to sin's enticements. His relationship with his Father in heaven and especially his knowledge of the Scriptures learned from childhood made him keenly <u>discerning</u>. (There are <u>other voices</u> out there that are not saying what God is saying.) When a suggestion was contrary to God's will and the nature of the kingdom and could only have come from the devil, Jesus was spiritually <u>equipped by Scripture</u> to detect the deception.

Marcus Aurelius: The Reason [Logos] which rules the universe has no cause in itself for doing wrong.[13]

Three Fascinating Proposals For Missing God's Plan

**GOSPEL QUARTET
IN HARMONY**

Matthew 4:3–10
Luke 4:3–12

For 40 days, Jesus faced the barren waste, braved the wild beasts (Mark 1:13), and fielded deceptive suggestions by a tempter intent on diverting him from the work to which God had sent him. On the surface every temptation seemed reasonable and each represented a less costly way to do God's work than the way called for in God's plan.

> **Matthew 4:3–4** The tempter came to him and said, "If you are the Son of God, tell these stones to become bread." Jesus answered, "It is written: 'Man does not live on bread alone, but on every word that comes from the mouth of God.'"

KEY POINT

God's priorities take precedence over felt human needs.

Proposition 1: You've Gotta Feed Yourself First

Jesus had the power to change stones to bread. Miracles would be a daily occurrence for him. Later he would turn <u>water to wine</u>. He would feed <u>5,000</u> hungry hangers-on with a child's lunch. He would do it again for <u>4,000</u>. In the desert, toe to toe with the enemy, he had not eaten for nearly six weeks. Matthew's matter-of-fact understatement says *"he was hungry."* Hungry? By this time his ribs were showing! How could it possibly upset some great eternal plan if a couple of rocks became breakfast? On the surface, the suggestion made sense and seemed harmless.

☞ **GO TO:**

John 2:1–11 (water to wine)

John 6:1–13 (5,000)

Mark 8:1–9 (4,000)

Why Turning Rocks To Bread Was A Bad Idea

It was a devilish strategy to get Jesus to divert the gifts of God from the "others-focus" that Saviorhood requires. At no time did Jesus use his miraculous powers to gratify himself. Even at his arrest he could have called a <u>legion of angels</u> to rescue him, but he refused. The work of God cannot be accomplished through self-indulgence. The gifts God gives—<u>spiritual gifts</u> or <u>material possessions</u>—are not for the receiver's personal benefit alone, for pride of ownership, or to gain power over others. They are given to meet the needs and hungers of others, as well as our own.

The suggestion to turn stones to bread was a bad idea because it challenged the wisdom that God's priorities take precedence over felt human needs. Jesus chose to be guided by the Word and wisdom of God, not merely his appetites and wants (Matthew 4:4).

☞ **GO TO:**

Matthew 26:53–54 (legion of angels)

Romans 12; 1 Corinthians 12 (spiritual gifts)

Acts 4:32–35; 2 Corinthians 8–9 (material possessions)

Revell Bible Dictionary: Basic to Jesus' response to temptation was his recall of biblical principles and his commitment to live according to the Word of God (Scripture). A believer who seeks to overcome temptations needs to be a student of the Word, committed to obey it.[14]

What Others are Saying:

Something to Ponder

In 200 A.D. some desperate Christians came to the Christian theologian Tertullian with the argument that if they did not burn incense to Caesar (a form of idolatry) they would lose their jobs. "We have to eat," they said. The always tough-minded Tertullian answered: "You do not need to eat. You need to obey God."

> **Matthew 4:5–7** Then the devil took him to the holy city and had him stand on the highest point of the temple. "If you are the Son of God," he said, "throw yourself down. For it is written: 'He will command his angels concerning you, and they will lift you up in their hands, so that you will not strike your foot against a stone.'" Jesus answered him, "It is also written: 'Do not put the Lord your God to the test.'"

Proposition 2: Choose Sensationalism As A Shortcut To Acceptance

Either the devil was allowed to physically transport Jesus to the **Temple pinnacle** or, as I've suggested, Jesus imagined himself on that high perch looking down on the gathering worshipers below.

In his mind's eye, Jesus saw himself standing on that high point. All he would need to do to attract Israel's attention would be to jump from the platform as worshipers gathered, land on his feet 450 feet below, and walk away unharmed. The Jews (who were always looking for miraculous signs) would be convinced by this phenomenal feat to instantly accept him as Messiah (at least that's how the tempter's reasoning went).

To make resisting temptation tougher, this brainstorm came with the refrain of an Old Testament hymn which seemed to say it was consistent with Scripture (Psalm 91:11–12).

Jesus was not fooled by the suggestion. The whole idea contradicted the principles by which his relationship with God was guided. Jesus recognized the suggestion as (1) a temptation to circumvent the cross and (2) a temptation to misuse Scripture to manipulate God into acting contrary to his character and will.

Why A Quantum Leap Off The Temple Peak Was A Bad Idea

The rule of God is not established by sensational display. It grows like <u>yeast</u>, quietly taking over a batch of bread dough, or a <u>mustard seed</u> germinating and growing into a sheltering bush without fanfare. Jesus is credited with many miracles. A few were spectacular. But he healed people and asked them not to tell. People looking for spectacles of power were disappointed. He repeatedly proved his messiahship, but never by putting on a flashy show of power. He **de-emphasized** visible proofs, expecting people to believe based on <u>his words</u>, <u>without visible proof</u>.

Jesus rejected the intriguing suggestion he take a quick leap to

---

Temple pinnacle: platform where a trumpeter sounded the call to the morning sacrifice; a 450-foot drop to the Kedron Valley below

☞ **GO TO:**

Matthew 13:33 (yeast)

Matthew 13:31–32 (mustard seed)

John 4:48 (de-emphasized)

John 7:16–17 (his words)

John 20:29 (without visible proof)

de-emphasized: played down

---

celebrity, because it would violate the delicate trust relationship between himself and his Father God. When Jesus cited the Scripture, *"Do not put the Lord your God to the test"* (Matthew 4:7; Deuteronomy 6:16), he used a different Greek word for *test* than the one used in Matthew 4:1. The new word means "to test as an attempt to coerce." The Old Testament verse Jesus quoted means, "Don't try to force God to do what you want him to do by contriving a test to make him prove himself."[15] The devil was suggesting Jesus back God into a corner to make him act the way he wanted God to act.

People who must have sensational proofs in order to believe usually <u>stumble</u> over the cross (Jesus' least sensational moment), and concepts like <u>self-denial</u>, long-suffering, commitment, and the kind of <u>humble service</u> Jesus says makes for greatness.

Demanding that God do what we choose is not an act of mature, genuine faith. <u>Real faith</u> always involves <u>submission</u> to the will, wisdom, and timing of God. Demanding God do something is a camouflage for dissatisfaction with God's will. Hebrews 11:1 defines faith as *"being sure of what we hope for and certain of what we do not see."*

> **Matthew 4:8–10** Again, the devil took him to a very high mountain and showed him all the kingdoms of the world and their splendor. "All this will I give you," he said, "if you will bow down and worship me." Jesus said to him, "Away from me, Satan! For it is written: 'Worship the Lord your God, and serve him only.'"

Proposition 3: Follow The Bloodless Road To The Kingdom

Jesus found himself on the summit of a peak so high all the earth's empires were visible. Spread before him were splendid palaces, shining thrones, gleaming cities, fabulous wealth, beauty, and political power. He thought of what he wanted to do for the millions of souls represented by this awesome exhibition. What an opportunity!

"All this will I give you, if you will worship me" (Matthew 4:9).

Remember This . . .

☞ **GO TO:**

1 Corinthians 1:22–23 (stumble)

Mark 8:34 (self-denial)

Matthew 10:42 (humble service)

2 Corinthians 5:7 (real faith)

Luke 22:42 (submission)

KEY POINT

The rule of God is not established by sensational display, but by quiet, constant submission to his will.

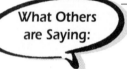
Walter Wangerin Jr.: "Jesus of Nazareth, look! . . . See the kingdoms one by one, the jewels of creation. Mark their power and their glory. Review their histories from the beginning till now, from now until forever. All this, all these wonders I will give into your hands—to rule them all—if you but bow down and worship me."[16]

KINGDOM
OF GOD

What Sort of Suggestion Was This, Really?

The original Greek word for *worship* (verse 9) literally means "to kiss." To the early Greeks it meant "to do homage by kissing the hand." The word was not primarily used to describe worship of deity, but respect for a prince or king.[17] Jesus was being tempted to grant the devil respect as a legitimate ruler—perhaps an equal—as a way to find an easier, less painful way than death on the cross to bring the world's kingdoms under the reign of God.

"*Away from me, Satan!*" shouted Jesus. "*It is written: 'Worship the Lord your God, and serve him exclusively'*" (Matthew 4:10; Deuteronomy 6:13).

Walter Wangerin Jr.: But Jesus does not look at the kingdoms of the world. He sits down on the terrible mountain and closes his eyes and whispers, "But I know you. I know what sort of angel you are. Satan, tempter, betrayer—begone!"[18]

☞ **GO TO:**

1 John 5:19; Ephesians 6:12
(devil-dominated)

KINGDOM
OF GOD

Why Legitimizing the Enemy Is a Bad Idea

Jesus knew: Acknowledgment that Satan has legitimate authority at any level is a compromise guaranteed to scuttle the plan of salvation and roadblock the kingdom of God. Thinking the enemy has even one thought, one bit of wisdom worthy of serious consideration, is a shortcut to disaster.

Human beings can only enjoy the benefits of life in God's realm if they are committed to worship God alone, acknowledge the exclusive finality of his authority, and resist the temptation to think the values of this <u>devil-dominated</u> world might be compatible with the values of God.

**Something
to Ponder**

William Barclay: What the tempter was saying was, "Compromise! Come to terms with me! Don't pitch your demands quite so high! Wink just a little at evil and questionable things—and then people will follow you in their hordes."[19]

Larry Richards: Subject, as you and I are, to the hungers and drives and needs which throb within and seek to pull us into sin, Jesus met Satan's temptations. He would continue to meet each earthly trial in all the vulnerability and weakness that are ours. Rejecting the privilege that was his by virtue of his deity, Jesus cast his lot totally with you and me.[20]

Passing With Flying Colors

For six weeks the black-hearted <u>world ruler</u> had done his dirt. But now it was clear that his sulfur-yellowed teeth would have nothing to chew on but the bitter, gritty grist of failure. He had failed to deter the young Messiah from his mission. So the devil left Jesus (Matthew 4:11), planning to resume his attack at another time when his intended victim was again vulnerable (Luke 4:13). As Satan leaves we learn three important things about him:

1. He is not able to be everywhere at once.
2. He has limited access to people.
3. We can expect him to be relentless—to attack again.

As for Jesus, passing the test seemed to invigorate him. Matthew and Mark tell of angels ministering to him following the temptation. This desert duel confirmed four realities for Jesus:

1. His oneness with human beings in their vulnerability to temptation
2. The genuineness of his faith and messianic vision
3. The reality of his relationship with God as Son
4. The presence and power of the Holy Spirit in his life

Study Questions

1. Give four Bible names for the tempter and what they reveal about him.
2. Which of the following tactics did Jesus use in dealing with each temptation: (a) called for angels to help him, (b) gritted his teeth and dug in his heels—willpower, (c) tried to reason with the tempter, (d) quoted Scripture to expose the deception, (e) ignored the temptation until it went away, and (f) ordered Satan to leave?
3. What were the three things the devil tempted Jesus to do? Why might each have appealed to Jesus?

What Others are Saying:

GO TO:

John 12:21
(world ruler)

KEY Outline:

Three Temptations
Stones to bread
- use God's gifts selfishly

Jump off Temple
- sensationalism instead of submission

Legitimize the devil
- bloodless road to rule

4. What would have been wrong with (a) turning stones to bread, (b) jumping off the Temple, or (c) showing the devil some respect?

5. What is your greatest temptation right now? What does Jesus' experience teach you about how to deal with it?

CHAPTER WRAP-UP

- Jesus was led by the Holy Spirit into the desert to be tempted. Temptation is a fact of life for every human being; it demonstrates our readiness to do God's will. (Matthew 4:1–11)

- The devil is a real person to whom the Bible gives many names describing his wicked character. He tempted Jesus when he was most vulnerable. (Mark 1:12–13)

- The devil proposed that Jesus (1) turn stones to bread to feed his hunger, (2) leap off the Temple to demonstrate how God would protect him, and (3) give the devil respect as an equal in exchange for control over the nations of the world. (Luke 4: 3–12)

- Using Scripture, Jesus exposed the deceptiveness of each temptation, passed the test, and ordered the devil to leave. Angels ministered to him. (Matthew 4:4, 7, 10, 11)

6 DESCENT FROM SPLENDOR

CHAPTER HIGHLIGHTS

- A Hymn to Him
- Distilled Faith
- Cosmic Secret
- Knowable God
- God's Ultimate Expression
- Big Three-in-One
- God's Children
- What's God Like?

Let's Get Started

Who is Jesus Christ, really? What makes him so important that Satan would offer him the kingdoms of the world as a carrot to detour him from his divine calling? Where does he come from? Bethlehem? Nazareth? The planet Crypton?

In his introduction to the Life of Christ, the apostle-historian-author John takes us back, back, back—into the mysterious sphere we call **eternity**. There we are introduced to a person with a history like no other born on this planet. There we discover answers to questions raised by the angelic announcements to Mary, Joseph, and the shepherds, and the amazing pilgrimage of the Magi. A tantalizing string of unusual events and pronouncements mark Jesus' early life. This **homo sapien** was not "usual." He was not just another religious leader like Buddha or Mohammed. Jesus was and is unique.

eternity: reality outside and not limited to time

homo sapien: scientific name for "human being"

> **John 1:1–2** In the beginning was the Word, and the Word was with God, and the Word was God. He was with God in the beginning.

☞ **GO TO:**

Luke 1:40–55, 68–79;
Colossians 1:15–20;
Philippians 2:6–11;
1 Timothy 3:16 (early Christian hymn)

A Hymn To Him

The first sentences of John 1 are the lyrics of an <u>early Christian hymn</u> sung in first century churches, accompanied by simple stringed instruments—lyre or harp—or without accompaniment. John adapted this hymn and made it "the overture to the **gospel** narrative of the career of the **incarnate Word**."[1]

gospel: good news

incarnate Word: God's expression of himself in human form

Michael Card: I find it touching that before this passage was ever made the topic of theological debate, it was a simple hymn. Before it was preached, it was sung. Without reasoning and argumentation the early believers embraced these complex incarnational truths by means of a simple melody. . . . And so with music those early saints sang their way to belief in the unbelievable.[2]

The Heady Wine Of Distilled Faith

Why is John's version of the Jesus story different from Matthew, Mark, and Luke? The operative word is *different,* not "contradictory." His account was written around 80 to 90 A.D. A generation had passed since he and the others spent those three years with Jesus. With the passage of time, their understanding of Jesus and what they experienced with him became clearer. The Holy Spirit, given to them at <u>Pentecost</u>, interacting with them daily, ignited <u>new insights</u>. In the process of telling and retelling the story to the growing band of **disciples** and their **pagan** neighbors, the Christians improved their ability to communicate the truth that had captivated them. Under the Spirit's inspiration and protection, these insights and experiences distilled into an orderly understanding of the person and work of Jesus Christ.

By the time John wrote, most of the other **apostles** had been **martyred**. After 50-plus years of walking with Jesus <u>in the Spirit</u>, John was the only one of the <u>original 12</u> left to write from the vantage point of a half century of experience with him.

EARLY CHURCH LIFE: Practice telling the good news helps Christians understand it.

The Cosmic Secret Of Christ's Uniqueness

In a stroke of communication genius, John introduced the principal character of his Life of Christ by building on an idea with which his readers, both Jews and Gentiles, were already familiar. Thinking people of that day believed in the existence of a spiritual force in the universe called *"the Word."* In Greek, the universal language of the Roman Empire, this force was known as the **Logos**.

J. I. Packer: This is the deep end of theology, no doubt, but John throws us straight into it. "In the beginning was the Word, and the Word was *with* God, and the Word *was* God." The Word was a person in fellowship with God, and the Word was himself personally and eternally divine. He was, as John proceeds to tell us, the only Son of the Father. John sets this mystery . . . at the head of his gospel because he knows nobody can make head or tail of the words and works of Jesus of Nazareth till he has grasped the fact that this Jesus is in truth God the Son.[3]

ACT OF THE HOLY SPIRIT

Gave insights and guided development of the disciples' understanding of Christ

First Century Ideas about the Logos (Word)

Group	Who/What They Believed the "Word" to Be
Greeks (Plato's disciples)	Divine wisdom that directs everything in the universe
Greeks (Stoics)	Soul of the universe
Romans	Universal principle by which life exists and is sustained
Assyrians/Babylonians	Raging cosmic power from which there is no escape
Egyptians	Creative substance from mouth of deity that maintains the universe
Jews (Old Testament)	Action of the Almighty (Psalm 33:6). Means by which God accomplishes his purpose in history (Isaiah 55:11).
Jews (Philo of Alexandria)	Agent of creation, God's thought, expression of wisdom, medium through which he governs the world, means by which humans know God—Advocate/High Priest through which people find God and forgiveness

Lawrence O. Richards: In Hebrew thought, "the Word of God" was his active self-expression, that revelation of himself to humanity through which a person not only receives truth about God, but meets God face-to-face.[4]

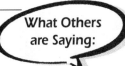

What Others are Saying:

An Opening You Could Drive a Truck Through

The "Word" was a concept first century people already believed (see Acts 17:22–23). Early Christian communicators didn't have to break down this door—it was already wide open. New Testament writers, preachers, and witnesses could simply affirm truth the world's thinkers had already discovered and proceed from there to share the good news about Jesus Christ.

Something to Ponder

EARLY CHURCH LIFE: Early Christians communicated with pagans starting with affirmation of truth pagans already believed.

Robert E. Coleman: Evangelism centers in a personality—Jesus Christ. He is the message and the medium.[5]

What Others are Saying:

The God Who Wants People To Know Him

☞ **GO TO:**

John 17:3 (full life)

agnostic: one who believes knowing God is impossible

The Bible, from Genesis to Revelation, describes God as a God who talks to people. God speaks, in all the ways he speaks, to help people know him. Knowing God is the key to experiencing the <u>full life</u> humans were created to experience. As important as it is to know God, people still respond like C. S. Lewis says he did before he became a Christian. The former **agnostic** describes God's persistence as "the steady, unrelenting approach of him whom I so earnestly desired not to meet."[6]

What Others are Saying:

R. Bultmann: From the outset God must be understood as the "one who speaks," the God who reveals himself.[7]

Henry H. Halley: We believe the Bible to be, not man's account of his effort to find God, but rather an account of God's effort to reveal himself to man . . . his unfolding revelation of himself to the human race.[8]

KEY POINT

God speaks so people will know him.

> **John 1:3** Through him all things were made; without him nothing was made that has been made.

The Word Of God Expressed In Creation

the beginning: before the material universe first came into being

made: created

life: "to make vital"—used 36 times in John's book

light: consciousness of being alive; spiritual enlightenment

The "Word" first appears *"with God"* in the creation story in the first chapter of Genesis. The story of how the universe *"was made"* is organized around the repeated statement, *"God said."* God brought the universe into existence by his Word! The New Testament reveals that the creative Word of God is a living person who was *"with God and was God"* from *"**the beginning**"* (John 1:1–2). When Genesis says, *"God said,"* it is describing the activity of the living "Word" <u>by whom</u> *"all things were **made**"* and without whom *"nothing was made that has been made."*

☞ **GO TO:**

Colossians 1:16–17 (by whom)

Acts 17:25–28 (life principle)

> **John 1:4–5, 9** In him was **life**, and that life was the **light** of men. The light shines in the darkness, but the darkness has not understood it. . . . The true light that gives light to every man was coming into the world.

The Word Of God Expressed In The Awareness Of Life

The "Word" (whom the New Testament reveals as Christ) is the <u>life principle</u> that vitalizes every living creature—the factor distinguishing inanimate things from things that are alive, growing, and moving. The New Testament teaches these things:

- Christ is the source of all biological life—he created and sustains all living things (Colossians 1:16–17).
- Christ is the source of eternal life—"the spiritual dynamic that shatters the power of death in the human personality"[9] and assures believers of everlasting life in fellowship with God (John 5:24–26).
- Christ is the source of spiritual life—the vitality and energy needed to live the Christian life from day to day (Romans 5:10; Galatians 2:20; Philippians 4:13).

With life consciousness goes an inborn God consciousness. John describes this God consciousness as *"the light of men"* (verse 4) and *"light to every person"* (verse 9). Every living human being has some basic <u>sense of God</u>. **Theologians** call this "first light." First light is a combination of (1) what may be learned about God through <u>observing nature</u>, (2) an inner sense of right and wrong called <u>conscience</u>, and (3) the universal awareness of God expressed in the human <u>inclination to worship</u> something or someone.

It's a light that won't stop shining. Eugene Peterson translates John 1:5, *"The light kept shining in the dark, and the darkness couldn't put it out!"*[10]

☞ **GO TO:**

Ecclesiastes 3:11; Acts 17:26–28; Titus 2:11 (sense of God)

Romans 1:18–21 (observing nature)

Romans 2:14–15 (conscience)

Acts 17:22–23 (inclination to worship)

Genesis 3 (Adam's choice)

Theologians: *students of the science of God*

Candy Paull: Anyone who has taken a look at the zillions of different kinds of bugs or fish or birds or tress or landscapes or noses or animals is aware of a world so filled with diversity and glorious variety that it becomes obvious our minds cannot contain all that God has created. . . . Seeing His abundant surprises at every turn, I am able to open the door to hope and be released from fear, limitation, poverty, and diminished expectation—because God is bigger than my little boxes.[11]

What Others are Saying:

Spiritual darkness, rebellion against God's person and purpose, in every conceivable form has tried repeatedly through history to extinguish the light of God's living Word. Every attempt—from <u>Adam's choice</u> and Israel's rejection of the Ten Commandments to the martyrdom of the prophets and the crucifixion of Jesus to the modern attacks of humanism and atheism—has failed. Every future attempt to deny the truth of Scripture, obliterate the name of Christ, or pronounce God dead, will meet with the same failure. The light just keeps shining!

Remember This . . .

Lawrence O. Richards: Where do human religions gain the moral insights they display? John may be saying that all genuine light is shed by Christ, and that the glimpses of truth the lost do have are themselves sourced in his matchless grace.[12]

KEY Outline:

God's Self-Expression

Creation (order, power)
Life consciousness
God consciousness
Law (morality)
Christ (Jesus)

Don Richardson: In actual fact, more than 90 percent of this world's folk religions acknowledge at least the existence of God. Some even anticipate his redeeming concern for mankind.[13]

> **John 1:6–9** There came a man who was sent by God; his name was John. He came as a witness to testify concerning the light, so that through him all men might believe. He himself was not the light; he came only as a witness of the light. The true light that gives light to every man was coming into the world.

The Word Of God And John The Baptist

When asked if he was the Messiah, the John this passage refers to answered unequivocally, "No!" He went on to describe a person greater than himself who was coming. Later the <u>Holy Spirit revealed</u> to John that Jesus of Nazareth was that "greater" person. From then on he preached, *"This was he of whom I said, 'He who comes after me has surpassed me because he was before me'"* (John 1:15). John said Christ *"surpassed"* him in four ways:

☞ **GO TO:**

John 1:32–34
   (Holy Spirit revealed)

1. In preexistence: Christ *"was before me"* (John 1:15)
2. In power: Christ is *"more powerful"* (Matthew 3:11)
3. In worthiness: "I am not worthy to untie Christ's sandals" (John 1:27)
4. In changing lives: Christ *"will **baptize with** the Holy Spirit"* (John 1:33)

baptize with: introduce
into, place in, saturate, fill

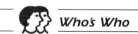

Who's Who

JOHN: This *"John"* is not the writer, but the desert preacher whose story is told in chapters 1 and 4.

> **John 1:14, 17** The word became flesh and made his dwelling among us. We have seen his glory, the glory of the One and Only, who came from the Father, full of grace and truth. . . . Grace and truth came through Jesus Christ.

The Ultimate Expression Of God

The Word is bigger than language. The Word of God has never been an impersonal force, but an extension of God himself, a living person. The Word has a name, *Jesus*, and has a title, **Christ** (John 1:17). The clearest, most complete communication of God's character in language human beings can understand is visible in the life, personality, words, and works of Jesus of Nazareth. Jesus is the expression of God in human form. Anyone who wants to know what kind of person God is, how God thinks, what God cares about, what God is doing, and what God expects from us, needs to look no further than the <u>face of Jesus Christ</u>. Know Jesus, and you <u>know God</u>.

Christ: *Anointed One, Messiah, King*

Lawrence O. Richards: John reminds us . . . that we must never forget that Jesus, carpenter of Nazareth, teacher and miracle worker of Israel, crucified and risen Savior, is also God **enfleshed**.[14]

What Others are Saying:

The Big Three-In-One

The four historians who wrote the New Testament's Lives of Christ were committed to the distinctive Hebrew concept of monotheism. With Jews everywhere they confessed the traditional faith: "The Lord is one!" (<u>the *Shema*</u>). None of these men would ever deny that truth. There is and always has been only one God. His expression of himself in Jesus Christ does not change that.

The introduction of the concept of the living Word who existed with God and is the co-Creator through whom God made the universe, opens up a mind-bending mystery! Struggling with this mystery has led Christians to the belief that the one, true God is a **Trinity** (see illustration, page 85). The word "Trinity" is not found in the Bible. But Old Testament references to God in plural terms, coupled with New Testament references to God the Father, Son, and Holy Spirit <u>together</u>, lead Christians to conclude the Bible's one God is "God in three persons, Blessed Trinity."[15]

enfleshed: *in human form*

☞ **GO TO:**

2 Corinthians 4:6; Hebrews 1:2–3 (face of Jesus Christ)

John 14:7–11 (know God)

Deuteronomy 6:4 (the *Shema*)

Matthew 28:19 (together)

Trinity: *one Being expressed in three personalities*

One God in Three Persons: Father, Son, and Holy Spirit

Old Testament Plural References to God:

Genesis 1:26
Genesis 3:22
Isaiah 6:8
Psalm 33:6 with John 1:1–3; 20:22
(*Elohim*, Hebrew name for God, is "a plural noun, generally taken as a plural of majesty."[16])

Dig Deeper

Dig Deeper

Father, Son, and Holy Spirit Identified Together as God:

Isaiah 42:1 with Matthew 12:15–18
Luke 3:21–22
John 3:34–35
John 14:16–26
John 15:26
John 16:13–15

Father, Son, and Holy Spirit Identified Together as God:

Acts 2:32–33
Acts 10:36–38
Romans 1:3–4
Romans 8:9–11
2 Corinthians 1:21–22
2 Corinthians 13:14
Galatians 4:4–6
2 Thessalonians 2:13–14
Titus 3:4–6
Hebrews 9:14
1 Peter 1:2

Jesus' Claims of Oneness with God:

John 10:30
John 14:9
John 9:38
John 20:28–29
Matthew 28:19

What Others are Saying:

Robert E. Coleman: Any formulation of the triune nature of God proves inadequate, for the very reason that human intelligence cannot explain the divine mind. Yet only by the Trinity can the person and mind of God be understood.[17]

> **John 1:10–13** He was in the world, and though the world was made through him, the world did not recognize him. He came to that which was his own, but his own did not receive him. Yet all who received him, to those who believed on his name, he gave the right to become children of God—children born not of natural descent, nor of human decision or a husband's will, but born of God.

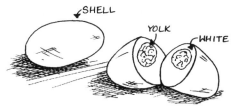

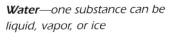

Egg—one entity with three parts:
shell, white, and yolk

Analogies from the natural world illustrate
the possibility of a single entity having three
distinct forms, all sharing the same basic
nature. God is a single being, or entity,
having three forms.

Water—one substance can be
liquid, vapor, or ice

LIQUID   ICE

VAPOR

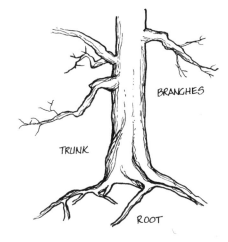

Tree—one woody plant with three parts:
root, trunk, and branches

The Right To Become God's Children

Being born a human being does not make a person a son or daughter of God in the way John is describing. He names two things people often think give them the right to be called "children of God" and declares that neither of them is enough!

1. Becoming children of God has nothing to do with *"natural descent."* Racial or national heritage or being born on the right side of the railroad tracks does not make a person a child of God.

2. Becoming children of God is not as simple as a mental *"human decision."* A person can't become God's child by gritting his or her teeth and determining to do it . . . somehow!

A "husband's will" (verse 13) is an unfortunate translation. It would be better if it read: "the will of man," which simply repeats, for emphasis, the truth that nobody simply makes up his or her mind to be a Christian and, bingo! He's a Christian. Uh, uh! Becoming God's child is something *God* must do for us and in us. Coming into God's family requires another kind of *birth*—a person must be "*born of God*."

There is a decision to be made, but the other kind of birth that makes us children of God is a miracle.

☞ **GO TO:**

John 3:3–8; 1 Peter 1:23 (born of God)

☞ **GO TO:**

John 3:5–8 (Spirit of God does)

John 3:19–21 (light)

John Bunyan: The egg's no chick by falling from the hen, Nor man a Christian till he's born again.[18]

How Can An Ordinary Person Be Born Again?

Being born of God and gaining the right to become children of God is something the Spirit of God does in the life of a person who welcomes Christ's light. From the human perspective spiritual birth hinges on two attitudes (John 1:12):

1. *"Receive him."* The original word for *receive* was used to describe a man taking a wife or adopting a child. It implies entering a committed, lifelong relationship with Jesus Christ.

2. *"Believe on his* [Jesus Christ's] *name."* The Amplified Bible gives additional meanings hidden in the original word for believe: "believe in—adhere to, trust in and rely on—his **name**."[19]

name: stands for everything Christ is, character, values, and person

Something to Ponder

The Meaning Of Believe

Did you hear the one about the high-wire walker performing his act over Niagara Falls? After he walked, ran, and danced several times across the falls, he brought a wheelbarrow up on the wire. He asked the audience how many believed he could push the wheelbarrow across the falls on the wire. All applauded and raised their hands. They believed. When he asked for a volunteer to get into the wheelbarrow and let him push it across the falls with the person in it, not a single hand was raised. Nobody believed that much!

The difference between mental assent to facts about Christ and faith that gives a person the right to become a child of God is that real faith involves a decision to get in the "wheelbarrow"—to trust your spiritual safety to Jesus Christ.

ACT OF THE HOLY SPIRIT

Enables spiritual rebirth

☞ **GO TO:**

John 1:12 (right)

Billy Graham: It is only when you are born again that you can experience all the riches God has in store for you. You are not just a living person, you are truly ALIVE![20]

> **John 1:14, 18** The word became flesh and made his dwelling among us. We have seen his glory, the glory of the One and Only, who came from the Father, full of grace and truth. . . . No one has ever seen God, but God the One and Only, who is at the Father's side, has made him known.

flesh: real humanity

made his dwelling: became like one of us

One and Only: Christ is unique

grace: favor, generosity, joy, mercy

truth: complete reliability, integrity, reality

What's God Really Like?

In the person and life of Jesus Christ, God

- exhibited himself in human form—*"the Word became* **flesh***,"*
- exhibited himself up close and personal—*"****made his dwelling*** *among us,"*
- exhibited himself in one special person—*"the* **One and Only** *who came from the Father,"* and
- exhibited himself as kind, loving, benevolent, and truthful—*"full of* **grace** *and* **truth***."*

Robert E. Coleman: God's plan to take upon himself the experience of man assumed material form in the incarnation of Christ. . . . The new being was not a man who became God; he is God who became man, coming into history from the outside.[21]

Leon Morris: The Greeks thought of the gods as detached from the world, as regarding its struggles and heartaches and joys and fears with serene divine lack of feeling. John's idea of the *Logos* conveys exactly the opposite idea. John's *Logos* does not show us a God who is serenely detached, but a God who is passionately involved.[22]

The Visible God

When you look into the face of Jesus, you see humanity at its finest. But that's not all. New Testament writers insist when you look at Jesus you are looking into God's face. They invite you to put aside childish notions of God as an angry, unapproachable tyrant with a long, white beard and fire in his eyes, sitting in the clouds waiting to get you if you aren't good. Jesus' life story invites us to discover a whole new picture of God.

William Barclay: In Jesus Christ the distant, unknowable, invisible, unreachable God has come to men; and God can never be a stranger to us again.[23]

Something to Ponder

Bird Talk

Looking out the window into our yard one day, Audrey saw a flock of robins fighting over access to the birdbath. As the angry birds attacked each other she wished she could tell them there was enough water for all! If they'd simply take turns, they could all bathe and drink! Suddenly she realized how inadequate she was to communicate with birds. The only way would be to become a robin herself. But that was impossible.

Not impossible for God, however. If earthlings were ever to understand his thoughts, a radical and imaginative communication strategy was called for. Could any act be more imaginative and radical than for God to wrap himself in human flesh and live among us as one of us, getting right down in the muck and struggles of this sin-bashed world? This is what God did in Christ, so people could actually look into his face, hear him talk their language, and come to know him, firsthand.

Study Questions

1. Name two of the ways God has expressed himself, according to John 1.
2. What facts about the Word are told in John 1:1–5?
3. Jesus Christ is the Word John says was *"in the beginning," "was with God,"* and *"was God"* (verse 1). What great mystery is suggested by these facts?
4. Identify the three kinds of life of which the New Testament claims Christ is the source?
5. What did the Word (Christ) do to show human beings what God is really like?
6. How does a person become a child of God?

CHAPTER WRAP-UP

- In his approach to telling the Life of Christ, John drew on a half century of experience with Christ and sharing the Good News with all sorts of people.

- The Bible's God is a God who speaks to people. His clearest expression of himself is Christ, whom early Christians identified as God's living Word. (John 1:1–2)

- When Christ came into the world, many failed to recognize him for who he was. Those who do recognize, receive, and believe in him are spiritually reborn as God's children. (John 1:10–13)

- John's viewpoint in his Life of Christ is that Jesus is God's clearest expression of himself to people and people can know what God is really like by looking at Jesus. (John 1:14–18)

7 CHOICES AT JORDAN

CHAPTER HIGHLIGHTS

- Interrogation of the Baptizer
- The Warrior Lamb
- Connecting with God's Lamb
- Ladder to God

Let's Get Started

John the Baptist's preaching attracted increasing attention from the people living in Palestine about 30 A.D. They flocked out into the desert to hear the man some said was the first bonafide prophet in 400 years. Others dared to speculate that he might even be the promised Messiah arriving at long last to rescue the oppressed nation from its Roman captors.

> **John 1:19–20** Now this was John's testimony when the Jews of Jerusalem sent priests and Levites to ask him who he was. He did not fail to confess, but confessed freely, "I am not the Christ."

Interrogation Of The Baptizer

As John's crowds increased it was inevitable that the authorities would take notice. Representatives of Jerusalem's religious intelligentsia were sent to the wild country near the Jordan River town of **Bethany** (see appendix A) to question the feisty prophet about his message and work. The writer who is telling the story is not anti-Semitic—he himself is a Jew, as is Jesus. When he uses the term, "*the Jews*," he does not refer to rank-and-file Jewish people, but to the Jewish leaders who wielded power through an official governing body known as the Sanhedrin. Thousands of Jewish people—an estimated one-third of the world's Jewish population in the first century—embraced Jesus as their Messiah. Eventually even many of the <u>leaders believed</u>. But the majority of Jewish lead-

Bethany: not Bethany near Jerusalem, but another town east of the Jordan, 12 miles from Jericho (see appendix A)

☞ **GO TO:**

John 19:38–40;
  Acts 6:7; 15:5
  (leaders believed)

ers opposed Jesus to the death. The three groups mentioned as John's interrogators were the priests, the Levites, and the Pharisees.

Who's Who

PRIESTS: (verse 19)—descendants of Aaron, Moses' brother, in charge of religious services at the Temple. John's father Zechariah was a priest (Luke 1:5). The priests would be especially interested in the activities of a member of a priestly family.

Who's Who

LEVITES: (verse 19)—descendants of the <u>patriarch</u> Levi (Moses and Aaron's ancestor) who were the Temple police, musicians, and teachers. Their teaching role explains their concern about the content of John's teaching.

Who's Who

PHARISEES: (verse 24)—Israel's "pure religionists." They portrayed themselves as serious students of the **Law** of God, but in practice were more committed to their **traditions**. Some were genuinely godly men, but their outward legalism usually led to spiritual pride that hid real godliness behind a smokescreen of rule-bound religion.

☞ **GO TO:**

Genesis 29:31–30:24, 35:16–18, 49:1–28 (patriarch)

Law: Old Testament commandments

traditions: extrabiblical religious rules and regulations

Day of the Lord: time when God implements some specific act of salvation: judgment, Christ's coming

☞ **GO TO:**

Malachi 3:1; 4:5–6; 1 Kings 18; Matthew 11:14 (Elijah)

> **John 1:21** They asked him, "Then who are you? Are you Elijah?" He said, "I am not." "Are you the Prophet?" He answered, "No."

Who Did John Think He Was, Anyhow?

This committee demanded to see John's credentials. Who did he think he was? He had not gone through the proper channels nor was he sanctioned by anyone in authority.

John stuck to his guns. His response to those who questioned his identity was always the same: *"I am not the Christ."*

People speculated on two other possible identities for the River Prophet. John said "No" to both.

First, he insisted he was not *"Elijah"* (John 1:21). An Old Testament prophecy predicted <u>Elijah</u> would come to prepare Israel for the **Day of the Lord**. Many believed this meant the famous Old Testament prophet would be literally resurrected. In that sense, John was not Elijah, so he denied it. However, the angel who spoke to John's father before his birth promised he would minister *"in the spirit and power of Elijah"* (Luke 1:17).

Second, John denied he was one known as *"the Prophet."* All sorts of <u>prophets</u> were expected before Messiah's coming. Centuries earlier, Moses told Israel to be ready to welcome a prophet <u>like himself</u>. (Early Christians believed the miracle-working, Moses-like prophet was Christ.)

Who John Was

Between the lines we sense that John disliked answering questions about himself. In the original Greek his "No!" (John 1:21) is the strongest negative he could have used. They simply could not get him to make claims they could attack.

John knew he was the fulfillment of the prophecy of Isaiah 40:3—a *"voice"* pointing the way to Christ (John 1:23). Beyond that he claimed nothing.

Lawrence O. Richards: The fact is that few of us understand the role we are playing in God's great plan. John was more significant than he suspected, even though he recognized his commission to call Israel back to God in preparation for the coming of the Messiah. You and I as well may be more significant in accomplishing God's purposes than we suspect![1]

> **John 1:24–25** Now some of the Pharisees who had been sent questioned him, "Why then do you baptize if you are not the Christ, nor Elijah, nor the prophet?"

Upsetting Institutional Protocols

Dissatisfied with John's answers, *"some Pharisees"* pressed the cross-examination, "Where then did you get your authority to baptize?" Baptism was normally administered by Temple priests to pagan proselytes converting to Judaism. John upset the applecart by baptizing people who were already (they thought) "God's people." Grassroots Jews readily admitted their **spiritual poverty** and came to him for baptism like brand new converts. None of this had been approved by the established authorities, nor was it likely to be!

 The possibility of <u>offending</u> established authorities was, from the beginning, one of the risks connected with proclaiming the kingdom of God and calling for visible change in people and institutions. <u>Jesus</u> and the <u>early church</u> would also be accused of it.

☞ GO TO:

Matthew 16:14; Mark 6:15; Luke 9:19 (prophets)

Deuteronomy 18:15–22 (like himself)

What Others are Saying:

KEY Outline:

John's Inquisitors
- Priests
- Levites
- Pharisees

spiritual poverty: sense of something lacking in one's spiritual life

---

☞ GO TO:

Mark 6:3; Matthew 11:6; 13:57; 24:9 (offending)

John 7:15, 45–52; Luke 20:1–2 (Jesus)

Acts 4:5–7, 13–21; 5:17, 27–33 (early church)

What Others are Saying:

Lewis Sperry Chafer: John did not preach Moses and the prophets. The law and the prophets were *until* John. It is to be concluded that the preaching of John the Baptist was wholly new, and was according to his mission as herald of the King."[2]

> **John 1:26** "I baptize with water," John replied, "but among you stands one you do not know."

Who's On First?

John did not directly answer the Pharisees' question. He picked up on the subject of baptism to explain where his work fit on the list of spiritual priorities. But water baptism was not the gut issue; it was merely a warm-up for the main event. Top priority was the Christ-issue. Christ was in the wings, ready to take center stage. You don't know him, John said. But he is *"among you,"* even as we speak!

among you: in Israel or there in the crowd

While the religious establishment was worrying about maintaining their positions of authority, the Messiah (Christ) for whom the nation had pined for centuries was among them, incognito. This exchange took place after Jesus' baptism. By this time John knew Christ's identity (see John 1:32–33). Christ's worth surpassed the value of any worldly protocol. The only response appropriate in the presence of such greatness was recognition of personal unworthiness (verse 27).

☞ **GO TO:**

Matthew 3:13–17 (Jesus' baptism)

What Others are Saying:

Leon Morris: This should not be taken as indicating that (John) did not regard his baptism as important. He did. He does not depreciate it. But his baptism is not an end in itself. Its purpose is to point men to Christ. John's interest is in the Christ and nothing less.[3]

> **John 1:29, 34** The next day John saw Jesus coming toward him and said, "Look, the Lamb of God, who takes away the sin of the world! . . . I have seen and I testify that this is the Son of God."

Identity Of The Warrior Lamb

The day after his official interrogation, John was back on the job. As Jesus came toward him, John announced to the people around him, *"Look, the Lamb of God."* When they heard Jesus identified as *"the Lamb of God,"* every Jew listening would have had a mental picture of the meaning of that description. Lambs played a giant part in Jewish worship.

Bible Pictures of the "Lamb of God"

If John was thinking of . . . **the God-provided Ram** Abraham found on Mt. Moriah which became the substitute sacrifice for his son Isaac (Genesis 22:8),

Then he was saying: . . . "This man is the substitute sacrifice for your sins, who can save your life."

If John was thinking of . . . **the Passover Lamb** whose blood was splashed on the lintel and doorposts to save Israelites from the death angel and free them to escape Egyptian slavery (Exodus 12:1–11),

Then he was saying: . . . "This man is the one true sacrifice who can deliver you from slavery to sin." The Morning and Evening Lambs offered at the **Temple**, whose daily sacrifice assured the continuity of God's presence (Exodus 29:38–46). "This man is the sacrifice that can take away your sins and assure daily fellowship with God."

If John was thinking of . . . **the Suffering Servant of the Lord** Isaiah described as *"a lamb led to the slaughter"* (Isaiah 53:7–8),

Then he was saying: . . . "This man is God's submissive servant who suffers and gives his life for the transgression of the people, including yours."

If John was thinking of . . . **the Horned Lamb**, during the days of the Maccabees, between the Old and New Testaments, which became the symbol of the conquering champion of God's people,

Then he was saying: . . . "This man is your champion who will give you victory over sin."

If John was thinking of . . . **the Triumphant Lamb** who, at the price of his blood, won the right to open the seals of God's judgment (Revelation 5:1–14),

Then he was saying: . . . "This man will judge the universe, after taking your judgment upon himself."

Dig Deeper

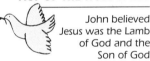

ACT OF THE HOLY SPIRIT

John believed Jesus was the Lamb of God and the Son of God

☞ **GO TO:**

Matthew 3:16–17; Luke 3:21–22 (for baptism)

John 3:16; 20:31 (Son of God)

Son of God: *Chosen One; Messiah; extension of God; Revealer of God*

What Others are Saying:

The Ultimate Fingerprint

John did not know Jesus was the promised Messiah until he saw the ultimate proof. The Lord had told him to watch for a special sign—a dove-like form descending from heaven to settle upon a certain man. The dove-form would be the Holy Spirit, and the man upon whom it fluttered down would be *"the Son of God."* It happened when Jesus came to John <u>for baptism</u>.

Prophets throughout Bible history had visions of spiritual realities not seen by others. John the Baptist, last of the Old Testament-style prophets, saw the most amazing vision of all. And it identified Jesus of Nazareth as the **Son of God**!

Dom J. Howton: Whereas God of old chose a nation (Israel) to work out his purpose in the world, and in that nation raised up prophets to direct his people, now he has chosen only one individual (Christ) who in himself represents God active in the world.[4]

John 1:36–37 When [John the Baptist] saw Jesus passing by, he said, "Look, the Lamb of God!" When the two disciples heard him say this, they followed Jesus.

Connecting With God's Lamb

John the Baptist's effectiveness in preparing people to receive Christ is seen in what happened the next day. He was in conversation with two of his **disciples** when Jesus walked by. John's greatness was most conspicuous in the selfless way he released his closest followers to switch their allegiance to Jesus.

The two disciples to whom John had spoken hurried to catch up. Jesus turned around and asked what they were looking for. They called him **Rabbi** or "Teacher," and asked where he was staying. He motioned for them to come. One of two who spent time with Jesus that day was a man named Andrew.

Immediately after spending time with Jesus, Andrew went looking for his brother Simon Peter. *"We have found the Messiah."*

Christian leaders and teachers are not called to make disciples who cling to themselves. They are called to make disciples for Jesus Christ who, as soon as possible, learn to listen to his voice and follow him with a healthy independence from the teacher's influence.

KEY POINT

Jesus' first disciples were introduced to him by John the Baptist. They had been John's disciples.

disciples: *learners, students*

Rabbi: *Hebrew for "my great one"*

Remember This . . .

It's amazing that in one meeting Andrew became convinced of Jesus' true identity. Of course his understanding was incomplete at this point. Full impact of the significance of Jesus as the Christ would not come until Jesus rose from the dead.

Something to Ponder

> **John 1:42** And [Andrew] brought [Simon] to Jesus. Jesus looked at him and said, "You are Simon son of John. You will be called Cephas" (which, when translated, is Peter).

You Are Rocky!

Meeting Simon for the first time, Jesus could see his potential. He gave Simon a new name in keeping with the change their encounter would bring and the destiny toward which it would lead. All three of Simon's names mean the same thing: "Rock."

KEY Outline:

Peter's New Name
Character change
Worldwide mission

- *Simon* is Aramaic
- *Petros* ("Peter" in English) is Greek
- *Cephas* is Syriac

The changing of Simon's name may have more significance than appears on the surface. In Bible days a person's name stood for his or her character. Simon was volatile, impulsive, and unreliable—not the solid character his new name suggests. Jesus intended to remake him into the "Rock Man." The two foreign names—Petros and Cephas—may have hinted at the worldwide dimensions Peter's **apostolic** ministry would have.

apostolic: related to being an ambassador for Christ

EARLY CHURCH LIFE: Early Christians sometimes changed their names when they met Christ.

First Five Alive

The next day Jesus left for Galilee. Five men—from the Galilean town of **Bethsaida**—joined him. Three he had met the day before: Andrew, John (the unnamed disciple), Simon Peter. The other two would be added on the way. Either before he headed north along the Jordan River road or after they got to Bethsaida (see appendix A), Jesus looked up the fourth man, Philip, and said, **"Follow me."** Philip, in Andrew-like fashion (compare John 1:41 and 45), went looking for his friend (or brother) Nathanael and told him what he believed about Jesus.

Bethsaida: town north of Sea of Galilee with suburb across the Jordan River

Follow me: Greek for "continue to follow me" (as a disciple)

Philip said to Nathanael: *"We have found the one Moses wrote about in the Law, and about whom the prophets also wrote—Jesus of Nazareth, the son of Joseph"* (John 1:45).

The Honest Skeptic

When Nathanael heard that Jesus was from Nazareth, Galilee, he was scandalized. Nazareth was a caravan town with a reputation for low morals. Could such a "Nowhere Town" produce the Messiah? And the people of the province of Galilee were considered by Judeans—especially the Jewish leaders—as lawless and rebellious. Religious leaders in Jerusalem dismissed Jesus and all Galileans as *"This mob that knows nothing of the law—there is a curse on them!"* (John 7:49). Nathanael, an honest Jewish believer from Galilee, would not have gone that far, but his thinking was colored by popular opinion, and his shock is understandable. He did not understand how absolutely essential it was for Christ to be identified with sinners. On that basis, there was no more appropriate place to be from than insignificant Nazareth!

What Others are Saying:

George R. Beasley-Murray: The residence of Jesus in Nazareth is akin to his birth in a stable; it is part of the offense of the incarnation.[5]

Skeptic No More

Philip did not argue with his friend. He simply said, *"Come and see"* (for yourself). As the two of them approached, Jesus called Nathanael *"a true Israelite, in whom there is nothing false."*

"How do you know me?" asked Nathanael.

Two things are notable about this exchange:

1. Jesus affirmed Nathanael's honesty and straightforwardness.

2. Nathanael's question about how Jesus knows him is just another honest question consistent with an open, inquiring mind. There is no suspicion of trickery or deceit on Jesus' part.

Son of God: *person in "the closest possible relationship to God"*[7]

King of Israel: *Jewish title for the Messiah*

☞ **GO TO:**

2 Kings 6:8–12; Ezekiel 8 (prophetic revelation)

Jesus answered: *"I saw you while you were still under the fig tree before Philip called you."* A Christian Arab commentator suggests this is a Middle Eastern idiom for "I know you very well."[6] But the fact that Nathanael immediately confessed a fairly advanced faith in Jesus—*"You are the **Son of God**; you are the **King of Israel**"*—indicates that what Jesus saw in Nathanael under the fig tree was a secret Jesus could only have known by God-given <u>pro-</u>

phetic revelation. He was convinced Jesus was a true prophet . . . and more.

What Others are Saying:

Lawrence O. Richards: How wonderful it is when you and I can say to anyone, "Come, and you will see." Jesus is in heaven, but through his body here on earth he maintains a living presence in our lost world. When our congregations are filled with the love and presence of our Lord, we can gladly invite inquirers to come, knowing that in the warmth of the loving relationships which marks people in whom Jesus now dwells, they will see—and find—him.[8]

Six Titles For Jesus In John 1:29–50

1. Lamb of God (verses 29, 35)
2. Son of God (verses 34, 49)
3. Rabbi (verses 38, 49)
4. Messiah (Christ) (verse 41)
5. King of Israel (verse 49)
6. Son of Man (verse 51)

> **John 1:51** He then added, "I tell you the truth, you shall see heaven open, and the angels of God ascending and descending on the Son of Man."

Ladder To God

Jesus assured the honest Israelite, Nathanael, that before their relationship was over he would experience and understand magnificent spiritual truths. Jesus' statement looked ahead to his entire ministry on behalf of people. He was saying "I, personally, am the point of access and communication between heaven and earth—between God and human beings."

The testimonies of
- the author of this New Testament version of the Life of Christ (John 1:18),
- the Holy Spirit (verses 32–33),
- John the Baptist (verse 34),
- Andrew (verse 41),
- Philip (verse 45), and
- Nathanael (verse 49)

KEY POINT

Jesus claims to be the point of access between people and God.

☞ **GO TO:**

John 14:6; Acts 4:12 (point of access)

Something to Ponder

. . . all agree that Jesus is God in the flesh, Messiah (Christ), source of light, life, and access to God. Others also testified to the same thing, and their testimony is recorded in the New Testament. The experience of multitudes who have trusted him since the first century confirms this conclusion. In the face of such evidence can anyone remain indifferent?

Many have concluded that the only reasonable response is to receive Jesus as the God-provided Savior he claims to be, and to gain the personal access to God that Jesus Christ makes possible.

Then to pass it on!

Study Questions

1. What three religious-political groups were represented in the investigative delegation sent to establish John's identity?
2. Who did John the Baptist claim to be? Where did he get his authority?
3. Identify three possible meanings of the title John gave to Jesus: "Lamb of God."
4. How did John know Jesus was the Son of God?
5. Of the first five disciples who joined up with Jesus, which two were introduced to Jesus by a friend or relative?
6. List the six titles for Jesus used by people in John 1:29–51 to describe him. Which one best describes the way you see Jesus today? Why?

CHAPTER WRAP-UP

- The Jewish religious authorities in Jerusalem sent a team of investigators to John the Baptist to check out his claims. He denied that he was Christ, Elijah, or the prophet Moses promised. He claimed only to be a voice sent to prepare the way for the Lord. (John 1:19–28)

- John the Baptist introduced Jesus as the Lamb of God and told how he knew the truth about Christ. (John 1:29–34)

- John the Baptist introduced two of his own disciples to Jesus, and they left John to follow Jesus. This started a chain reaction in which three others were introduced to Christ and began to follow him as serious disciples. (John 1:35–49)

- Jesus claimed to be, personally, the point of access and communication between God and people. (John 1:50–51)

8 THE GUSH OF NEW WINE

CHAPTER HIGHLIGHTS

- The Worrisome Wedding
- Temple Rock
- Superficial Faith
- Nick at Night

Let's Get Started

Jesus upsets all the stereotypes of a religious leader. He shows up in the most down-to-earth places, says the most shocking things, and gets far too personal for most people. The Jesus of the gospels seems strangely out of place in church! He has this disturbing way of being the "first responder" right smack in the middle of the latest crisis. It started at a party.

> **John 2:1–2** On the third day a wedding took place at Cana in Galilee. Jesus' mother was there, and Jesus and his disciples had also been invited to the wedding.

The Case Of The Worrisome Wedding

Three days after John the Baptist introduces Jesus to his Jordan River audience as *"the Lamb of God,"* the scene shifts to the sleepy up-country village of Cana, about nine miles from Nazareth, Galilee (see appendix A). A wedding festival was in progress. Jesus' mother was there—she was probably a relative. Jesus and his five **new compadres** were among the invited guests.

A **Coptic** gospel says Mary was a sister of the bridegroom's mother. The Monarchian Prefaces to the New Testament say the groom was John, author of the fourth Gospel, whose mother was Mary's sister, Salome.

☞ **GO TO:**

John 1:35–51 (new compadres)

new compadres: *friends; Andrew, John, Peter, Philip, and Nathanael*

Coptic: *the church in Egypt and North Africa*

Michael Card: Whenever Jesus wasn't preaching or teaching you'd find him at a party. It might be at a tax collector's or a Pharisee's home. The guests might include powerful men in the community or the riff-raff. What seemed to bother the stuffy, "religious" types wasn't that Jesus went to parties, but that he seemed to enjoy himself too much. . . . It was at just such a party that Jesus performed his first miracle.[1]

Wedding Protocols—First Century Jewish Style

At night, with torches blazing, the groom and his friends paraded noisily through the town to the bride's house. At her home, a feast was held, with speeches and expressions of good will. Then, that same night, the bride and groom paraded back through the streets to the groom's house where the wedding banquet took place—taking the longest route possible, so the whole town would have a chance to wish the couple well.

For a week the couple held open house, dressed in wedding clothes (see illustration this page) and wearing crowns. The whole town treated them like royalty.

Alfred Edersheim: The pious fasted before [a wedding], confessing their sins. It was regarded almost as a sacrament. . . . The bridal pair, on the marriage day, symbolized the union of God with Israel.[2]

Bridal Dress

Brides decorated their dresses by adding colorful embroidery rather than by altering the design and style of their clothing as we do today.

Bubbly Boo-Boo

A strong element of reciprocity attached itself to wedding customs. If a guest did not bring an appropriate gift, he might, in certain situations, face legal action. If the groom did not properly entertain his guests, he could face censure.

At the Cana nuptials such a social disaster raised its ugly head out of the wine barrels like the Loch Ness Monster and threatened to destroy the celebration. A miscalculation occurred so serious that it had the ominous potential to bring repercussions on the bridegroom's family, cloud the marriage, and disrupt the couple's standing in the community. The problem? The wine—which was supposed to be enough for a week of celebrating—ran out! (The wine shortage may have been caused by Jesus bringing five unexpected guests!)

Supermom To The Rescue!

Mary, Jesus' mother, was apparently responsible for some of the festival arrangements—at least she felt responsible. She had authority over the servants—when she gave orders, they obeyed (John 2:5). Aware of the far-reaching consequences of the waning drink, she immediately swung into action to solve the problem.

Did Jesus Talk Back To His Mom?

From the moment of his conception <u>Mary knew</u> her son had a special destiny. By now she'd probably heard about the things <u>John the Baptist said</u> introducing him as the Messiah. But she was his mother. She naturally thought of him as the <u>obedient son</u> she had raised. Furthermore, after the **death of Joseph**, Jesus had likely taken over responsibility for the care of his mother and family. So it was understandable for her to go to him for help. *"They have no more wine,"* she said.

☞ **GO TO:**

Luke 1:32–35
(Mary knew)

John 1:29, 34
(the Baptist said)

Luke 2:51
(obedient son)

death of Joseph: *not recorded in Scripture, he died sometime during the "silent years"*

> **John 2:4–5** "Dear woman, why do you involve me?" Jesus replied. "My time has not yet come." His mother said to the servants, "Do whatever he tells you."

Same Son, New Relation

At first glance, Jesus' response to his mother's implied suggestion that he do something about the wine shortage seems harsh. It was an unusual way for a son to address his mother, but the Greek word for "woman" is not disrespectful or harsh. One translator

KEY POINT

Mary had to recognize Jesus not only as her son but as her Messiah.

☞ **GO TO:**

John 7:6, 8, 30; 12:23; Matthew 26:18, 45; Mark 14:41 (timetable)

John 13:4–16; 1 Timothy 5:10 (foot-washing)

Deuteronomy 21:6; Psalm 26:6; Mark 7:2–5 (hand-washing)

master of the banquet: master of ceremonies, emcee, or headwaiter

180 gallons: enough for the feast plus leftovers for a wedding gift

What Others are Saying:

interprets it: "Lady, let me handle this in my own way."[3] His response signals a new phase in the relationship between himself and Mary. He is no longer merely her obedient son, but also her Messiah. From now on he must call the shots.

 When Jesus said, *"My time has not yet come,"* it was a thinly veiled hint that even he was not ultimately in charge. The shape and timing of his activities was determined by the <u>timetable</u> of God's will. He would act when the time was right. Mary, never slow to catch on, always desiring God's best, got the message. But she did not take Jesus' response as a no.

Steps To A Miracle

Every Jewish home in those days had large containers reserved for water used in the ceremonial washings involved in day-to-day Jewish life. At this home in Cana, there were six stone pots that held 120 to 180 gallons of water. Stone pots were used because it was thought that in them water was less likely to become ceremonially contaminated. Clean, pure water was important for two Jewish rituals:

1. <u>Foot-washing</u>, to remove the dust and other road filth from sandaled feet
2. <u>Hand-washing</u>, an elaborate ceremony performed by the strictest Jews not only before meals but between courses

"Fill the jars with water," Jesus instructed the servants. They did as he said. The jars were filled *"to the brim,"* leaving no room for additional ingredients.

"Now draw some out and take it to the **master of the banquet***"* (John 2:8).

The servants obeyed, without a recorded doubt or sideways glance that asked, "Are you crazy, man?" Sometime between the ritual pots and the emcee's lips the ceremonial wash water had changed to the best wine at the feast (John 2:10)—**180 gallons** of it!

Leonard I. Sweet: Instead of showing up at the door with the gift of a bottle of wine, as moderns particularly are wont to do, he made 180 gallons of wine after he got there.[4]

Wine Drinking in Bible Times

FACT: There was no known festival protocol which demanded the best wine be served first, and the wine of lesser quality be saved until *"after the guests have had too much to drink."* The banquet master's comment in verse 10 was not necessarily a criticism.

FACT: In Middle Eastern cultures, before wine was drunk it was usually mixed with water.

FACT: Straight water was often unsafe. The easiest way to make it safe was to mix it with wine.

FACT: Jewish Passover wine, which would have been shared by Jesus and his friends at the <u>Last Supper</u>, was mixed three parts water to one part wine.

FACT: A mixture of one part wine to one part water or less fell into the category of "strong wine" or "strong drink," against which the Bible issues <u>strong warnings</u>.

Robert H. Stein: To consume the amount of alcohol that is in two martinis by drinking wine containing three parts water to one part wine, one would have to drink over 22 glasses. In other words, it is possible to become intoxicated from wine mixed with three parts of water, but one's drinking would probably affect the bladder long before it affected the mind.[5]

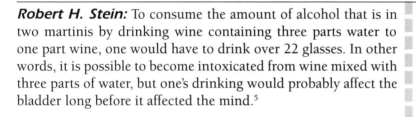

> **John 2:11** This, the first of his miraculous signs, Jesus performed at Cana in Galilee. He thus revealed his glory, and his disciples put their faith in him.

Signs Of Saviorhood

The changing of ceremonial water into the best wine at the wedding was, the author John notes, *"the first sign"* proving Jesus was the special, God-sent person John the Baptist, the New Testament writers, and he himself insisted he was. John's Life of Christ lists seven such signs. John chose these seven from a much <u>larger number</u> of Jesus' known miracles and uses them to illustrate specific aspects of Jesus' personality and ministry.

Something to Ponder

☞ **GO TO:**

Luke 22:17–18 (Last Supper)

Proverbs 20:1; 23:29–35; Ephesians 5:18; 1 Timothy 3:3; Titus 2:3 (strong warnings)

What Others are Saying:

KEY POINT

The miracle of changing water to wine was the first supernatural evidence ("sign") of messiahship.

☞ **GO TO:**

John 21:25 (larger number)

The Wine Of Cana Signals Vital Realities

- The ancient rules of purification were replaced by the "new wine" of Jesus' personal authority.
- The first five disciples put their trust in Jesus.
- God's **glory** was seen in down-to-earth terms in everyday situations—a new picture of "the domesticated God"[6] who cares about the ordinary lives of people.
- God is a God who joins the party, not merely somber "religious" events.
- Jesus' authority extended to created things, like water, wine, and weddings.

☞ **GO TO:**

John 1:14 (glory)

glory: *manifestation of God's character and splendor*

Dig Deeper

Seven Signs in John to Back up Jesus' Claims

John's Report	Sign	Response
John 2:1–11	Water changed to wine	(2:11) Disciples trusted him
John 4:46–54	Royal official's son healed	(4:50, 53) Official and family believed
John 5:1–18	Paralyzed man healed at Bethesda Pool	(5:9) Man's faith seen in his actions; (5:18) Leaders wanted to kill Jesus.
John 6:1–14	Feeding of the 5,000	(6:14) People believed Jesus a prophet; (6:66) Many disciples left him
John 6:16–21	Walking on water	(6:21) Disciples took Jesus into the boat
John 9:1–41	Restored blind man's sight	(9:11, 17, 33, 36) Man's faith developed; (9:16, 24, 29, 40, 41) Pharisees opposed Jesus
John 11:1–44	Raised Lazarus from the dead	(11:27) Martha confessed faith; (11:45) Many Jews believed; (11:53) Sanhedrin plots to kill Jesus

What Others are Saying:

Henry H. Halley: This first miracle was done at a wedding feast, on a festive occasion, ministering to human joy, making people happy, as if Jesus wanted to announce, right at the start, that the religion which he was now introducing into the world was no religion of asceticism, but a religion of natural joy.[7]

I. Howard Marshall: It is argued that science rules out the possibility of miracles. In fact, however, this argument is nothing more than the statement of a presupposition, namely that in a purely material universe nothing can happen that cannot be accounted for in terms of natural causes. But that is purely an assumption about the nature of the universe which cannot be proven to be true. At most it could be argued from it that normally miracles do not occur; but it is illegitimate to claim that therefore miracles can never occur.[8]

Temple Rock

After the wedding, Jesus and his five friends spent a few days in Capernaum where his mother and brothers now lived, then headed for Jerusalem. It was spring—time for the annual Feast of Passover celebrating Israel's freedom and nationhood. This would be the first of at least <u>three Passovers</u> Jesus attended during his brief ministry.

> **John 2:14–16** In the temple courts he found men selling cattle, sheep and doves, and others sitting at tables exchanging money. So he made a whip out of cords, and drove all from the temple area, both sheep and cattle; he scattered the coins of the money changers and overturned their tables. To those who sold doves he said, "Get these out of here! How dare you turn my Father's house into a market!"

New Wine Floods The Temple Swap Meet

New Testament historians record two times when Jesus angrily invaded the Temple, driving out people conducting for-profit business in its courts. This one came just as his public ministry was starting and introduced his authority. <u>The other</u> happened during the last week of his life.

What Made Jesus So Angry?

What brought the "gentle" Jesus to a point of violent outrage was the misuse of God's house and God's law to make a fast buck! The rules of Jewish religious life required Jewish males living within walking distance to come to Jerusalem every year for the Passover. If they lived outside the homeland, they were to make it to the festival as often as possible—at least once in their lifetime. This brought huge crowds—sometimes as many as two and a quarter million—to the feast.

Three additional regulations made these throngs easy pickings for enterprising profiteers:

- **Rule 1: Temple Tax.** Every Jewish male over 19 years of age was required to pay a half-shekel tax (two days' wages) for Temple maintenance. This could only be paid in official

☞ **Check It Out:**

John 2:12–22

☞ **GO TO:**

John 2:13; 6:4; 11:55 (three Passovers)

☞ **GO TO:**

Matthew 21:12–13; Mark 11:15–17; Luke 19:45–46 (the other)

KEY Outline:

**Sins of the Temple
Swap Meet**

Oppressing the poor

*Using God's law for
selfish advantage*

*Using people's faith to
manipulate them*

Cheating

Misusing power

*Hindering Gentile
access to Temple*

*Distorting the picture of
God*

Temple coinage; foreign money had to be exchanged. Shrewd money changers made huge profits charging the equivalent of one-fourth of a day's wage for each half-shekel. For the poor this rate constituted a real hardship.

- **Rule 2: Paschal Lambs.** Each man was required to sacrifice a lamb without blemish the afternoon before the Passover meal. Temple inspectors, appointed by the high priest, examined all animals before sacrifice. If a lamb was purchased outside the Temple it was more likely to be rejected by the inspectors than if bought from Temple marketeers. Guess what? The price of lambs available inside was several times higher than those outside. The worshiper was over a barrel. Again, the poor suffered most from this scam.

- **Rule 3: Alternate Sacrifice.** Those too poor to offer a lamb were allowed by law to offer a pair of doves. Sacrificial doves had to have a stamp of approval from the same Temple inspectors as those who ruled on the lambs. Temple dove-sellers were known to charge as much as a hundred times more than their outside counterparts.

Is it any wonder there was fire in Jesus' eyes as he chased the cheats from the courtyard? The whole system reeked of injustice and avarice. And worse, this smelly business created in people's minds a distorted idea of God. It made God seem not to be the welcoming <u>God revealed</u> in Christ, but a **capricious** deity who throws barriers in the way of people who want to come to him, a God whose favor must be bought.

According to some sources, the geniuses behind this profitable conspiracy were the high priest and his family. People appointed to lead worship padded their greedy pockets by scamming the faithful—especially the poor.

KINGDOM
OF GOD

The brains behind the exploitive sanctuary swap meet demanded Jesus produce the credentials that gave him the right to close down their lucrative swindle. They did not argue that the seamy business was out of place in God's house. They seemed to understand that cleaning corruption out of the church was appropriate messianic activity. Jesus' zeal for God's house amounted to a <u>claim to messiahship</u>. What they were looking for was a *"miraculous sign"* to back up his claim (verse 18). They demanded he prove his authority by putting on what Ed Sullivan would have called "a really big shew"—a colossal and impressive demonstration of power.

> **John 2:19** Jesus answered them, "Destroy this temple, and I will raise it again in three days."

The Ultimate Proof Of Jesus' Authority

Talk about rocking the Temple! The author explains that *"this temple"* Jesus was talking about *"was his body"* (verse 21). His statement was a metaphor meaning "Watch for the greatest proof of all—the miracle of my resurrection!" Even his disciples did not fully grasp his meaning until *"after he was raised from the dead"* (verse 22).

He might as well have been talking to the wall. The Jewish leaders were looking for trouble, and they completely misconstrued his words. They would later use his statement to accuse him <u>at his trial</u> and mock him with it <u>as he died</u>!

KINGDOM OF GOD

The Beat of the Temple Rock

Jesus' whip-swinging, table-smashing, money-scattering purge of the Temple introduces important realities:

- Christ heads a new order of <u>grace and truth</u> replacing the old system of **legalism** and ritual.

- God's <u>Temple</u> ignites Christ's **zeal**, stirs <u>his passions</u>, moves him to action, and consumes his life.

- Appropriate respect for God's Temple is demonstrated in worship and living that is <u>free of prejudice</u>, selfishness, manipulation, injustice, and exploitation.

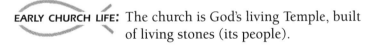

EARLY CHURCH LIFE: The church is God's living Temple, built of living stones (its people).

No Distant God

Christ, becoming flesh and living among us, discloses before our eyes the truth about God to replace childish notions about him we've clung to in the past: God is not a detached deity coolly monitoring our lives "from a distance." He's a disturbingly involved God who is angered when people take unfair advantage of others and when human institutions muddy people's concept of him.

☞ **GO TO:**

Matthew 26:59–61 (at his trial)

Matthew 27:39–40 (as he died)

John 1:17 (grace and truth)

1 Corinthians 3:16; Ephesians 2:19–20; 1 Peter 2:5 (Temple)

Ephesians 5:25 (his passions)

James 2:1–9 (free of prejudice)

legalism: religion based on rules and regulations

zeal: jealousy, passionate concern

Something to Ponder

> **John 2:23–24** Now while he was in Jerusalem at the Passover Feast, many people saw the miraculous signs he was doing and believed in his name. But Jesus would not commit himself to them, for he knew all men. He did not need man's testimony about man, for he knew what was in man.

☞ **Check It Out:**

John 2:23–3:12

miraculous signs: Greek word means "authenticating evidence"

The Cure For Superficial Faith

Many people *"saw the* **miraculous signs***"* Jesus did in Jerusalem during the Passover and *"believed in his name."* No specific signs or miracles are described, other than shutting down the illegal Temple market. In Bible terms the phrase *"his name"* often refers to a person's character. The greatest sign of Jesus' authenticity went deeper than miracles. People became convinced he was the genuine article by simply observing the character and personality of the man himself.

Leading In The Polls

Even though many "believed," Jesus did not commit himself to them. Something was missing. A less perceptive politician might have taken advantage of these first signals of popular confidence, openly declared himself, and tried to ride the balloon of early popularity into national leadership. Wasn't that, after all, what he wanted?

KINGDOM OF GOD | ### Heart Scan

Jesus was not blinded by his ego. *"He knew what was in man"* (verse 25). He knew the people expressing early faith in him did not really understand what kind of leader he intended to be or what sort of kingdom he intended to establish. It was not that there was anything wrong with believing in miracles. It was simply that believing Jesus could do miracles was only the first step. A deeper, more life-changing spiritual breakthrough must come if faith was to become an informed persuasion that sees Christ in his true significance as Revealer of God, Lord of life, and God's Provision for human salvation—the kind of faith on which his kingdom is founded.

KEY POINT

Christ knows what's in human hearts.

What Others are Saying:

Billy Graham: I had heard the message. . . . Intellectually, I accepted Christ to the extent that I acknowledged what I knew about him to be true. That was mental assent. Emotionally, I felt that I wanted to love him in return for his loving me. But the final issue was whether I would turn myself over to his rule in my life.[9]

> **John 3:2** He came to Jesus at night and said, "Rabbi, we know you are a teacher who has come from God. For no one could perform the miraculous signs you are doing if God were not with Him."

Nick At Night

Before the Passover ended and Jesus returned to Galilee, he was visited by an influential man named Nicodemus.

Nicodemus came to Jesus after dark, perhaps because he did not wish to be seen by his religious and political colleagues who were already lining up against Jesus. Considering his position in the community, it was amazing that he would risk coming at all. Considering the Sanhedrin's negative stance toward Jesus, Nicodemus said three startling things:

- He called Jesus *"Rabbi"*—respected teacher.
- He recognized Jesus was *"from God."*
- He acknowledged that Jesus' works showed God was *"with him."*

His greeting also discloses a startling revelation concerning the ruling council: *"We know"* indicates the Sanhedrin understood that Jesus had been sent from God. And they opposed him anyway!

NICODEMUS: A Pharisee (verse 1) committed to high moral values based on the **Law of Moses** and the religious traditions of Judaism. A member of the Sanhedrin (verse 2), the ruling council which directed Jewish life. A teacher of national prominence (verse 10).

In Hebrew, Nicodemus was *Naqdemon.* A prominent family by that name appears in first century Jewish history. A "Nicodemus" was envoy to the Roman general Pompey during the first century B.C. Gorion, a "son of Nicodemus," negotiated the end of the war of 66–70 A.D. when Jerusalem was destroyed. A prominent citizen named Nicodemus is reported to have survived that war. Could he have been the one who came to see Jesus?[10]

 Who's Who

Law of Moses: *Ten Commandments*

Something to Ponder

> **John 3:3** In reply Jesus declared, "I tell you the truth, no one can see the kingdom of God unless he is born again."

What Was Really Bugging Nicodemus?

Jesus *"knew all men"* (John 2:24). He did not need a ton of bricks to fall on him to know why Nicodemus took the risk to come. Without polite chitchat, he went directly to the point. He knew the famous Pharisee was thinking about the *"**kingdom of God**."* Nicodemus had seen something in Jesus that ignited a spark of messianic hope.

kingdom of God: place where God reigns as King

Like most of his countrymen, he expected Messiah to come as a conquering king, fulfill Israel's dreams of national liberation, destroy its enemies, and restore the lost glory of David's kingdom. The things Jesus was doing did not fit the general Jewish picture of the promised Liberator.

The truth was, as brilliant a student of the Bible as Nicodemus was, he did not really understand the nature of God's kingdom as Jesus modeled it in his actions and attitudes. Like a lot of religious people, if the kingdom of God suddenly materialized before Nicodemus' eyes, he wouldn't have recognized it (verse 3: *"see"*) and, if he did, he wouldn't have had the foggiest idea how to live there (verse 5: *"enter"*).

KINGDOM OF GOD Jesus immediately hit Nicodemus twice with the hard truth that if he expected to see or live under the reign of God, he would need to be *"born again."* Jesus said it twice. Each time he prefaced it with, *"I tell you the truth."* Literally, his words were *"Amen! Amen!"* To the Hebrew listener this meant the statement about to be made was absolutely certain, dependable, truthful, and binding.

> **John 3:4** "How can a man be born when he is old?" Nicodemus asked. "Surely he cannot enter a second time into his mother's womb to be born!"

The Intellectual Response

Chalk one up for the brilliant lawyer-teacher. Nicodemus knew the biological facts of life. But, even though he was one of Israel's top thinkers, he was ignorant of the spiritual facts of life.

Spiritual Obstetrics 101

The word Jesus used, translated "again" (in *"born again"*), has four meanings:

1. "From the beginning." To be *born from the beginning* means to scrap one's old <u>way of thinking</u> about the world and life and start over from scratch.
2. "For the second time." To be *born for the second time* means to experience a birth subsequent and superior to the physical birth by which you entered this world.
3. "Anew." To be *born anew* means to have a <u>fresh start</u> totally different from the physical birth experience.
4. "From above." To be *born from above* means to be the object of an <u>act of God</u>, a new beginning beyond what can be produced depending on human resources.

"Born Again" Has A Familiar Ring

Various cultures include the idea of being born again. In Jewish thought, when a Gentile turned from paganism to Judaism, rabbis referred to him as a "newborn child" and as "born anew." Embracing faith in Yahweh-God made him a new person.

In early Gentile life, first century pagans also spoke of new birth. In one "mystery religion" the candidate for membership was buried alive up to the neck. When he emerged from this "burial" he was declared "born anew." In another, the candidate was placed in a pit, a bull was killed on the grate over the pit, and the initiate bathed himself in the blood of the sacrificial animal. Emerging, he was declared "reborn for all eternity."

Don Richardson, missionary to the Asmat people of New Guinea, describes a ritual in which two enemy tribes come together to make peace. The men of the two tribes mingle, unarmed, on a grassy knoll. Then the men lie face down, beside each other in a long row. Each man's wife stands beside her husband, with ankles apart, one foot under his chest, the other under his hip, forming a human tunnel through which the children from each tribe squirm over the backs of their fathers, between the ankles of their mothers.

When they emerge from this living tunnel, each child is welcomed by an adult of the enemy tribe. Others from the enemy tribe wash the child as if it were a newborn. Each is cuddled and rocked and lullabied. The human passageway

☞ **GO TO:**

Romans 12:2
(way of thinking)

Ephesians 2:1–7
(fresh start)

John 1:13; 1 Peter 1:23
(act of God)

**Something
to Ponder**

KEY Outline:

"Again"
New
Better
Fresh
Different
*Beyond previous
experience*

represents a communal birth canal. The children passing through are considered *born again* into the kinship system of their enemies. Through their children the factions become members of each other's extended family.[11]

The whole world cries out to be born again. Millions are looking for somewhere to begin again. The Bible teaches that the incompleteness people feel is a longing for God. Jesus insists the rebirth needed to fill our emptiness comes from him.

What Others are Saying:

Blaise Pacal: There is a God-shaped vacuum in every man that only Christ can fill.[12]

What Do You Mean, "Born Again"?

Jesus was not telling Nicodemus he needed a religious ceremony. He was talking about an inner spiritual transaction that can only be called "miraculous." Trace Jesus' reasoning in John 3:3–8. Jesus said five things about spiritual rebirth:

1. New birth is an eye-opening experience that makes a person able to "*see*" God's kingdom (verse 3) and enables him or her to "*enter*" it (verse 5).

2. New birth involves "*water*" (verse 5). Water is a reference to the cleansing (<u>washing</u>) away of past sins and the guilt for them.

3. New birth is a work of the Holy Spirit (verses 5–6), a miracle of God's life-restoring <u>power</u>, not the result of human effort or <u>willpower</u> apart from God.

4. Spiritual rebirth is a "*must*" and that should surprise no one (verse 7). Stacking the weaknesses that go with being human against the challenging teachings of Scripture, an honest seeker is forced to admit that living well without some sort of radical personal renewal is a "mission impossible."

5. New birth is a mysterious work of God's Spirit the <u>effects</u> of which can be observed but never fully explained (verse 8). Trying to explain being "*born of the Spirit*" is like trying to explain the wind. You can hear the rustling of trees and grass and observe the effects of a hurricane, but to control or fully explain where the wind "*comes from or where it is going*" is beyond even the most brilliant meteorologist.

☞ **GO TO:**

Ephesians 5:26–27;
Titus 3:5 (washing)

1 Peter 1:3, 23
(power)

John 1:12–13
(willpower)

1 Corinthians 13;
Ephesians 2:10
(effects)

KEY Outline:

Born Again Is
Eye-opening
Cleansing
A miracle
Power
A mystery

Taking a purely intellectual approach to this discussion of being born again will almost always leave us baffled and confused. The only way to grasp this life-changing spiritual phenomenon is to take Jesus' later advice and receive the kingdom of God *"like a little child"* (Luke 18:17). The best way to understand the new birth is to admit that it is beyond you and to simply accept it, like a wide-eyed, gullible toddler, based on faith in Jesus and his Word.

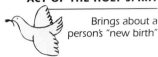

ACT OF THE HOLY SPIRIT

Brings about a person's "new birth"

> **John 3:10, 12** "You are Israel's teacher," said Jesus, "and do you not understand these things? . . . I have spoken to you of earthly things and you do not believe; how then will you believe if I speak of heavenly things?"

Dig Deeper

The New Birth in Other Words

Scripture	Words Used to Describe New Birth
Ezekiel 11:19; 36:26	A new heart and a new spirit
Romans 6:4	Newness of life
Romans 6:4–6; Ephesians 2:5; Colossians 2:12	Spiritual resurrection
Romans 7:6	The new way of the Spirit
Romans 8:15	Received the Spirit of sonship
1 Corinthians 6:11	Washed . . . sanctified . . . justified
2 Corinthians 5:27; Galatians 6:15	A new creation
Ephesians 4:24	The new self
Colossians 1:13	From the dominion of darkness to the kingdom of the Son he loves
Titus 3:5	Washing of rebirth and renewal by the Holy Spirit
2 Peter 1:4	Share the divine nature

New Birth—A Simple, Earthy Thing

Nicodemus shook his head in disbelief. He's thinking, "This is the most incredible idea I've ever heard!"

Jesus found it incredible that Nicodemus, Israel's top teacher, should be so baffled by the simple concept. Lost pagans believe in it, for heaven's sake! They perform mysterious rituals dramatizing new birth. Why should it be so difficult for a brilliant Bible scholar?

KEY POINT

The best way to understand the new birth is to approach it like a little child.

Jesus calls new birth an *"earthly"* thing. Like birth of an earth-child, being born again often involves three stages:

1. Conception—implantation of the "sperm" (*seed*) of truth (1 Peter 1:23)

2. Gestation—time lapse in which God oversees the development of the seed (Psalm 139:13; Galatians 4:19)

3. Viability—spiritual birth, the emergence of the "baby" believer, marked by

   - Life—the Holy Spirit resuscitates the dead (dormant) human spirit (1 John 5:12; Galatians 5:22–25)

   - Consciousness of relationship with the Father (Romans 8:16)

   - Moral transformation—desire to do right (1 John 2:29, 5:18)

   - Love for God and others (1 John 4:7, 5:1–2)

   - Development of the likeness of Christ (Romans 8:29)

New birth answers the human need for a new start with God, a change in direction, renewal of mind and spirit. It's simple. Don't complicate it. Just follow your sense of emptiness to Christ and <u>invite him</u> to fill you with himself. Expect to be <u>changed</u>.

Something to Ponder

What Others are Saying:

☞ **GO TO:**

Revelation 3:20 (invite him)

Romans 12:1–2 (changed)

Oswald Chambers: Our part as workers for God is to open men's eyes that they may turn themselves from darkness to light; but that is not salvation, that is conversion—the effort of a roused human being. I do not think it is too sweeping to say that the majority of nominal Christians are of this order; their eyes are opened, but they have received nothing. . . . When a man is born again, he knows that it is because he has received something as a gift from Almighty God and not because of his own decision.[13]

Johnny Cash: A few years ago I was hooked on drugs, I dreaded to wake up in the morning. There was no joy, peace, or happiness in my life. Then one day in my helplessness I turned my life completely over to God. Now I can't wait to get up in the morning to study my Bible. Sometimes the words out of the Scriptures leap into my heart. This does not mean that all my problems have been solved, or that I have reached any state of perfection. However, my life has been turned around. I have been born again![14]

Study Questions

1. Identify two spiritual realities demonstrated in Jesus' miracle of turning water into wine at the wedding?

2. Why was Jesus so angry with the profit-making businesses in the Temple?

3. What three rules of Jewish religious life were the Temple businesses misusing? How were they misusing each rule?

4. What answer did Jesus give to the demand that he prove with a sign his authority to cleanse the Temple? What sign was he telling them to watch for?

5. What did Nicodemus believe about Jesus when he came to him at night?

6. Identify at least three meanings of the word "again" in the phrase "born again."

7. What first aroused your interest in Jesus? Why?

CHAPTER WRAP-UP

- At a wedding in Cana, Galilee, Jesus performed his first miraculous proof that he was the Messiah—turning water into wine. His disciples became convinced. His relationship with his mother entered a new phase. (John 2:1–11)

- Jesus angrily drove the sacrifice-sellers and money changers out of the Temple of Jerusalem, closing down their illicit and spiritually destructive business and establishing his authority over Jewish worship. (John 2:12–22)

- Many people believed Jesus' claims after his purge of the Temple and confrontation with the leaders, but he knew their faith was shallow and uninformed, so he held back from committing himself to them as their king. (John 2:23–25)

- Nicodemus, the influential Pharisee, visited Jesus to check his legitimacy as Israel's Messiah-Savior. Jesus told Nicodemus he needed to be spiritually reborn if he expected to understand and experience God's kingdom. (John 3:1–12)

9 OPERATION RESCUE

Let's Get Started

The first recorded in-depth theological conversation Jesus had with anyone was with a skeptical Pharisee who came to him secretly. Nicodemus was not all that sure he wanted to believe Jesus was who he claimed to be. The issues Jesus discussed with him were some of the most basic and important he would raise with anyone. He spoke of the universal need for spiritual <u>renewal</u>. The only way to such renewal was to experience a radical new beginning initiated by the Spirit of God.

> **John 3:16** For God so loved the world that he gave his one and only Son, that whoever believes in him shall not perish but have eternal life.

The Love Connection

John 3:16 is "the background of the canvas on which the rest of the Gospel is painted."[1] It's "the golden text of the Bible." It's "the Gospel in a sentence."

Love Shock

The idea that God loves all people came as a shock to Nicodemus. Israelites believed <u>God loved them</u>. They were, after all, "God's chosen people." No Hebrew commentary on Scripture ever suggested that God loved *all* people.[2] Hatred of sinners and Gentiles was considered appropriate. Jesus exploded this cherished bit of

CHAPTER HIGHLIGHTS

- Love Connection
- Healing Snake
- Changing the Guard
- Rendezvous at Jake's Place
- Muddying the Living Water
- Right Place to Meet God
- Harvest of Hearts

GOSPEL QUARTET IN HARMONY

John 3:13–4:42
Luke 3:19–20; 4:14
Matthew 4:12
Mark 1:14

 **GO TO:**

John 3:3, 5–8 (renewal)

Deuteronomy 7:7–9; 23:5; Isaiah 63:9; Jeremiah 31:3 (God loved them)

first century Hebrew theology and practice when he declared God's love, not just for the "chosen," good, religious, and God-fearing, but also for skeptics, God-haters, pagans, and synagogue drop-outs—the world!

John 3:16 turns an outdated picture of God on its ear. God is not an angry, unforgiving heavenly sourpuss who holds nothing but contempt for people who have messed up and can't wait to send them to hell. Nothing could be farther from the truth!

Augustine: God loves each one of us as if there was only one of us to love.[3]

> **John 3:13–15** No one has ever gone into heaven except the one who came from heaven—the Son of Man. Just as Moses lifted up the snake in the desert, so the Son of Man must be lifted up, that everyone who believes in him may have eternal life.

Remember
This . . .

Love Gift

When God offered the world *"his one and only Son"* it was the all-time greatest gift ever given. The <u>one and only</u> is Jesus Christ. His coming as God's gift to the world came in four phases:

1. Descent *"from **heaven**"* (verse 13). New Testament historians contend Christ originated "with God" (see John 1:1–2, 9–14). This is the first time Jesus claims this for himself.

2. **Incarnation**, a <u>miracle conception</u> in the womb of a human woman, the virgin Mary, making it possible for God's Son to arrive on this planet as a human being, *"the Son of Man"* (John 3:13–14).

3. Christ *"lifted up"* (verse 14). Jesus and the New Testament writers use this phrase to mean several things:
   - *"Lifted up"* to die on the cross (John 12:32–33).
   - *"Lifted up"* to honor after completing the work God sent him to do (John 12:23; 13:31; Philippians 2:9).
   - *"Lifted up"* in the **ascension** when Christ returned to his Father in heaven (Luke 24:50; Acts 1:9).
   - *"Lifted up"* to supremacy in the life of the church (Colossians 1:18).

☞ **GO TO:**

John 1:14, 18, 34, 49, 51 (one and only)

Luke 1:35 (miracle conception)

heaven: *unseen, spiritual dimension; God's home; created universe beyond earth*

incarnation: *God assumed humanity in the person of Jesus Christ*

ascension: *return of Christ to his Father in heaven*

- *"Lifted up"* in the climax of history when the universe confesses Christ as Lord (Philippians 2:9–11).

4. Christ *believed* (John 3:14–15). The final word is in the hands of the people to whom God's gift is offered. God's Son must be <u>received</u> by a personal decision to accept God's offer of life.

The Healing Snake

Jesus' reference to Moses lifting up *"the snake in the desert"* illustrates the place personal faith plays in experiencing the benefits of God's love gift. The original story is in Numbers 21:4–9. The Israelites followed Moses out of Egypt on the way to the **Promised Land**. The Lord fed them with a miracle food called **manna**. Seven days a week they ate nothing but manna from heaven!

They soon got sick and tired of manna and complained. Their sin of ingratitude brought an infestation of poisonous snakes into the camp and many died of snakebite. When the poisoned people faced up to their sin, God told Moses to craft a **bronze snake** and lift it up on a pole in the midst of the camp (see illustration below). Anyone who had been bitten could be healed by simply looking at the snake. It wasn't magic. The bronze snake had no therapeutic power in itself. Looking at the snake represented four essentials vital to healing and **salvation**:

1. Acceptance of personal responsibility for sin

2. Trust in the reliability of God's instructions

3. Obedience to God's instructions

4. Turning to God in faith

 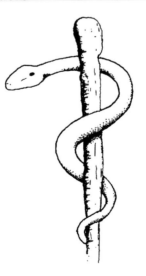

☞ GO TO:

John 1:11–12 (received)

🔑 *KEY Outline:*

God's Gift
Descended
Incarnate
Lifted up
Received by faith

Promised Land: *God promised Canaan (Palestine) to Abraham's offspring*

manna: *Hebrew means "What is it?"; a nourishing, sweet-tasting wafer that appeared on the desert floor*

bronze snake: *snake on a pole; symbol of the medical profession*

salvation: *rescue from sin's destructive power, assurance of eternal life*

Bronze Snake

The bronze snake Moses crafted and placed on a pole, right, is similar to the symbol, left, used by today's medical profession.

The spiritual processes involved in healing from the snake-bite correspond with the processes involved in healing from the poisonous effects of sin. Looking in faith to Christ on the cross assures the responsive looker eternal life.

> **John 3:17–18** For God did not send his Son into the world to condemn the world, but to save the world through him. Whoever believes in him is not condemned, but whoever does not believe stands condemned already because he has not believed in the name of God's one and only Son.

Christ's Mission: Love, Not Judgment

High on the list of Nicodemus' expectations for the Messiah was that he would bring judgment. The sight of Jesus, eyes blazing, chasing profiteers out of the Temple (John 2:15–16) may have been what convinced some people to believe he was the One (John 2:23). Pharisees like Nicodemus, who instinctively mistrusted the priestly establishment that ran the Temple, were probably among those who tentatively applauded the Nazarene's brash action. When Nick saw the merchants scrambling to escape Jesus' whip, visions of the purifier-Messiah-judge leaped to mind (Malachi 3:1–5). He was right. Jesus was all of that.

Pharisees thought Christ's judgment would be directed mainly against Gentiles. His initial purge was against Jewish religious leaders using God's house for personal profit. Now he was telling Nicodemus his mission was not to bring God's wrath to sinners, but to rescue them (John 3:17). One by one the Pharisee's cherished prejudices were being overturned.

Condemned In The Presence Of Love

God's purpose in sending his Son was salvation. The driving force in the Son's life was the same as his Father's—love for lost people. Christ did not come to condemn people. No one need be lost. Yet many are.

How can this happen?

It is a paradox of biblical proportions: Jesus came to save, not judge, but his presence judges everyone. The choice of some to believe and be rescued cannot save those who refuse to be rescued. Refusal is a self-condemning decision.

KEY Outline:

Four Essentials to Healing
Accept responsibility
Trust God's Word
Obey God's instruction
Turn to God in faith

KEY POINT

Christ's mission was to rescue, not to condemn.

Lewis Sperry Chafer: The ground of universal divine condemnation is no longer the sins which men have committed and which Christ has borne; but rather the condemnation is now because of the personal rejection of the Savior who bore the sin.[4]

Leon Morris: Salvation . . . judgment. These are the two sides to the same coin. The very fact of salvation for all who believe implies judgment on all who do not.[5]

> **John 3:19–21** This is the verdict: Light has come into the world, but men loved darkness instead of light because their deeds were evil. Everyone who does evil hates the light, and will not come into the light for fear that his deeds will be exposed. But whoever lives by the truth comes into the light, so that it may be seen plainly that what he has done has been done through God.

The "Guilty" Verdict

Wherever Jesus went some people were attracted to the genuineness and purity of the life they saw in him. They came to him and believed, even though it meant exposure of personal sin. They faced up to their sins and committed themselves to <u>walk in the light</u>. Others hated the self-exposure that came with listening to Jesus. They rejected the truth, persisting in dishonesty and denial. They did not welcome his light. But it was too late. Light had come. Sin had been exposed. They stood condemned by their choice to turn away from the light.

- *Light* stands for truth, understanding, honesty, genuineness, integrity, purity.
- *Darkness* stands for falsehood, blindness, dishonesty, deceit, hypocrisy, denial.

Christ calls us to live in light—to tell the truth and live honestly and openly before God and people. The choice is ours.

☞ **GO TO:**

1 John 1:5–10
(walk in the light)

Remember This . . .

Something to Ponder

What Others are Saying:

KEY POINT

Walking in the light means living transparently, honest, and pure.

☞ **Check It Out:**

John 3:22–4:4

Luke 3:19–20; 4:14

Matthew 4:12

Mark 1:14

☞ **GO TO:**

Matthew 3:13–17 (baptized)

John 3:29 (friends)

Compare Matthew 3:2 and 4:17 (John's echo)

Luke 1:36 (cousins)

repentance: *willingness to turn to God and change one's way of living*

cousins: *mothers of John and Jesus were relatives*

Aenon: *"place of springs"; seven springs pour into the Jordan in a quarter mile*

William Barclay: If, when a man is confronted with Jesus, his soul responds to that wonder and beauty, he is on the way to salvation. But if, when he is confronted with Jesus, he sees nothing lovely, he stands condemned. His reaction has condemned him. . . . It is not God who has condemned the man; God only loved him; the man has condemned himself.[6]

John 3:22 After this, Jesus and his disciples went out into the Judean countryside, where he spent time with them, and baptized.

Changing Of The Guard

Soon after his conversation with Nicodemus, Jesus left Jerusalem for Jordan River country where he and his disciples apparently linked up for a while with John the Baptist. It was a natural association. Jesus' first disciples had first been disciples of John. John had baptized them and Jesus. In the process, John and Jesus had become close friends. When Jesus began to preach he sounded like John's echo, preaching the same message of **repentance** John preached. The inference in John 3:22–26 is that there was a brief time when Jesus and John worked side by side, preaching and baptizing. People kept coming. The spiritual awakening grew as the **cousins** and their coworkers ministered together at **Aenon** on the Jordan.

John 3:26 They came to John and said to him, "Rabbi, that man who was with you on the other side of the Jordan—the one you testified about—well, he is baptizing, and everyone is going to him."

Sunrise, Sunset

While they worked together, something happened that pointed up the necessity for the two ministries (Jesus' and John's) to separate. It also demonstrated John's integrity as a man of God. John's ministry began to fade. Fewer people came to him for baptism, while increasing numbers flocked to the nearby venue where Jesus was preaching. Some of John's disciples became alarmed. It was a human response, but showed they did not fully understand John's mission. John understood. It was he who sent many of his disciples to Jesus (see John 1:35–36). God's design was for the crowds around John to dwindle while those around Jesus increased.

> **John 3:27–30** To this John replied, "A man can receive only what is given him from heaven. . . . The friend who attends the bridegroom waits and listens for him, and is full of joy when he hears the bridegroom's voice. That joy is mine, and it is now complete. He must become greater; I must become less."

Big John Goes Down

The great **forerunner** explained to his nervous supporters what was going on. Big John the Baptist made a statement calculated to encourage his disciples to follow Christ. He compared his ministry with Christ's. There was no contest.

John

Earthborn, earthbound

Speaks as a man

Certifies God's truthfulness by accepting Christ's testimony

Possesses the Holy Spirit in limited measure

Christ

Heavenborn, <u>above all</u>

Speaks God's words, speaks of heavenly things
he has personally <u>seen and heard</u>

Although the majority <u>reject</u> his testimony

Possesses the Holy Spirit **without limit**

Son of God, intimate with the Father in heaven

<u>Controls everything</u> including the destiny of human beings

Trusting him brings eternal life

Rejecting him brings **God's wrath**

John stated important principles to guide every authentic Christian ministry:

- John 3:27—The <u>size and power</u> of one's ministry is determined by the Lord.
- John 3:28—No one's ministry should ever obscure the ministry of Christ.
- John 3:29—The bride (God's people) belongs to the <u>bridegroom</u> (Christ), not to the **bridegroom's friend** (servant, minister, helper).

☞ **GO TO:**

Ephesians 1:21–22
(above all)

John 3:13
(seen and heard)

John 1:10–11; 6:66
(reject)

Colossians 1:17
(controls everything)

forerunner: advance man

without limit: Holy Spirit's power in humans is limited by their sin

God's wrath: conscious, determined hostility of God toward sin[7]

☞ **GO TO:**

1 Corinthians 3:6–7;
12:4–6
(size and power)

2 Corinthians 11:2;
Ephesians 5:25–27
(bridegroom)

Remember This . . .

bridegroom's friend: best man, who saw to the wedding arrangements

- John 3:29—A ministry is successful if the bride and groom come together.
- John 3:30—A ministry is effective if it enhances Christ's greatness, not its own.

> **Luke 3:19–20** But when John rebuked Herod the tetrarch because of Herodias, his brother's wife, and all the other evil things he had done, Herod added this to them all: He locked John up in prison.

Jailhouse John

After John urged his disciples to shift their allegiance to Jesus, the end of the Baptist's ministry came abruptly. On a trip to Rome, Herod Antipas, tetrarch of Galilee (see illustration, page 40), had seduced his brother's beautiful young wife Herodias and convinced her to leave her husband for him. The sordid process involved divorcing his own wife. The Jewish people were outraged. Courageously, John publicly rebuked Antipas and Herodias. Herodias never forgave him. The prophet's arrest was the first step toward execution.

First century Jewish historian Josephus reports Herod had a second reason for John's arrest: He feared the popular prophet was about to lead a revolution against him.[8]

Hightailing It For Home

Jesus had two good reasons to leave Judea:

- The Pharisees were beginning to notice the growth of Jesus' following, hinting at potential opposition from Jewish religious leaders (John 4:1). The timing was not right for intensification of the opposition.
- Jesus had an "appointment" to meet someone in Samaria on the way home (verse 4). The Greek uses the word *dei* or "had to," meaning "it was necessary" (because of the need to get out of Judea quickly) or that Jesus felt a compelling sense of obligation.

THE BIG PICTURE

> **John 4:1–9** On his way to Galilee Jesus traveled through Samaria. At noon he sat down at a well to rest. A Samaritan woman came to draw water, and Jesus asked her to give him a drink.

GOSPEL QUARTET IN HARMONY

Matthew 4:12
Mark 1:14
Luke 3:19–20

☞ **GO TO:**

Mark 6:17–29
(execution)

GOSPEL QUARTET IN HARMONY

Matthew 4:12
Mark 1:14
Luke 4:14
John 4:1–4

☞ **GO TO:**

John 2:4 (timing)

John 3:14; 9:4; 10:16; 12:34; 20:9
(appointment)

Rendezvous At Jake's Place

"He had to go through Samaria" does not mean the only route to Galilee was through Samaria. Most travelers took the Samaritan route because it was the shortest. But strictest Jews took the Jordan River road around Samaria in order to avoid contact with its racially and religiously mixed citizens. The distance from Jerusalem to Nazareth through Samaria was 75 miles. To bypass Samaria on the Jordan River road, travelers went 97 miles (see appendix A).

Jesus did not allow ethnic prejudice to affect his choices. He headed north across the border into Samaritan territory: by divine arrangement, he had a date with destiny at **Jacob's well** near Sychar. He and his companions arrived at the well at **high noon**.

The prejudice of Jews against Samaritans was based on a history of bad feelings:

- Samaritans were a <u>mixed race</u> whose ancestors were relocated in northern Israel after the <u>Assyrian conquest</u> in 722 B.C.

- Samaritans practiced a <u>corrupted</u> form of Jewish <u>worship</u> centered at Mt. Gerazim rather than Jerusalem.

- Samaritans <u>hindered</u> the rebuilding of Jerusalem after the **Babylonian exile**.

Weary God-Man

"Jesus, tired as he was from the journey, sat down by the well" (John 4:6). John's simple report of the weariness, hunger, and thirst of Jesus reveals an important fact: Jesus, who would one day be worshiped throughout the world as God's Son, was an authentic human who experienced the physical needs common to human beings.

EARLY CHURCH LIFE: From early church history to the present Christians have taught that Jesus Christ is the "God-Man"— undiminished deity and perfect humanity united in one person forever, with no loss in the identity of the two natures, no mingling of the attributes, no confusion of the natures, and no separation of the person.[9]

Jacob's well: dug by Jacob; still used today

high noon: sixth hour of the day which began with the first hour (sunrise)

Remember This . . .

☞ **GO TO:**

Genesis 33:18–19; 48:22; Joshua 24:32 (Jacob's well)

2 Kings 17:24 (mixed race)

2 Kings 17 (Assyrian conquest)

2 Kings 17:25–41 (corrupted worship)

Nehemiah 4 (hindered)

2 Kings 24:14 (exile)

Babylonian exile: 586 B.C. Nebuchadnezzar destroyed Jerusalem, deported Jews to Babylon

Dig Deeper

The God-Man: The Deity of Jesus Christ

Bible Passages	How the Passage Stresses Christ's Divinity
John 1:1–4	Christ with God in the beginning as the Word; with God in creation; source of life
John 1:10	The world made through Christ
John 1:14	Christ's glory the glory of God's one and only Son
John 1:14	Christ came from the Father, bringing God's grace and God's truth to the world
John 1:18	Christ the only one who has ever seen God the Father as he really is
John 1:18	Christ intimately related to God the Father; shows humans God as he really is
John 1:34, 49	Christ God's Son in a way no one else is
John 1:51; 3:13	Christ the point of access between earth and heaven, man and God
John 3:14–18	Faith in Christ the way to be assured of eternal life
John 3:21–36	Christ from above, sovereign over everything earthly

The God-Man: The Humanity of Jesus Christ

Bible Passages	How the Passages Stress Christ's Humanness
Matthew 1:18; Galatians 4:4	Christ's mother was a Jewish virgin named Mary
Luke 2:40, 51–52	Christ grew through all the human growth stages from child to adult
Hebrews 5:8	Christ learned obedience through painful experiences
Matthew 26:38; Mark 10:14; Luke 7:13; 22:44; John 12:27; 13:21; 15:11	Christ experienced the full range of human emotions: sorrow, anger, compassion, anguish, troubled spirit, frustration, joy
John 4:6–7; 19:28; Luke 4:2	Christ experienced tiredness, hunger, thirst
Hebrews 2:18; 4:15	Christ was tempted in every way humans are tempted
John 19:30; Luke 23:46; 1 Corinthians 15:3–4; Philippians 2:8	Christ was mortal—he died a human death
John 8:46; Hebrews 4:15; 2 Corinthians 5:21; 1 Peter 2:21–22; 1 John 3:5	Christ was human, yet he was sinless—never sinned

Harold O. J. Brown: The claims the New Testament makes for Jesus Christ, and the impression he made on his followers, were so overwhelming that it was very difficult to conceive of him as really ever having been a man. The early Christians found it easier to accept Christ as God than to admit that, being God, he was also truly man.[10]

Ronald B. Allen: We must learn to think rightly about the One who is God and man. To learn to think rightly about his humanity is to rediscover the meaning of our own humanity created in the image of God.[11]

The Naughty Lady Of Sychar

Jesus' men went into the town of Sychar, about a half mile away, to buy lunch. Jesus sat alone at the ancient well. A woman approached to draw water. *"Will you give me a drink?"* Jesus asked. It was the beginning of a conversation that was unlikely to have taken place in polite society of those times.

- First, she was a Samaritan (John 4:7). "Let no man eat of the bread of the [Samaritans]," the rabbis taught, "for he who eats their bread is as he who eats **swine's flesh**!"[12]
- Second, she was a woman (verse 7). The rules of etiquette stated it was improper for a man to talk to a woman in public.
- Third, she was a social pariah. It was noon, the hottest part of the day. Respectable ladies came to draw water in the cool of morning or evening. She came to the well alone to avoid their stares.

The woman was shocked that this Jewish male should speak to her. *"How can you ask me for a drink?"* (verse 9). The statement, *"For the Jews do not associate with Samaritans,"* may also be translated, "Jews do not use dishes Samaritans have used." With no bucket of his own with which to draw water (verse 11), Jesus the Jew was asking this Samaritan to give him a drink out of hers.

Jesus treated with contempt the rules and regulations that tradition had built up to separate people from each other and from God on the basis of race, nationality, gender, lifestyle, social status, reputation, and religion. He had one mission in this conversation: to satisfy this socially and spiritually thirsty person with the life-giving "water" of **grace**.

What Others are Saying:

KEY Outline:

Jewish Prejudice against Samaritans
Mixed race
Corrupt worship
Historical hindrance

swine's flesh: *pork was ceremonially unclean, eating it was forbidden*

grace: *undeserved kindness, acceptance, forgiveness, favor*

Something to Ponder

> **John 4:10–15** Jesus answered her, "If you knew the gift of God and who it is that asks you for a drink, you would have asked him and he would have given you living water." "Sir," the woman said, "you have nothing to draw with and the well is deep. Where can you get this living water? Are you greater than our father Jacob, who gave us the well . . . ?" Jesus answered, "Everyone who drinks this water will be thirsty again, but whoever drinks the water I give him will never thirst. Indeed the water I give him will become in him a spring of water welling up to eternal life."

Cool, Clear Water

Jesus swept aside the woman's first response and cut to the real issue. He knew she was thirsty physically and spiritually.

She misunderstood his first statement (perhaps purposely), but it grabbed her attention nonetheless. As the story unfolds we get a clear picture of this woman. She was acquainted with failure, having five failed marriages, but she was no dummy. The man before her was making outrageous claims. The well dug by forefather Jacob was over 100 feet deep. In spite of social protocols and prejudices, she was willing to converse with Jesus.

The promise of <u>living water</u> sounded glorious. She probably envisioned a stream or spring from which she could draw water. No more hot, dusty trips to this well. Her comment to Jesus also showed that she was not an atheist—she believed in God, the **patriarchs**, and the **messianic promises** (verses 12, 19–20). One day, she knew, Christ (the Messiah) would unravel the mysteries of life (verse 25).

The Ultimate Thirst Quencher

In every human heart there is a thirst that can only be satisfied if a person has a vital relationship with God. There is a discontent—a sense of something missing—which frustrates the quest for peace and meaning. My wife, Audrey, remembers the emptiness she felt every time she listened to Charles E. Fuller, popular radio preacher of the 1930s and 1940s. When she welcomed Christ into her life the emptiness disappeared.

☞ **GO TO:**

John 7:37–39 (living water)

patriarchs: Jacob and his sons (Genesis 49)

messianic promises: Old Testament predictions concerning Christ

Something to Ponder

Dipping into the "Living Water" Metaphor from Old Testament Prophecies of the Messiah

Dig Deeper

Living water is . . .

Psalm 36:8–9—abundant spiritual nourishment from *"the river of [God's] delights"*

Isaiah 35:6–7—healing, joy, spiritual refreshment in life's desert, fruitfulness

Isaiah 44:3–4—satisfaction of spiritual thirst, drenching with the Holy Spirit, fruitful offspring

Isaiah 49:10—protection, Christ's compassion, guidance, spiritual refreshment, and restoration

Jeremiah 17:13—hope for God's people, escape from shame and rejection (being forgotten)

Zechariah 13:1—cleansing from sin and impurity

Zechariah 14:8–9—perpetual spiritual refreshment flowing from Jerusalem to the whole world

> **John 4:15–17** The woman said to him, "Sir, give me this water so that I won't get thirsty and have to keep coming here to draw water." He told her, "Go, call your husband and come back." "I have no husband," she replied.

Muddying The Living Water

The woman's response was flippant. But Jesus cut to the chase and cornered her about her life of sin. The woman told the truth but not the whole truth.

Her eyes popped wide open when he revealed that he knew about her five failed marriages and the "significant other" she was now living with without marriage (verses 17–18).

The woman at the well was convinced the man talking to her was a prophet (verse 19). According to Samaritan theology there had not been a real prophet since Moses. God promised to send another prophet <u>like Moses</u>. This Moses-like prophet would be the Messiah. The woman may have begun to wonder if the man talking with her might be that prophet—Messiah.

So she brought up a religious controversy: Samaritan worship on Mt. Gerazim is just as good as Jewish worship in Jerusalem (verse 20). Or she may have been expressing honest spiritual need, like saying, "Where can I find God?"

☞ **GO TO:**

Deuteronomy 18:18 (like Moses)

☞ **GO TO:**

Genesis 22:1–18
(offered Isaac)

Genesis 14:18–20
(Melchizedek)

Remember This . . .

☞ **GO TO:**

Romans 12:1
(whole person)

Revelation 5:9–13
(the worth)

Luke 10:27 (adoration)

worship: *reverence, respect, adoration, praise (Greek: "to kiss the hand")*

Mt. Zion: *hilltop site of the Temple in Jerusalem*

Something to Ponder

Samaritans recognized only the first five books of the Old Testament and rewrote parts of the Old Testament to make Mt. Gerazim, not Jerusalem, the focal point of important events in the history of Israel. According to revisionist Samaritan history Abraham offered Isaac on Mt. Gerazim, he and Melchizedek met there, and most of the significant events in the lives of the patriarchs took place near there.

A woman could be married five times and not be guilty of breaking the letter of the Law, though its spirit would certainly have a few puncture wounds! The rules of Middle Eastern culture tolerated two or three marriages depending on whether the husbands died or divorced the woman. But the neighbors could be expected to look down their collective noses at numbers four and five. "Shacking up" was definitely forbidden.

> **John 4:21–24** Jesus declared, "Believe me, woman, a time is coming when you will worship the Father neither on this mountain nor in Jerusalem. You Samaritans worship what you do not know; we worship what we do know, for salvation is from the Jews. Yet a time is coming and has now come when the true worshipers will worship the Father in spirit and in truth, for they are the kind of worshipers the Father seeks. God is spirit, and his worshipers must worship in spirit and in truth."

The Right Place To Meet God

The woman was thirsty for peace. She sincerely wanted to know the right place to offer a sacrifice to atone for her sins, where peace with God could be made.

Worship Revolution

Jesus turns typical thinking about **worship** upside down. Everything he said about it was based on the fact that *"God is spirit"* (verse 24) and can't be limited to a geographical location—neither Mt. Gerazim nor **Mt. Zion**. Because he is spirit, worshiping him is not a matter of sacred locations, shrines, or ceremonies, but of the whole person acknowledging the worth of God in sincere adoration. So what is the state of your worship?

J. I. Packer: Christ's point is that while man, being "flesh," can only be present in one place at a time, God, being "spirit," is not so limited. God is non-material, non-corporeal, and therefore non-localized. Thus . . . the true condition of acceptable worship is not that your feet should be standing in either Jerusalem or Samaria, or anywhere else for that matter, but that your heart should be receptive and responsive to his revelation.[13]

What Others are Saying:

☞ **GO TO:**

Matthew 18:19–20 (anywhere)

2 Timothy 3:15–17 (Scripture)

Principles Of Worship 101

According to Jesus

1. the physical location of worship is irrelevant—God may be worshiped <u>anywhere</u> (verse 21);
2. God must be worshiped as he is, not as people would like to think he is (verse 22);
3. who God is and how he wants to be approached are revealed in the history of his dealings with the Jews—that is, in <u>Scripture</u> (verse 22); and
4. two things characterize true worship: *spirit* and *truth* (verses 23–24).

spirit: emotions, intellect, will—the inner person

EARLY CHURCH LIFE: Early Christians had no church buildings; they met around Christ.

☞ **GO TO:**

Ephesians 2:19–22 (living temple)

Matthew 18:20 (meets)

Acts 7:48–50 (not essential)

The Holy Place

Worship has both personal and corporate dimensions. It is important for worshipers to join together to express praise and love for God. Christ and his followers form a <u>living temple</u>. Christ is the sanctuary. He <u>meets</u> his people wherever a few are together in his name. Man-made structures for worship are not forbidden, but they are <u>not essential</u>.

Remember This . . .

EARLY CHURCH LIFE: Early Christians met in homes or some borrowed place. Jesus met with them wherever two or three gathered in his name.

Tim Stafford: What the phrase "personal relationship with God" claims, most basically, is that God is a person. Since I am a person, I must therefore know him through means peculiar to persons. My relationship with him is not institutional, though I am part of religious institutions. My relationship is not with a force, though I recognize that God is a force who affects my every breath.

What Others are Saying:

My relationship is not with an idea, though Christianity includes ideas. Those who know God only as an institution or a power or an idea miss knowing him as he wants to be known. God chose to give himself to us as a person.[14]

> **John 4:25–26** The woman said, "I know that Messiah" (called Christ) "is coming. When he comes, he will explain everything to us." Then Jesus declared, "I who speak to you am he."

Harvest Of Hearts

The cat is out of the bag. Jesus is the promised Messiah. His clear claim affirmed the woman's suspicions. As Jesus' disciples approached with lunch, she left her water pot and headed for the village on her first mission sharing her discovery. This woman of questionable character was uniquely qualified to attract the attention of the men of the village, who immediately headed out to see for themselves if what she was telling them was true.

The disciples were surprised to see Jesus talking with the woman (verse 9). They were equally amazed that he had no interest in the food they brought. He said he'd already eaten (verse 32). *"Could someone have brought him food?"* they muttered under their breath. Doing the work of God had satisfied his hunger (verse 34).

Motioning toward the group of Samaritans making their way toward the well, Jesus added, "Don't tell me it's still four months to harvest. Look at the fields. They are already ripe. It's time for harvest—now!" He was right. Many of the Samaritans the woman rounded up put their faith in Jesus. When they met him for themselves, they too became convinced he was *"the Savior of the world"* (verse 42).

THE WOMAN AT THE WELL: A social outcast with women, but a hit with men. She's never named but famous for being the first female Samaritan to believe in Jesus and for bringing her whole town to Christ.

Jesus was always more concerned for people than for unloving social protocols. He did not miss this chance to bring salvation to a thirsty woman and her thirsty town. His Samaritan stopover gave him a lift. The fact that these new "converts" were all socially disfranchised Samaritans only

KEY Outline:

True Worship

Location irrelevant
God as he really is
Scripture tells how
In spirit
In truth

KEY POINT

It's fine to hear someone else tell about Jesus. It's better to meet him for yourself.

Who's Who

Something to Ponder

added to the sweetness of the Harvester's joy and made him more determined than ever to make the good news of God's love available to everyone—beginning with the most needy.

Study Questions

1. Identify the four essentials to spiritual healing and salvation represented by the act of looking to Moses' bronze snake in the desert.
2. If Christ came into the world to save not to judge, how did his coming result in judgment for many?
3. Did John the Baptist see himself as a success or a failure when more people began to follow Jesus than followed him? Explain.
4. Why did Jesus head for Galilee after John was arrested?
5. What was the basis for the mutual animosity between Jews and Samaritans?
6. Identify three of the four principles of worship Jesus gave in John 4:21–24.

CHAPTER WRAP-UP

- In conversation with Nicodemus, Jesus revealed God's motive of love in sending him to bring eternal life to people who put their faith in him. (John 3:13–21)

- Though it is painful for John's disciples, John the Baptist explained that his ministry had to fade away so the ministry of Jesus Christ could grow. (John 3:22–36)

- In order to avoid a premature confrontation with the Pharisees, Jesus headed north to Galilee. He felt compelled to stop at Jacob's well for a strategic encounter with a spiritually needy woman. (John 4:1–15)

- The woman was surprised when she discovered how much Jesus knew about her. She brought up the controversy between Samaritans and Jews over worship, and Jesus used it to teach important and revolutionary principles of true worship. (John 4:16–34)

- Jesus confirmed the woman's growing faith in him, directly claiming to be Christ. She returned to the village to tell the men about him. Many came to see him and believed. (John 3:35–42)

Part Three

GALILEE: BATTLE FOR HOME TURF

REVEREND FUN

Peter's early attempts to walk on water with Jesus displayed an inadequate amount of faith.

10 THE RUGGED HILLS OF HOME

CHAPTER HIGHLIGHTS

- Prophet's Honor
- Long Distance Service
- Hometown Chill
- In Command

Let's Get Started

Jesus and his compadres stayed in Sychar, Samaria, for two days, "harvesting." Then they moved on, heading north into the Galilean hill country—the hills of home.

> **John 4:43–45** After the two days he left for Galilee. (Now Jesus himself had pointed out that a prophet has no honor in his own country.) When he arrived in Galilee, the Galileans welcomed him. They had seen all that he had done in Jerusalem at the Passover Feast, for they also had been there.

Prophet's Honor

Jesus made the statement about a prophet having *"no honor in his own country"* on three other occasions recorded in the New Testament. In all the others it came in the midst of conflict or rejection. Here there is no conflict. Jesus' ministry is off to a flying start. Three days earlier he left Judea because his success was attracting too much attention (John 4:1–3). In Samaria, an entire town confessed him as *"Savior of the world"* (verse 42). On arrival in Galilee, the Galileans welcomed him (verse 45). So why this sour note?

Jesus was no dummy. He knew people. Despite his early welcome in Galilee, his own hometown people would soon turn on

**GOSPEL QUARTET
IN HARMONY**

Matthew 4:13–22;
8:14–17; 13:53–58
Mark 1:14–34; 6:1–6
Luke 4:14–41
John 4:46–54

☞ **GO TO:**

Mark 6:4; Matthew
13:57; Luke 4:24
(three other occasions)

John 2:24
(knew people)

Luke 4:16–30
(hometown people)

☞ **GO TO:**

John 6:60–66
(dump him)

John 4:48
(diet of miracles)

☞ **Check It Out:**

Matthew 4:17

Mark 1:14–15

Luke 4:14–15

*synagogue: literally
means "to bring together"*

**What Others
are Saying:**

*Sabbath: seventh day of
the week; day of rest and
worship*

*Spirit: The Holy Spirit or
Spirit of God*

☞ **GO TO:**

Acts 1:8 (Spirit)

Compare Matthew 3:2
with 4:17 (message)

him. Many Galileans who hung around him at first would <u>dump
him</u> when he started saying things they didn't want to hear. He
knew the faith of many was not soundly based because it depended
on a steady <u>diet of miracles</u>. Knowing all this, he launched the
Galilean phase of his ministry with power and courage.

> **Luke 4:14–15** Jesus returned to Galilee in the power
> of the Spirit, and the news about him spread through
> the whole countryside. He taught in their synagogues,
> and everyone praised him.

Galilean Power Play

Galilee means "circle." The northern hill-country province was
surrounded on the north, south, and east by pagan nations under
Roman control and on the west by the Mediterranean Sea. Because Galilee was encircled by pagan cultures and because important trade routes (see illustration, page 141) crossed the province
bringing a constant flow of foreigners, Galilean citizens were continually exposed to non-Jewish influences. Many Galileans spoke
Greek as well as Hebrew and Aramaic. Galileans hated the Romans and did not trust the religious establishment in Jerusalem.
If you wanted to start a revolution among the Jews, Galilee was
the ideal place to kick it off.

Josephus: They [Galileans] were fond of innovations and by
nature disposed to changes and delighted with seditions. They
were ready to follow a leader who would begin an insurrection.
They were quick in temper and given to quarreling. . . . They were
more anxious for honor than for gain.[1]

Synagogue Agog

The **synagogue** was the center of Galilean life, ever since the days
of the Babylonian exile when the Jews had no temple in which to
meet. By lifelong family custom Jesus attended synagogue every
Sabbath (Luke 4:16). He knew how to use it to introduce his
message. Standard synagogue practice was to invite visiting rabbis to expound on the Scripture. With his fame spreading, Jesus
became increasingly recognizable and was invited to speak in synagogues across Galilee. He spoke with unusual power—*"the power
of the **Spirit**"*—and his message in Mark 1:15 echoed John the
Baptist's <u>message</u>:

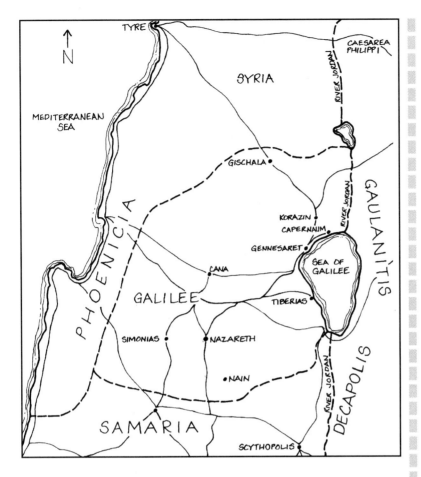

Trade Routes through Galilee

Trade routes through Galilee, shown as solid lines, brought outside influences to Jesus' hometown. Boundaries between regions are shown as dashed lines.

- *"The time has come"*—the time of the Messiah the prophets predicted and for whom <u>Israel had waited</u> for hundreds of years.
- *"The kingdom of God is near"*—a <u>community</u> of people who recognized God's reign in their day-to-day lives.
- *"Repent"*—a decision to turn from sinful independence from God to righteousness and dependence on God that resulted in personal <u>spiritual renovation.</u>
- *"Believe"*—"put all your eggs in one basket." Stake your life and destiny on the <u>trustworthiness</u> of God and his Word.
- *"The good news"*—God's <u>love</u> for the world, his visit to <u>earth</u> in the person of his Son Jesus Christ, the Son's redeeming death and resurrection assure spiritual recovery and eternal life for all who believe.

☞ **GO TO:**

Luke 2:28–32, 38 (Israel had waited)

Matthew 5:14 (community)

Luke 3:7–14; John 3:3, 5 (spiritual renovation)

John 1:12 (trustworthiness)

John 3:16 (love)

John 1:14, 18 (earth)

Galilean Honeymoon

The earliest response to Jesus in his home province was positive (Luke 4:15). News of the young Galilean rabbi with the flare for preaching traveled fast. The revolutionary implications of his preaching were slow to penetrate the beginning flush of popularity. He was getting rave reviews along the Galilean grapevine.

> **John 4:46–47** And there was a certain royal official whose son lay sick at Capernaum. When this man heard that Jesus had arrived in Galilee . . . he went to him and begged him to come and heal his son.

Long Distance Service

News of the young miracle worker reached all levels of Galilean society. Twenty miles away in the lakeside city of Capernaum (see appendix A) one of King Herod's top officials was desperate. His son was near death. He heard Jesus was in Cana. So he mounted his horse and made the daylong trip to the one person he believed could help.

Herod's name is not mentioned in the story. The father is simply called *basiliko*, a Greek word meaning a high official on the king's staff, royal family member, or ranking military officer. Jewish historian Josephus uses that term exclusively for people associated with Herod.

begged: *persistent asking*

This frantic father, like many people today, was forced by a family emergency to turn to Jesus. He might never have come if his son had not been desperately ill, since Jesus did not regularly move in royal circles. The man laid aside his aristocratic pride and **begged** Jesus to help his son.

Something to Ponder

What Others are Saying:

signs: *proofs, evidence, convincing works*

wonders: *miracles, acts of power, events beyond explanation*

William Barclay: There could be no more improbable scene in the world than an important court official hastening 20 miles to beg a favor from a village carpenter. First and foremost, this courtier swallowed his pride. He was in need, and neither convention nor custom stopped him bringing his need to Christ.[2]

The Quest For Real Faith

"*Unless you people see miraculous* **signs** *and* **wonders**," Jesus told him, "*you will never believe*" (John 4:48). This was not just for the frantic father, but for the gawking Galileans craving the spectacular, withholding full acceptance until Jesus gave proof after proof of his power. In the original language, the *"never"* in his statement is an emphatic double negative, indicating the intensity of his feelings. He welcomed people who believed <u>because of the miracles</u>, but he longed for those who would believe because of his character and teachings.

☞ **GO TO:**

John 6:26; 14:11 (because of the miracles)

Lawrence O. Richards: What's wrong with a faith that is rooted in miracles? Simply that a fascination with the miraculous is no substitute for a settled confidence in the person of Jesus, or for obedience to his Word.[3]

What Others are Saying:

> **John 4:49–50** The royal official said, "Sir, come down before my child dies." Jesus replied, "You may go. Your son will live." The man took Jesus at his word and departed.

Taking Jesus At His Word

The anxious royal restated his request, more urgently this time. Jesus did not give the man exactly what he asked for. The request was based on the faulty belief that, for healing to take place, Jesus had to be physically present with the sick person. Jesus gives the father what he wants but in an unexpected way.

The man's departure for home was evidence of his faith and recognition of Jesus' authority. No tangible sign was given, just Jesus' word. It was all the man had to hang on to. On his way, servants met him with the news of his son's recovery. Synchronizing their sundials they discovered the fever had broken at the very moment Jesus said, *"Your son will live"* (verses 52–53).

Jesus Christ quietly gained a foothold in the circle close to King Herod as family and servants of this royal official became believers. None of the Herods personally believed, as far as we know. But this did not keep the Christian faith from growing right under Horrid Herod's princely **proboscis**!

proboscis: nose, snout

Faith Infiltrates Herod's Family

John 4:46–50—Royal official comes to Jesus to plead for son's healing; takes Jesus at his word

John 4:51–53—Royal official's entire household (family and servants) believe on Jesus

Dig Deeper

Luke 8:3—Joanna, wife of Chuza, manager of Herod's household, follows Jesus, provides support

Acts 13:1—Manaen, raised with Herod, member of the leadership team in the Antioch church

**GOSPEL QUARTET
IN HARMONY**

Matthew 13:54–58

Luke 4:16–31

bima: *platform*

migdal ez: *"wooden tower," lectern*

chazzan: *attendant in charge of the sacred scrolls*

Hebrew: *language used in religious activities*

Aramaic: *most commonly used language in daily conversation*

anointed: *granted authority and power*

year of the Lord's favor: *time of grace; also Year of Jubilee*

What Others
are Saying:

☞ **GO TO:**

Leviticus 25:8–55
(Year of Jubilee)

> **Luke 4:16** He went to Nazareth, where he had been brought up, and on the Sabbath day he went into the synagogue, as was his custom. And he stood up to read.

Hometown Chill

The Sabbath custom in first century synagogues was for seven men to mount the **bima** and read from the sacred scrolls (see illustration, page 145) of Holy Scripture spread out on the **migdal ez**. They stood to read, sat to explain. As a young man who had grown up in the synagogue, Jesus served as one of these reader-explainers. Home again, he was asked to fulfill his old duties. Stories of his preaching and wonderworks had preceded him (verse 23). The hometown folk were anxious to see if the stories were true—if their "hometown boy" had made good. The **chazzan** handed him the scroll of Isaiah. He opened it to chapter 61. According to custom, he read in **Hebrew** while an interpreter translated it into **Aramaic**. This is what Jesus read:

> "The Spirit of the Lord is on me,
> because he has **anointed** me
> to preach good news to the poor.
> He has sent me to proclaim freedom for the prisoners
> and recovery of sight to the blind,
> to release the oppressed,
> to proclaim the **year of the Lord's favor**" (Luke 4:18–19).

Robert E. Coleman: Intuitively the Old Testament became [Jesus'] textbook of life. His thought was literally cast in the spirit of the ancient patriarchs, kings, and prophets of Israel. . . . So saturated was his utterance with the words and principles of Scripture, it is difficult to tell them apart. Where distinction can be made in the gospels, there are at least 90 separate instances in which Jesus referred to the inspired writings, either by direct quotation, allusion to an event, or language similar to biblical expressions.[4]

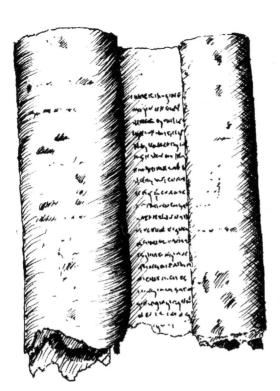

Papyrus Scroll

Egyptian papyrus paper made of river reeds was the primary writing material in the Roman world in New Testament times. A typical scroll might be 30 feet (9 meters) long.

KINGDOM OF GOD

"I'm the One!"

Jesus sat down. What he said next immediately divided the congregation: *"Today this scripture is fulfilled in your hearing."* In plain English, he claimed himself to be Isaiah's *"anointed"* One. He explained that it was he who was commissioned by the Lord God and given authority

- to give hope and dignity to the poor, downtrodden, and underprivileged;
- to liberate people in bondage physically, psychologically, and spiritually;
- to give sight to people who are blind because of physical disability, spiritual darkness, or lack of insight into God's perspective;
- to release the oppressed, those weighed down by spiritual, political, social, psychological, or economic forces; and
- to announce that the long-awaited day of God's grace had arrived, that all debts were cancelled and all slaves were freed, as in the Year of Jubilee.

KEY Outline:

Jesus' Mission
Hope for poor
Freedom for captive
Sight for blind
Release for oppressed
Debts cancelled

Matthew 13:55–58
Mark 6:1–6
Luke 4:22–30

☞ **GO TO:**

1 Kings 17:7–24
(pagan widow)

2 Kings 5:1–19
(Naaman)

🔑 *KEY Outline:*

Nazareth Reacts
Amazed at grace
Familiarity's contempt
Claims offend
Mob scene
Assassination try

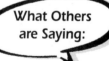

What Others
are Saying:

A Prophet From God? Naw. He's Just Joe's Kid!

At first they were amazed at the grace flowing with such authority from their young neighbor's lips (Luke 4:22). Then, as if to deny the hope his words inspired, they began to express doubts.

"Isn't this Joseph the carpenter's son? Isn't his mother's name Mary? Aren't his brothers James, Joseph, Simon and Judas? Aren't all his sisters with us living in Nazareth? Where then did this man get all these things he says and does?" Initial admiration changed to offense.

Nazareth would see no great miracle that day—only a few sick people healed.

"*No prophet is accepted in his hometown,*" Jesus said. Then he reminded them of stories from the lives of two esteemed Bible prophets:

1. Elijah found refuge in the home of a <u>pagan widow</u> and miraculously supplied her needs, while Israel suffered under famine because of unfaithfulness to God.

2. Elisha healed the leprous pagan military commander, <u>Naaman</u>, while Israel's lepers remained unhealed because of the nation's idolatry.

Jesus forced acceptance or rejection of his claims by suggesting through these stories that God loved pagans as well as Jews, and would bypass "the chosen people" if they refused to honor him and rescue needy Gentiles. This was not what the home folks wanted to hear. Suddenly the synagogue became a mob! They drove Jesus from the platform. People who had known him all his life—neighbors and relatives—pushed and shoved him out to the edge of the cliff on which the town was built. They would silence his unwelcome voice once and for all!

With the same authority with which he had offered them grace, Jesus now turned to face the angry mob. Shaking his head over their disbelief, he walked straight through the crowd, left Nazareth, and never looked back.

Lawrence O. Richards: Don't be surprised when words you speak about the grace of God first amaze others—and then bring angry rejection. Many people resent the notion that they need to rely on God's grace, supposing that God simply must give them credit for their good deeds![5]

Leslie F. Brandt: Many who heard his message that day took offense and cast him out of the synagogue. They could not endure being reminded that the God of history was as concerned about the poor and foreign widows as he was about the children of Israel and that he sent his prophets to minister to them.[6]

Christ In Command

Luke 4:31 reports that, after the heartbreaking fiasco at Nazareth, Jesus moved to the town of Capernaum, on the shore of Lake Galilee. From then on Capernaum became his Greater Galilean Campaign headquarters. Once a sleepy fishing village, Capernaum in New Testament times had grown into a city.

What Others are Saying:

☞ **Check It Out:**

Matthew 4:13–22; 8:14–17

Mark 1:16–34

Luke 4:31–41

Dig Deeper

Capernaum, Galilee—"Jesus' Town"

Scripture	What Happened at Capernaum
John 2:12	Jesus' mother and brothers lived at Capernaum
Matthew 4:13	Jesus' home base for his ministry in Galilee was there
Matthew 4:18–22; Mark 1:16–20	Andrew, Peter, James, and John ran fishing businesses there
Matthew 8:8–9	The Roman Garrison at Capernaum was commanded by a believing Centurion
Luke 7:4	A Jewish synagogue at Capernaum was built by the Roman Centurion
Mark 5:22	One of the synagogue officials was Jairus whose daughter Jesus raised from the dead
Matthew 8:14–17	Jesus healed many people from demon possession and sicknesses
Matthew 9:9	A Roman tax office was at Capernaum, where Jesus met Matthew (Levi)
John 6:59	Jesus preached at the Capernaum synagogue

Matthew 4:18 As Jesus was walking beside the Sea of Galilee, he saw two brothers, Simon called Peter and his brother Andrew. They were casting a net into the lake, for they were fishermen. "Come, follow me," Jesus said, "and I will make you fishers of men." At once they left their nets and followed him.

Gone Fishin'

The recruitment of the 12 men Jesus trained for leadership in his movement did not happen with a single encounter. John the Baptist introduced the first five men to Jesus. They <u>followed him</u> for several weeks. Upon return to Galilee, some apparently went home to Capernaum, rejoined their families, and resumed their previous jobs, while Jesus preached his way to Nazareth. Now it was time for phase two in their progress toward **apostleship**.

KEY POINT

Jesus called ordinary working people to lead his movement.

☞ **GO TO:**

John 1:35–4:54 (followed him)

apostleship: ambassadorship, oversight of church development

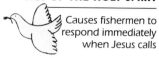

casting net: circular net nine feet across, weighted with pellets of metal to make it sink, cast from shore, surrounding the fishes[8]

dragnets: rectangular net with ropes at each of four corners, cast from a boat or two boats working together[9]

Two sets of brothers, Peter and Andrew, and James and John, were working down by the lake. All fishermen by trade. Not poor, not rich. Just ordinary "working stiffs" with families to support and mundane jobs to do. Peter and Andrew were "***casting a net into the lake.***" The other two, James and John, were in a boat with their senior fishing partner, their father Zebedee, *"mending their nets"* (**dragnets**) in preparation for a fishing trip (Matthew 4:21). First Jesus called Peter and Andrew to join him. Then he called James and John. *"I will make you fish for people,"*[7] he said.

EARLY CHURCH LIFE: Jesus recruits the apostles. The work of the early church was spearheaded by these apostles.

KINGDOM OF GOD The immediacy (verses 20, 22) with which these four men left their fishing, and in the case of James and John, their father, is almost unbelievable. Having spent considerable time with Jesus, they had a pretty good idea what he was about. They had, no doubt, thought a lot about the things they'd seen and heard with him, already feeling the urge to spend more time with him. They may already have discussed their thoughts and aspirations with their families. Besides, no one they had ever met before spoke with such authority.

What Others are Saying:

Jerome: There must have been something divinely compelling in the face of the Savior. Otherwise they would not have acted so irrationally. . . .Does one leave a father to follow a man in whom he sees nothing more than he sees in his father? They left their father of the flesh to follow the Father of the spirit. They did not leave a father; they found a Father.[10]

Stuart Briscoe: When the Master called men "fish," he used a term full of meaning. Men are darting hither and thither in the shallows of aimlessness, busy doing nothing, and getting nowhere. They swim in shoals because they lack the moral caliber to think, decide and act independently on the basis of what they know to be right. Consequently, they are jumping for the tiniest, gaudiest flies in an effort to satisfy their hunger, only to return to the depths of despair, emptiness and futility.[11]

> **Luke 4:32** They were amazed at his teaching, because his message had authority.

"This Is Your Captain Speaking!"

Next Sabbath, Jesus and his fishing crew went to the synagogue in Capernaum. Jesus was asked to teach. The congregation sat on the edge of its seats. He did not sermonize like the scribes, drawing authority from the ancient's interpretations of Scripture. He seemed to speak directly from <u>God</u>, backing up what he said with Holy Scripture, the visible self-authenticating quality of his life and character, and the <u>empowerment</u> of the Spirit.

Robert E. Coleman: Borne along with this sense of divine authenticity, he never hesitated with doubt, nor apologized for errors in judgment. . . . Never did Jesus offer an opinion subject to rebuttal, nor even venture a hypothesis relatively correct, for he realized that every word he spoke would count for eternity.[12]

Albert Barnes: Jesus was open, plain, grave, useful, delivering truth as became the **oracles** of God; not spending his time in trifling disputes and debating questions of no importance, but confirming his doctrine by miracles and argument. . . . He showed that he had authority to explain, to enforce, and to change the **ceremonial laws**.[13]

The Shootout At The Old Synagogue

As the spellbound audience listened, the meeting was interrupted by the screams of a man possessed by a *"demon."* The controlling spirit cried out, identifying Jesus as *"the Holy One of God."*

The Old Testament does not speak of demons, though some incidents are told involving <u>spiritual personalities</u> that are God's enemies. In the New Testament there is a great outburst of demon activity, presumably because Satan focused his forces to oppose the work God was doing through Jesus Christ.[14] According to the experiences described in the New Testament, destructive spirits sometimes take control of people, causing emotional, spiritual, and physical <u>problems</u>.

DEMON: The terms "evil spirit," "unclean spirit," and "demon" all refer to the same thing. Demons are part of <u>organized evil forces</u> opposed to God. Apparently, unholy spirits are able to take advantage of early ignorance, fear, rejection, grief, absence of love, abuse, chemical misuse, or involve-

☞ **GO TO:**

John 12:49, 50 (God)

John 6:63 (empowerment)

What Others are Saying:

oracles: *messages directly from God rather than through a messenger*

ceremonial laws: *religious rules in Exodus, Leviticus, Numbers, Deuteronomy*

☞ **GO TO:**

Genesis 3; Job 1 and 2; Daniel 10:12–13 (spiritual personalities)

Matthew 8:28; 9:32; Luke 8:29; 9:39; 22:3; Acts 16:16 (problems)

Ephesians 6:12 (organized evil forces)

Who's Who

ment in occult activities to take control over some area of an individual's life.

Not every sickness or emotional disorder is caused by an evil spirit. The normal way to deal with a compulsive pattern of evil is not to try to exorcise a demon, but to acknowledge personal sin and its destructiveness, to quit sinning, and to accept God's <u>forgiveness</u>, trusting that Jesus has <u>won our deliverance</u> by his death and resurrection.

☞ GO TO:

1 John 1:9 (forgiveness)

Colossians 2:13–15 (won our deliverance)

Luke 9:1–2; Mark 16:17 (authority to command)

KINGDOM OF GOD The man in the synagogue—and others from whom Jesus is reported to have driven evil spirits—was evidently the victim of destructive spiritual compulsions set so deeply that the only solution was to command the evil thing to leave. The voice of supreme authority triumphed. At Jesus' command the foul personage left the man's body and he was free.

EARLY CHURCH LIFE: Jesus has given the church <u>authority to command</u> evil spirits when necessary to liberate harassed people. But shouting, "Demon be gone!" will not solve the spirit problems of most people. Multitudes bound by evil spirits cannot be unchained without time and sacrifice by someone spiritually sensitive and willing to invest an effort in their lives. Christians must pray and fast for others.

What Others are Saying:

KEY POINT

Christ's power over evil spirits and authority in preaching are the same power.

Neil T. Anderson: When Satan harasses you, you may be prone to languish in the shadows of your misery. . . . You cry out for God to deliver you, like Jesus miraculously and instantaneously delivered the demonized people in the Gospels. But when you read through the epistles it is obvious that your deliverance has already been accomplished in Christ's work on the cross and his resurrection. . . . But it is your responsibility to exercise your authority and resist the devil, renounce participation in his schemes, confess sin, and forgive those who have offended you.[15]

Ten Confrontations with Evil Spirits

CONFRONTATION:

Luke 4:33–35	SYMPTOMS:	screaming, disruptive, fear Jesus will destroy him
	DIAGNOSIS:	"demon," "evil spirit," "unclean spirit"
	TREATMENT:	spirit ordered to be silent, to come out
	PATIENT RESPONSE:	expressed fear, fell down
	EVIDENCE OF CURE:	people saw the difference
Mark 5:1–17	SYMPTOMS:	antisocial, super strength, screams, self-destructive, thinks God will hurt him
	DIAGNOSIS:	"evil spirit"
	TREATMENT:	spirits identified, ordered to leave
	PATIENT RESPONSE:	fear, begged not to be tortured
	EVIDENCE OF CURE:	sitting, dressed, sanity returned, wants to be with Jesus
Matthew 9:32–34	SYMPTOMS:	muteness, inability to speak
	DIAGNOSIS:	"demon-possessed"
	TREATMENT:	not specified
	PATIENT RESPONSE:	he spoke
	EVIDENCE OF CURE:	ability to speak
Matthew 12:22–23	SYMPTOMS:	blindness, muteness
	DIAGNOSIS:	"demon-possessed"
	TREATMENT:	Jesus healed him
	PATIENT RESPONSE:	he spoke and saw
	EVIDENCE OF CURE:	ability to speak and see
Matthew 15:21–28	SYMPTOMS:	"suffering terribly"
	DIAGNOSIS:	"demon-possession"
	TREATMENT:	her mother's great faith
	PATIENT RESPONSE:	not specified
	EVIDENCE OF CURE:	not specified
Mark 9:14–29	SYMPTOMS:	deaf, mute, convulsions, foaming mouth, rigid, self-destructive
	DIAGNOSIS:	"a spirit," "evil spirit"
	TREATMENT:	father brings son to Jesus, faith order to leave, prayer/fasting
	PATIENT RESPONSE:	shriek, convulse, passed out
	EVIDENCE OF CURE:	stood up
Luke 4:41	SYMPTOMS:	shouting, religious speech
	DIAGNOSIS:	"demons"
	TREATMENT:	rebuked demons, didn't let them speak
	PATIENT RESPONSE:	not specified
	EVIDENCE OF CURE:	not specified
Luke 13:11–13	SYMPTOMS:	physical deformity
	DIAGNOSIS:	"a spirit," "Satan" (v.16)
	TREATMENT:	assurance of healing, touched her
	PATIENT RESPONSE:	came forward
	EVIDENCE OF CURE:	straightened up, praised God
Acts 5:16–18	SYMPTOMS:	torment
	DIAGNOSIS:	"evil spirits"
	TREATMENT:	brought to apostles for healing
	PATIENT RESPONSE:	not specified
	EVIDENCE OF CURE:	not specified
Acts 16:16–24	SYMPTOMS:	clairvoyance, shouting, religious speech, disturbance
	DIAGNOSIS:	"a spirit"
	TREATMENT:	Paul's concern, command in Jesus' name
	PATIENT RESPONSE:	stopped predicting the future (implied) and disturbing
	EVIDENCE OF CURE:	her owners' anger over lost revenue

☞ GO TO:

Luke 4:14; John 3:2
(power of God)

Something to Ponder

GOSPEL QUARTET IN HARMONY

Matthew 8:14–17
Mark 1:29–34
Luke 4:38–41

fever: *Malta fever, intermittent fever (like typhoid), or malaria*

sunset: *Sabbath is from sunset Friday to sunset Saturday*

Remember This . . .

KINGDOM OF GOD

Authority and Power

The people who witnessed the deliverance of the demonized man used two words to describe Jesus' command of evil spirits (Luke 4:36):

- *"Authority"*—the Greek word means "freedom of choice and action." Jesus acted spontaneously, of his own will, without regard to accepted protocols.
- *"Power"*—the Greek word sounds like "dynamite" and means "strength," "energy," "effectiveness," or "force." It's the term used for the <u>power of God</u>.

The people recognized that the power Jesus had over evil spirits and the authority with which he taught were the same power (Luke 4:32, 36). If he controlled demons with his words, whatever he said should be listened to attentively!

The Power To Heal

From the synagogue, Jesus and his companions went to Simon Peter's house where Peter's mother-in-law lay sick with a high **fever**. Jesus took her hand and the fever subsided, she got out of bed and served him tea.

It was the Sabbath, so not much else happened until **sunset**. Then the crowds gathered outside Peter's house, bringing mentally and physically ill people plagued with all sorts of diseases. Mark 1:33 says the *"whole town"* gathered. That was quite a crowd since Capernaum's population was about 20,000. Matthew reports that Jesus healed all the sick (8:16)! As he watched the events of that evening, Matthew concluded that he was witnessing the fulfillment of a 700-year-old prophecy—*"He took up our infirmities and carried our diseases"* (Isaiah 53:4).

Jewish tradition held that sickness was caused, either directly or indirectly, by sin. By quoting the passage in Isaiah, Matthew is saying that Jesus' healing ministry is part of Christ's ultimate purpose to bear in his own body the pain and penalty of our sin. For Matthew, Jesus' healing miracles pointed to the cross.

Statements like these about Jesus' power over disease convince his modern day followers that his authority extends to and his power can impact every problem people face.

Study Questions

1. What kind of believers is Jesus looking for?
2. How did Herod's royal official demonstrate his faith?
3. Name three of the five things Jesus said the Lord had anointed him to do. Which comes closest to the thing you personally need most?
4. Why did his hometown folk fail to believe in him?
5. Identify six or more symptoms the gospel writers mention that accompanied the activity of an evil spirit in a person's life.
6. What does Jesus' power to command evil spirits and heal diseases tell us about his teachings?
7. How has Jesus' authority grabbed your attention recently? How is it freeing you?

CHAPTER WRAP-UP

- Jesus' return to Galilee was met with a warm reception by the Galileans. But he knew as he launched his preaching tour of Galilean towns that warmth would soon change to a mix of acceptance and opposition. (John 4:43–45; Luke 4:14–16)

- Upon arrival in Cana, Galilee, a royal official came from Capernaum with an urgent request that Jesus go there and save the official's dying son. Jesus healed the son without going to Capernaum. The official's entire household believed on Jesus. (John 4:46–54)

- In his hometown of Nazareth, Jesus revealed he was the fulfillment of Old Testament prophecies concerning the Messiah. He told them God loved Gentiles too. His former neighbors ran him out of town. (Luke 4:16–30)

- Jesus moved his headquarters to Capernaum. He demonstrated his messianic authority by calling four men to follow him, by powerful teaching, and by acts of healing and deliverance from evil spirits. (Matthew 4:13–22; 8:14–17)

11 THE MIGHTY KINGDOM OF THE WEAK

CHAPTER HIGHLIGHTS

- The Real Kingdom
- King of the Powerless
- Fishing for Sinners
- Raggedy Man
- The Unforgiven
- Party at Matt's
- Shredding Old Shirts

Let's Get Started

The collection of people around Jesus gave huge hints as to the kind of movement he was leading. One government official and one scholar had sought him out, but mostly the politicians and intellectuals left him alone. Except for the day he whipped the money launderers out of the Temple, there had been only hints of conflict with the religious establishment. Most Galilean synagogues were still open to him.

In and around Capernaum the ordinary people—the religious and political nobodies—thronged him. His following was mostly what the snobbish power brokers referred to as "this cursed mob that knows nothing!" (John 7:49).

> **Mark 1:35–38** Very early in the morning, while it was still dark, Jesus got up, left the house and went off to a solitary place, where he prayed. Simon and his companions went to look for him, and when they found him, they exclaimed: "Everyone is looking for you!" Jesus replied, "Let us go somewhere else—to the nearby villages—so I can preach there also. That is why I have come."

Pursuit Of The Real Kingdom

The young Messiah faced crucial decisions. In the dizziness of celebrity he must talk with his <u>Mentor</u>. He had to pray. As he would often do during the next three years, he got up before sunup,

GOSPEL QUARTET IN HARMONY

Matthew 4:23–24;
8:2–4; 9:1–17
Mark 1:35–2:22
Luke 4:42–44; 5:1–39

GOSPEL QUARTET IN HARMONY

Mark 1:35–39
Luke 4:42–44
Matthew 4:23–24

☞ **GO TO:**

John 7:16 (Mentor)

What Others are Saying:

☞ **GO TO:**

Matthew 4:17 (first)

Matthew 5–7; 13; 25; Luke 6:17–49 (large sections)

Isaiah 66:1–2 (universe)

Isaiah 9:6–7 (government)

Luke 1:32–33 (a king)

Isaiah 2:1–4; 11:1–5; Jeremiah 23:3–8; Hosea 3:4–5 (kingdom)

prophecies: *predictions given in visions and "words" from the Lord*

rabbinical teaching: *rabbi's teaching, ancient commentaries on Scripture*

hiked to a quiet place, and before the rest of the world opened its eyes, he had a conversation with his Father in heaven. He cleared his mind of distractions, asked directions, and got a fresh grip on the vision of what he had been sent to do. By the time Simon and the others found him, he knew what he must do next. His decision blew away the smokescreen of success.

Elizabeth O'Conner: We came to know that if we were going to learn to pray, we were going to have to pray. Christ ever remains the great teacher of prayer.[1]

KINGDOM OF GOD

The Kingdom—Hottest Thing in Jesus' Oven

Sweeping aside the "urgent" clamor of the city's needy, Jesus, with fresh orders from his Father, left Capernaum to take his message to other towns (Luke 4:43). This is Luke's first mention of the subject of Jesus' preaching: the kingdom of God.

To many Galileans, Jesus' cry, *"The kingdom of God is near!"* must have sounded like a rebel yell—the rallying cry for a revolution. It was that slogan the young Nazarene paraded across the politically volatile Jewish province of Galilee. *"The kingdom of God"* is the subject Jesus talked about more than any other. (Matthew, with his Jewish reluctance to speak or write the name of deity, calls it, the kingdom of *heaven.*) It was the theme of his <u>first</u> sermon. It consumed <u>large sections</u> of his recorded teaching.

What Is This Thing Called "The Kingdom Of God"?

The kingdom of God was not a new concept to the Jews. Every synagogue attendee listening to Jesus already had some idea what he was talking about. The kingdom was an Old Testament concept, rooted in the history of the Jews and deeply imbedded in their belief system. To the first century Israelite the kingdom of God was

1. the entire <u>universe</u>—God was sovereign over all creation;
2. the <u>government</u> on the shoulders of the promised Messiah—he would be <u>a king</u>; and
3. a political <u>kingdom</u> in which the Messiah-King would defeat his enemies, save Israel from oppression, and rule the entire world from Jerusalem.

These beliefs were based on Old Testament **prophecies**. However, the expectations of most Jews were off target because of missing links in most **rabbinical teaching**. Most failed to grasp another vital messianic principle: The necessity for the Messiah to <u>suffer and die</u> as a **sacrifice** to **atone** for human sin before God's kingdom could be established on earth.

The dream of God's rule in the hearts and lives of humans could never be realized without the <u>spiritual renewal</u> Christ's sacrifice would make possible. This missing piece of the prophetic puzzle left many in Israel confused and hanging on to incomplete and unrealistic expectations. When it became apparent Jesus would be a servant and sacrifice instead of a military leader, many of his disciples <u>jumped</u> ship. Even John the <u>Baptist questioned</u> for a while if Jesus was the expected one.

> Jews did not expect their King would suffer and die. Many people were so busy looking for political victory they missed Jesus as the Messiah.

☞ **GO TO:**

Isaiah 53 (suffer and die)

Isaiah 55; John 3:3, 5 (spiritual renewal)

John 6:66 (jumped)

Matthew 11:3 (Baptist questioned)

Remember This . . .

sacrifice: an offering to God

atone: to pay for a wrong, cleanse, purify, restore harmony

Unwrapping the Kingdom Dream

KINGDOM OF GOD

So far in the New Testament's telling of Jesus' story, the kingdom of God has not been defined. Jesus' teachings and the model of his life with his disciples put flesh on the bones of the kingdom concept. He challenges the Jews' ultranationalistic expectations. His followers are shown how to enter in and experience the kingdom. In the process it becomes clear that the kingdom of God is not merely something that happens in the hearts of individuals who get right with God, one by one. Jesus is clearly intent on leading the development of a new society, a new nation, a distinct counterculture that exists and thrives, and pledges allegiance to Christ as King, right smack dab in the middle of the kingdoms, societies, nations, and cultures of this rebellious world!

What Does The Kingdom Have To Do With The Church?

From Jesus' teachings concerning the kingdom of God we see his strategy: When it came time for him to return to his Father in heaven, he planned to leave behind a close-knit, mutually dependent, believing community, including people of all nations who acknowledge Jesus as King. The **church**, with its confession of allegiance to Jesus and its network of supportive spiritual relationships, is the advance contingent of the kingdom of God on earth. The church is a human, earthly entity. Its flaws and weaknesses stick out like a parade of sore thumbs! Perfection of the kingdom dream is a <u>future promise</u>. But fulfillment of the dream of a community under God's reign has already begun. Jesus gives clear instructions concerning how, if they are willing to do as he

☞ **GO TO:**

Matthew 16:16–19; 18:15–20 (church)

Isaiah 65:17–25; Zephaniah 3:11–13; Revelation 21:1–4 (future promise)

church: community of people called out from the world, trusting in Jesus, living under God's reign

says, his followers can live together in an authentic expression of the kingdom society in the here and now of their lives.

Howard A. Snyder: I am convinced that a properly biblical understanding of the Kingdom of God is possible only if the church is understood—predominantly, if not exclusively—as a charismatic community and God's pilgrim people, his kingdom of priests . . . a radically biblical, caring community of believers totally sold out to Jesus Christ. . . . [The church] must be seen as God's people in relation to God's kingdom or, in other words, the messianic community, the community of the king.[2]

Audrey I. Girard: We spend all our lives praying "Thy kingdom come," because the true kingdom is an unfulfilled desire within us to see total justice, total love, total mercy, and total purity—but the kingdom hasn't yet come in completeness (Hebrews 2:8–9).[3]

KEY Outline:

The Kingdom
Reign of God
  • now: the church
  • future: the whole world

> **Matthew 4:42** Jesus went throughout Galilee, teaching in their synagogues, preaching the good news of the kingdom, and healing every disease and sickness among the people.

Kingdom Of The Powerless

GOSPEL QUARTET IN HARMONY

Matthew 4:23–24
Mark 1:39
Luke 4:44

Christ breaks all the rules that normally govern where and how a kingdom gets its power. History has shown him to be the most powerful monarch who ever reigned, but there is no similarity to the way he builds his kingdom and the way the world's great leaders—the Nebuchadnezzars, Alexanders, Caesars, Napoleons—have gone about building theirs. In the societies of the world in which we live, to exercise power is to dominate and control other people. Jesus' strategies all reflect "God's descending way of becoming a servant."[4] Greatness is measured in terms of servanthood and sacrifice.

☞ **GO TO:**

Matthew 20:25–28 (greatness)

Galilee: Luke 4:44 (NIV) says "Judea." Original Greek: "country of the Jews" (including Galilee)

As Matthew tells the story (4:23–24), Jesus preached *"the good news of the kingdom"* wherever people would listen. News quickly spread that he had power to heal. They came from everywhere around **Galilee.** Soon his crowds took on a distinct flavor: the diseased, pain-wracked, mentally and emotionally disturbed, epileptics, quadra- and paraplegics—the broken, weak, harassed, suffering, sick, vulnerable, confused, driven, and addicted. The most needy people of that day were brought by friends or dragged themselves out of their sickbeds and places of confinement and loneliness. They found their way to Jesus because they had heard from somebody that he could help.

What a way to build a kingdom!

EARLY CHURCH LIFE: The early church began among the weakest, neediest people in the world.

Joni Eareckson Tada: It is the "<u>least</u> of the brethren" and "the <u>weakest members</u> of the body" who are to be given special places of honor. . . . Those who are helpless, no matter what their handicap, see themselves in the Man of <u>Sorrows</u> because he became one of them. Jesus' message was clear. We are all without help or hope as long as we are without him. But he was also clear that his good news was, in some way, especially for those who suffer the helplessness and hopelessness that physical infirmity can often bring.[5]

Gordon Cosby: When people have a hunger, one beggar will tell another where to find food.[6]

Fishing For "Sinners"

Simon Peter, his brother Andrew, James, and John had followed Jesus on his Galilean preaching tour. When he returned to his Capernaum home, the four fishermen returned to their trade.

Capernaum (see appendix A) was on the north shore of the body of water that forms the headwaters of the Jordan River. This small inland sea in New Testament times was known by three different names: Sea of Galilee, Sea of Tiberias, or Lake or Sea of Gennesaret (named for the fertile plain west of the lake). "The Lord has created the seven seas," said the rabbis, "but the sea of Gennesaret is his delight."[7] This blue lake fills the crater of an extinct volcano. Surrounded by black basaltic rock, it has sandy beaches and plenty of fish.

Offshore Pulpit

One morning Jesus again walked by the lake. The ever-present crowds surrounded him. It was the same stretch of beach where earlier he had called four fishermen to leave their work and join him. Again the boats were pulled up to shore and the men were washing their nets. Needing a better vantage point from which to

KEY POINT

In God's kingdom greatness is measured by servanthood.

What Others are Saying:

☞ **GO TO:**

Matthew 25:40, 45 (least)

1 Corinthians 12:22 (weakest members)

Isaiah 53:3 (Sorrows)

☞ **Check It Out:**

Luke 5:1–11

talk to the crowd, Jesus climbed into the boat belonging to his friend Simon (Peter) and asked him to anchor the boat a little offshore. Jesus sat down in the boat to teach. His voice resonated off the water, which acted like a megaphone, so the crowd on shore could hear him.

Go Fish!

His talk ended. Jesus turned to his friend and said, "Let's go catch some fish!" (Luke 5:4).

Simon, fastest tongue in the west, thought Jesus needed to be better informed about the ins and outs of Galilean fishing. He and his partners were exhausted. They'd fished these waters all night and caught nary a minnow!

"But at your bidding I will let down the nets," Simon says with resignation.

Suddenly, **denizens** of the deep began to hit the nets! It was more than Peter and Andrew could handle. They called for James and John to row over and help. Both boats were soon full of fish. Water began to lap up over the sides, and a new danger presented itself—the distinct possibility of a quick descent into Davy Jones' Locker!

As the overloaded boats struggled to make shore, Peter fell to his knees before Jesus, overcome by awareness of his unworthiness to be in the presence of such authority, confessing himself a **sinful man**. The whole fishing crew shared the same awe.

"Do not fear, from now on you will be catching men," Jesus said. This was the third time he had approached these four about being his disciples. This time, they burned their bridges behind them— *"left everything and followed him."*

Something about realizing that you are in the presence of the Lord makes confessing your sins seem a <u>most appropriate</u> thing to do.

The four fishermen were not priests, Levites, or Pharisees, any of whom might be expected to engage in religious work. They were not the worst sinners in town. Neither were they particularly known for their righteousness. Peter was a synagogue dropout. They could read and write, but they were <u>not educated</u>. They had demonstrated eagerness for Messiah's coming. They were willing to learn and change. They were willing to leave everything to be with Jesus (Luke 5:11).

denizens: *residents (fish)*

sinful man: *a first century Jewish idiom for a synagogue dropout*

Something to Ponder

☞ **GO TO:**

Isaiah 6
(most appropriate)

Acts 4:13
(not educated)

> **Luke 5:12** While Jesus was in one of the towns, a man came along who was covered with leprosy. When he saw Jesus, he fell with his face to the ground and begged him, "Lord, if you are willing, you can make me clean."

Raggedy Man

Society's only defense against leprosy was quarantine. <u>By law</u>, the **leper** was required to live alone or with other lepers *outside the camp*. He or she could have no normal human contact. Untouchable, a leper was unemployable and reduced to begging, although he or she could expect to suffer nine years before dying. Josephus reports lepers were treated as if they were dead men.

"Never, No Never, Touch A Leper!"

To the Law, society added its own restrictions.

- Lepers were prohibited from entering Jerusalem or any walled town.
- It was illegal to greet a leper even in an open area.
- No one was allowed to approach within six feet of a leper.
- Downwind from a leper, the distance was increased to 150 feet.
- Rabbis urged people to run and hide from an approaching leper.
- One rabbi bragged about throwing stones to keep lepers away.[8]
- Lepers were feared, hated, and driven away like animals.

The psychological effects were the worst aspects of the leper's suffering. A sense of guilt and rejection by God often went with the disease, even though the leper was not personally responsible for acquiring it. No one needed to be touched more than the outcast leper. Jesus knew this.

According to society's customs, the leper who threw himself down in front of Jesus approached with his hand over his face, loudly warning, "**Unclean**! Unclean!" The leper reminded everyone, "Contact with me could be injurious to your health." As an identifying "uniform" the leper wore torn clothing and unkempt hair, permanent signs of mourning. Hearing the rasping cry from ulcerated vocal chords, the crowd instinctively backed away, giving the raggedy man a wide birth.

As he lay before Christ, this leper felt something he may not

GOSPEL QUARTET IN HARMONY

Matthew 8:2–4
Mark 1:40–45
Luke 5:12–16

☞ **GO TO:**

Leviticus 13, 14 (by law)

---

leper: person with Hanson's disease; incurable in Bible times, ulcers eat away at skin, tendons, muscle, and bone

Unclean: physically or morally polluted and unfit to participate in Temple worship

Jesus never let social or religious rules keep him from helping someone in need.

Remember This . . .

☞ **GO TO:**

Matthew 9:30; 12:16; Mark 1:34; 5:43 (instruction)

☞ **GO TO:**

Leviticus 14 (God's Law)

have felt for a very long time. A hand reached down and touched his diseased flesh. *"I am willing. Be clean!"* Jesus said. The horrors of the awful disease were swept away in a word and a touch.

People need to be touched and loved and accepted. If we recoil from touching or refuse to be touched, we may actually hinder the healing process in our own lives.

Joyful Disobedience (Otherwise Known as "Dumb Love")

Jesus gave the cleansed leper two commands:

1. *"Tell no one."* Jesus often gave this <u>instruction</u> to healed people. Reasons?

   - To forestall a premature popular movement to crown Jesus king before he had a chance to demonstrate the kind of kingdom he was building

   - To keep the cleansed leper from getting sidetracked retelling his story instead of following the procedure Moses prescribed for verification of the cure

   - To keep crowds to manageable size so as not to hinder his freedom to go anywhere he needed to go in ministry (see Mark 1:45)

2. *"Go and show yourself to the priest."* This involved a sacrifice and two examinations by a priest, a week apart, to officially certify healing had taken place. Reasons?

   - To obey <u>God's Law</u>

   - To officially remove the stigma of leprosy

   - To give *"a testimony"* to the priests of Jesus' messiahship

We can't be sure the man ever went to the priests. We know he disobeyed Jesus' first instruction till the cows came home! This exuberant blabbermouth simply could not or would not be quiet about the wonderful thing Jesus had done for him. As a result, the numbers of people coming to see Jesus exploded. He could no longer take his message inside the city limits, but was forced to meet people in the countryside.

> **Matthew 9:2** Some men brought to him a paralytic, lying on a mat. When Jesus saw their faith, he said to the paralytic, "Take heart, son; your sins are forgiven."

The Paralysis Of The Unforgiven

On Jesus' return to Capernaum, representatives of official Judaism showed up at **his home**. He was surrounded by Pharisees and lawyers when four men came carrying a paralyzed friend on a stretcher. Unable to get through the door, they climbed to the roof, removed some tiles, and let the man down into the room in front of Jesus.

To the shock of the gathered Bible scholars, Jesus said to the paralyzed man, *"Your sins are forgiven."*

The room became deafeningly silent. The religionists stared at Jesus, incredulous. No one spoke but they were thinking volumes! "**Blasphemy**! Only God can forgive sins!"

"Which is easier to say, 'Your sins are forgiven you,' or 'Rise and walk'?" Jesus asked. The deafening silence persisted. *"That you may know that the Son of Man has authority to forgive sins,"* Jesus turned to the paralytic, *"Take your stretcher and go home."*

The man got up, picked up his bed, and walked out the door shouting "Hallelujah!" (or "Goody gumdrop!" or some expression of thanks to God).

The Baloney Of Unforgiveness

"Only God can forgive sins?" The learned religionists made this error sound so pious! In Matthew's version of this story, Jesus responds by asking, *"Why are you thinking evil in your hearts?"* (Matthew 9:4). To think only God can forgive was a diabolical distortion—a wicked rationalization to justify failure to do what they knew was the right thing to do—forgive!

Jesus admitted forgiveness isn't easy. It's as great a miracle as healing paralyzed legs (Luke 5:23). To prove he, a human being—*"the Son of Man"*—had authority to do both, he ordered the man to get up and go home.

The Healing Power Of Forgiveness

1. Not only is the authority to forgive sins given to Jesus, but all human beings (sons and daughters of men) have the right, responsibility, and God-given <u>authority to forgive</u> the sins of others.

GOSPEL QUARTET IN HARMONY

Matthew 6:1–8
Mark 2:1–2
Luke 5:17–26

his home: probably the home of his mother

Blasphemy: slanderous speech directed toward God or man

☞ **GO TO:**

Matthew 18: 21–22; John 20:22–23 (authority to forgive)

Remember This . . .

Something to Ponder

2. Physical healing and forgiveness of sins are <u>often linked</u>.

3. Forgiveness is <u>proof</u> God is at work in a person or situation (Luke 5:25–26).

Forgiving Each Day Keeps The Doctor Away

Modern medical science agrees that unresolved emotional and spiritual conflicts involving anger, bitterness, and fear can have such negative effects on physical health as arthritis, ulcers, heart disease, stroke, and depression. Forgiving and being forgiven can help keep the immune system strong and ward off many maladies.

Jesus on Forgiveness

Scripture	What He Taught about Forgiveness
Matthew 6:12	We need to pray for forgiveness of our sins and for ability to forgive others
Matthew 6:14–15	Our personal experience of God's forgiveness is linked to forgiving others
Matthew 9:2	Happiness and hope are linked with forgiveness
Matthew 18:21–22	We should always forgive no matter how often the other person sins
Matthew 18:23–35	The person who does not forgive will experience torment
Mark 11:25	Unforgiveness affects the effectiveness of prayers
Luke 7:47	Ability to love is proportional to forgiveness received
Luke 7:47–50	Accepting forgiveness is an act of faith and brings peace
Luke 11:4	If we forgive others we can expect God to forgive us
Luke 23:34	Jesus demonstrated true forgiveness by forgiving the people who crucified him
Other verses for study:	Mark 2:10–12; Luke 15:11–24; 17:3–6; John 8:3–11; 20:22–23

☞ **GO TO:**

James 5:16
(often linked)

Romans 5:8 (proof)

GOSPEL QUARTET IN HARMONY

Matthew 9:9–13
Mark 2:13–17
Luke 5:27–32

Matthew 9:9–12 As Jesus went on from there, he saw a man named Matthew sitting at the tax collector's booth. "Follow me," he told him, and Matthew got up and followed him. While Jesus was having dinner at Matthew's house, many tax collectors and "sinners" came and ate with him and his disciples. When the Pharisees saw this, they asked the disciples, "Why does your teacher eat with tax collectors and 'sinners'?" On hearing this, Jesus said, "It is not the healthy who need a doctor, but the sick."

The Party At Matt's House

The paralytic was not the only one experiencing the freedom, power, and joy of forgiveness. More shock waves rolled when Jesus called a tax collector named Matthew to join his team. To the intelligent people of the day this staff addition was a political nightmare. What was Jesus thinking?

The Fishing Crew Welcomes The Crooked Tax Man

Tax collectors, also called Publicans, each added their "cut" to the amount required by the government. They became rich bilking their countrymen. They levied import and export duties, bridge and road tolls, and town and city dues gathered at the gates of each town. People they cheated had no recourse in the courts because the judges were part of the corrupt system. Publicans also did a brisk business in loan-sharking. The government praised them. Their fellow citizens considered them the same as prostitutes, highwaymen, murderers, and traitors.[9]

> PUBLICANS: *Tax collectors.* Low-class Jews working for the *Publicani,* an order of Roman knights who had won government contracts to conduct its tax-gathering enterprises.

Why Are These Sinners Celebrating?

The Pharisees watched Jesus enter Matthew's house, accompanied by a notorious aggregation of Roman collaborators and **sinners**. As food was consumed and wine flowed and noise increased, the whole neighborhood could tell the party was gettin' a glow on!

To Pharisees, those self-righteous killjoys, and **scribes**, those champions of the Olympic wet blanket throw, everyone was having too good a time. Such unbridled joy couldn't be spiritual. No good Pharisee would be caught dead in such a gathering. They were disappointed in Jesus. If he was the Messiah, why was he hangin' around with the irreligious rabble?

> "These are the ones I came to heal," Jesus replied. He did not defend their lifestyle. He called them to change (Luke 5:32). Jesus was concerned with the social outcasts of his day. He spent time with them. He loved them. They <u>listened</u>, and many became disciples.
>
> In contrast, the Pharisees believed it was their religious duty to stay so far away from the ungodly that they would not even teach them the Law. Eating with these people was worse than talking to them, so the Pharisees thought, because sharing a meal meant you recognized and welcomed the sinners.
>
> To Jesus, political and religious correctness was useless. Introducing wandering souls to God's grace was what he lived for.

KEY Outline:

Forgiveness
Our choice
Heals
Proves God is working

KEY POINT

Acceptance by God is reason enough to celebrate.

Who's Who

sinners: *irreligious Jews, synagogue dropouts*

scribes: *scholars, experts on the Law of Moses*

☞ **GO TO:**

Luke 15:1–2; Matthew 11:19; 21:31–32; 7:29–35 (listened)

Something to Ponder

KEY POINT

Christ came to save sinners, not to feed religious egos.

> **Matthew 9:16–17** But no one puts a patch of unshrunk cloth on an old garment; for the patch pulls away from the garment and a worse tear results. Nor do men put new wine into old wineskins; otherwise the wineskins burst, and the wine pours out, and the wineskins are ruined; but they put new wine into fresh wineskins, and both are preserved.

**GOSPEL QUARTET
IN HARMONY**

Matthew 9:14–17
Mark 2:18–22
Luke 5:33–39

Shredding Old Shirts And Busting Old Bottles

Jesus' response to his critics was to compare the joyous celebration at Matt's place with a happy seven-day Jewish wedding festival (Matthew 9:15). The bride and groom and their guests dressed in their finest and feasted for seven days.

Jesus used three illustrations to describe religious people who could not force such an idea into the narrow package of their preconceptions:

1. They were old shirts on which new patches had been sewn (verse 16). When washed, the new patch would shrink and tear the old shirt apart!

2. They were old wineskins (see illustration below) unsuitable to handle the fermenting process of new wine (verse 17). As grape juice ferments it gives off gasses, causing pressure. Old, inflexible wineskins explode. The skin is ruined. The wine is lost.

3. They were addicted to *"old wine"* (Luke 5:39).

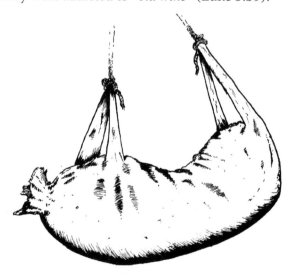

Goatskin Wine Bottle

In first century Israel, wine was kept in goatskins. New skins were supple and elastic. In time, they became hard and inflexible.

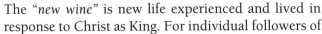

KINGDOM OF GOD

What Is the "New Wine"?

The "*new wine*" is new life experienced and lived in response to Christ as King. For individual followers of Christ and for their religious structures and institutions, the person responsive to Christ must be flexible—willing to change and grow. Old wineskins represent the rigidity of religion by rules, regulations, and ritual. New wineskins represent the flexibility of personal relationship with the King.

Old wine can become habit-forming and dull one's taste for real life and joy! It happened in Christ's day. It happens now.

Remember This . . .

Study Questions

1. What did Jesus do when success at Capernaum threatened to deter him from his main mission?
2. What did Jews hearing Jesus preach the nearness of the kingdom already believe about the kingdom of God? What did they fail to understand, which caused them confusion?
3. How are the kingdom of God and the church related?
4. When Simon saw the power of Christ, what did he confess?
5. What was wrong with the scribes' and Pharisees' belief that only God can forgive sins?
6. What did Jesus do to prove he had the authority to forgive sins?

CHAPTER WRAP-UP

- The greatest concern in Jesus' preaching and ministry was and is the establishment of the kingdom of God. As crowds gathered, it became apparent his kingdom was not built on the exercise of power, but on weakness, servanthood, and sacrifice. (Matthew 4:17–25)

- Jesus demonstrated his authority over nature and men. He issued the final call for four fishermen to join him in catching people. They left everything and followed. (Matthew 4:18–22; Luke 5:1–11)

- Jesus broke social rules by touching and healing a leper. The leper told everyone, making it impossible for Jesus to take his ministry into some cities. (Mark 1:40–45)

- Jesus healed a man whose paralysis was linked with guilt for unforgiven sin, and confronted hypocritical reasoning about forgiveness. (Luke 5:17–26)

- Jesus called Matthew to leave his crooked tax-collecting job to follow him as a disciple. Matthew invited his friends to dinner to meet Jesus. The Pharisees became unglued. Jesus reminded them that it was the sick who need a doctor. (Matthew 9:9–13)

- Jesus warned the Pharisees that their rigid attitudes kept them from enjoying the new spiritual relationship he was offering, as surely as a new patch destroyed an old shirt and new wine busted an old wineskin. (Luke 5:33–39)

12 RELIGION GONE RIGID

- Stirring the Water
- Did Jesus Claim to Be God?
- "Picking" a Fight
- Retreat to the Sea

GOSPEL QUARTET IN HARMONY

Matthew 12:1–14
Mark 2:23–3:12
Luke 6:1–11
John 5

Let's Get Started

Miracles happened wherever Jesus went. All four New Testament historians report his miracles. One New Testament historian, John, organizes his telling of the Life of Christ around what he calls seven "signs"—supernatural works of power demonstrating Christ's compassion for individuals and his ability to meet their needs—proofs to convince people to believe in him as the Messiah. But, people being what they are, the same works that caused some to believe caused others to oppose everything Jesus stood for!

Stirring The Water

The Pool of Bethesda was not far from the Temple area in Jerusalem (see illustration, page 170). Its five porches were always filled with sick people. Jesus visited the place during a feast (likely the **Feast of Tabernacles**). His attention was drawn to a man who had been unable to walk for 38 years.

☞ Check it Out:

John 5:1–47

Feast of Tabernacles: festival commemorating Israel's 40 years of desert wandering

> **John 5:7** [Jesus] asked him, "Do you want to get well?" "Sir," the invalid replied, "I have no one to help me into the pool when the water is stirred. While I am trying to get in, someone else goes down ahead of me."

Last One In The Pool Is A Rotten Egg!

Popular belief said, "From time to time an angel of the Lord would come down and stir the waters. The first one in the pool after

☞ GO TO:

John 5:4, NIV margin (popular belief)

This map of Jerusalem shows the location of the Pool of Bethesda where the paralyzed man had come for 38 years hoping to be healed. The name of the pool is Hebrew for "house of mercy" or "place of salt." Many believed the water had healing properties.

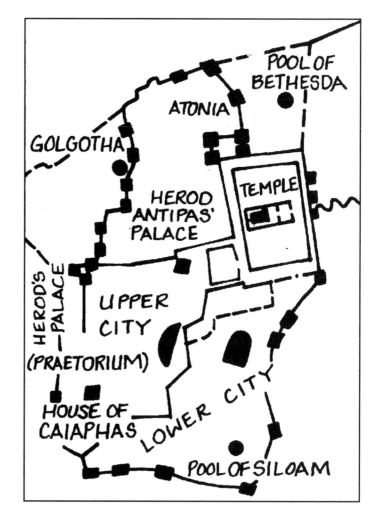

each such disturbance would be cured."[1] It was a highly questionable notion. The idea that God works in "lottery-like" fashion seems grossly inconsistent with what the Bible reveals about God.

The $64,000 Question

"Do you want to get well?" Someone might wonder why Jesus asked this question. This man had been incapacitated for 38 years. Of course he wanted to get well. Duh!

Something to Ponder

Actually, it's a pretty good question. Nearly four decades of helplessness can leave a man hopeless, depressed, and passive. Suddenly being able to do things for yourself after 38 years of depending on other people, means having to take responsibilities you're not used to and may not want!

> **John 5:8–9** Then Jesus said to him, "Get up! Pick up your mat and walk." At once the man was cured; he picked up his mat and walked. The day on which this took place was a Sabbath.

The Unexpected Cure

The cure was instantaneous. The man must have been shocked out of his wits! He got up, folded his **mat**, threw it over his shoulder, and walked away. It wasn't an act of faith, but obedience. The man didn't even know who the healer was (verse 13)!

The simplicity in the way the healing is reported masks the bomb blast detonated in the last phrase of verse 9: *"The day on which this took place was a Sabbath."* (Gasp!)

You had to be seriously Jewish to understand the fuss that simple fact set off. When religious leaders saw the man carrying his bed through the streets on the Sabbath they made a citizen's arrest— "It is against the law to carry a bed on the Sabbath day." If you know the <u>Ten Commandments</u> that sounds reasonable.

> **Exodus 20:8–10** Remember the Sabbath day by keeping it holy. Six days you shall labor and do all your work, but the seventh day is a Sabbath to the Lord your God. On it you shall not do any work.

Stirring The Sabbath Pot

When ancient Israel neglected the Sabbath principle, <u>spiritual leaders</u> rightly refocused its importance. But over the 15 centuries since God commanded it, Jewish scholars added all sorts of rules and regulations, which turned this **unique principle**—one day of rest each week—into a painful, ultra-restrictive burden.

Here are some examples:

- The maximum legal weight to be carried on Sabbath was about the weight of a teaspoon.
- The distance a person could travel was no more than the distance to the nearest synagogue.
- To untie a knot on the Sabbath was to engage in forbidden labor (in case of pain it could be untied by a Gentile).
- A tailor sinned if he carried a needle (the tool of his trade) in his robe on the Sabbath.
- Later rabbis argued about whether a person could break the Sabbath by wearing false teeth or a wooden leg!

mat: a light, stretcher-like conveyance

Sabbath: *the seventh day, meant for rest*

☞ **GO TO:**

Exodus 20:3–17 (Ten Commandments)

Jeremiah 17:19–27; Nehemiah 13:15–19 (spiritual leaders)

unique principle: no other nation gave its people one day in seven for rest

KEY POINT

Religious rules turned the Sabbath blessing into a Sabbath burden.

Sabbath Keeping: A Matter Of Life And Death

The official Jewish rulebook read: "If anyone carries anything from a public place to a private house on the Sabbath intentionally he is punishable by death by stoning."[2] The healed man's only defense was, *"The man who made me well said to me, 'Pick up your mat and walk.'"* The authorities were not impressed. They could only see him disobeying a rule they considered on the same level as the Law of God!

> **John 5:16** So, because Jesus was doing these things on the Sabbath, the Jews persecuted him.

Jesus The Sabbath Breaker

This story pinpoints the issue over which the opposition against Jesus began to crystallize. He had two strikes against him. (Strike one: He told the man to carry his bed on the Sabbath. Strike two: He healed on the Sabbath. One more strike and he's out!)

Jesus <u>loved the Scriptures</u>, and he <u>kept the Sabbath</u>. But he despised freedom-robbing, joy-killing traditions added by teachers seeking to leave their mark on Judaism. The story of the healing at the pool was a mere sample of how Jesus treated the religious establishment's **extrabiblical** prohibitions. For him, Sabbath breaking was premeditated and habitual. He did it publicly and with gusto!

☞ **GO TO:**

Luke 4:18–19; 24:27, 44–46
(loved the Scriptures)

Luke 4:16
(kept the Sabbath)

extrabiblical: *outside of or in addition to the Bible*

What Others are Saying:

KEY POINT

Jesus loved the Bible but hated man-made additions to it.

Bill Comeau:

No waves, please,
heaven help the man
who maketh waves. . . .
And along comes
the troublemaker
from Nazareth
and right away he starts
challenging the rules
offending the establishment
calling everybody to rethink their faith
or for the first time
really to come to grips with
their beliefs. . . .[3]

> **John 5:17–18** Jesus said to them, "My Father is always at his work to this very day, and I, too, am working." For this reason the **Jews** tried all the harder to kill him; not only was he breaking the Sabbath, but he was even calling God his own Father, making himself equal with God.

Jews: not the Jewish people, but the religious leaders

Jesus' Bizarre Defense: "Even God Breaks The Sabbath!"

Jesus' response to persecution from the picayunish purveyors of pretended piety was to argue that since the Father in heaven works on the Sabbath, as the Father's Son, he had authority to do the same. A highly unusual defense wrapped in a bold claim.

KEY POINT

Religious rules and rituals can distort people's perception of God.

The religious authorities thought Jesus was claiming to be bigger than the Sabbath traditions. They were right! They understood him to be dispensing with their authority to tell people what they could or couldn't do on the Sabbath. They were right! When he identified his works with God's works, and called God "*Father*," they understood him to be claiming equality with God. Again, they were right! Red lights were flashing in their rule-bound brains: This was **blasphemous** insanity! (It would turn out to be strike three for Jesus.)

blasphemous: slander against God

Religious Rigidity And The Perception Of God

The issue of who is Lord and what the Lord is like was at the heart of the Sabbath issue as well as other issues Jesus forced. The greatest problem with religious rigidity is that it warps the worshipers' perception of God, making God seem concerned mainly with outward religion rather than personal relationships with people.

Lawrence O. Richards: The religious leaders either had to accept Jesus' claim and worship him as God, or reject Jesus' claim. They refused to believe that Jesus was God's Son, and instead tried to kill him![4]

What Others are Saying:

Did Jesus Christ Claim To Be God?

☞ **Check It Out:**

John 5:19–47

Did Jesus claim to be God, or was deity something claimed for him by the apostles and early Christians? If he was trying to stay out of trouble with the authorities, he never should have said the things he said in John 5:19–47. And he certainly should not have been surprised that his unbelieving listeners concluded he was a dangerous man.

1 John 5:19a: *"The Son can do nothing by himself; he can only do what he sees his Father doing."*

Jesus' claim: He never acts independently from the Father; everything he does is something he has seen God do.

2 John 5:19b: *"Whatever the Father does the Son also does."*

Jesus' claim: All his actions mirror the acts of God.

What Others are Saying:

John Pollock: His accusers demanded to know why he worked on the Sabbath. He answered by words which made them certain that he claimed to be equal with God, whom he called "my Father," an expression no Jew would dare to use. Not denying their interpretation, Jesus emphasized his relationship with God until no one present remained in doubt of his claim that his life and actions revealed the life and action of God. . . . His claims were uncompromising, forceful, and put him beyond retreat, being blasphemous delusion or fraud unless true.[5]

ACT OF THE HOLY SPIRIT

Brings spiritually dead people to life

3 John 5:20: *"The Father loves the Son and shows him all he does."*

Jesus' claim: He and God share unbroken intimacy in which there are no secrets; they are in constant communication and God reveals to Jesus everything he is doing.

What Others are Saying:

Lawrence O. Richards: In the East great emphasis was placed by artisans on trade secrets. The metalworker, the glassworker, the maker of dyes—all guarded their processes and skills jealously. Typically these were family secrets, passed on from one generation to the next. While apprentices outside the family might be employed, even those who served loyally for years were unlikely to be taught all the family secrets, lest they leave and establish a competing establishment. By contrast, the son works with his father from childhood. The son watches the father mix his compounds or add distinctive finishing touches to work done in his shop. As they work together day by day, the father teaches his son all his secrets. Such a son can "do nothing by himself" but instead can do "only what he sees his father doing." In time the work of the father and the son becomes indistinguishable because the father "loves the son and shows him all he does."[6]

4 John 5:21: *"Just as the Father raises the dead and gives them life, even so the Son gives life to whom he is pleased to give it."*

Jesus' claim: He and God are equal in lordship over life and death; both can <u>raise the dead</u>.

5 John 5:22, 27: *"The Father judges no one, but has entrusted all judgment to the Son . . . He has given him authority to judge because he is the Son of Man."*

Jesus' claim: God so completely trusts him he has placed mankind's judgment totally <u>in Jesus' hands</u>, because, being human, Jesus can judge from the human perspective.

6 John 5:23: *"All may honor the Son just as they honor the Father. He who does not honor the Son does not honor the Father who sent him."*

Jesus' claim: He is worthy of the same honor as God—failure to honor Jesus is failure to honor God.

7 John 5:24–25: *"Whoever hears my word and believes him who sent me has eternal life and will not be condemned; he has crossed from death to life . . . a time is coming and has now come when the dead will hear the voice of the Son of God and those who hear will live."*

Jesus' claim: Spiritual resurrection and eternal life depend on listening to what he says and believing God is the One who sent him; paying attention to Jesus' words can bring spiritually dead people to life . . . now.

8 John 5:26: *"As the Father has life in himself, so he has granted the Son to have life in himself."*

Jesus' claim: Just as the Father's existence depends on no one but himself, so the Son's existence depends on no one but himself.

Dallas Willard: Nothing other than God has this character of *totally* self-sufficient being, or self-determination.[7]

9 John 5:28–29: *"A time is coming when all who are in their graves will hear his [the Son's] voice and come out—those who have done good will rise to live, and those who have done evil will rise to be condemned."*

☞ **GO TO:**

Deuteronomy 32:39; 1 Samuel 2:6; John 4:47, 49–50 (raise the dead)

Acts 17:31 (in Jesus' hands)

KEY Outline:

Jesus' Claims
He does what God does
He knows God's secrets
He raises the dead
God made him judge
He shares God's honor
He gives eternal life
Like God he's self-existent
The dead rise at his call
He always pleases God

What Others are Saying:

☞ **GO TO:**

Revelation 20:11–13
(the dead)

Jesus' claim: He has the power to call <u>the dead</u> from their graves to face their eternal destinies, and one day he will do precisely that.

10 John 5:30: *"By myself I can do nothing; I judge only as I hear, and my judgment is just, for I seek not to please myself but him who sent me."*

Jesus' claim: As God's Son, Jesus' judgment is always absolutely just, because he lives for one purpose—to please his Father.

What Others are Saying:

J. I. Packer: Jesus constantly affirmed that, in the day when all appear before God's throne to receive the abiding and eternal consequences of the life they have lived, he himself will be the Father's agent in judgment, and his word of acceptance or rejection will be decisive. . . . God's own appointment has made Jesus Christ inescapable. He stands at the end of life's road for everyone without exception.[8]

C. S. Lewis: A man who said the sort of things Jesus said wouldn't be a great moral teacher. He would either be a lunatic on the level of a man who says he's a poached egg, or else he would be the devil of hell; you must take your choice. Either this was and is the Son of God, or else a mad man or something worse. You can shut him up for a demon; or you can fall at his feet and call him Lord and God. But don't come up with any patronizing nonsense about his being a great moral teacher. He hasn't left that alternative open to us.[9]

Corroborating Witnesses

☞ **Check It Out:**

John 5:31–47

☞ **GO TO:**

Deuteronomy 19:15
(Jewish . . . law)

In first century courts, according to <u>Jewish</u>, Roman, and Greek <u>law</u>, no witness could testify in his own behalf. Other witnesses must be called to testify for him. Jesus didn't need human testimony to prove his equality with God. But if Jewish leaders needed witnesses, he provided them, hoping to convince them to believe (verse 34). In verses 33–40 Jesus called four "witnesses" to substantiate his claims. Here they are with the gist of their testimony:

Witness 1: John the Baptist: *"This is the Son of God"* (John 1:34).

Witness 2: The saving mission on which God sent Jesus: *"It is finished!"* (John 19:30).

Witness 3: The Father's voice (1) heard at Jesus' baptism: *"You are my son, whom I love; with you I am well pleased"* (Luke 3:21–22); and (2) heard by people, like Peter: *"You are the Christ, the Son of the Living God"* (Matthew 16:16).

Witness 4: The Old Testament Scriptures (Luke 24:44–47; John 1:45):

1. The Law of Moses <u>pictured</u> Christ's work in its rituals and sacrifices.
2. The prophets <u>predicted</u> details of his person and work.
3. The Psalms <u>foreshadowed</u> his death and resurrection.

These witnesses can still be heard speaking from the pages of the Bible. Knowing who Christ really is depends, to some degree on spending time studying the Bible and <u>applying</u> (living) its principles. Without applying the teachings of Scripture to our everyday living, Bible study becomes an exercise in spiritual arrogance. This is precisely what kept the rule-bound religionists of Jesus' day from accepting the testimony of Jesus and his "witnesses" (above), recognizing him as their Messiah, and submitting to his authority (John 5:37–47). They knew the <u>*letter*</u> of the Scripture but they failed to catch its <u>*spirit*</u>.

John Masefield:

The trained mind outs the upright soul,
As Jesus said the trained mind might,
Being wiser than the sons of light,
But trained men's minds are spread so thin
They let all sorts of darkness in;
Whatever light man finds they doubt it,
They love not light, but talk about it.[10]

John Charles Ryle: If a man is not thoroughly honest in his professed desire to find out the truth in religion—if he secretly cherishes any idol which he is resolved not to give up, if he privately cares for anything more than God's praise—he will go on to the end of his days doubting, perplexed, dissatisfied, and restless, and will never find the way to peace.[11]

> **Luke 6:1–2** One Sabbath Jesus was going through the grainfields, and his disciples began to pick some heads of grain, rub them in their hands and eat the kernels. Some of the Pharisees asked, "Why are you doing what is unlawful on the Sabbath?"

☞ **GO TO:**

Hebrews 10:1 (pictured)

Hebrews 1:1; Matthew 1:22; 2:6; 4:15–16 (predicted)

Psalm 22 (foreshadowed)

John 7:17 (applying)

Something to Ponder

What Others are Saying:

☞ **GO TO:**

2 Corinthians 3:6 (letter . . . spirit)

☞ **GO TO:**

Deuteronomy 23:25
(permitted to pluck)

1 Samuel 21:1–6
(violated a law)

Leviticus 24:5–9
(consecrated bread)

Numbers 28:9–10
(priests working)

Matthew 12:41–42
(greater than)

David: Israel's most
illustrious king

Pentateuch: First five
books of the Old
Testament

Tabernacle: Jewish tent
of worship during desert
wanderings

consecrated bread: 12
loaves kept on a table,
symbol of communion
with God

"Picking" A Fight

Back in Galilee, Jesus and his disciples again ran head-on into the Sabbath issue. One Sabbath day as they walked through ripened grainfields, they plucked a few heads of grain, rubbed them in their hands, and snacked on the kernels. With one mouthful of seeds they busted five Sabbath rules to smithereens! Count 'em:

1. The rule against reaping on the Sabbath (plucking the heads)
2. The rule against threshing on the Sabbath (rubbing the heads between their hands)
3. The rule against winnowing grain on the Sabbath (tossing the shucks aside)
4. The rule against preparing food on the Sabbath (all of the above)
5. The rule against eating food that had been prepared on the Sabbath

The "Sabbath police" (otherwise known as Pharisees) were out in force, and immediately questioned the "offenders'" actions.

According to Moses' law, the poor were <u>permitted to pluck</u> standing grain in order to sustain life and limb. But according to the Sabbath traditions, hunger was no excuse for breaking the law.

Jesus disagreed with the Pharisees and stated six reasons:

1. **David** <u>violated a law</u> actually found in the **Pentateuch** and was never punished for it (Matthew 12:3–4). On the run from King Saul, David and his hungry men went into the **Tabernacle** and ate **consecrated bread**, which could legally be eaten only by priests. He was excused because of his hunger and his greatness.

2. <u>Priests working</u> at the Temple technically *"break the Sabbath"* every week, and the Law declares them exempt (Matthew 12:6) on the basis that service at the Temple is more important than strict adherence to the Sabbath regulations.

3. *"Something"* (Someone) *"<u>greater than</u> the temple is here"* (Matthew 12:6). That Someone is Christ. Those who serve him (his disciples) are exempt from some Sabbath rules simply because of the greatness of the One they serve.

4. The Sabbath was set aside for the spiritual and physical refreshment of people; people were not created to be drudging slaves of <u>burdensome</u> Sabbath restrictions (Mark 2:27).

5. God's purpose in the no-work-on-the-Sabbath commandment was never to stifle <u>concern for people</u>. The leaders' condemnation of the disciples for eating was evidence they misunderstood the true spirit of the Sabbath (Matthew 12:7).

6. Christ is ultimately Lord and has the last word on the Sabbath, its meaning and purposes (Matthew 12:8; Mark 2:28; Luke 6:5).

The Reach For Renewal

Given Jesus' compassion for the physically challenged, what happened next was to be expected. He was teaching in a synagogue in Galilee. In the congregation were the ever-present religious establishment spies—*"the scribes and the Pharisees."* Also in attendance was a man with a withered right hand. It was a situation for which the scribes and Pharisees had waited: *"They watched him closely to see if he would heal on the Sabbath"* (Luke 6:7).

In "an atmosphere of glorious defiance,"[12] Jesus called the man forward so no one would miss what was about to take place. The rabbis taught that it was okay to rescue a farm animal who had fallen into a pit on the Sabbath, even if the animal was in no danger of dying (Matthew 12:11). But, unless the disease or injury was life threatening, a person could not be given medical treatment until another day.

Jesus disdained such compassionless reasoning: *"Of how much more value . . . is a man than a sheep!"* he demanded. Then he swept aside the whole catalog of nit-picking Sabbath regulations with one straightforward declaration: *"It is lawful to do good on the Sabbath"* (Matthew 12:12). Turning to the man he said, *"Stretch out your hand!"* The man did, and his hand was restored.

Athanasius: In the synagogue of the Jews was a man who had a withered hand. If he was withered in his hand, the ones who stood by were withered in their minds.[13]

☞ **GO TO:**

Acts 15:10
(burdensome)

Hosea 6:6
(concern for people)

**GOSPEL QUARTET
IN HARMONY**

Matthew 12:9–13
Mark 3:1–5
Luke 6:6–10

KEY Outline:

Christ, Greater than
King David
The ministering priests
The Temple
The Sabbath

**What Others
are Saying:**

GOSPEL QUARTET
IN HARMONY

Matthew 12:14
Mark 3:6
Luke 6:11

**Something
to Ponder**

**What Others
are Saying:**

Gentile church: churches
composed mostly of non-
Jews

first day: Sunday

☞ **GO TO:**

Romans 14:5–8 (any)

Hebrews 4:9–11 (rest)

Matthew 11:28–30
(with Christ)

***Dig
Deeper***

An Assassination Conspiracy Is Born

The Pharisees stormed out of the synagogue. They had found what they were looking for—a reason to condemn Jesus. The Sabbath issue became his enemies' immediate charge against him. From then on they would be in every crowd that gathered to hear him, listening, building their case for his execution.

These experts had read, studied, and dissected the Old Testament from Genesis to Malachi, and they took pride in their Bible knowledge. But with all their scholarship they missed the meaning. Christians must be careful of the same error— to read the words of Jesus and remain unchanged—to take our theology *to* the Bible and read into it our preconceived ideas, instead of taking our theology *from* the Bible, allowing it to change the way we think and live.

Philip Lloyd: When we read the Bible, how little compunction and honest heart-searching it often arouses in us! When we hear sermons, how much more apt we are to apply their rebukes and warnings to our neighbors than to ourselves! And therefore the sermon is only just one more sermon, and not Jesus himself speaking in our heart.[14]

The Sabbath Today

The early **Gentile church** moved away from Jewish-style observance of the Sabbath. In his New Testament letters, Paul teaches Christians have freedom to hold as special <u>any</u> day they are convinced in their minds is the right one, or, if they choose, to make every day special. Most Gentile Christians gathered on the **first day** of the week and never adopted the Jewish Sabbath regulations. The original Sabbath commandment is the only one of the Ten not repeated in the New Testament. Christians—even Christian Jews—are encouraged to find the Sabbath's original purposes fulfilled in the Sabbath-like <u>rest</u> of a living relationship <u>with Christ</u>.

The Sabbath in the New Testament Letters

Passage	What It Teaches about the Sabbath
Romans 14:5–6	Differing personal convictions regarding sacred days must never divide Christians.
Colossians 2:16–17	No one should judge others over the Sabbath. Sabbath foreshadows realities *in* Christ.

Hebrews 4:4–11	Sabbath keeping pictures the spiritual rest of God's people, which they experience by depending on what he has done for them rather than on their own works.

The Lord's Day in the New Testament

Passage	What Happened the First Day of the Week
Matthew 28:1; Mark 16:1; Luke 24:1; John 20:1	Jesus rose from the dead, met with disciples, showed wounds, taught Scriptures.
John 20:26	A week later the risen Christ meets Thomas and the other disciples.
Acts 20:7	Christians at Troas meet to share a meal, celebrate communion, hear teaching.
1 Corinthians 16:2	Christians at Corinth regularly meet, collect money for poor Jewish Christians.
Revelation 1:10	John, *"in the Spirit"* on *"the Lord's Day,"* receives the Revelation vision of Christ.

 **EARLY CHURCH LIFE:** Early Christian congregations met on either Saturday or Sunday, in some cases, both.

Under the New Testament no legal condemnation attaches to a seven-day workweek. In our clock-punching technological age, however, anyone who regularly takes one day in seven to relax from the pressures of work and to gather with others for <u>mutual encouragement</u> in the Christian faith will have more energy and inspiration for the other six days of work. The Sabbath-rest principle is a gracious gift.

Retreat To The Sea

After Jesus exposed them before the synagogue congregation for theological inconsistency and lack of compassion, the scribes and Pharisees were *"furious"* (Luke 6:11). Mark reports they were so determined to destroy Jesus they were even willing to conspire with their worst political enemies, the **Herodians** (Mark 3:6).

> **Matthew 12:15–16** Aware of this, Jesus withdrew from that place. Many followed him, and he healed all their sick, warning them not to tell who he was.

Too Soon For The Cross

For Jesus to continue to preach in the synagogues would be to risk all-out public opposition from the forces joined against him. The final confrontation that would end in crucifixion would eventually come, and he knew it. But it was too soon. His own people did not yet understand the kind of king he was and the kind of kingdom he would establish. He had not yet trained leaders to shepherd his movement after his death. To buy time, he left the synagogues and moved to the open-air setting of the Galilean shore.

Too Soon For The Crown

Crowds of Galileans followed him to the sea. The throngs became more cosmopolitan as people came from greater distances and all directions—Judea and Jerusalem, Idumea (Edom, far to the south, bordering Arabia), east of Jordan, and Tyre and Sidon (pagan cities on the Mediterranean coast northwest of Galilee) (Mark 3:7–8). The sick rushed to touch him. His men readied a boat to whisk him from the danger of being overwhelmed.

As he healed people Jesus warned them not to openly confess him as Messiah (Mark 3:12). He was Messiah. But popular belief was that Messiah would be a conquering king who would lead Israel in military victory over its enemies. He had not been sent for that kind of conquest, but to rescue believers from sin through his death on the cross. Development of a premature movement to crown him king might lead to badly timed conflict and scuttle the work he had been sent to do.

Matthew understood. He quotes the prophet Isaiah to explain (Isaiah 42:1–4; Matthew 12:19–21). The ancient prediction makes it clear:

- Christ would first be a *"servant,"* not warrior (verse 18).
- He would not be a combatant or politician (verse 19).
- He would not inflict harm (verse 20).
- Instead of smashing the Gentiles, he would offer them hope (verse 21).

Study Questions

1. Name two rules Jewish teachers had added to the Sabbath commandment that helped make it a burden instead of a blessing. Why was carrying one's bed on the Sabbath considered so terrible?

☞ **GO TO:**

John 12:22–33; Luke 19:31–33; Mark 8:31–32 (he knew it)

Matthew 26:18; John 2:4; 7:6, 8, 30 (too soon)

2. What was the healed man's defense when questioned about carrying his bed? What was Jesus' defense when they accused him of breaking the Sabbath?
3. In what ways is Christ equal to his Father in heaven?
4. Who and what are the four witnesses Jesus calls to verify his claims?
5. How had the scribes and Pharisees neglected the meaning of "I desire mercy, not sacrifice?" (Matthew 12:7)
6. By healing a man's withered hand on the Sabbath in the synagogue, what did Jesus demonstrate?
7. When have you fallen into the trap of *"offering sacrifice"* while *"neglecting mercy"*? What can you do today (or this week) to change that?

CHAPTER WRAP-UP

- Jesus healed a lame man at the Pool of Bethesda on the Sabbath; religious leaders questioned the man for carrying his bed; Jesus deliberately ignored unreasonable and unmerciful Sabbath regulations. (John 5:1–15)

- Jesus defended his actions by claiming equality with God in work, authority to raise the dead, and as giver of eternal life; he cited four witnesses to his claims. (John 5:16–47)

- The Sabbath issue was pressed when Jesus' disciples picked grain on the Sabbath; he healed a man on the Sabbath, declaring the Sabbath was for doing good and showing mercy, and that he was Lord of the Sabbath. His enemies conspired to kill him. (Luke 6:1–11)

- To avoid a full-scale confrontation with his enemies, he took his ministry outdoors; crowds came from all directions and were healed; he warned them not to tell. (Matthew 12:15–21)

13 THE INNER CIRCLE

CHAPTER HIGHLIGHTS

- The Power Team
- School of Kingdom Life
- Bill of Rights
- Jesus and the Old Testament
- No Phony Baloney Spirituality
- First Things First
- Da Judge

Let's Get Started

Jesus would have only three years to prepare the kingdom-of-God movement to carry on without his visible leadership. Powerful political and religious forces were already looking for the right moment to terminate him. He met the challenge with a simple but brilliant strategy. He would leave behind a cadre of spiritually powerful people. They would be equipped with careful instruction, the living model of his life, each other's support, and the gifts and power of the Holy Spirit.

GOSPEL QUARTET IN HARMONY

Matthew 5–7
Mark 3:13–19
Luke 6:12–49

> **Mark 3:13–15** Jesus went up on a mountainside and called to him those he wanted, and they came to him. He appointed twelve—designating them apostles—that they might be with him and that he might send them out to preach and to have authority to drive out demons.

The Power Team

To this point, the New Testament historians have named seven men who spent time with Jesus in the early days of his public ministry: Andrew, Simon Peter, James, John, Philip, Nathanael, and Levi (Matthew). They are identified as "**disciples**." Unnamed others also were identified that way. Luke describes *"a large crowd"* as *"disciples"* of Jesus (Luke 6:17). According to Jesus' strategy, the time came to select from the growing number of his followers those who would form the leadership team to lead the assault on the world.

☞ **Check It Out:**

Mark 3:13–19

Luke 6:12–16

disciples: pupils, followers

"The Twelve"

After spending a *"night in prayer"* (Luke 6:12), Jesus called his disciples together to announce his choice of 12 to be trained as *"apostles."* The men he chose would be <u>foundation stones</u> in the <u>living temple</u> of his Spirit—men equipped to continue Christ's ministry on earth.

By worldly standards the people Jesus chose were poorly qualified for leadership. They were ordinary working stiffs, mostly poor but not impoverished. All were skilled at some trade or craft (like Levi's genius for cheating taxpayers!). They could read and write but were not well educated. They were untrained in theology—not a clergyman among 'em. Polite society denounced some of them as "<u>sinners</u>"—meaning they didn't obey the religious rules. By association with John the Baptist, several showed eagerness for Messiah's arrival. They were part of the responsive group who'd already indicated a desire to be with Jesus (Luke 6:13).

☞ **GO TO:**

Matthew 10:2–4; Mark 3:16–19; Luke 6:14–16; Acts 1:13 (apostles)

Ephesians 1:19–20 (foundation stones)

1 Corinthians 3:16 (living temple)

Luke 5:8, 30; 15:1–2 (sinners)

EARLY CHURCH LIFE: Jesus' choice of apostles shows that, just as with everything else in Scripture, church leaders are to be mutually dependent, to share the responsibility, and to work together.

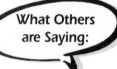
What Others are Saying:

KEY POINT

Christ chooses leaders who are responsive to him.

William Barclay: They had two special qualifications. First, they had felt the magnetic attraction of Jesus. . . . And second, they had the courage to show that they were on his side. Make no mistake that did require courage. Here was this Jesus calmly crashing through the rules and regulations; here was this Jesus heading straight for an inevitable collision with the orthodox leaders of his day; here was this Jesus already branded as a sinner and labeled as a heretic; and yet they had the courage to attach themselves to him. No band of men ever staked everything on such a forlorn hope as these Galileans, and no band of men ever did it with opener eyes.[1]

Who's Who

PETER: Also called Simon and Cephas ("Rock"). Fisherman. Impulsive, brash. Introduced to Jesus by his brother Andrew. One of the first five to follow Jesus. First to confess Jesus as *the Son of God* (Matthew 16:15–16). One of the three closest to Jesus.

Who's Who

ANDREW: Peter's brother. Fisherman. Son of John (Jonah). Introduced to Jesus by John the Baptist. Brought his brother Peter to Jesus. Left fishing trade to follow Jesus.

JAMES: Brother of John. Son of Zebedee and Salome. Fisherman. Left father and fishing business to follow Jesus. Volatile personality. The brothers were nicknamed "sons of thunder" (Mark 3:17; Luke 9:51–55). One of the three closest to Jesus.

JOHN: Brother of James. Son of Zebedee and Salome. Fisherman. Ambitious (see Matthew 20:20–28). "Son of thunder." May be the "disciple Jesus loved" in the gospel of John (see John 13:23; 19:26; 20:2; 21:7, 20–24). One of the three closest to Jesus.

PHILIP: Name means "lover of horses," which may describe either him or his father. One of the first to meet Jesus. Brought his friend (or brother) Nathanael to Jesus. Slow to catch on who Jesus really was (John 14:7–11).

BARTHOLOMEW: Name means "son of *tolmai*." *Tolmai* is Hebrew for "plowman"—may have been a farmer. May be the same as Nathanael, Philip's friend from Cana (John 21:2). Bartholomew/Nathanael was skeptical of Jesus at first because he came from Nazareth.

MATTHEW: Name means "gift of God." Son of Alphaeus (Mark 2:14). Possibly James the Younger's elder brother. Also called Levi. Customs officer. Probably hated by fellow Jews for collecting foreign taxes.

JAMES: Son of Alphaeus and Mary, also called "James the Younger" (Mark 15:40) to distinguish him from John's brother (who may have been older). Probably Matthew's brother (compare Matthew 10:3 and Mark 2:14).

THOMAS: Nicknamed Didymus, "the twin." Cautious. Yet willing to follow Jesus into danger (John 11:16). Genuine believer who struggled with uncertainty. "Doubting Thomas."

SIMON: Also called "the Zealot" or "the **Cananaean**" (Mark 3:18). The "Zealot" I.D. indicates he was zealous for the Jewish Law and/or he was a member of the movement committed to violent overthrow of Roman rule and assassination of Jewish collaborators.

Cananaean: an Aramaic word meaning "Zealot"

Who's Who

THADDAEUS: Also called "Judas the son of James" and "Jude." "Judas" is the Greek, "Jude" the Latin, for "Judah," a common Jewish name (Matthew 10:4; 13:55; Acts 5:37; 9:11; 15:22). May have been son of the apostle James and grandson of fisherman Zebedee.

Who's Who

JUDAS ISCARIOT: *Iscariot*, may mean "man of Kerioth." Kerioth was a Judean town. This may indicate Judas was the only non-Galilean apostle. Father's name: Simon. Treasurer (John 12:5–6) of the apostolic group.

Why Did Jesus Choose These Twelve?

KEY Outline:

Jesus' Team
Disciples
Apostles
Friends

First, they were *"disciples"* (Luke 6:13). They were chosen because they were teachable, moldable, and eager to learn from him. Second, they would become *"apostles"* (Luke 6:13). He would train them as ambassadors for his kingdom and give them authority to preach and drive out evil spirits (Mark 3:14–15). Third, he wanted them with him (Mark 3:14), as intimate friends. Through personal relationship with him and each other, they would become like him (Luke 6:40).

KEY POINT

People work better in teams.

KINGDOM OF GOD

Church and kingdom leadership develops and operates best in a context of personal friendship, not through a system of powerful "bosses."

What Others are Saying:

Stu Weber: A flock of geese, by flying in the "V" formation, actually adds at least 71 percent more flying range than if each bird were flying on its own. As each bird flaps its wings, it actually creates an updraft for the bird immediately following. Left to itself, the lone goose experiences a drag and resistance that causes it to long for the flock. When the lead bird in the formation tires, it simply rotates back in the wing and another flies the point. . . . If our feathered friends know it . . . why should we be so slow to learn it? Together is better. . . . Some men have caught it. They've reached out toward other men in moments of need and vulnerability. They've taken the risk and grabbed a few friends. And they've changed their world! . . . The strength of two or more can make you fly higher and longer, pull bigger loads, and be more of the man you were meant to be.[2]

GOSPEL QUARTET IN HARMONY

Matthew 5–7
Luke 6:17–49

Christ's School Of Kingdom Life

Jesus' teachings are the constitution and bylaws of *"the kingdom of heaven."* The most basic "kingdom teachings" are concentrated in two major "sermons": The Sermon on the **Mount** (Matthew 5–7) and the Sermon on the **Plain** (Luke 6:17–49). These may be two **versions** of the same message, or they may be two sermons delivered on separate occasions. Jesus preached these ideas <u>all over Galilee</u> and Judea.

What on Earth Is "the Kingdom of Heaven"?

Three interchangeable terms are used in the New Testament to identify the movement of God on earth: (1) *"the kingdom of **heaven**"* (used mainly by Matthew who wrote for a Jewish audience because Jews tended to avoid direct use of God's name), (2) *"the kingdom of God,"* and (3) *"the kingdom."*

A kingdom is (1) the sphere (domain) of a king's rule, (2) a form of government (monarchy), (3) the people who submit to the rule of the king, (4) the society and culture that develops under the king's rule, and (5) the nation, municipality, or community in which people ruled by the king live their daily lives in relationship with the king and one another.

The kingdom of God is all those things. The Bible teaches that the kingdom of God will <u>never end</u>. It will ultimately reach perfection at a time in the future when <u>every person</u> on earth bows to Jesus Christ as Lord and <u>King of Kings</u>. Until that time, the **church**, the kingdom's <u>advance contingent</u>, provides <u>glimpses</u> of that future kingdom in the way it applies Jesus' principles to its relationship with God and its life together as the **community** of believers.

THE BIG PICTURE 🔍

> **Matthew 5–7** Jesus' dream is not merely of believing individuals living heroic Christian lives alone against the world. His dream is of his followers facing the challenges of faith together, in a close-knit community guided by principles like the ones he taught in the Sermon on the Mount.

Bill Of Rights For The King's Country

Jesus begins his description of the Christian life with nine statements known as "The **Beatitudes**." A play on words calls them "*be*-attitudes" because they describe attitudes that produce the kind of *be*-havior that makes possible the unique lifestyle of the kingdom of heaven community. The Beatitudes introduce a cata-

---

Mount: Greek: mountain, hill

Plain: Greek: level place, plateau, valley

versions: Matthew's eyewitness account; Luke's from interviews with witnesses

☞ **GO TO:**

Matthew 4:17, 23 (all over Galilee)

Luke 1:32–33 (never end)

Philippians 2:10–11; Revelation 5:13 (every person)

Revelation 19:6–16 (King of Kings)

Matthew 16:15–19 (advance contingent)

Ephesians 2:6–7; 3:10–11 (glimpses)

heaven: created universe beyond earth; invisible spiritual dimension; God's home

church: original word means "those who are called out"

community: network of relationships, city, family, fellowship

Beatitudes: from Latin word for "blessed" or "fortunate"

KEY POINT

The Beatitudes de-scribe "be-attitudes."

☞ **Check It Out:**

Matthew 4:24–5:1

Luke 6:17–20

born again: *God's children through believing and receiving Jesus*

Remember This . . .

Jesus is Lord: *commitment to let Jesus run one's life*

☞ **GO TO:**

John 1:12–13; 3:3–8
(born again)

1 John 5:19
(unbelieving world)

Matthew 16:15–17;
Romans 10:9
(conviction)

Luke 9:59–62
(Do it now!)

John 7:38; Acts 1:8;
Philippians 4:13;
1 Thessalonians 5:24
(resources and energy)

log of teachings designed to pull the kingdom of God idea down from the ivory towers of heady theology and put it right smack dab in the middle of down-and-dirty situations of the everyday lives and relationships of earthlings.

Who's This Sermon For?

From celebrity seekers and enemy spies to serious truth seekers, they flocked to hear him preach. But the primary target of these teachings was the believing minority scattered among the crowds—his disciples (Matthew 5:1–2; Luke 6:20). He was drawing true believers—the **born again**—into a special community through which his Good News could be carried to the world.

If you expect the <u>unbelieving world</u> to adopt Jesus' teach-ings as its way of life . . . fahgeddaboudit! Unless he specifi-cally states otherwise, Jesus does not expect these values to be adopted by secular societies to make this a "kinder, gen-tler" world. The kingdom community is founded on the <u>con-viction</u> that **Jesus is Lord**.

Gentlemen, Start Your Engines!

The ideals in Jesus' sermons are not for some groovy future world we can only dream of till this one gets its act together. Every word has a "<u>Do it now!</u>" ring. Sure, this is difficult stuff. Perfection waits until God's reign is recognized worldwide. But Christ's fol-lowers are expected to apply these principles now . . . with the <u>resources and energy</u> available in their relationship with him. The apostle Paul said it: *"I can do everything through him who gives me strength"* (Philippians 4:13).

The Less-Traveled Road To Success

The *Amplified Bible* lists meanings of the original word for *blessed*: "happy, to be envied, and spiritually prosperous [that is, with life-joy and satisfaction in God's favor and salvation, regardless of their outward conditions]" (Matthew 5:3). In other words, successful!

Jesus turns accepted formulae for success and happiness up-side down. Success has nothing to do with wealth, power, or worldly honor. Such things may actually undermine true success. Personal success revolves around character issues, attitudes, val-ues, and behavior. These are also the issues that guide successful development of the community of faith.

F. R. Maltby: Jesus promised his disciples three things—that they would be completely fearless, absurdly happy, and in constant trouble.[3]

Jesus' Formula for Success: The Beatitudes

MATTHEW 5:3–10

> ***Blessed*** (happy, spiritually prosperous, successful) *are . . .*
>
> The poor in spirit—*The vulnerable*, confess their poverty (material/spiritual), forced to depend on God. *"The kingdom of heaven belongs to them."*
>
> Those who mourn—*The broken*, who weep over their sins, allow their hearts to break over what breaks God's heart. *"They will be comforted."*
>
> The meek—*The gentle*, who demand nothing, give themselves to God and others, teachable, flexible. *"The earth is their inheritance."*
>
> Those who hunger and thirst for righteousness—*The intense*, who are dissatisfied with the depth of their own spirituality, obsessed with desire for justice, fairness. *"Their desire will be satisfied."*
>
> The merciful—*The compassionate*, whose lives are marked by the "inefficiency" of concern for cripples, misfits, the hurting. *"They will be given mercy."*
>
> The pure in heart—*The single-minded*, who are surrendered to Jesus, and are undefiled by their own evil and their own virtues.[4] *"They will have a clear view of God."*
>
> The peacemakers—*The reconcilers*, who are actively involved in healing troubles and conflicts between people. *"They will be recognized as true children of God."*
>
> Those who are persecuted because of righteousness—*The despised*, whose living, radical contradiction to cultural values and ways brings them rejection and trouble. *"The kingdom of heaven is theirs."*

KEY Outline:

Success Involves
Relationship with God
Character
Attitudes
Values
Behavior

Larry Richards: When first heard by the disciples, the familiar words of the beatitudes must have sounded jolting and strange. . . . Implicit is a rejection of the values which lie at the core of human civilizations and which shape most individual personalities. . . . Jesus . . . sets up a whole new package of values, proclaiming that in *these* you and I will find fulfillment.[5]

> **Luke 6:22–23** Blessed are you when men hate you, when they exclude you and insult you and reject your name as evil, because of the Son of Man. Rejoice in that day and leap for joy, because great is your reward in heaven. For that is how their fathers treated the prophets.

Strange Reasons To Celebrate

For people looking for real success, it is good to know that when you're poor, hungry, shedding tears, rejected, and hated for telling the truth, you are in excellent company—it's how God's witnesses have always been handled by a world rejecting him!

What Others are Saying:

Polycarp [about to be burned at the stake for his refusal to renounce Christ]: O Lord God Almighty, the Father of thy well-beloved and ever-blessed son, by whom we have received the knowledge of thee . . . I thank thee that thou has graciously thought me worthy of this day and this hour.[6]

☞ **Check It Out:**

Luke 6:24–26

The Millionaires' Club

Ah, to be "blessed" with mountains of moolah, sacks of simoleons, freight cars full of filthy lucre, tens of tons of legal tender, surrounded by all the toys and trash the green stuff can buy, laughing one's way through life among phawning, phlattering (phony) "phriends!" What could be more wonderful?

Jesus chooses the word "**woe**" to describe such a situation! To be satisfied with what wealth can get is a spiritual disaster. It hides a shriveling soul settling for less than the best life has to offer.

woe: *Greek: ouaí!, a wail of anger, pain, frustration, bitterness*

Remember This . . .

Jesus was laying the groundwork for a new society. In his kingdom community, citizens <u>care for</u> one another. They are generous. They have a kingdom-shaped view of material possessions. Unless they learn the value of poverty, hunger, sorrow, rejection, and the dangers of wealth, they cling too tightly to the things of the world and are never free to help in a liberality of spirit that demonstrates true love for Jesus.

☞ **GO TO:**

Luke 12:32–34; Acts 2:44–46; 4:32–35; 6:1–7 (care for)

> **Matthew 5:13–16** You are the salt of the earth. But if the salt loses its saltiness, how can it be made salty again? It is no longer good for anything, except to be thrown out and trampled by men. You are the light of the world. A city on a hill cannot be hidden. . . . Let your light shine before men, that they may see your good deeds and praise your Father in heaven.

KEY POINT

Materialism is a shortcut to "woe."

Salty Saints, Shining Cities, And Flaming Lamps

The old baloney about religion being "a private thing" (meaning: "It's none of your business!") is out the window. Jesus' followers make a visible difference. Jesus uses three homely illustrations to get this point across.

1. *"Salt."* Emphasis is on the distinctive flavor life lived by the values of the kingdom brings to the world. There's a difference. You can taste it.

2. *"City on a hill."* Nazareth, Jesus' hometown was on a hill. At night its lights were visible from Cana, nine miles away. The emphasis is on the high visibility of a community of people living together by Jesus' happy values.

3. *"Lamp."* Christ's followers are *"the light of the world."* The lamp Jesus was thinking of was a pottery bowl full of olive oil with a wick set ablaze. It only fulfilled its purpose when the wick was lit and the lamp was put where it illuminated the house.

What Others are Saying:

William Barclay: In a worried world, the Christian should be the only man who remains serene. In a depressed world, the Christian should be the only man who remains full of the joy of life. There should be a sheer sparkle about the Christian, but too often he dresses like a mourner at a funeral, and talks like a spectre at a feast. Wherever he is, if he is to be the salt of the earth, the Christian must be the diffuser of joy.[7]

Robert Weber: The church is to be the one institution on earth not ruled by the gods of this world. It does not accommodate itself to cultural norms. It functions differently than other institutions because it is rooted in a confession which stands in radical antithesis to the worldly ideologies which rule the institutions of society. Therefore the church as church is a radical witness to the world, a community of different people, a light set on a hill, a salt which has not lost its strength.[8]

Harry Emerson Fosdick: They were a fallible group and he knew it, but he called them "the light of the world" and the "salt of the earth." The modern reader of the Gospels often wonders at Jesus' faith in God the Father, despite his life's tragedy, but that is easier to understand than his faith in those disciples. He demanded of them a quality of life far above the average.[9]

> **Matthew 5:17, 20** Do not think that I have come to abolish the **Law or the Prophets**; I have not come to abolish them but to fulfill them. . . . For I tell you that unless your righteousness surpasses that of the Pharisees and the teachers of the law, you will certainly not enter the kingdom of heaven.

KEY POINT

God's Law is "fulfilled" when we understand and live by its spirit, not just by its letter.

righteousness: moral harmony with God's character

Something to Ponder

What Others are Saying:

Jesus And The Old Testament

Jesus declared in no uncertain terms that nothing he taught contradicted the Old Testament Law or Prophets. His mission was to *"fulfill"* the Law (Matthew 5:17). "Fulfilling the law" was the way rabbis described what they were doing when they sought to give their students a true and full understanding of God's Word. Jesus says that's what he's doing. The **righteousness** of kingdom citizens can *"surpass the righteousness of the Pharisees and the teachers of the law"* because in the ideal of the kingdom community people face up to and deal with their heart motives as well as their actions.

A Pharisee could hate someone and still pride himself in being law-abiding because he'd never killed anyone. Technically he was right. But according to Jesus he was tromping all over the spirit of the law and would be judged as certainly as a murderer.

R. T. France: The Old Testament . . . remains a permanent and crucial revelation of the will of God, but its application can no longer be by the simple observance of all its precepts as literal regulations for Christian conduct. The key to its interpretation is in Jesus and in his teaching, with its sovereign declaration of the will of God at a far deeper level than mere rule-keeping.[10]

KINGDOM OF GOD *Where the Rubber Meets the Road*

Jesus cites six Old Testament commandments and goes behind the scenes to show God's concern not only with sinful acts, but also with motives and hypocritical practices that, in effect, break the commandments. These six examples show the difference his teachings make and how the new kingdom society is able to fill up the spiritual blank spaces left by the letter of Old Testament Law.

1. **The Law:** *"Do not murder"* (Matthew 5:21; Exodus 20:13).

   Lawbreaking Motives and Practices: Disrespect and derision (**Raca!**), slander, anger, hatred, are a murderer's attitudes and will be judged (Matthew 5:22; 1 John 3:15).

2. **The Law:** *"Do not commit adultery"* (Matthew 5:27; Exodus 20:14).

   Lawbreaking Motives and Practices: Looking at a woman (not one's wife) wishing to have sex with her is mental and spiritual adultery (Matthew 5:28).

3. **The Law:** *"A man may divorce his wife if he gives her a divorce certificate"* (Matthew 5:31; Deuteronomy 24:1).

   Lawbreaking Motives and Practices: The cause of divorce is hardness of heart; God's original intent is lifelong commitment (see Matthew 19:8).

4. **The Law:** *"Do not break your oath, but keep the oaths you have made to the Lord"* (Matthew 5:33; Exodus 20:16).

   Lawbreaking Motives and Practices: First century Jews had an elaborate system of breakable and unbreakable promises, depending on the precise words spoken (Matthew 5:34–36). For example, an oath was binding if spoken "toward Jerusalem" and not binding if spoken "by Jerusalem."[11]

5. **The Law:** Revenge is permissible: *"Eye for eye, and tooth for tooth"* (Matthew 5:38; Exodus 21:24).

   Lawbreaking Motives and Practices: This rule was intended to limit revenge, to keep simple offenses from escalating into wars of vengeance. But it came to be used as an excuse for retaliation. For Christ's follower, retaliation is out (Luke 6:27–36).

6. **The Law:** *"Love your neighbor and hate your enemy"* (Matthew 5:43; Leviticus 19:18).

   Lawbreaking Motives and Practices: They interpreted *"your neighbor"* to mean "your fellow Israelite." *"Hate your enemy"* was never God's instruction, it developed as a rationale for prejudice, bitterness, and vengefulness.

Raca!: *Aramaic for spitting; epithet of contempt; like saying: "You're worthless!"*

KEY Outline:

Cause and Effect
Anger—Murder
Lust—Adultery
Hardheartedness—
  Divorce
Rationalizing—Promise
  breaking
Unforgiveness—
  Revenge
Bitterness—Hate for
  enemies

Dig Deeper

Murderous attitudes	Deuteronomy 19:1–13; Matthew 18: 15–19
Adultery	Deuteronomy 22:13–30; Proverbs 5:3–22; 6:20–35
Divorce	Deuteronomy 24:1–4; Matthew 19: 1–11; 1 Corinthians 7:10–16
Oaths	Exodus 23:1; Psalm 24:3–4; James 5:12
Revenge	Exodus 21:23–25; Deuteronomy 19: 16–21; Romans 12:19
Love for all	Exodus 23:4–5; Proverbs 25:21–22; Romans 12:14, 17–21

What Others are Saying:

Henri J. M. Nouwen: What my enemy deserves is not my anger, rejection, resentment, or disdain, but my love. Spiritual guides throughout history have said that love for the enemy is the cornerstone of the message of Jesus and core of holiness.[12]

Jesus' Dream For Life In The Kingdom

Jesus expected his teachings to make a difference in the way his followers lived and related to one another. Following each "fulfilled" (fully explained) commandment, he describes a new way of responding to everyday moral challenges which can contribute to the development of a corporate lifestyle in radiant contrast to the lifestyle of the world. The ideal lifestyle that Jesus hopes his followers will experience together has these six characteristics:

1. Peace is so important that personal conflicts are dealt with even if you have to skip church to do it! (Matthew 5:22–26).

2. Sexual purity is so prized that individuals are willing to take radical steps to control what they look at, touch, and imagine (Matthew 5:29–30).

3. Lifelong commitment and marital faithfulness are the norm (Matthew 5:32).

4. A Christian always keeps his promises: He is so honest that when he says yes it always means yes; when he says no it always means no (Matthew 5:34–37).

5. Retaliation is out. Relinquishment of personal rights is in, along with liberal sharing of material possessions, and forgiveness of debts. Christians are free in Christ to go beyond the demands of the law into love and liberality (Matthew 5:39–42).

KEY POINT

Jesus expects his followers to treat their enemies the way God treats his.

6. The response to one who insults or injures (whether inside or outside the community of faith) is love, expressed in three ways (Luke 6:27–28): (1) going out of our way to be **deliberately kind** and to do our enemies good, (2) countering their insults with **blessing**, and (3) praying for them.

deliberately kind: Greek word for love here is agape—*deliberate, active kindness*

No Phony Baloney Spirituality

Using three religious practices that first century Jews considered true *"acts of righteousness,"* Jesus attacks **hypocrisy** and shows it has no place in the kingdom society:

1. Giving to the needy (verses 2–4)
2. Praying (verses 5–15)
3. Fasting (verses 16–18)

☞ **Check It Out:**

Matthew 6:1–18

blessing: word means to speak well of and wish them well

hypocrisy: playing a part that masks the actor's real self and motives

All three are good things to do, but not if the motive is *"to be honored by men."* Show-offy piety is as phony as a three-dollar bill and has no eternal value. It's an act of arrogance and quite disgusting. Christians are to do these things quietly, for the Lord's eyes only, with the goal of pleasing him.

Once again, as in Matthew 5, the issue is not the act itself but the motive and attitude behind it. The prayer Jesus taught his disciples to pray—"The Lord's Prayer"—reveals the secret attitudes that are to mark Christians, their work, worship, and sacrifice.

The Lord's Prayer is set in the middle of Jesus' warning against spiritual dishonesty. Was that prayer intended to become what it has for many Christians—a rote recitation for formal worship—or was it intended as a practical guide for expressing the attitudes toward God necessary for living together in his kingdom?

Something to Ponder

The Lord's Prayer[13]

Words of the Prayer: Matthew 6:9–13	Kingdom Attitude Expressed
Our Father	Affirms the pray-er's personal relationship with God
in heaven	Recognizes God as Lord over the whole universe
hallowed be your name	Expresses deep respect for God and his holy character
your kingdom come	Invites God's rule in our lives and relationships
your will be done on earth as it is in heaven	Complete, personal surrender to God's will
Give us today our daily bread	Dependence on God's involvement and supply of needs
Forgive us our debts, as we also have forgiven	Readiness to be forgiven and to forgive others
Lead us not into temptation but deliver us from the evil one	Looks to God for protection from temptations and trials that go with living together in the kingdom community

William Barclay: The highest reward never comes to him who is seeking it. If a man is always seeking reward, always reckoning up that which he believes himself to be earning, then he will in fact miss the reward for which he is seeking. And he will miss it because he is looking at God and looking at life in the wrong way.[14]

Richard Foster: In the same way that a small child cannot draw a bad picture so a child of God cannot offer a bad prayer.[15]

Martin Luther: The fewer the words, the better the prayer.[16]

> **Matthew 6:19–21** Do not store up for yourselves treasures on earth, where moth and rust destroy... but store up for yourselves treasures in heaven.... For where your treasure is, there your heart will be also.

First Things First

Jesus now moves to deal with another area of human life in which the priorities of the world and the priorities of the kingdom collide. To the consternation of all who are trying to balance a quest for material success with life in the kingdom society, Jesus states flat out that it is not possible to focus on both God and money. We cannot seek what can be gained in this world and single-mindedly serve God and tend kingdom business at the same time.

> **Matthew 6:22–24** The eye is the lamp of the body. If your eyes are good, your whole body will be full of light. But if your eyes are bad, your whole body will be full of darkness. If then the light within you is darkness, how great is that darkness. No one can serve two masters. Either he will hate the one and love the other, or he will be devoted to the one and despise the other. You cannot serve both God and **Money**.

Money: "Mammon," meaning wealth or property; here it's personified as if a rival god

Remember This . . .

It's impossible to focus on worldly riches and kingdom riches at the same time.

Time To Redraw The Old Treasure Map?

The direct connection between this section of Jesus' sermon and life in the church (the present earthly contingent of kingdom society) is in his statements about the eyes: *"If your eyes are good . . . if your eyes are bad"* (verses 22–23). The original word for *"good"* is used other places in the Bible to mean "generous," and the word for *"bad"* means "grudging" or "stingy." A clue to whether or not your eyes are focused (and your heart set) on earthly instead of heavenly treasure is the way you respond to people in need. If your sharing is grudging, it's time to redraw your treasure map (that is, rethink your priorities).

☞ **GO TO:**

Romans 12:8;
  2 Corinthians 9:11;
  James 1:5 (generous)

Deuteronomy 15:9–10;
  Proverbs 23:6; 28:22
  (grudging or stingy)

2 Corinthians 9:6–11
  (sharing)

> **Matthew 6:25–28** Therefore I tell you, do not worry about your life, what you will eat or drink; or about your body, what you will wear. Is not life more important than food, and the body more important than clothes. Look at the birds of the air; they do not sow or reap or store away in barns, and yet your heavenly Father feeds them. Are you not much more valuable than they? Who of you by worrying can add a single hour to his life?

Job One: The Kingdom

Jesus goes on to point out that temptation to focus one's energy on worldly things is not just a problem for the rich. Anxiety about the lack of worldly things like food, drink, clothing, health, and longevity, is the flip side of the same broken record! Worry about such things is unnecessary since our Creator, who knows we have such needs, is also our Father who is committed to care for us as certainly as he cares for birds and wildflowers. Birds and flowers *never* worry about such stuff!

☞ **GO TO:**

Romans 8:15–17
  (our Father)

Matthew 7:7–11;
  Philippians 4:19
  (committed to care)

Remember This . . .

Materialism is a problem for two groups of people: the greedy rich and the anxious poor. It is possible for the poor to love money as much as the rich do. While the poor may worry about how they will pay the rent and still have money to buy food, the rich may worry that people will try to cheat them and steal their money and their things. Both groups can be equally preoccupied with money. Their focus on material things hinders their contentment and their relationship with God. (To learn more about what the Bible says about money, see WBFW, pages 125–147.)

Matthew 6:29, 33 And why do you worry about clothes? See how the **lilies** of the field grow. They do not labor or spin. Yet I tell you that not even **Solomon** in all his splendor was dressed like one of these. If that is how God clothes the grass of the field, which is here today and tomorrow is thrown into the fire, will he not much more clothe you, O you of little faith? But seek first his kingdom and his righteousness, and all these things will be given to you as well.

KINGDOM OF GOD

Seek His Righteousness

The key to understanding this teaching and reaping its restful benefits is in the phrase *"seek first his kingdom and his righteousness."*

- God's kingdom is his rule. Seeking his righteousness revolves around committing to please God ahead of everything else.
- God's kingdom is the community of believers. Seeking his kingdom revolves around serving the needs of your fellow Christians and contributing to the peace and spiritual prosperity of the community of faith.

These two priorities can provide both the divine and human support needed to enjoy a worry-free life now and tomorrow (verse 34).

Remember This . . .

When tempted to worry, seek God's righteousness and fellowship with other believers. Take your problems to God in prayer (see WBFW, page 20).

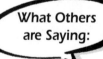

What Others are Saying:

Leonard I. Sweet: There is no excuse for a sadsack, wallflower spirituality. God's pantry is never bare. God's party is never dull.[17]

Luke 6:37 Do not judge, and you will not be judged. Do not condemn and you will not be condemned. Forgive, and you will be forgiven. Give and it will be given to you.

Here Come Da Judge!

Someone might ask, "What if I join the kingdom and I'm the only one who gets it right?" (I won't even discuss how arrogant that question is.) Just when we thought we'd found heaven on earth, Jesus does a reality check!

Here's the reality: My fellow citizens in the kingdom community are all at different stages in their spiritual development. If that weren't enough, they have strange personalities—quirks, blind spots, neuroses, bad breath, weird ways of looking at things, and a ton of baggage they brought with them when they stumbled through the <u>narrow gate</u>! And I've gotta live with 'em!

Dial 911! How am I supposed to deal with the weaknesses and spiritual lapses of these people?

Got your pencil and paper ready? Here's the plan:

1. Don't **judge** (Luke 6:37).

2. Don't **condemn** (verse 37).

3. **Forgive** (verse 37).

4. Give what people most need: grace. The more you give the more you get (verse 38).

5. Clean up your own <u>act</u> (get honest about your own faults) before you try to clean up theirs! (verses 41–42).

Why should you do these things? Because somebody's watching. And it's not Big Brother. In this case, it's not even God. It's your fellow disciples. They are learning what it's like to be like Jesus by watching you! (verses 39–40).

Other believers learn how to live the Christian life by watching you! Conscious mentoring and being mentored is what the Christian life is all about. Jesus was the original mentor, and he calls his followers to show others what they have learned.

Oswald Chambers: Never water down the word of God, preach it in its undiluted sternness; there must be unflinching loyalty to the word of God; but when you come to personal dealing with your fellow men, remember who you are—not a special being made up in heaven, but a sinner saved by grace.[18]

☞ **Check It Out:**

Matthew 7:1–6

Luke 6:37–42

☞ **GO TO:**

Matthew 7:13–14
 (narrow gate)

judge: Greek: krino, evaluate, assess, select, prefer

condemn: to pass sentence on someone, disapprove

forgive: cancel the debt you feel they owe you

☞ **GO TO:**

Galatians 6:1 (act)

Remember This . . .

What Others are Saying:

thornbushes: buckthorn
bush whose black berries
resemble tiny grapes

thistles: desert thistle
whose flower resembles a
fig blossom

**GOSPEL QUARTET
IN HARMONY**

Matthew 7:15–23
Luke 6:43–45

ACT OF THE HOLY SPIRIT

Helps Christians
to be discerning

KEY POINT

Living in the kingdom
community means
accepting a broad
variety of people.

Christianese: the right
religious words

Remember
This . . .

What Others
are Saying:

> **Matthew 7:15–16** Watch out for false prophets. They
> come to you in sheep's clothing, but inwardly they are
> ferocious wolves. By their fruit you will recognize them.
> Do people pick grapes from **thornbushes**, or figs from
> **thistles**?

KINGDOM ![crown] **OF GOD**

Fruit Inspecting 101 or How to Tell a Wolf from a Shepherd

"Judge not!" Jesus says. Then in the next breath he adds:
"Except when it comes to spiritual leaders." There are wolves
among the shepherds. Sour grapes on the trellis. How can you tell
a pseudo prophet from the real McCoy? Two clues:

1. Inspect his or her *"fruit."* A good grape . . . uh, er, I mean
   spiritual leader . . . will be a good character. Galatians
   5:19–23 says, *"The acts of the sinful nature are obvious:
   sexual immorality, impurity and debauchery; idolatry and
   witchcraft; hatred, discord, jealousy, fits of rage, selfish
   ambition, dissensions, factions and envy; drunkenness, orgies,
   and the like. . . . The fruit of the Spirit is love, joy, peace,
   patience, kindness, goodness, faithfulness, gentleness and
   self-control."*

2. Check out his or her obedience (Matthew 7:21–23).
   Speaking **"Christianese"** and even preaching powerful
   sermons or doing miracles are not the signs of a sound
   spiritual guide. Jesus states the issue clearly: *"Not everyone
   who says to me, 'Lord, Lord,' will enter into the kingdom of
   heaven, but only he who does the will of my Father who is in
   heaven"* (verse 21).

The first thing a person must know to be Christ's follower is
that Christ is Lord. Verbal confession is not enough. The
outcome (fruit) of a person's life is determined by whether
or not that person really pays attention to Jesus' teachings
and seeks to put them into practice.

Oswald Chambers: These messages of Jesus Christ are for the
will and the conscience, not for the head. If you dispute the Sermon on the Mount with your head, you will blunt the appeal to
your heart.[19]

> **Matthew 7:24** Therefore everyone who hears these words of mine and puts them into practice is like a wise man who built his house on the rock.

A Tale Of Two Builders

There are, Jesus insists, only two ways to build a life—one leads to success; the other, to disaster. Consider two housebuilders:

1. The *"wise builder"* gives prime attention to the foundation, being careful to build his house on bedrock. What's this bedrock? Listening to and putting into practice the teachings of Jesus.

2. The *"foolish builder"* builds his dream house in a dry wash, without a foundation. What is the nature of this sandy footing? Letting Jesus' teachings go in one ear and out the other, without making a difference.

Push comes to shove when both houses are struck by a violent storm. Life throws its worst at both, as life will do. The life built on Jesus and his wisdom weathers the storm; the life built without him collapses! The "gut issue" is the choice to submit all of life to the authority of Christ.

C. S. Lewis: Never, never pin your whole faith on any human being: not if he is the best and wisest in the whole world. There are lots of nice things you can do with sand; but do not try building a house on it.[20]

Study Questions

1. How many of his disciples did Jesus choose to be apostles? How many of the apostles can you name? Which one was a tax collector? Which ones had been fishermen? Which were brothers? Which one was a political radical?
2. Identify four of the five definitions of a kingdom.
3. Who does Jesus expect to be able to live by the teachings in the Sermon on the Mount?
4. In Luke 6, what word does Jesus use to describe the situation and future of the rich? Why does he state so strongly the dangers of material possessions and the value of poverty?
5. How does Jesus "fulfill" the Old Testament Law?

KEY POINT

To tell good leaders from bad ones, check their fruit and their obedience.

☞ **Check It Out:**

Matthew 7:24–27

Luke 6:46–49

KEY Outline:

Wisdom
Builds on Jesus' teachings

Foolishness
Ignores Jesus' teachings

What Others are Saying:

6. What are three ways Jesus teaches us to express love for our enemies? (See Luke 6:27–28.)

7. Considering this past week in the light of the Sermon on the Mount (Matthew 5–7), is your "bank" on earth or in heaven? What needs to be done to change accounts?

CHAPTER WRAP-UP

- Jesus chose twelve men to be with him and to become his apostles to lead his movement after his death and resurrection. (Luke 6:12–16)

- Jesus taught his disciples the basic principles of the kingdom of God, the community of believers in which they would live their lives. (Matthew 5–7; Luke 6:17–49)

- Jesus turned the world's view of success and happiness upside down with nine statements called "the Beatitudes." (Matthew 5:3–12)

- Jesus said he did not come to abolish the Old Testament but to fill up what was lacking in it by dealing with the motives behind the Ten Commandments, and showing how life among his followers was radically different from the world. (Matthew 5:17–48)

- He attacked religious hypocrisy and called his followers to attitudes and actions based on honesty, humility, and dependence on the Father in heaven. (Matthew 6:1–18)

- He taught the importance of having our hearts set on heavenly rather than earthly treasures. If we seek the kingdom of God first, all our needs will be supplied. (Matthew 6:19–34)

14 REVOLUTION OF LOVE

Let's Get Started

Jesus, the young prophet from Nazareth, preached the ancient truths in a strange and powerful new way, pressing each issue deeper to deal in startling new ways with his hearers' values, attitudes, and allegiances. This brash sermonizer spoke straight from the heart. He dared to challenge familiar interpretations of Scripture and accepted social protocols. He called for radical change in the way people related to friends, enemies, the world, and God. He called for an end to rationalizing a way around the great fundamental moral values. His reasoning was so clear and honest there was no room for debate. And he had the audacity to claim listening to his teachings and putting them into practice was the only way to avert disaster!

All his speechless enemies could do was look for some violent way to silence his piercing preachments.

GOSPEL QUARTET IN HARMONY

Matthew 8:1, 5–13; 11:2–30; 12:22–50
Mark 3:20–35
Luke 7:1–8:3, 19–21

THE BIG PICTURE

> **Matthew 7:28–8:1** When Jesus had finished saying these things, the crowds were amazed at his <u>teaching</u>, because he taught as one who had authority, and not as their teachers of the Law. When he came down from the mountainside, large crowds followed him.

 **GO TO:**

Matthew 5–7; Luke 6:17–49 (teaching)

A Walk On The Wild Side

People stuck to him like glue, though they scarcely understood where being with him would take them. Even those who believed he was the Messiah were far from comprehending what messiahship actually involved. Hebrew nationalism dominated their messianic dreams. The idea of a crucified Messiah was unthinkable. The amazing things the New Testament reports Jesus did from then on would demonstrate three things: (1) God had sent him, (2) he was who he claimed to be, and (3) he was a completely unique commander-in-chief leading a completely unique army of revolutionaries in the most unique revolution ever to disturb the status quo.

If they stayed on the path he was traveling, they would find themselves out on a limb, cut off from the security of the ancient ways, on a scary, new walk on the wild side! They would be there to see the old religious structures collapse in a Christ-led revolution of love.

> **Luke 7:1–6** Jesus . . . entered Capernaum. There a centurion's servant, whom his master valued highly, was sick and about to die. The centurion heard of Jesus and sent some elders of the Jews to him, asking him to come and heal his servant. When they came to Jesus, they pleaded earnestly with him, "This man deserves to have you do this, because he loves our nation and has built our synagogue." So Jesus went with them.

A Revolutionary Model Of Faith

The Roman army maintained a military presence at Capernaum. A **centurion** stationed there had a dearly loved slave who was disabled with painful paralysis and near death. Slaves in Roman culture were treated as property to be used, so this owner displayed an unusual attitude toward his worker. The officer was not a Jew; he was a Roman. Most Romans would do anything to avoid duty in Israel, but this soldier loved the Jews. While he had not formally **converted** to Judaism, he was one of the non-Jewish believers called "<u>God-fearers</u>," who, in many cities, attended the synagogue, believed in God, studied the Scriptures, and lived by many of the Jewish rules.

This centurion's faith in Jesus was real (verse 9), but as a Gentile, he wasn't sure how the Jewish Jesus would respond. He knew legalistic protocols barred strict Jews from entering **Gentile houses**. He evidently didn't know how much Jesus delighted in dispensing with man-made regulations that got in the way of helping people in need.

**GOSPEL QUARTET
IN HARMONY**

Matthew 8:5–13
Luke 7:1–10

☞ **GO TO:**

Acts 10:2 (God-fearers)

centurion: commander of 100 men; "backbone of the Roman army"

converted: circumcised, living by Jewish religious rules

Gentile houses: homes of non-Jews

At first, the centurion sent Jewish friends with the request for Jesus to come (Luke 7:3). Jesus was on his way to the centurion's house when the Roman dispatched a second group to tell Jesus he didn't deserve to have him come into his home (verse 6), nor did he feel worthy to approach him personally (verse 7). At some point, according to Matthew's account, the centurion himself came and expressed his urgency (Matthew 8:5). Jesus was **amazed** at the soldier's attitude (Luke 7:9). He shocked Jewish onlookers by asserting that nowhere in Israel had he found faith as great as this Gentile's faith! The servant was healed (verse 10).

amazed: the original word indicates high admiration

Two things were admirable and different about the centurion's faith:

1. He acknowledged the principle of **grace**. While the Jews who recommended that Jesus help him thought his good works made him "deserving" (Luke 7:5), the centurion appealed for help, fully understanding he did not deserve it (verses 6–7).

2. He recognized the uniqueness of Jesus' authority—that (a) his authority is similar but superior to earthly authority; (b) Jesus has authority over people and created things (i.e., disease); and (c) his authority transcends space and distance. In other words, the Roman soldier recognized Jesus as more than "just another teacher."

Something to Ponder

☞ **GO TO:**

Ephesians 2:8–9 (grace)

grace: God's kindness to the undeserving

Centurions—New Testament Good Guys

Luke 7:1–10—Centurion of Capernaum: *"Not . . . such great faith even in Israel"*

Luke 23:46–47—Centurion at the cross: *"Surely this was a righteous man!"*

Acts 10—Centurion of Caesarea: *"Devout and God-fearing"*

Acts 23:17–18—Centurion of Jerusalem: Uncovers assassination plot against Paul

Acts 23:23–24—Two centurions of Jerusalem: Took Paul safely to Governor Felix

Acts 27:42–43—Centurion aboard ship: *"Wanted to spare Paul's life"*

KEY Outline:

Jesus' Authority
Is superior to earth's
Is over people and disease
Transcends space/ distance

☞ **Check It Out:**

Luke 7:11–17

☞ **GO TO:**

Luke 8:52 (professional mourners)

Nain: near Shunam, where Elisha raised a widow's son from the dead 800 years earlier (2 Kings 4:18–37)

cemetery: 10-minute walk from Nain is a burial ground, still used today

☞ **GO TO:**

Matthew 9:36; 15:32; Mark 8:2 (feeling compassion)

KEY POINT

God feels our pain.

☞ **GO TO:**

John 1:1–18 (God's expression)

expression: "the Word"

A Revolutionary Picture Of God

Jesus and his men took a hike to the village of **Nain** (see appendix A). The crowd went along. As they approached the town gate a funeral procession was headed for the **cemetery**. As a typical Jewish funeral, the pathetic procession would have been led by professional mourners, loud wailing, doleful flutes, crashing symbols, and the grief-stricken shrieks of the mourning mother. Her husband had died earlier. Now the bier carried the body of her **only son**. The mother was in bad shape. A woman seldom owned property; if her husband died and she had no children to care for her, she was often left destitute.

> **Luke 7:13** When the Lord saw her, his heart went out to her and he said, "Don't cry."

This God Has Feelings

The original language says, "*he was moved in his inner body parts.*" He cared deeply. When Jesus cared it was never just empty emotion. Whenever the New Testament records Jesus feeling compassion or sympathy toward someone, it also records him doing something about the situation.

> **Luke 7:14–16** Then he went up and touched the coffin, and those carrying it stood still. He said, "Young man, I say to you, get up!" The dead man sat up and began to talk, and Jesus gave him back to his mother. They were all filled with awe and praised God.

This God Has Come To Help

Witnesses drew two conclusions: (1) "*A great prophet has appeared among us,*" and (2) "*God has come to help his people.*"

Among first century Jews, a God who let himself be bothered by a widow's grief was a theological scandal! Theologians thought if God could be moved emotionally—with sadness, happiness, compassion, and anger—he would be changeable and not in control.

Jesus corrects that grotesque idea. As God's **expression**, he shows us a God who not only cares about people and their pain, but actually feels their pain with them! As he and his entourage left town, a widow's tear-stained face wore a smile. She and her dazed son, who'd just been to death and back, hugged each other for dear life. People knew they'd been **visited** by God (Luke 7:16).

visited: *"come to help"—God personally dropped in on his people*

> **Matthew 11:2–4** When John heard in prison what Christ was doing, he sent his disciples to ask him, "Are you the one who was to come, or should we expect someone else? Jesus replied, "Go back and report to John what you hear and see."

Medal Of Honor For A Revolutionary Hero

John the Baptist had stood toe-to-toe with powerful people and <u>courageously confronted</u> them with their need for spiritual change. He was there when the Holy Spirit came down like a <u>dove</u> and identified Jesus as God's *"beloved Son."* He was the first to <u>introduce</u> Jesus as *"the Lamb of God."* Because he <u>dared to confront</u> a wicked king about the illegitimacy of his marriage, John was arrested and thrown in the dungeon at **Machaerus Castle**, "one of the loneliest and grimmest and most unassailable fortresses in the world."[1]

Just Checking

Why then did such a man of faith and power send disciples to ask Jesus if he was really the Messiah? Was it his own need for comfort as his execution approached? Did he have doubts even after all he had seen and said about Jesus? Or was it to redirect the allegiance of his disciples from himself to Jesus? Whatever the reason, Jesus knew John would recognize the fulfillment of Old Testament <u>prophecies</u> of things Messiah would do.

So while John's messengers watched, Jesus healed the sick, freed the demon-harassed, restored sight to the blind, cured lepers, made the deaf hear, raised the dead, and cared for the poor.

> **Matthew 11:11** I tell you the truth: Among those born of women there has not risen anyone greater than John the Baptist; yet he who is least in the kingdom of heaven is greater than he.

First Prize Goes To . . . (Drum Roll, Please)

When the messengers left, Jesus paid John a high tribute. In giving this compliment, Jesus was spotlighting three things:

GOSPEL QUARTET IN HARMONY

Matthew 11:2–15
Luke 7:18–28

☞ **GO TO:**

Luke 3:19–20 (courageously confronted)

Luke 3:21–22 (dove)

John 1:35–36 (introduce)

Matthew 3:7–10 (dared to confront)

Machaerus Castle: Herod's fortress in the desert east of the Dead Sea

☞ **GO TO:**

Isaiah 61:1–2 (prophecies)

1. His character: In the raging wind of opposition to truth and justice, John was an immovable tree! No overindulged yes-man lolling about a king's palace, he was a tough-minded, rugged, uncompromising man of God (Luke 7:24–25; Matthew 11:7–8).

2. His work: John was a special kind of prophet. First, he prepared Israel for Messiah's arrival (Luke 7:26–27; Matthew 11:9–10). Second, in Spirit, power, and the strategic nature of his work, he was an "<u>Elijah</u>" (Matthew 11:14; Malachi 4:5–6; Luke 1:17. See also GWMB, pages 130–144).

3. His place in history: John was the living bridge between Old Testament prophecy and Law and the kingdom led by Jesus Christ (Matthew 11:12–13). John was the first hero of the revolution of love.

☞ **GO TO:**

1 Kings 18:16–45 (Elijah)

ACT OF THE HOLY SPIRIT

Empowered John for Elijah-like ministry

GOSPEL QUARTET IN HARMONY

Matthew 11:16–19
Luke 7:29–35

> **Luke 7:33–34** For John the Baptist came neither eating bread nor drinking wine, and you say, "He has a demon." The Son of Man came eating and drinking, and you say, "Here is a glutton and a drunkard, a friend of tax collectors and 'sinners.'"

"No Matter The Game, We Won't Play!"

As Jesus paid his tribute to the greatness of John the Baptist, the audience divided itself as it had from the baptizer's first desert cry for repentance. It was a divide that carried over into Jesus' ministry and would finally culminate in his death on the cross.

On one side were grassroots Israelites, including tax collectors—those turncoats who had long ago been written off by the nation's "patriots." They represented the varied multitude of ordinary sinners and spiritual desperados, weary of sin's "rewards," who found hope in John's call for repentance and his announcement that Messiah was coming. Now Jesus was building his kingdom society out of the same people (Luke 5:27–31). They applauded Jesus' tribute to the Baptist.

On the other side were the religious leaders—official and self-appointed. Since John's call to all regardless of status was a call to repent, being **baptized** by him would be admission they were not as righteous as they wanted everyone to think. So they rejected him and his roughshod crusade. Luke says it was because they *"rejected God's purposes for themselves"* (Luke 7:30).

baptized: *dipped in water as declaration of intent to change*

The Pharisees and experts in the Law represented people of every generation who, in order to take the spotlight away from their own shortcomings, look down their noses at anyone who suggests they might need to change.

Jesus compared them to two groups of children playing in the street.

"Let's play weddings," one group says.

The other group answers, "That's a silly game."

"All right then," the first group responds, "Let's play funerals."

"No!" responds the second group, "That game is too sad." No matter what game is suggested, they simply do not want to play.

John lived a strictly disciplined life: Ate simple food; drank no wine. The religious establishment wrote him off as a crazy ascetic living on bugs and honey. Jesus joined the party, ate and drank and spent time with sinners. They dismissed him as a glutton and a drunk. Spoiled brats! They refused to join the fun no matter how the game was played!

KEY POINT

Since they rejected God's will, the religious leaders rejected John and Jesus.

Leonard I. Sweet: John the Baptist's . . . funeral ethic with its fasting and flailing, its eating nothing but wild honey and locusts, its wearing nothing but a hair shirt, didn't appeal to you, Jesus is saying. But neither did my wedding ethic with its eating and drinking. What more do you want? God gave you a choice . . . a funereal faith or a dance spirituality. You rejected both.[2]

At Risk Of Scandal

Jesus never did anything that was morally questionable—except in the eyes of those looking for the slightest excuse to accuse him and willing to twist the truth to find it. But at the same time he never thought twice about risking his reputation to be there for some hurting, love-starved soul.

What Others are Saying:

GOSPEL QUARTET IN HARMONY

Matthew 12:22–50
Mark 3:20–35
Luke 7:36–8:3, 19–21

THE BIG PICTURE

Luke 7:36–39 A Pharisee invited Jesus to his house for dinner. During the meal, a woman who had lived a sinful life came and stood by Jesus, weeping. Her tears washed Jesus' feet. Then she wiped them with her hair, broke open a bottle of perfume she had brought, kissed Jesus' feet, and poured perfume on them.

Kiss Of The Forgiven

Jesus went to dinner at the home of a Pharisee named Simon. Proper etiquette dictated a respected guest should be greeted with

KEY Outline:

The Forgiven Prostitute

Washed Jesus' feet with tears

Wiped them with her hair

Kissed his feet

Bathed them in perfume

denarii: *money, one denarius equaled a day's wage*

KEY POINT

The more one is forgiven, the more one loves.

three gracious acts: (1) The host should greet him with the kiss of peace; (2) a servant should kneel and wash his feet; and (3) a pinch of incense should be sprinkled on his head.[3] This host's disrespect was obvious when none of these things were done for Jesus (verses 44–46).

The meal was served in the central courtyard around which finer Middle Eastern houses were built. Guests reclined on one elbow on couches around a low table, their unsandaled feet stretching out behind.

When the guest was a teacher, custom allowed for anyone to come into the courtyard and listen to the table talk. Among those who came to the Pharisee's house was the town prostitute. (We won't ask how these gathered religious leaders instantly recognized this woman of ill repute!) Bringing with her a jar of expensive perfume she stood behind Jesus, at his feet. As she stood there, she wept. Some of her tears fell on his bare feet. She bent over and wiped her unintentional tears from his feet with her hair. Then, quite intentionally, she kissed his feet, broke open the container of perfume, and emptied its fragrant oil on his feet.

While the Pharisee and his cronies squirmed, Jesus quietly accepted the woman's expressions of adoration and worship. Simon thought, *"If this man were a prophet, he would know who is touching him and what kind of woman she is—that she is a sinner!"* (Luke 7:39).

THE BIG PICTURE

Luke 7:40–50 "Simon," Jesus said, "I have a story to tell you about two debtors, one owed 500 **denarii** and the other 50. Neither could repay his debt, so the moneylender canceled both debts. Who will love him more?" Simon answered, "The one with the bigger debt." Jesus replied, "You didn't wash my feet when I came to your house, but this woman has poured perfume on them. Therefore, her many sins have been forgiven—for she loved much. But he who has been forgiven little loves little."

The Telling Story

Aware of the Pharisee's secret thoughts, Jesus told a story about two debtors. The two debtors represented Simon and the woman. The amounts owed represented how deeply each felt his or her need for forgiveness. The woman had a monumental sense of guilt.

Simon considered his sins minor. She was overwhelmed with gratitude for forgiveness and compelled to express it in a spendthrift demonstration of love for Jesus. Simon had so thoroughly rationalized his sin he failed to show Jesus even the simplest courtesies! Jesus gladly accepted her adoration, completely carefree of whether others were bothered by it or not.

> **Luke 8:1–3** . . . The Twelve were with him, and also some women who had been cured of evil spirits and diseases: Mary (called Magdalene) from whom seven demons had come out; Joanna the wife of Cuza, the **manager** of Herod's household; Susanna; and many others. These women were helping to support them out of their own means.

manager: Greek: epitropos—king's financial adviser, administrator

The "Impossible" Fellowship

Jesus traveled from town to town proclaiming the kingdom of God. He did not travel alone. The 12 apostles-in-training were with him along with *"many other"* disciples, including a group of women whose involvement with him had led to their personal transformation and healing, and who traveled with them and paid the bills. Two things are impressive about this group of fellow travelers:

KEY POINT

Faith is best expressed not independently, but in community.

1. The invitation to enter the kingdom of God was given in a context of sharing, fellowship, and mutual care. Seeing Jesus and his disciples living together provided an instant illustration of the community life into which he was calling them.

2. The mix of people who made up this early Christian fellowship was revolutionary: a woman with a dark past, a royal lady of the king's court, a carpenter, a couple of "super-patriots," a tax collector, some pugnacious fishermen, healed psychotics, poor and rich, male and female, and at least one potential traitor. It was a group too varied to get along. They were a microcosm of the diverse peoples who make up the church—the advance contingent of the kingdom of God—today. The thing that holds such a lumpy mix of souls together and makes it an indivisible family is Jesus Christ at the center.

Remember
This . . .

GOSPEL QUARTET
IN HARMONY

Matthew 12:22–50
Mark 3:20–35
Luke 8:19–21; 11:14–32

Beelzebub: *Meaning "lord of flies" or "lord of filth"; Satan*

Son of David: *title for Messiah based on prophecy he'd be from David's lineage*

KEY POINT

Jesus' enemies would stoop to anything to smear his reputation.

EARLY CHURCH LIFE: The early church was composed of a highly diverse group of people.

Jesus was the center, which kept the diverse group around him together. His teachings proved, *"There is neither Jew nor Greek, slave nor free, male nor female, for you are all one in Christ Jesus"* (Galatians 3:28).

> **Luke 11:14–15** Jesus was driving out a demon that was mute. When the demon left, the man who had been mute spoke, and the crowd was amazed. But some of them said, "By Beelzebub, the prince of demons, he is driving out demons."

The Attack Of The Mudslingers

If Jesus were in a modern political race, the last hours of the campaign would most certainly feature 30-second TV attack-ads. The ads would show the Nazarene standing over the quivering body of some pitiful foaming-at-the-mouth victim of evil spirit harassment. Headlines and an accusing voice would say, *"It is only by **Beelzebub**, the prince of demons, that this fellow drives out demons!"* (Matthew 12:24).

Fine print at the bottom of the screen would read: "Paid for by the Committee to Elect Pharisees."

The "politics of personal destruction" was not invented by late twentieth century Democrats and Republicans. Jesus had just healed a man who was blind and mute. Rank-and-file Jews were amazed. When they began to ask, *"Could [Jesus] be the **Son of David**?"* (Matthew 12:23), Jesus' enemies accused him of being in league with the devil.

> **Luke 11:17** Jesus knew their thoughts and said to them: "Any kingdom divided against itself will be ruined, and a house divided against itself will fall."

The Foolish "Wisdom" Of Belittling Christ

Jesus summoned the Jewish legal experts to a face-to-face meeting (Mark 3:23) and challenged the foolishness of their accusations with six powerful arguments:

1. Any kingdom, city, or family divided against itself is destined for collapse (Matthew 12:25). It is illogical to

214

GOD'S WORD FOR THE BIBLICALLY-INEPT

suggest Jesus drove out demons in cooperation with the prince of demons (verse 26). Would the devil make war on himself?

2. He threw their reasoning, that anyone casting out demons must be in league with the devil, back into their teeth: If his exorcism was of the devil, then the exorcism practiced by the Pharisee's **"sons"** was also of the devil! (verse 27). He knew they would never agree to that.

3. If, however, the **finger of God** (Luke 11:20) was the power behind what Jesus did, the only possible conclusion to be drawn was that God was present, in Jesus, establishing his kingdom and rule on earth (Matthew 12:28).

4. Jesus put the power of Beelzebub and the power of God at work in Jesus into perspective. *"How can anyone enter a strong man's house and carry off his possessions unless he first ties up the strong man? Then he can rob his house"* (Matthew 12:29). The *"strong man"* is Satan (Beelzebub). His *"house"* is the world (1 John 5:19). His possessions are men and women under his control. The power of the devil is no match for the power of *someone stronger* (Christ) who attacks and overwhelms him (Luke 11:22).

5. Jesus pressed the religious leaders for a personal decision concerning him: *"He who is not with me is against me, and he who does not gather with me, scatters"* (Luke 11:23). By trying to discredit him, the spiritual "shepherds" (Pharisees and Bible scholars) acted more like wolves, scattering the flock. Their responsibility was to gather the flock to their true Shepherd, Christ himself.

6. Jesus warned his enemies that mudslinging of the type in which they were indulging could be extremely dangerous to their health! They were telling people on the verge of trusting him (Matthew 12:23) that his works were of the devil (verse 24). They knew better. One of their group, Nicodemus, admitted he knew Jesus and his works were from God (see John 3:1–2). Any other sin a person may commit can be forgiven. But this sin—Jesus called it *"blasphemy against the Holy Spirit"*—is unforgivable.

Dan McCartney and Charles Clayton: With the casting out of demons, man's proper **viceregency** has already begun. Jesus did what Adam should have done; he threw Satan out of the Garden.[4]

☞ **GO TO:**

Exodus 8:19 (finger of God)

"sons": disciples

finger of God: *the Holy Spirit*

ACT OF THE HOLY SPIRIT

Gave Jesus power to work miracles

KEY POINT

Christ is stronger than the devil.

viceregency: *office of king's deputy*

What Others are Saying:

Remember This . . .

What puts blasphemy beyond pardon? For a person to be so set against God's purposes that, knowingly and with malice of forethought, he falsely identifies God's work as the devil's in order to keep others from believing in Jesus Christ, is to be so hard of heart and so seared in conscience that one is beyond hope of repentance or change. Jesus did not say they had crossed that line, but he threw up a blazing banner to warn them of the danger.

What Others are Saying:

John Charles Ryle: There is such a thing as a sin which is never forgiven. But those who are troubled about it are most unlikely to have committed it.[5]

☞ **GO TO:**

Jonah 1–4 (Jonah)

KEY POINT

Lying to keep others from believing in Jesus is extremely dangerous.

> **Matthew 12:38–41** Then some of the Pharisees and teachers of the law said to him, "Teacher, we want to see a miraculous sign from you." He answered, "A wicked and adulterous generation asks for a miraculous sign! But none will be given it except the sign of the prophet Jonah. For as Jonah was three days and three nights in the belly of a huge fish, so the Son of Man will be three days and three nights in the heart of the earth. The men of Nineveh will stand up at the judgment with this generation and condemn it; for they repented at the preaching of Jonah, and now one greater than Jonah is here."

"Show Us A Sign! Do Us A Miracle!"

Relentless in their rejection, the Pharisees and Bible scholars at the meeting changed the subject and demanded Jesus perform some sign to prove his messiahship. Blind liars, they had just seen him give a man who was blind and mute sight and speech, a miracle they immediately tagged as the work of the devil! They had no intention of believing in him.

sign: *proof, supernatural evidence*

Nineveh: *wicked city turned from its sins when Jonah preached*

He would not play their silly game! He told them to look for the one great proof of his authenticity and power: the **sign** of Jonah. As Jonah (see GWBI, pages 88–89) spent three days and nights in the stomach of a gigantic Mediterranean fish, so Jesus would spend three days and nights dead and buried in the earth, after which he would rise from the dead.

They would see it, and it would make no difference. Jonah's destination, the pagan city of **Nineveh**, repented in sackcloth when the fish released him. These hypocrites, for the most part, would not, although they would see someone **greater than Jonah**.

The ultimate sign of messiahship was Jesus' death, burial, and resurrection.

greater than Jonah: *Jesus' reference to himself*

"Big Brother's Flipped!"

The strain of Jesus' notoriety took its toll on his family. Seeing the crowds flocking to hear him, aware of the risk of making the revolutionary claims he made, watching the opposition intensify, Jesus' relatives began to think he'd gone too far. *"He is out of his mind!"* they concluded, and made plans to take him home and protect him from himself (Mark 3:20–21).

When they arrived to take him away, they were unable to get into the house where he was speaking, because of the crowd that had come to hear him. They sent word to Jesus that his *"mother and his brothers"* were standing outside and that they wanted to talk to him. There is no record they made contact. Their plans to take him into protective custody were frustrated.

> **Luke 8:21** He replied, "My mother and brothers are those who hear God's word and put it into practice."

A Real Family

Jesus used the occasion to announce that his true family (brothers, sisters, and mother) includes *"whoever does the will of God"* (Mark 3:35). Christ's revolution of love creates more than an audience or aggregation of unrelated adherents—our Elder Brother and Lord has made true believers members of his family!

I find few references to the **martial** character of the body of Christ in the New Testament. What is abundant are the references to the family life of the church. The most frequent biblical reference to fellow Christians is "brother" or "sister" or "**brethren**." "Brethren" is used 70 times. Older saints refer to younger believers as "dear children." And when they gather they greet each other with the kiss of love.

EARLY CHURCH LIFE: The church is Jesus' mother, brothers, and sisters.

GOSPEL QUARTET IN HARMONY

Matthew 12:46–50
Mark 3:20–21; 8:19–21
Luke 8:19–21

☞ **GO TO:**

Mark 6:3 (his brothers)

Mark 10:28–30
(brothers, sisters, and mother)

1 John 22:1, 12, 18, 28; 3:7, 18
(dear children)

Romans 16:16; 1 Peter 5:14 (kiss of love)

martial: *relating to war*

brethren: *fellow believers*

KEY Outline:

Jesus' Family
Hear the Word
Do God's will
Forsake old ties for new

Study Questions

1. What did the centurion recognize as unique about Jesus' authority?
2. What does Jesus' response to the sorrow of the widow at Nain teach us about God?
3. How did the lifestyle of John the Baptist differ from that of Jesus? Why did the religious leaders reject both of them?
4. What did the "sinful woman" do for Jesus that his Pharisee host did not do? Why the difference?
5. What did Jesus mean when he told the Pharisees and Bible scholars to look for the "sign of Jonah"? In what way were Jesus and Jonah alike?
6. Considering your life right now, would others see you as Jesus' "brother or sister" or as a distant relative? Why?

CHAPTER WRAP-UP

- For his disciples, following Jesus was a march into unfamiliar territory. Examples of faith came from unexpected sources (a Roman centurion). The picture of God that emerged was different from the picture they had grown up with, personal, caring. (Luke 7:1–17)

- John the Baptist sent messengers from his prison cell to Jesus to ask if he was, for sure, the Messiah. Jesus demonstrated his authenticity by the works he did. Then he gave John high praise and explained why the Pharisees refused to listen to him. (Matthew 11:2–19)

- While Jesus dined at the home of a Pharisee, a prostitute scandalized the gathering with emotional expressions of appreciation toward Jesus because of his message of forgiveness. Jesus used it to teach the Pharisee a lesson in forgiveness. (Luke 7:36–50)

- Jesus' enemies attacked with the slander that he did his miracles by the power of the devil. He showed them how illogical such a suggestion was, and how dangerous it was to knowingly attribute the work of the Holy Spirit to Satan. (Matthew 12:22–50)

- The Pharisees and Bible scholars demanded a sign to prove that Jesus was the Messiah. He told them to look for the sign of Jonah—a veiled prophecy of Jesus' death, burial, and resurrection. (Matthew 12:38–45)

15 THE STORYTELLER

CHAPTER HIGHLIGHTS

- Tales from the Trail
- A Seedy Saga
- Why Parables?
- Jesus' Parables

Let's Get Started

Who comes to mind when you think of the world's great storytellers? Aesop? Hans Christian Anderson? Mother Goose? Mark Twain? Edgar Allen Poe? C. S. Lewis? Stephen King? Walt Disney? Jesus?

The yarns Jesus spun captured the imagination of people who talked with him one-on-one, the 12 who hung out with him, and the crowds who came to hear him preach. Still today many who have never read the Bible refer in ordinary conversation and public speeches to the Prodigal Son, the Good Samaritan, the salt of the earth, and others of Jesus' punchy **parables** and biting one-liners. The Greek word *paraballein* means "to throw one thing down alongside another." Jesus' parables are sayings, stories, or metaphors he used to communicate truth by comparison.

Tales From The Trail

A group of men and women tagged along as Jesus hoofed it from one Galilean town to the next. As they walked the roads Jesus told true-to-life stories, using familiar objects and incidents to set priorities, correct misconceptions, shape attitudes, and teach concepts they must learn if they were to be part of the Jesus movement. For many, Jesus' stories were just stories. But for his inner circle, they became "revelations that pushed them to examine their understanding of God and themselves."[1]

**GOSPEL QUARTET
IN HARMONY**

Matthew 13:1–52
Mark 4:1–34
Luke 8:4–18

*parables: earthly stories
with heavenly meaning*

Emily Dickenson: The truth must dazzle gradually, or every man be blind.[2]

> **Matthew 13:3** Then he told them many things in parables, saying, "A farmer went out to sow his seed."

A Seedy Saga About Listening

The trail took them past a farmer seeding his field. "Look!" Jesus said, "a sower planting his crop!" Like a play-by-play announcer Jesus described the scene as he and his companions watched. It was a familiar sight. A man with a sack of grain walked up and down the field, "broadcasting" (see illustration, page 221). Again and again, his hand reached into the bag of seed, and scattered each handful in a circular motion. A wind gust caught some seed, depositing it on the beaten footpaths between the fields. Other seed fell where the Palestinian limestone was scarcely covered with a thin layer of dirt. Still others fell into the weedy soil at the corners of the field. Most fell where the sower intended—in good soil, rich and deep enough to produce a harvest.

"That's us and the people who listen to us!" Jesus may have said. Then, without explaining the meaning of the story, he added, *"He who has ears to hear, let him hear!"* (Matthew 13:9; Mark 4:9; Luke 8:8) which freely translated means, "Wake up and smell the coffee!"

> **Luke 8:9** His disciples asked him what this parable meant.

What Mysteries Lie Buried In The Seeding Story?

Jesus' disciples, seeing the puzzled looks on the faces of the crowd and struggling themselves to wrap their minds around the story's meaning, wished he'd put it in "plain English" (excuse me! "plain Aramaic"). They were frustrated and said, *"Why do you speak to the people in parables?"* (Matthew 13:10).

The key to understanding this parable is to focus on four types of listeners.

- *The seed* is the word of God—the Good News of the kingdom taught by Jesus (Matthew 13:19; Mark 4:14; Luke 8:11).

- *The hard-packed path* represents people who listen to Jesus'

Farmers in the ancient world walked through the fields, throwing handfuls of seed in a circular motion so that it scattered evenly on the ground. Then they used a plow to scratch the soil and lightly cover the seed.

words with closed minds ("My mind is made up; don't confuse me with facts!"). They have built around their hearts a comfort zone of religious habits, preconceived ideas, and prejudice. The Word never sinks in, and the **enemy** whisks away the new info like a buzzard snatching a scrap of road kill! (Matthew 13:19; Mark 4:15; Luke 8:12).

enemy: Satan

- *The rocky places* are people who look like they are listening, but beneath the façade of initial openness lie concretized prejudice, stubbornness, and fear. The Word of God sends down roots but runs with a dull thud into hidden resistance to anything that might disturb the comfy spiritual status quo of their shallow faith. Growth stops. Pressure comes. Faith makes like a dandelion doused in Weed-Be-Gone! (Matthew 13:20–21; Mark 4:16-17; Luke 8:13).

- *The thorny ground* pictures the listener who is genuinely receptive. Christ's words take root, sprout, and start to grow. But the listener's head is turned by distractions— anxiety, the seduction of wealth, and the nearly irresistible siren call to wallow in the world's voluptuous vanities. The gagging sound you hear is the life being strangled out of some split-hearted fool trying to sing the songs of the kingdom in harmony with the discordant serenade of **the world** (Matthew 13:22; Mark 4:18–19; Luke 8:14).

the world: everything in the present order of things that appeals to the soul as an object of desire apart from and in rivalry to God[3]

☞ **GO TO:**

John 15:2; Galatians
 5:22 (fruit)

1 Samuel 3:1–14
 (Samuel)

What Others
are Saying:

KEY Outline:

**Responses to Good
News**
Closed mind
Hidden resistance
Distraction
Teachableness

- *The good soil* is the responsive, teachable mind that lets
  Christ's teachings sink down deep, take root, wrap themselves around the hearer's welcoming heart, grow, and
  produce practical, profitable <u>fruit</u>. No secondary concerns
  are allowed to choke out the Word. Resistance to change is
  displaced by teachability and responsiveness. Kingdom-of-
  God values (values that promote the development of the
  kingdom community) become apparent in the lifestyle,
  priorities, and personal relationships of this person.

A. W. Tozer: Lord, teach me to listen. The times are noisy and
my ears are weary with a thousand raucous sounds which con-
tinuously assault them. Give me the spirit of the boy <u>Samuel</u> when
he said to thee, "Speak, for thy servant heareth." Let me get used
to the sound of thy voice, that its tones may be familiar when the
sounds of earth die away and the only sound will be the music of
thy speaking voice. Amen.[4]

> **Matthew 13:34–35** Jesus spoke all these things to the
> crowd in parables; he did not say anything to them
> without using a parable. So was fulfilled what was spo-
> ken through the prophet: "I will open my mouth in
> parables, I will utter things hidden since the creation
> of the world."

Why Did Jesus Speak In Parables?

New Testament Jesus-scholar Matthew, quoting Psalm 78:2, reminds us that the Old Testament promised that Messiah would be
a storyteller. Jesus was a brilliant teacher who never stopped teaching. Parables were a familiar teaching technique in Israel. He would
have first heard God's truth in parable form from his earthly father, Joseph. It was one of the ways Hebrew parents passed their
faith on to their children. Parables are a great way to teach for at
least six reasons:

1. Parables grab the listener's interest. Count on a good story
   to catch more listeners than a brilliant-but-abstract
   sermon . . . every time.
2. Parables turn abstract truth into pictures a listener can see
   clearly with the imagination. Stories magically turn words
   into flesh, ideas into tangible responses.

3. Parables start where a listener is—with what he already knows—and lead to where he should be and what he can know.

4. Parables disarm listeners' natural defenses against new ideas and change by letting them see themselves in the characters of a story.

5. Parables give listeners room to do their own thinking and make them responsible to discover truth for themselves. When a person thinks his or her own way to truth, that truth becomes more real and personal and potentially life-changing.

6. Parables—like any good joke or yarn—are easy to remember.

Jesus' teaching is so clear <u>even a child</u> can understand. But he does not feed it to us in pre-chewed form (like Gerber's baby food). He doesn't do our thinking for us.

KEY Outline:

Parables
Grab interest
Picture truth
Start with familiar
Disarm defenses
Allow thinking
Are memorable

Remember This . . .

Dallas Willard: Parables are not just pretty stories that are easy to remember; rather, they help us understand something difficult by comparing it to, placing it beside, something with which we are very familiar, and always something concrete, specific.[5]

Frank Peretti: Stories work. Jesus used them to capture the attention of his audience and drive home a point his listeners would long remember.[6]

> **Luke 6:40** A student is not above his teacher, but everyone who is fully trained will be like his teacher.

Jesus' Stories: Teaching With Its Feet On The Ground

Jesus' parables were part of a style of teaching in which the teacher does not depend on books or lecture alone to communicate truth. Jesus was not satisfied to cram his disciples' heads full of "amazing facts to impress their friends"! He was building lives—men and women who, under his tutelage, would become so much like him they could be mistaken for "<u>little Christs</u>." He wanted them to be *"fully trained."*

What Others are Saying:

☞ **GO TO:**

Luke 18:16–17;
 1 Corinthians 3:1–2;
 Hebrews 5:13
 (even a child)

☞ **GO TO:**

Acts 4:13; 1 Corinthians 4:15–16; Galatians 2:20; 2 Thessalonians 3:7–9 (little Christs)

To keep his disciples' learning experience close to the realities of their day-to-day lives, Jesus capitalized on what was happening around him as he went from town to town or taught down at the beach. A man in the crowd asks Jesus to order his brother to divide the family inheritance fairly. Jesus hands the responsibility back to the man to deal with his attitudes toward money, and spins the yarn about the <u>rich fool</u> who has succeeded at everything except getting ready to die.

☞ **GO TO:**

Luke 12:13–21
(rich fool)

Or he takes them back in memory to their mothers baking bread. While they are enjoying the sweet remembered smell of fresh-baked bread, he tells them that the growth of the kingdom of God in, among, and through them is not going to be what their rabbis have taught them to expect—a spectacular overthrow of occupation armies by a conquering messianic military general. Rather, it will be an almost invisible process of change—like the change yeast makes in bread dough (Matthew 13:33).

KEY POINT

Jesus teaches from life.

That is Jesus' teaching style: taking the familiar and concrete and using it to reveal the mysteries of life in the kingdom of God.

What Others are Saying:

Dallas Willard: By showing to others the presence of the kingdom in the concrete details of our shared existence, we impact the lives and hearts of our hearers, not just their heads. And they won't have to write it down to hold onto it.[7]

> **Matthew 13:11–13** He replied, "The knowledge of the secrets of the kingdom of heaven has been given to you, but not to them. Whoever has will be given more, and he will have an abundance. Whoever does not have, even what he has will be taken from him. This is why I speak to them in parables: 'Though seeing, they do not see; though hearing, they do not hear or understand.'"

Did The Great Storyteller Speak With "Forked Tongue?"

Jesus used stories to illustrate, reveal, and clarify spiritual truth. But often his parables hid spiritual truth from unbelievers while (in the same breath) revealing it to believers.

☞ **GO TO:**

Matthew 12:22–45
(the slander)

When Jewish leaders dragged their ugly opposition out into the open, spreading <u>the slander</u> that Jesus got his power not from God but from the devil, Jesus changed his storytelling style. He told more stories. At one point Mark comments that Jesus said nothing to the crowd that was not in parable form (Mark 4:34), but he crafted his stories to conceal truth from people who were too lazy or too prejudiced to do the thinking required to understand what he was illustrating. When they were alone, he would disclose the meaning of each parable to his closest followers. He explained: *"The knowledge of the secrets of the kingdom of heaven has been given to you, but not to them"* (Matthew 13:11).

People who are responsive and willing to know the truth can always unlock the secrets of the parables. But people who knowingly reject Jesus and turn a deaf ear to what God is saying through him develop a <u>hard-heartedness</u> that clamps their minds shut against the truth.

Deliberate spiritual deafness has the potential to make it <u>impossible</u> for a person to know the secrets of God's kingdom (Matthew 13:13–15). Those who reject the truth are responsible for their rejection.

Jesus' sense of mission urged him to teach and preach to everyone regardless of whether or not they believed. But his method of teaching, using parables, divided his audiences. Parables don't convey information or mask it. They present Christ's claims in such a way that the believers are challenged and the unbelievers are frustrated.

> Jesus' teaching style began with the familiar and concrete and moved from there to reveal mysteries in the kingdom of God.

William Barclay: The parable reveals truth to him who desires truth; it conceals truth from him who does not wish to see the truth.[8]

The Bazooka Factor

I hasten to add a disclaimer: Jesus' stories sometimes had the power to penetrate even closed minds, and to blast holes through even the most rigid walls of spiritual resistance. Some people, blind and deaf to the truth, can be touched by a story when nothing else will reach them. Even Jesus' worst enemies <u>sometimes understood</u> his parables and trembled in their sandals!

Henry H. Halley: The kingdom that Jesus intended to establish was so utterly different from what was commonly expected of the Messiah that it was necessary for him to be very tactful. So he used these stories, to illustrate the origin, development, mixed character, and consummation of the kingdom, which to us seem very plain, but were enigmas to his immediate hearers.[9]

☞ **GO TO:**

Isaiah 6:10;
   Romans 1:18–32;
   Hebrews 3:7–19;
   1 Timothy 4:2
   (hard-heartedness)

Mark 3:28–30
   (impossible)

ACT OF THE HOLY SPIRIT

Helped listeners to understand Jesus' parables

Remember This . . .

What Others are Saying:

☞ **GO TO:**

Luke 20:9–19 (sometimes understood)

What Others are Saying:

KEY POINT

Sometimes hard-headed people can be reached with a story.

☞ **GO TO:**

Luke 15:8–9 (lost coin)

What Others are Saying:

metaphors: figurative language

Decoding A Parable

Here are some things to remember that can help us discover the meaning of Jesus' parables:

1. *Note the context in which the story is told.* Jesus used parables to answer someone's question or to shed light on some issue. When trying to figure out the meaning, look at the verses leading up to the parable and following it. What triggered the story? What was the event, question, issue, or need which the parable was told to explain, answer, or address?

2. *Focus on the main point.* A parable is not the same as an allegory. In an allegory, every part of the story has meaning. In a parable, some details are simply part of the story. Usually a parable makes one point, and only the parts that focus on the main point are significant.

3. *Consider the culture and customs of the time.* It is valuable to know something of the culture and customs of Jesus' time. For example, to identify with the panic of the woman in Jesus' parable of the <u>lost coin</u>, we need to know that the 10 coins were probably her dowry, which many Jewish women strung and wore like a necklace. The missing coin was probably a family heirloom more prized for its sentimental than actual value.

Merril F. Unger: The mind takes a natural delight in this manner of teaching, appealing as it does not to the understanding only, but to the feelings, to the imagination, in short to the whole man . . . and all things thus learned with delight are those longest remembered.[10]

Jesus' Parables In The Four Gospels

Depending on how each defines them, various scholars say Jesus told 27 to 50 parables.[11] The difference is that some include Jesus' **metaphors** among the parables, while others define a parable more strictly as a short story. Using the story definition, the number is about 30.

The parables of Jesus fall into at least six categories:

1. Parables of the kingdom, present (see chart, page 227)

2. Parables of the kingdom, future

3. Parables about resources, priorities, and material possessions

4. Parables about grace and forgiveness

5. Parables about prayer

6. Parables about various spiritual issues

Tales of the Kingdom

The predominant theme of Jesus' stories is the kingdom of God—the structure, values, processes, attitudes, and expectations of life under God's reign. Day by day on the trail or from his Galilean boat-pulpit, in homes where he and his disciples were guests, and nights around the campfire, the people who spent time with him listened to these unforgettable stories. Later they would tell these stories to subsequent generations of people who joined up with Jesus through their ministry. The stories would help them catch Jesus' kingdom dream.

KEY Outline:

Jesus' Stories

Power to expose
- hypocrisy
- lovelessness
- prejudice

Eight Parables of the Kingdom from Matthew 13

Identified by phrases as, "The kingdom of God is like . . ."

Parable	Illustrated Truth	Matthew 13
Sower, seed, soils	Listening, receiving the Word	13:3–9, 18–23
Weeds (tares)	Dealing with enemies in the church	13:24–30, 36–43
Mustard seed	How the kingdom grows	13:31–32
Yeast (leaven)	Change, inner influence of the kingdom	13:33
Hidden treasure	The kingdom a priceless discovery	13:44
Fishnet	Separation of righteous from unrighteous	13:47–50
Pearl of great price	Total commitment to gain the kingdom	13:45–46
Old and new treasure	Sharing from experience	13:51–52

(For a more complete list of Jesus' parables, see appendix B.)

Teaching Life From Life

Jesus had a knack for telling a story or grabbing something that was happening in somebody's life and turning it into a life lesson. Whenever and whatever he taught was always firmly anchored on earth and immediately applicable to the real lives of his hearers. "Pie in the sky by and by" had little or no relevance. His stories and teachings, his questions and Bible lessons were never aimed at filling students' heads with knowledge or tickling their fancies. He took deadly aim at their mixed motives, unloving attitudes, and prejudices. Even though he always offered them grace, he never let them off the hook easily. He did not tolerate the unloving assumptions by which they had lived before they met him. His teaching style met their hypocrisy and legalism and phony baloney religiosity head on.

"Repent!" was a call that he never rescinded. The call to follow him was a call to be changed. The kingdom community he came to establish on this planet could never exist without radical, thorough, ongoing, life-transforming change—the kind that never stops because there is always more of ourselves to surrender to the rule of King Jesus, the reign of God.

What Others are Saying:

Dietrich Bonhoeffer: Costly grace is the treasure hidden in the field, for the sake of it a man will gladly go and sell all that he has. It is costly because it costs a man his life, and it is grace because it gives a man the only true life.[12]

Study Questions

1. Define a parable.
2. In the parable of the sower and seeds, what is the seed? What do the rocky places represent?
3. Identify four good reasons for using parables to teach.
4. What was Jesus' goal in his teaching, according to Luke 6:40?
5. What are three helpful things to remember when interpreting Jesus' parables?
6. When it comes to how you listen to God right now, are you (a) locked in on the signal, (b) moving with the music, (c) getting a lot of static, (d) channel surfing, or (e) barely picking up the signal? Why? What needs to happen to get tuned in on his voice?

CHAPTER WRAP-UP

- An important part of Jesus' teaching was the telling of special stories based on things familiar to his hearers, to set priorities, correct misconceptions, develop attitudes, and teach concepts necessary for life in the kingdom community. (Matthew 13:3)

- Through the parable of the sower, the seeds, and seed growth, Jesus taught about various ways of listening and responding to truth. (Matthew 13:3–9, 18–23; Luke 8:1–8, 11–15)

- Jesus' parables, like all of his teaching, were designed to help disciples keep their understanding of truth solidly related to life's realities and to pass on the teacher's likeness. His stories were crafted to hide spiritual truth from unbelievers while revealing it to believers. (Matthew 13:10–17, 34–35)
- Jesus' parables dealt with a variety of subjects. The predominant theme was life in the kingdom of God. (Matthew 13)

16 STORMS OVER GALILEE

Let's Get Started

The pattern of the New Testament historians is to report some aspect of Jesus' teaching or some claim he made concerning himself and then to show how he confirmed it by his actions. Following this pattern, after the seed-planting parable, which focuses on the importance of paying attention to Jesus' words, the Gospel writers report incidents which demonstrate the power of Jesus' words—to establish the fact that whatever he says deserves to be listened to. Each of these happenings revolves around some sort of life-threatening "storm" that went calm when he spoke.

GOSPEL QUARTET IN HARMONY

Matthew 13:53; 8:18, 23–34; 9:35–10:42; 14:1–12

Mark 4:35–6:30

Luke 8:35–9:10

> **Mark 4:35–38a** That day when evening came, he said to his disciples, "Let us go over to the other side." Leaving the crowd behind, they took him along, just as he was, in the boat. A furious squall came up, and the waves broke over the boat, so that it was nearly swamped. Jesus was in the stern, sleeping on a cushion.

Tranquilizing A Galilean Gale

Jesus was bone tired. He'd started the day by facing down an evil spirit that was destroying a man's life. He'd fielded lying accusations of Pharisees and Bible scholars who spread the ugly slander that he was in league with the devil. He'd stood toe-to-toe with these powerful men and warned them of dire spiritual consequences if they continued to oppose him. His day ended in a small fishing boat anchored just offshore on the north end of Lake

GOSPEL QUARTET IN HARMONY

Matthew 13:53; 8:18, 23–27

Mark 4:35–41

Luke 8:35–41

Galilee, not far from Capernaum, where he pressed a crowd gathered on the beach to accept the personal reign of God. The 12 disciples were with him in the boat.

The sun was setting and still the crowd stayed, begging for more. In need of rest, Jesus told his men to head across the lake. Several were experienced boatmen who'd grown up on these waters, so he left the sailing to them, grabbed a cushion, laid down in the back of the boat, and fell asleep.

Lake Galilee lies 600 feet below sea level. It is surrounded by plateaus and high mountains. The plateaus are streaked with deep ravines cut by rivers and washes. This normally peaceful inland sea, infrequently and without warning, is swept by winds rushing down from the mountains, intensifying as they funnel through the ravines, becoming roaring gales, suddenly turning the lake into a boiling cauldron.

> **Mark 4:38b–39** The disciples woke him and said to him, "Teacher, don't you care if we drown?" He got up, rebuked the wind and said to the waves, "Quiet! Be still!" Then the wind died down and it was completely calm.

Terror On The Poop Deck

Seasoned salts sailing with the sleeping Savior shook at the sight of the savage squall! Lightning flashed. Thunder crashed. Rain splashed. Wind whipped. Waves washed the wee watercraft. Sailors bailed and bawled and bellowed at each other over the storm.

Jesus slept.

"*Don't you care if we drown?*" The men with Jesus were not far from wrong. Drowning was a distinct possibility. They were afraid *they* would be drowned. And they were afraid *he* would be drowned along with everything his teachings had caused them to dream of. They might as well be saying, "Don't you care if the kingdom of God sinks?"

Jesus woke, yawned, rubbed his eyes, "*rebuked*" the wind, and told the roaring waves to "*be still!*" Two things happened: The wind stopped, and the <u>sea stilled</u>.

Robert L. Thomas and Stanley N. Gundry: Here is a double miracle, the cessation of the wind and the immediate calming of the water. Ordinarily the waters would remain rough for a time after the wind stopped, but not this time.[1]

KEY POINT

His need for rest demonstrates the humanness of Christ.

Remember This . . .

☞ **GO TO:**

Psalm 89:9 (sea stilled)

What Others are Saying:

The Elements Obey Christ's Word

Each of the three versions of this story puts a slightly different spin on Jesus' comment to his disciples:

- Matthew 8:26—*"You of little faith, why are you so afraid?"* Did he actually expect their faith to remove even fears related to the survival instinct? Or was it a **rhetorical** question to help them think through to the realization that no boat with Jesus aboard could possibly sink?

- Mark 4:40—*"Why are you so afraid? Do you still have no faith?"* After all he had taught them and all they had seen in their time with him, it had not yet dawned on them that God's own power and authority were present in Jesus.

- Luke 8:25—*"Where is your faith?"* They had faith. They'd left everything to follow him. When in danger, they'd asked him to rescue them (Matthew 8:25). They simply did not realize that the faith they already had demonstrated could make them able to handle any crisis, including a storm and the prospect of their own death.

The light dawned. As their jaws dropped open, their knees became spaghetti—this time out of sheer awe. The man whose concern they had the audacity to question when the storm hit (Mark 4:38) held power (including authority <u>over the sea</u> and the weather). They knew this power and authority belonged only to God! *"Who is this?"* they said.

They knew. And now they understood better why listening to his words was the only thing that made sense.

Leonard I. Sweet: The miracle Jesus wanted to show them was not the miracle of calming the storm, but the miracle of calming them in the storm. Think what it would have been like to have experienced the miracle of wave-riding, the joy of knowing that no matter how fierce the storm; no matter how many crises in your cruises, nothing of ultimate harm could happen to you as long as you were in the boat with Jesus.[2]

Ephrem the Syrian: The ship carried his humanity, but the power of his Godhead carried the ship and all that was in it.[3]

rhetorical: no answer expected

KEY Outline:

In the Storm
Wrong question:
- Don't you care?

Right question:
- Who is this?

☞ **GO TO:**

Psalm 89:8–9; 104:5–9; 106:8–9; 107:23–32 (over the sea)

What Others are Saying:

GOSPEL QUARTET IN HARMONY

Matthew 8:28–34
Mark 5:1–20
Luke 8:26–39

Calming Mental Tornadoes

The boat landed at a craggy limestone area overlooking the lake near Gadara (see appendix A). The cliffside was honeycombed with caves used to entomb the dead. On the grassy plateau above the tombs, a herd of some 2,000 pigs was rooting, watched over by local swineherds.

As Jesus and his men pulled the boat up on shore, a notorious madman emerged from the tombs, screaming and gesturing for the intruders to leave him alone. He and his equally tormented companion (Matthew 8:28 says there were two of them) ran down the rocky steep toward the boat. Both were naked and covered with filth. Their bodies were scarred from slashing themselves with sharp stones in attempts at self-punishment. The big one's ankles, legs, and arms bore the marks of chains and irons used to control his violence. This tortured soul, with demon-enhanced strength, had repeatedly broken the chains and escaped to haunt the tombs where together the two madmen of Gadara filled the night with deranged wails and by day poured threats and obscenities on passersby and those who came to bury their dead.

What Others are Saying:

Henry H. Halley: The rather plain implication of Scripture is that "demoniacs" were not mere lunatics, but cases of "invaded personality;" and that demons, whatever their origin or nature, were evil spirits that did actually enter and afflict, one way or another, certain persons. It is thought to have been a special exhibition of the devil against Jesus, permitted by God during Jesus' stay on earth, to demonstrate that Jesus' power extended even into the unseen realm.[4]

An Army Of Warrior Devils

Jesus knew what he was up against and as the harassed souls stumbled and screamed their way toward him, he commanded the evil spirits to free their captives.

"Don't hurt us!" the big man screamed. "Please, don't torture us!" echoed his partner in pain, as they fell to their knees.

"What is your name?" Jesus demanded, addressing the trembling hulk before him. "My name is **Legion**, for we are many!"

Legion: *an army of 6,000 men*

snarled the man. It was the cry of a man who felt like all the demon soldiers of hell had fastened themselves to him and were waging war against him from the inside.

> **Luke 8:31–32** And they begged him repeatedly not to order them to go into the **Abyss**. A large herd of pigs was feeding there on the hillside. The demons begged Jesus to let them go into them, and he gave them permission.

☞ **GO TO:**

Revelation 9:1–11; 11:7; 17:8; 20:1–3 (Abyss)

Abyss: Greek for "bottomless" pit; realm of the dead

Hog Hell

Suddenly there was a commotion in the porkers on the hill. They squealed and shook. Then they moved with increasing agitation toward the precipice. The swineherds ran here and there yelling, but nothing could stop the stampede. Down the rocky slope tumbled a thundering herd of 2,000 crazed oinkers, headlong straight into the Sea of Galilee, squealing and gurgling their last as they drowned in the blue waters of what the rabbis loved to call "the sea of God's delight."

Why did Jesus do as the evil spirits requested by letting them go into the pigs? Under the Law of Moses <u>pigs</u> were ceremonially unclean. This rule tested Israel's obedience and protected them from exposure to **trichinosis**. In rebellion, Israel sometimes ignored this ban. By sending the demons into the pigs, Jesus "killed two birds with one stone," getting rid of a man's demons and disciplining the illegal swine trade in one fell swoop!

☞ **GO TO:**

Leviticus 11:7–8; Isaiah 65:3–5 (pigs)

trichinosis: disease caused by trichinae, carried by pigs

No Pork Chops For Dinner Tonight!

To make a long story short, the madmen of Gadara were healed, cleaned up, put their clothes back on, stopped harassing the neighborhood, and found peace sweet peace. And the whole town turned out to ask Jesus to leave! (Mark 5:17). Which only proves some people would rather have pork than peace! The bottom had suddenly dropped out of the hog market!

But the cured crazies went home to their families and reported all the good things Jesus had done for them (Mark 5:19–20). Although the cured men asked to go with Jesus when he left (Mark 5:18), Jesus said, "no." He gave them the more difficult task of being witnesses for him in that Gentile region. The healed men's obedience gave that area the gift of a believable testimony of Christ's power and an opportunity to respond.

KEY Outline:

Proof Demoniac Is Cured

Sitting

Clothed

Sane

Sharing good news

Demons Obey Christ's Word

Even demons—the worst warriors of wickedness hell has to throw into the fray against us—have no choice but to obey when Jesus speaks. In this story, the whole attitude of the evil spirits changed when Jesus came on the scene. Until then they had been in total control of the men they possessed, and had terrorized the whole community. But when Jesus arrived, they immediately began to plead for mercy. And when he told them to leave, they left!

Do Demons Cause Trouble for People Today?

**Something
to Ponder**

Despite inclusion in the New Testament of many case histories in which Jesus and his disciples healed people by driving out evil spirits, modern Christians understand little of this process. We're more comfortable giving scientific names to our emotional problems and thinking of evil spirits as related only to voodooism, witchcraft, or Satanic cults. The Bible does not say every mental disorder is the activity of a devil. But we don't follow the story of Jesus far until we realize that he believed evil spirits were the cause of many such disorders. Apparently, some long-standing emotional response patterns are set so deeply they seem beyond the individual's power to choose. Could some emotional problems like this involve a struggle against an evil spirit? Apparently, Jesus thought so. If so, this is a legitimate target for prayer to set the troubled person free.

KEY POINT

Jesus is able to bring out-of-control people under his control.

**What Others
are Saying:**

Lawrence O. Richards: Are we in danger today from these evil beings? . . . It would be wrong to suggest that possession or oppression cannot happen today. . . . What the Scriptures emphasize, and what the Gospels prove, is that Jesus is <u>more than a match</u> for the evil powers of our universe.[5]

☞ **GO TO:**

1 John 4:4
(more than a match)

> **Mark 5:21–24** When Jesus had again crossed over by boat to the other side of the lake, a large crowd gathered around him. . . . Then one of the synagogue rulers, named Jairus, came there. Seeing Jesus, he fell at his feet and pleaded earnestly with him, "My little daughter is dying. Please come and put your hands on her so that she will be healed and live." So Jesus went with him.

Stilling Windstorms Of Worry And Grief

Galilean synagogues had been wide open for Jesus early in his ministry, but as official opposition mounted were rapidly closing to him. Jairus may have been initially opposed, but there is a big difference between taking an arrogant attitude toward Christ when the sun is shining and hanging on to that attitude when you're in trouble and need Christ's help! Pride isn't worth diddly when your kid is dying! So when Jesus' boat docked at Capernaum, Jairus was waiting on the beach.

As president of the synagogue, Jairus organized and directed Sabbath services. By rabbinical rule he was expected to be a man of high moral character, modest, God-fearing, truthful, not greedy, hospitable, and not a gambler. In some synagogues the president was the sole authority.[6] But he risked it all for his child.

Right there in front of God and everybody, the proud president pled with the controversial Nazarene to come to his house and save his 12-year-old from death.

JAIRUS: *"Synagogue ruler"* in Capernaum (Mark 5:22). President of the synagogue (*Archisynogogos*) and chairman of the local **Sanhedrin** or elders of the local congregation. Some synagogue rulers believed in Jesus. Jairus was apparently one of those.

> **Luke 8:42–44** As Jesus was on his way, the crowds almost crushed him. And a woman was there who had been subject to bleeding for twelve years, but no one could heal her. She came up behind him and touched the edge of his cloak and immediately her bleeding stopped.

Stopping A Blood Flood

On the way to Jairus' house, the crowd pushed and shoved like the paparazzi on a photo frenzy after the latest hot celebrity. They were in his face, asking questions, demanding attention. Someone was constantly pressing against him, touching him.

Suddenly Jesus spun around to face the swarming mass. *"Who touched my clothes?"* he asked.

The disciples thought it was a ridiculous question. "Who touched you?" they echoed incredulously. "Who *didn't* touch you? You're in the middle of a mob. Twenty-five people are touching

GOSPEL QUARTET IN HARMONY

Matthew 9:18–26
Mark 5:21–43
Luke 8:40–56

☞ **GO TO:**

1 Timothy 3:1–7;
Titus 1:5–9
(high moral character)

Who's Who

Sanhedrin: *board of elders*

GOSPEL QUARTET IN HARMONY

Matthew 9:20–22
Mark 5:24–34
Luke 8:42–48

you at any given moment. And you ask who touched you? Get real!"

Their sarcasm notwithstanding, Jesus knew he'd felt something unusual in the press of the crowd. Someone had touched him in *faith*. As he searched the faces, a frightened woman stepped out of the mass and blurted out her painful and embarrassing story: For 12 years she hadn't stopped **bleeding**!

Old Testament Law declared a woman with a chronic menstrual flow and anyone she touched ceremonially "unclean." She could not participate in worship or community life until bleeding stopped. The Jewish **Talmud** prescribed 11 different "cures" for her problem—several amounted to superstitious mumbo jumbo. She'd no doubt tried them all. Doctors had been unable to help (though they were more than willing to accept payment for their "services").

In a final act of desperation, the sick and lonely woman risked public condemnation, pushed through the crowd, and got close enough to reach out and touch the <u>edge</u> of Jesus' robe. Devout Jews wore a four-cornered outer robe with a tassel at each corner; the woman reached for the tassels.

As soon as she made contact, her bleeding stopped. She could feel it (Mark 5:29). *"Your faith has healed you,"* Jesus said. *"Go in peace"* (verse 34).

> **Mark 5:35** While Jesus was still speaking, some men came from the house of Jairus, the synagogue ruler. "Your daughter is dead," they said. "Why bother the teacher any more?"

Bad News: The Girl Is Dead!

No sense bringing Jesus to a funeral! Understandably, the synagogue president panicked!

"Don't be afraid," Jesus said. *"Just believe"* (verse 36).

Taking Peter, James, and John with him as witnesses, Jesus followed Jairus the rest of the way to his house. Sure enough, the funeral had already started! The sound coming from the house of Jairus was like the cacophony of a grade school band playing in a Machiavellian torture chamber! **Wailing women** filled the place with earsplitting, high-pitched moans and melodramatic pleas for the dead girl to speak. Others played mournful dirges on flutes. The house was a pandemonium of tragedy and grief.

☞ **GO TO:**

Leviticus 15:25–30 (bleeding)

Numbers 15:38–40 (edge)

bleeding: *chronic menstrual flow*

Talmud: *ancient commentaries; collections of insights of rabbis*

KEY Outline:

Woman Healed because
She believed
She acted on it
She risked censure
She touched Jesus

wailing women: *professional mourners hired to wail*

Good News: The Funeral Is Cancelled!

Jesus marched in and demanded the commotion stop! *"The child is not dead but asleep,"* he said.

The orderly mourning disintegrated into disorderly fits of cynical laughter.

"Out! All of you!" he demanded. Then, with only his three disciples and the girl's parents, Jesus went into the room where the child's body lay. He took her hand and told her to get up. She got up and walked through the house greeting gape-mouthed guests who had come to join the wailing! Those who were in the room were under strictest orders *"not to let anyone know about this."* What *this* did he mean? Since it would be hard to keep her resuscitation from the gathered mourners, Jesus must mean the process involved—the fact that he touched her dead body and raised her up by the hand.

Some suggest since Jesus said she was *"asleep,"* she was unconscious. He just woke her up. But Luke's statement, *"her spirit returned,"* (8:55) indicates she was dead.

The Compassionate Etiquette Buster

The bleeding woman touched Jesus and was healed; he touched the dead body and Jairus' daughter lived. He knew the Law said to be touched by a woman in her menstrual period or to touch a dead body would cut a person off from God until a cleansing ritual could take place. He knew that his actions would bring him criticism from his legalistic enemies.

- They would see only an "unclean" woman touching Jesus, *not* the joyous end of the woman's 12-year ordeal of loneliness and agony.

- They would see only that Jesus' hand touched a dead body, *not* the wonder of a little girl lost getting to live out her life or the inexpressible relief of the grieving parents whose child had been given back to them.

Jesus, as usual, ran roughshod over insensitive protocols that inhibited ministry to people in need. He risked condemnation from the religious establishment by acting out of compassion instead of anxious, overscrupulous rule keeping. He shows us that the God who <u>is love</u> never intended his laws to become excuses for ignoring people in their pain and grief. Jesus never broke a **moral law**, but his example

Remember This . . .

Something to Ponder

☞ **GO TO:**

1 John 4:16 (is love)

moral law: *the Ten Commandments*

teaches that there is a time for ceremonial rules to be set aside in order to act in love.

EARLY CHURCH LIFE: Jesus focused on people and their pain and taught his disciples to do the same.

The Power of Christ's Words

Read each statement below and think about (1) what Christ's words are and (2) what Christ's words can do.

1. Jesus: *"Heaven and earth will pass away, but* my *words will never pass away"* (Matthew 24:35).

2. John the Baptist: *"The one [Jesus] whom God has sent speaks the words of God"* (John 3:34).

3. Jesus: *"Whoever hears* my *word and believes him who sent me has eternal life and will not be condemned; he has crossed over from death to life"* (John 5:24).

4. Jesus: *"The* words *I have spoken to you are spirit and they are life"* (John 6:63).

5. Peter (to Jesus): *"You have the* words *of eternal life"* (John 6:68).

6. Jesus: *"If you hold to* my *teaching [word], you are really my disciples. Then you will know the truth, and the truth will set you free"* (John 8:31–32).

7. Jesus: *"Whatever I say is just what the Father has told me to say"* (John 12:50).

8. Jesus: *"If anyone loves me, he will obey* my *teachings [words]. My Father will love him, and we will come to him and make our home with him"* (John 14:23).

9. Jesus: *"You are already clean because of* the *word I have spoken to you"* (John 15:3).

10. Jesus: *"If you remain in me and* my *words remain in you, ask whatever you wish, and it will be given you"* (John 15:7).

11. Paul: *"Let the* word *of Christ dwell in you richly as you teach and admonish one another"* (Colossians 3:16).

12. Anonymous: *"The Son is the radiance of God's glory . . . sustaining all things by* his *powerful word"* (Hebrews 1:3).

Dig Deeper

KEY Outline:

Must Obey Christ's Word

Weather (elements)
Demons (mental illness)
Death (grief)

Study Questions

1. Where was Jesus when the storm threatened to sink the boat? When has Jesus seemed asleep in your life when you desperately needed to know he was awake?

2. How did the disciples react when the wind and waves obeyed Jesus? What does it tell us about who Jesus is?

3. How did the people of Gadara try to deal with the demon-possessed man? How is the way we treat mentally ill people today similar? Different?

4. How did the evil spirits react to the presence of Jesus? What does this say about Jesus' authority over evil spirits?

5. When they saw the former madman sitting, dressed, and in his right mind, how did the townspeople react? What does this say about their values?

6. By seeing only the religious rules Jesus broke, what important things did the legalistic religious leaders overlook? (Refer to page 239.)

CHAPTER WRAP-UP

- In a boat sailing across the northeast corner of Lake Galilee, Jesus and his disciples were caught in a ferocious gale that threatened to scuttle the tiny boat. Jesus woke up from his nap, rebuked the wind and the waves, and the storm stopped! (Mark 4:35–41)

- On the shore of Gadara, two madmen emerged from the tombs, one having been possessed by a legion of evil spirits. Jesus sent the spirits into a herd of pigs grazing nearby, whereupon the porkers plunged to their death in the sea. (Mark 5:1–20)

- On the beach as they returned, a synagogue president named Jairus met Jesus with the urgent request that he come and heal his young daughter who was near death. (Luke 8:40–42)

- On the way to Jairus' house, a suffering woman reached through the crowd and touched the tassel of Jesus' robe. She was instantly healed. (Luke 8:43–48)

- Word came from Jairus' house that his daughter was dead. Jesus ignored the bad news and encouraged her father to believe. The daughter was raised from the dead at Christ's word. (Luke 8:49–56)

17 CRUSADE FOR GALILEE

CHAPTER HIGHLIGHTS

- Help Wanted
- Offense! Offense!
- Go, Team, Go!
- Baptist Boogeyman

GOSPEL QUARTET IN HARMONY

Matthew 9:35–10:42;
14:1–12
Mark 6:6–30
Luke 9:1–10

Let's Get Started

The 12 apostles-in-training had spent more than a year with Jesus, listening as he stated, restated, and illustrated the basic concepts upon which his revolutionary society (the kingdom of heaven) was founded. In private moments, away from the crowds, they interacted with him at depth about the meaning of the stories he told and the things he taught. On the road with him they gained practical experience in the way the basic concepts worked out in day-to-day relationships. Most importantly, they observed him at work, watched how he dealt with people and problems. They experienced fear in some dangerous situations, and saw those fears melt before demonstrations of their teacher's authority over people, nature, the weather, disease, and nightmarish demons.

In the training timetable for these future leaders of the kingdom movement, it was time for the rubber to meet the road. The 12 must be sent out in specific ministry to preach his message and to duplicate his working style. It would be a temporary sending this time. They would be "on their own" for a short time, then return for debriefing and several more months with him. But it would be a real get-their-feet-wet event. And they'd never be the same after the experience.

> **Matthew 9:35–36** Jesus went through all the towns and villages, teaching in their synagogues, preaching the good news of the kingdom and healing every disease and sickness. When he saw the crowds, he had compassion on them, because they were harassed and helpless, like sheep without a shepherd.

☞ **Check It Out:**

Matthew 9:35–38

Mark 6:6

☞ **GO TO:**

Matthew 14:14; 15:32;
20:34; Mark 1:41
(he had compassion)

Compare Matthew
9:35; Luke 4:14; 8:1
(third preaching tour)

compassion: *feeling
moved by another's
situation, leading to
action*

KEY POINT

Jesus felt people's pain
and acted to help.

☞ **GO TO:**

Psalm 23; John 10:1–
16; 1 Peter 5:1–4
(shepherd)

KEY Outline:

People without Christ
Harassed
Helpless
Shepherdless

Help Wanted!

The endless crowds of needy people "got to" Jesus. By the principles of "good" management, an efficient leader who's really in
control keeps his head, maintains a cool distance, and doesn't let
himself get too emotionally entangled in people's problems. Jesus
could never do that. He was too vulnerable, intentionally. When
the Bible says "*he had* **compassion**," it means he put himself in
people's shoes, let himself feel their pain, and hurt with them.
The pain he shared with them moved him to help them. On his
third preaching tour of Galilee, his identification with hurting
people was multiplied by the hundreds of anxious faces surrounding him in each place.

Matthew infers that Jesus' emotional perception of the situation of the people he met from town to town was a signal to him
that it was time to take his training of the 12 to the next level.

Floundering Flock

When he looked at people, Jesus saw (1) a flock of wandering
sheep and (2) a precious ripe harvest waiting to be brought in
(Matthew 9:36). As sheep, they were a flock in trouble:

1. "*Harassed*"—the original Greek word was used to describe
   someone who was wounded, mangled, plundered, fleeced
   by robbers; troubled, bewildered, in a sorry plight; wea-
   ried by an endless journey.

2. "*Helpless*"—the original word could mean downcast,
   down and out, castaway, dejected; early Greeks used it to
   describe someone laid low with mortal wounds.

3. Shepherdless—lost, wandering, straying, unguided, unfed,
   unprotected—lacking the care of a good shepherd. The
   Jewish people had many leaders, but instead of leading
   them to sound spiritual health, they laid intolerable
   legalistic burdens on them and filled their ears with
   useless, endless arguments about the Law.

> **Matthew 9:37** Then he said to his disciples, "The har-
> vest is plentiful but the workers are few. Ask the Lord
> of the harvest, therefore, to send out workers into his
> harvest field."

Urgent Harvest

As *"a plentiful harvest"* (verse 36), the people represented a huge, critical task. The chief priests saw the people as a *"cursed mob ignorant of the Law"* (John 7:49); the Pharisees considered them chaff to be destroyed and burned up.[1] Jesus saw them, not as the objects of judgment and condemnation, moral refuse to be thrown away and burned, but as a <u>ripened crop</u> to be carefully, joyfully gathered and saved for God's good purposes.

Jesus ached deep inside to gather them to himself and to be their shepherd. However, there was one urgent need if this was to be accomplished: enough workers (Matthew 9:37). While physically among us, his was a single voice that could not possibly reach all the people who were ready to respond. Workers—hundreds, thousands of "harvesters"—must be put to work. The 12 willing men with Jesus represented the nucleus of that great force of reapers. But their sending must begin with prayer.

As they prayed, their hearts would share his concern. They would begin to see the task from his perspective. By the time he sent them out, they would not be draftees, but <u>volunteers</u>.

Robert E. Coleman: Like a mother eagle teaching her young to fly by pushing them out of the nest, Jesus pushed his disciples out into the world to try their own wings.[2]

Dietrich Bonhoeffer: Christ calls, the disciple follows; that is grace and commandment in one.[3]

> **Matthew 10:1, 7–8** He called his twelve disciples to him and gave them authority to drive out evil spirits and to heal every disease and sickness. . . . As you go, preach this message: "The kingdom of heaven is near." Heal the sick, raise the dead, cleanse those who have leprosy, drive out demons.

Offense! Offense!

Jesus gathered his 12 recruits for a strategy briefing. His instructions pulled together the things he'd been showing them by example all the time they'd been together. He specifically deputized them to do *his* work, assuring them they possessed the **authority** and **power** needed to do it.

KEY Outline:

People
Pharisees' view
- chaff

Jesus' view
- ripe grain

☞ **GO TO:**

John 4:35; Matthew 13:23 (ripened crop)

Isaiah 6:1–8 (volunteers)

What Others are Saying:

KEY POINT

In prayer we share Christ's concern.

authority: *jurisdiction, freedom to act; Jesus' delegated authority*

power: *spiritual energy to meet each challenge*

GOSPEL QUARTET IN HARMONY

Matthew 10:1–42
Mark 6:7–11
Luke 9:1–5

> **Matthew 10:5–6** . . . "Do not go among the Gentiles or enter any town of the Samaritans. Go rather to the lost sheep of Israel."

Go For The Easy Shots

Exciting things happened when Jesus' path took him into Gentile or Samaritan territory, but he stated clearly that his primary calling was to his own people—the Jews. They were the ones most likely to receive him, because the ancient prophecies had been given to them and they were expected to be expecting him. Likewise, the disciples' Jewish kinsmen were most like them in cultural and religious background: spoke the same language, attended the same synagogues and festivals, shared common enemies and problems and, of course, those messianic expectations.

☞ **GO TO:**

Mark 8:1–9; John 4
(Gentile or Samaritan)

Matthew 15:24; John
1:11–12
(his own people)

worthy: *receptive, welcoming, willing to listen*

greeting: *Shalom: peace, health, prosperity, God's blessing*

let your peace return: *withhold God's blessing*

> **Matthew 10:11–14** Whatever town or village you enter, search for some **worthy** person there and stay at his house until you leave. As you enter the home, give it your **greeting**. If the home is deserving, let your peace rest on it; if it is not, **let your peace return** to you. If anyone will not welcome you or listen to your words, shake the dust off your feet when you leave that home or town.

Assault Strategy

Jesus' assault strategy was to concentrate the most energy on receptive individuals and families. This requires discernment and sensitivity. Generally, if the door is open to the witness, it is not closed to Christ. The Christian workers' primary concentration is to be on people most likely to respond positively, to positively influence their neighbors, and to continue the work after the evangelists leave.

What if no such person can be found?

"If anyone will not welcome you or listen to your words, shake the dust off your feet when you leave that home or town" (Matthew 10:14).

☞ **GO TO:**

Matthew 10:40–42;
Luke 10:5–7, 16
(door is open)

Luke 10:11–12;
Acts 13:51
(shake the dust off)

Ooh! That sounds nasty! Ancient rabbis taught that even the dust of Gentile lands was defiled. Strict Jews, upon reentering the Holy Land from a foreign country, would literally shake their clothing and wipe the dust from their shoes. Jesus told his missionaries to warn residents of unresponsive communities that Jews who reject the Gospel are no better off than pagans—to reject Christ and his witnesses was to abandon the right to consider themselves God's people! (Pretty dire stuff!)

> **Matthew 10:8–10** Freely you have received, freely give. Do not take along any gold or silver or copper in your **belts**; take no **bag** for your journey, or extra tunic, or sandals or a staff, for the worker is worth his keep.

Getting Down To Fighting Trim

Jesus' ambassadors were to be dispensers of grace, <u>not profiteers</u> lining their pockets. They had nothing to offer that had not come to them freely through the loving-kindness of God. Everything they gave, every service they performed, was to be given without charge. For their support, they would depend on God and the hospitality of those to whom they ministered (Matthew 10:11; Luke 9:4). Yet they were to hold their heads up, knowing they were <u>worthy of their keep</u>. In a host home they were to eat and drink what was set before them (without complaining); they were not to move from house to house, as if looking for more comfortable accommodations or a better deal (Luke 10:7–8).

 **EARLY CHURCH LIFE:** Jesus set the standard for early missionary training. His specific instructions helped Gospel workers.

- Traveling light makes it easier to identify with and move among poor people, who are often more ready to accept the kingdom.

- The ambassador must not give the impression his movements are dictated by his own preferences and comfort or the profit motive.

- By being willing to depend on others for daily needs, the witness breathes life into the principle of <u>mutual dependence</u>, a vital principle for function within the body of Christ, the church, and the kingdom community.

KEY POINT

If the door is open to Christ's witness, it is not closed to Christ.

belts: money belts, purses

bag: knapsack or beggar's bag

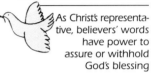 **ACT OF THE HOLY SPIRIT**

As Christ's representative, believers' words have power to assure or withhold God's blessing

☞ **GO TO:**

1 Corinthians 9:3–18; 2 Corinthians 2:17; 1 Timothy 6:3–10 (not profiteers)

1 Corinthians 9:7–11 (worthy of their keep)

Acts 2:42–47; 1 Corinthians 12:21–26 (mutual dependence)

 **KEY Outline:**

Effective Witnesses
Travel light
Forget the profit motive
Depend on others

Enables Christians to rejoice in suffering

☞ **GO TO:**

1 Peter 4:14–16 (innocent)

shrewd: practical, sensible, decisive

innocent: not devious, not misleading

Remember This . . .

☞ **GO TO:**

John 15:18–16:3 (they will persecute)

Matthew 5:10–12; Luke 6:22–23, 26; Acts 5:40–41 (reason to rejoice)

> **Matthew 10:16–17** I am sending you out like sheep among wolves. Therefore be as shrewd as snakes and as innocent as doves. Be on guard against men.

No Pain, No Gain

Jesus did not sugarcoat the hardships his witnesses would face. Every prediction he made ultimately came true, if not on this trip, then later in the course of their Christian service. This short-term missionary jaunt in Galilee was the start of the toughest job these men had ever undertaken. But he wasn't a glutton for punishment. He wanted them to be "*shrewd*" and avoid it if they could. He urged them to be "*innocent*;" "don't give your persecutors a legitimate reason to attack."

He told them to expect trouble from town officials and abuse from religious leaders (Matthew 10:17), arrest by rulers—Jewish and pagan (verse 18), betrayal by members of their own families (verse 21), hatred for no better reason than their association with Jesus (verse 22), and to be driven from place to place by persecution (verse 23).

In effect, he was saying, "Face it! Not everyone is going to be happy you came with the Good News. In fact, most people are going to do everything they can to get you to shut up."

Persecution was and is inevitable because of identification with the Lord. Christians get tarred with the same reputation, are charged with the same indictments, as people level at Christ. If they persecuted him, they will persecute his disciples. This is, in the same breath, a reason to understand why painful things happen, and a reason to rejoice when they do.

> **Matthew 10:19–20** But when they arrest you, do not worry about what to say or how to say it. At that time you will be given what to say, for it will not be you speaking, but the Spirit of your Father speaking through you.

Don't Worry, Be Happy

Even though they were to be ready to die for Christ if necessary, nobody should seek martyrdom. If the witness for Christ can escape persecution without denying the Lord, he should do it (Matthew 10:23). But, if there's no way to keep the "wolves" at bay, hang on for dear life to these promises, and get ready for the ride of your life!

- God's Spirit will never leave you speechless, so trouble can be turned to opportunity for witness (verse 20).
- Even if they take your life, they cannot kill your soul (verses 22, 28).
- Your Father in heaven is aware of every detail of your life (even the number of hairs on your pointy little head!): He will take care of you (verses 29–31).
- Jesus is in your corner: He'll never let the Father forget you (verse 32).

KEY Outline:

Persecution Promises
Something to say
They can't kill your soul
Your Father cares
Jesus in your corner

Dietrich Bonhoeffer: When we are called to follow Christ, we are summoned to an exclusive attachment to his person.[4]

What Others are Saying:

J. I. Packer: For a final example and proof of the truth that following God's guidance brings trouble, look at the life of the Lord Jesus himself. No human life has ever been so completely guided by God, and no human being has ever qualified so comprehensively for the description "a <u>man of sorrows</u>."[5]

☞ **GO TO:**

Isaiah 53:3
(man of sorrows)

> **Matthew 10:34–37** Do not suppose that I have come to bring peace to the earth. I did not come to bring peace, but a sword. For I have come to turn
>
> "a man against his father,
> a daughter against her mother,
> a daughter-in-law against her mother-in-law—
> a man's enemies will be the members of his own household."
>
> Anyone who loves his father or mother more than me is not worthy of me; anyone who loves his son or daughter more than me is not worthy of me.

Swords In The Family Room

The cost of throwing in with Jesus Christ is revealed in startling reality when Jesus reminds his men that the message they are being sent to preach can be painfully divisive and will demand total commitment.

They can expect splits in the family tree. Since Christ's invitation is to repentance (the forsaking of sin), and since the kingdom lifestyle is so revolutionary and demands such sweeping changes in values, priorities, and personal relationships, it is inevitable that family feathers will be ruffled. Anyone digging in against change is going to be deeply disturbed when someone close to them embraces Jesus, begins to try to live by Jesus' ideas, and tells others about it. To emphasize his point Jesus quotes Micah 7:6.

Not every Christian may have to choose between love of family and love of Christ, especially if his family joins him in the commitment to follow the Lord. But for some people, linking up with Jesus and doing God's will means moving a direction the family doesn't understand or approve.

What Others are Saying:

William Barclay: A man has to choose sometimes between the closest ties of earth and loyalty to Jesus Christ. . . . all loyalties must give place to loyalty to God.[6]

> **Matthew 10:38–39** Anyone who does not take his cross and follow me is not worthy of me. Whoever finds his life will lose it, and whoever <u>loses his life</u> for my sake <u>will find it.</u>

☞ **GO TO:**

Luke 14:26–27
(loses his life)

Matthew 5:10–12; Luke 6:22–23 (will find it)

Acts 5:37
(Judas of Galilee)

The High Cost Of Winning

"Total commitment" is a phrase tossed around glibly in athletic and military circles. No one ever called for a commitment more total than Jesus did. From the men about to take his kingdom dream to the cities of Galilee he demanded the ultimate.

Galileans listening to Jesus say these words had vivid images of the cross in their minds. A few years before, the Romans had crushed a rebellion led by <u>Judas of Galilee</u>. In reprisal, the Roman General Varus crucified 2,000 Galileans and lined the roads of Galilee with their crosses. Now Jesus' friends were being told that following him was going to be no less costly. For every man or woman who joined his uprising there awaited . . . a cross!

KINGDOM OF GOD Jesus wants his foot soldiers to understand they are being called to lay down their lives just as he was doing. Most if not all the original 12 were martyred for Christian witness, some on literal crosses.

EARLY CHURCH LIFE: In its first 250 years, the church with-
stood 10 Roman Imperial persecutions
and hundreds of local persecutions
trying to silence the Christian witness.

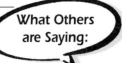
What Others
are Saying:

Audrey I. Girard: Denial of self-interests leads to meaningful
vocations, unselfish actions, discovery of meaning in suffering,
and ability to accept the difficult and uncomfortable.[7]

Robert E. Coleman: One cannot help being impressed with the
realistic way that Jesus never let his disciples underestimate the
strength of the enemy, nor the natural resistance of men to his
redeeming Gospel. They were not looking for trouble . . . but in
spite of all their precautions, the fact remained that the world was
not likely to receive the disciples with favor when they faithfully
preached the Gospel.[8]

> **Matthew 10:40; 11:1** He who receives you receives
> me, and he who receives me receives the one who sent
> me. After Jesus had finished instructing his twelve dis-
> ciples, he went on from there to teach and preach in
> the towns of Galilee.

Player-Coach

The mission on which his disciples were being sent was not different in principle or method from Jesus' own mission. As he sent
them out, he himself continued to work at the same work. They
went out equipped with his authority and power (Luke 9:1). As
they did what they did, it was as though he was <u>doing it himself</u>
through them (Matthew 10:40). As people responded to them—
positively or negatively—it was as though they were responding
<u>not merely to them</u>, but to Christ himself.

> **Mark 6:7** Calling the Twelve to him, he sent them out
> two by two. . . .

Go, Team, Go!

General Jesus divided his stormtroopers and sent them out in two-
man teams. Christian work is expected to be an exercise in <u>spiri-
tual teamwork</u>. The teamwork <u>principle</u> provides team members
with companionship, mutual support, and accountability.

☞ **GO TO:**

John 15:4–5; Galatians
2:20; Philippians
2:12–13; 4:13
(doing it himself)

Luke 10:16; John
13:20; Acts 9:5
(not merely to them)

Romans 12,
1 Corinthians 12
(spiritual teamwork)

Ecclesiastes 4:9–12
(principle)

What Others are Saying:

Dig Deeper

Unknown: One horse can pull six tons, but a team of two horses harnessed together is able to pull not 12, but 32 tons!

Early Christian Teams Jesus Sent

- He sent the 12, 2 by 2, to the cities of Galilee (Mark 6:7).
- He sent the 72, 2 by 2, to prepare for his arrival in the cities of Perea and Judea (Luke 10:1).
- He taught that 2 or 3 together should confront a sinning brother (Matthew 18:16).
- He taught that 2 or 3 agreeing in prayer have power with God (Matthew 18:19).
- He sent 2 disciples to borrow a donkey for his Triumphal Entry (Mark 11:1–7).
- He sent 2 disciples to arrange for the last meal in the upper room (Mark 14:13–16).

Spiritual Teamwork in the Early Church

Examine the teamwork principle in operation:

Acts 1:12–13; 2:14	Acts 6:1–6
Acts 8:4–8, 14–17	Acts 10:23; 11:12
Acts 11:25–26	Acts 13:1–3
Acts 13:4–5	Acts 15:22–29
Acts 15:39	Acts 15:40–41
Acts 16:1–5	Acts 18:1–5

> **Mark 6:14–16** King Herod heard about this, for Jesus' name had become well known. Some were saying, "John the Baptist has been raised from the dead, and that is why miraculous powers are at work in him." Others said, "He is Elijah." And still others claimed, "He is a prophet, like one of the prophets of long ago." But when Herod heard this, he said, "John, the man I beheaded, has been raised from the dead!"

GOSPEL QUARTET IN HARMONY

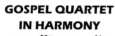

Matthew 14:1–12
Mark 6:12–29
Luke 9:6–9

Baptist Boogeyman

The success of the Jesus-teams was phenomenal. As Jesus' 12 fledgling ambassadors, in teams of two, fanned out over the hills and villages of Galilee, the impact of their ministry and of Jesus himself became, more than ever, the talk of the province. The disciples were powerfully preaching the Good News of the kingdom and calling people to turn from their sins (Mark 6:12). Demons were releasing their hold on their victims. The sick were healed (verse 13). The impact of Jesus was being multiplied through his men.

The news of the word and work of Christ reached the centers of power, making its way even to the court of **Herod** (see illustration, page 40). The powers-that-be had a "movement" on their hands! People on the street were identifying it all as the work of a resurrected John the Baptist or this or that Old Testament prophet.

King Herod was looking under his bed for the headless ghost of John the Baptist!

Flashback: The Courage And Arrest Of Big John The Baptist

At this point in the story, Matthew and Mark pause for a flashback. The last time we heard from John the Baptist he was cooling his heels in the dungeon at Herod's Machaerus Castle. Herod had arrested him for publicly pointing the finger at the "king" and his new wife, Herodias, whom he had seduced and stolen from his brother Philip (see illustration, page 40). In the process, Herod had divorced his legitimate wife to clear the way for the new romance. John had dared to declare the whole sordid affair illegal!

Herodias never forgave him. She would not be happy until John was dead. Herod too wanted John dead (Matthew 14:5) but he feared the prophet's political influence and, superstitiously, his spiritual power. So he kept John alive, albeit in prison. He'd been there for a year and a half.

John the Baptist is an example of courageous witness and laying one's life on the line for the truth.

> **Matthew 14:6–7** On Herod's birthday the daughter of Herodias danced for them and pleased Herod so much that he promised with an oath to give her whatever she asked.

When Salome Danced—Oh How She Danced!

At Herod's birthday party, Herodias' beautiful and voluptuous young daughter, Salome, danced for the king and his invited guests. In an expansive statement of inebriated and sexually aroused appreciation (and to impress the high mucky-mucks at the party) the tetrarch issued the above oath offering the girl "... *up to half my kingdom*" (Mark 6:23).

Herod: *Tetrarch Antipas, son of Herod the Great, called himself a "king"*

☞ **Check It Out:**

Matthew 14:3–11

Mark 6:17–29

KEY POINT

Jesus' message and work was so similar to John's that Herod thought he'd seen a ghost!

Remember This . . .

After conferring with her mother, Herodias, Salome immediately returned to the banquet hall with her request: "I want you to give me right now the head of John the Baptist on a platter!"

Herod kept his promise. The illustrious career of Christ's forerunner came to a sudden end on the chopping block, but his influence lives today.

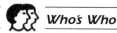

Who's Who

SALOME: Teenage daughter of Herodias by her first husband, Philip; her name is known from sources outside the Bible. Her dancing so pleased the king that John the Baptist lost his head.

What Others are Saying:

John Chrysostom: So the princess danced and, after the dance, committed another more serious sin. For she persuaded that senseless man to promise with an oath to give her whatever she might ask. . . . The request was abominable, but she persuaded him, and he gave the order to bridle John's holy tongue. But even now it continues to speak. For even today in every church, you can hear John still crying aloud through the Gospels and saying: "It is not lawful for you to have the wife of your brother Philip." He cut off the head but he did not cut off the voice.[9]

Study Questions

1. What convinced Jesus the crowds needed a shepherd (Matthew 9:36)? Describe his feelings toward people. What was the first thing he asked his disciples to do about it?

2. What did Jesus mean when he told his disciples he was sending them out "like sheep among wolves"? (Matthew 10:16–17)

3. How has Christ's teaching united your family? How has it divided your family? (Matthew 10:34–37). Why?

4. What is the principle of "spiritual teamwork"? How did Jesus use it?

5. Who did King Herod think Jesus was when his disciples fanned out across Galilee casting out demons and preaching the kingdom of God? What had he done that was probably bothering his conscience?

CHAPTER WRAP-UP

- Filled with compassion for the lost, harassed, and helpless crowds, Jesus asked his disciples to pray for workers to send into the fields to "harvest" those willing to be saved. (Matthew 9:35–38)

- Jesus gathered his disciples and gave them instructions on how to go throughout Galilee preaching the message of the kingdom and carrying on his work, what to expect in the way of opposition, and their need for total commitment. (Matthew 10:1–42)
- He sent them out on their mission in teams of two. (Mark 6:7)
- Many people, including King Herod, misread the effective evangelism and miracles done by Jesus and his men as evidence that the martyred John the Baptist had returned from the dead. (Mark 6:14–16)

18 GOOD BREAD

CHAPTER HIGHLIGHTS

- Power Lunch
- Royalist Movement
- Sea Walker
- Bread of God
- Captured by Life

Let's Get Started

Always in the backdrop of the story of Jesus Christ is the deep poverty that gripped most of the people of Israel in the first century. Rome's occupation forces controlled the tiny nation. Most of the land was owned by a few wealthy land barons and worked by sharecroppers for percentages too low to offer any hope of ever getting off the cycle of deprivation and hardship.

The Jewish people despised the Roman conquerors more than most conquered countries. There was always an insurrection brewing somewhere in Israel. Nowhere was anti-Roman sentiment more explosive than in Galilee. The atmosphere of political unrest had a negative effect on trade. Goods did not flow to Israel as freely as to other parts of the Empire. High taxation and reluctant trade assured that food would always be in short supply. Prices were high. The rich, as usual, had all they needed. The poor, always the first to suffer under such conditions, existed on the brink of starvation.

GOSPEL QUARTET IN HARMONY

Matthew 14:13–36; 15:1–6; 15:10–16:12
Mark 6:31–56; 7:1–8:26
Luke 9:10–17
John 6:1–71; 7:1

> **Mark 6:34–36** When Jesus landed and saw a large crowd, he had compassion on them, because they were like sheep without a shepherd. So he began teaching them many things. By this time it was late in the day, so his disciples came to him, "This is a remote place," they said, "and it is already very late. Send the people away so they can go to the surrounding countryside and villages and buy themselves something to eat."

GOSPEL QUARTET
IN HARMONY

Matthew 14:13–15
Mark 6:31–35
Luke 9:10–12
John 6:1–5

Passover: *celebration of Israel's liberation from Egyptian slavery*

other side: *where Jordan flows into northern end of Lake Galilee*

☞ **GO TO:**

Luke 9:10; John 1:44;
6:5 (Philip)

1 Peter 1:6–7
(their own faith)

Power Lunch

The season was spring. The time of the **Passover** approached (John 6:4). Passover, to the Jews, was like the Fourth of July to Americans or Bastille Day for the French. Nationalist feelings always ran high as they prepared for this festival.

Getting Away From Getting Away From It All

Because of the clamoring crowds, Jesus and his apostolic teams, who had just returned from their preaching sweep of Galilee, couldn't find time to be alone to share what they'd experienced. Jesus suggested a getaway ("just the 13 of us") to the desolate hill country north of the Sea of Galilee (see illustration, page 259).

As they boarded a fishing boat to escape across the lake, someone saw them. Word of their departure and direction spread like wildfire and, by the time they got to the **other side**, a crowd was waiting on shore. Even though his plan for time alone with his compadres was disrupted, Jesus' compassion for the crowds moved him to temporarily lay aside retreat plans for his two primary people-helping ministries—teaching and healing.

The Miracle Picnic

The people followed Jesus and his men into the hills near Bethsaida (see illustration, page 259). They stayed with him all day. The gathering had happened so spontaneously, few had brought food. Their hunger combined with Christ's powerful compassion to bring about one of the most spectacular miracles of Jesus' career. The four New Testament historians tell how he did many miracles, but only two are recorded by all four—his resurrection from the dead and the feeding of the 5,000.

Each gospel storyteller—Matthew, Mark, Luke, and John—gives details not noticed by the others. All four number the crowd at *5,000 men*. Many may have been armed,[1] thinking Jesus was a "new Moses" who would lead in a war of liberation from Roman oppression. Matthew adds that this number did not include women and children. The actual size of the crowd has been estimated at between 10,000 and 15,000, depending on how many women and children were there. As the day wore on and the crowd stayed, his disciples suggested Jesus send them into neighboring villages to buy food. He turned to <u>Philip</u>, who was from the area, and asked where food might be purchased to feed the crowd.

Jesus knew what he was going to do. His question was designed to reveal to Philip and the others the strength of <u>their own faith</u>.

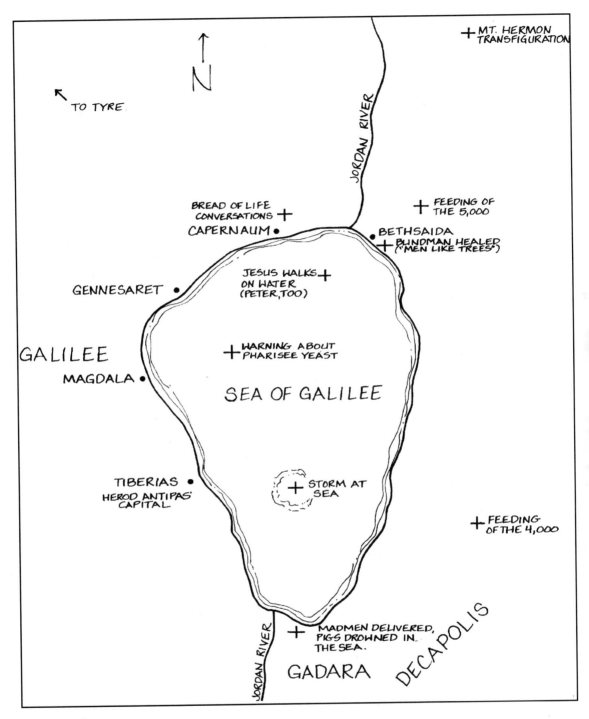

Sea of Galilee

Map of the Sea of Galilee shows the locations of many of Jesus' miracles, including the feeding of 5,000 and his walk on water as well as his bread-of-life conversations.

wages: a laborer's pay for a day's work was one denarius

barley loaves: rough bread of the poor; three loaves made an adult's meal

small fish: dried or pickled, to help the barley bread go down

satisfied: original word means not a token meal but abundant feast

surreptitious: secret

baskets: long, wicker baskets in which Jews carried travel provisions [2]

What Others are Saying:

🔑 **KEY Outline:**

Steps to Miracle
Need: hunger
Shortage of food
Concern
Offering (boy's lunch)
Thanksgiving
Lord's hands
Satisfied on poor food
Preserve leftovers

Two responses are noted:

1. The response of hopelessness based on mathematical calculation. Philip says, *"Eight months' __wages__ would not buy enough bread for each one to have a bite!"* (John 6:7; Mark 6:37).

2. The response of hopelessness based on a survey of available resources. Andrew says, *"Here is a boy with five small __barley loaves__ and two __small fish__, but how far will they go among so many?"* (John 6:8–9). The boy may have come from nearby Bethsaida on his way to bring supper to his father or brothers herding sheep in the hills.

Jesus took the loaves in his hands and offered thanks as if presiding over a family dinner. Then he broke the bread and fish (Luke 9:16) and handed the pieces to the 12 to distribute to the people who were seated in the soft grass. Everyone in the crowd, from all economic levels, was *"__satisfied__"* (Matthew 14:20; Mark 6:42; Luke 9:17) or *"had enough"* (John 6:12). While thousands were being fed an adequate lunch from a couple of pickled fish and five biscuits, there was **surreptitious** marvel taking place—everyone in that mixed crowd, rich and poor together, was *"satisfied"* and content with the food of the poor!

To avoid waste of God's gifts and to emphasize the preciousness of food, after everyone had eaten his fill, the disciples collected 12 **baskets** of leftovers!

Ray E. Baughman: Notice the difference between this miracle and the manna that was given to the children of Israel. God provided manna directly to the Israelites, but on this occasion he used human instruments to supply the need and distribute to the people. [3]

Augustine: Certainly the government of the whole world is a greater miracle than the satisfying of 5,000 men with 5 loaves; and yet no man wonders at the former; but the latter men wonder at, not because it is greater, but because it is rare. For who even now feeds the whole world, but he who creates the cornfield from a few grains? [4]

EARLY CHURCH LIFE: Jesus set the pattern of sharing for early Christians (see Acts 2:42–46; 4:32–36).

> **John 6:14–15** After the people saw the miraculous sign that Jesus did, they began to say, "Surely, this is **the Prophet** who is to come into the world."

The Royalist Movement

Powerful forces at work in first century Jewish society shaped the people's response to the supernatural supper. Many battled the persistent problem of poverty and hunger. The Jews hated the Roman occupation of Israel. Jewish teachers reminded the people of the messianic prophecies.

Add to these a general confusion about the miracle in which they had just participated. The feeding of the 5,000 demonstrated Jesus' phenomenal ability to supply human needs—and perhaps, they reasoned, this also meant he could lift them out of near-starvation and grinding poverty. Jesus intended the miracle of the loaves and fishes to do four things:

1. To feed over 5,000 hungry people
2. To be a sign to people expecting Messiah's arrival that he was the One
3. To open the way to introduce himself as the Bread of Life
4. To show that the kingdom of God had arrived

 The kingdom was certainly on their minds but, in their confusion, they saw the bread-giver as a "second Moses" who would form a political government and mount an army to deliver them from Roman oppression.

The Draft Jesus Campaign

They had been exposed to enough of Jesus' **kingdom teachings** to know he would likely be <u>reluctant to accept</u> a political crown, so some of them planned to force it on him.

This demonstrates the people's confusion about the Messiah-King. Unwilling to submit to Jesus' leadership, they intended to impose their will upon him, to put him under pressure to further their political agenda—which they saw as their only hope of deliverance. They had their own plans for solving their problems their own way. God's plans were not on their minds. It has a familiar ring. Christians often try to force Christ to bless their plans, preferences, and goals rather than allowing him to shape their plans, preferences, and goals from the ground up to harmonize with his.

☞ **GO TO:**

Deuteronomy 18:15–19 (the Prophet)

GOSPEL QUARTET IN HARMONY

Matthew 14:22
Mark 6:45–46
John 6:14–15

the Prophet: catchphrase for Moses-like leader expected in the last days

 **KEY Outline:**

Why This Miracle?
Feed people
Messiah sign
Prep for Bread of Life
Kingdom demo

☞ **GO TO:**

John 18:36
(reluctant to accept)

kingdom teachings: Sermons on the Mount (Matthew 5, 6, 7) and Plain (Luke 6)

Something to Ponder

☞ **GO TO:**

Matthew 4:1–7;
Luke 4:5–8
(old temptation)

Luke 4:42; 6:12
(alone with God)

withdrew: *mild word for "fled"*

What Others
are Saying:

☞ **GO TO:**

Mark 12:12; Luke
20:19; John 12:12–
13, 19 (at his feet)

KEY POINT

Christ's kingdom
cannot be established
through human
politics.

**GOSPEL QUARTET
IN HARMONY**

Matthew 14:24–33
Mark 6:47–52
John 6:16–21

> **John 6:15** Jesus, knowing that they intended to come and make him king by force, **withdrew** again to a mountain by himself.

The Case Of The Reluctant Royal

To the young Messiah, this royalist movement was neither a compliment nor an asset. It was a "summer rerun" of an <u>old temptation</u>—the enticing prospect of becoming ruler of the world in some way other than the Father's plan, which involved the cross. Whenever such temptations came, Jesus knew what to do. He hightailed it out of there and found a place to be <u>alone with God</u>. He climbed a mountain . . . *"to pray"* (Mark 6:46).

Robert E. Coleman: If Jesus had only accommodated himself to their natural appetites, the multitudes would have been <u>at his feet</u> and the cross could have been avoided. . . . He could have set himself upon the throne of the world. Was not this his temptation in the wilderness? That he viewed the suggestion as a satanic deception poses a bewildering problem for those activists who see his mission only in terms of social and political reformation.[5]

Christ's Kingdom—No Political Solution

By refusing to accept the crown Jesus threw down a marker at this strategic point in his ministry. The royalists would try again, but he had made it clear that he was not seeking a political solution to Israel's problems. From this time on desertions from his ranks increased. Especially at risk were the 12. As close as they were and as much time as they had spent with him, they still shared the deep-seated misunderstanding of the crowds—that Christ had come to revive David's earthly, military-political kingdom. They were to serve as founders of his church, the advance contingent of the heavenly kingdom. What happened that night further opened the eyes of the apostles to Jesus' true identity and what his kingdom was really about.

Sea Walker

Moving quickly to keep them from getting trapped in royalist politics, Jesus directed them to get into the boat and to proceed to the other side of the lake. It was getting dark when they took oars in hand and headed out across the water. Jesus didn't go with them—he needed time on the mountain.

The cooling of the air at nightfall often causes the wind to rush into the Galilean basin churning the lake into wild foam. The disciples had rowed about three miles when this unpredictable weather pattern struck from the west, and they found themselves rowing hard against the wind (John 6:18). Sometime during *"the fourth watch of the night"* (Mark 6:48) the struggling oarsmen saw a terrifying sight: In a flash of lightning or moonlight they caught sight of a lone ghostly figure walking on top of the water, catching up to them!

fourth watch: 3 to 6 A.M.

The water walker spoke. The voice was familiar: *"It is I. Don't be afraid."* It was Jesus.

> **Matthew 14:28–29** "Lord, if it is you," Peter replied, "tell me to come to you on the water!" "Come," he said. Then Peter got down out of the boat, walked on the water and came toward Jesus.

Dancing, Dancing, Over The Bounding Main

Matthew remembers part of the story the others fail to mention. Peter, ever the compulsive faith-leaper, responded to Jesus' voice with a daring request.

"Come," Jesus said.

Peter climbed over the side and found himself walking on top of the water, just like Jesus! What faith! But wait. What's this? Peter, God's "man of faith and power" looked around as he walked with Jesus on the surface of the water. The wind whipped the waves. Suddenly fear scared the faith right out of his heart! He began to sink.

KEY Outline:

Peter
Willing to believe
Willing to risk
Willing to yell for help

"Lord, save me!" he screamed in desperation. Jesus reached out his hand and pulled Peter to safety, giving him a mild reprimand for his doubt.

Upon reflection, the sting of the **Master's** reprimand must have been slight. Peter's faith may have *wave*-ered (pardon the pun), but it had been enough to make possible an experience with Christ none of the other guys in the boat experienced. None of them even dared to try walking on water by faith. Peter tried, succeeded for a moment, then failed. But he tried!

Something to Ponder

Master: title for Jesus, meaning "Teacher"

The 12 confessed
Jesus was God's Son.
He accepted it.

Matthew 14:33 Then those who were in the boat worshiped him, saying, "Truly you are the Son of God."

With Eyes (And Mouths) Wide Open

Jesus and Peter climbed into the boat and immediately its prow made a grinding sound in the sand as the skiff beached on the western lakeshore. What did the 12 do? What would you do? They got on their knees right then and there and worshiped Jesus!

The spiritual significance of the incident of the loaves and fishes had failed to penetrate their spiritual dullness (Mark 6:52).

But after the night on the lake, the truth began to trickle through the cracks in their preconception-hardened minds that Jesus' messiahship could not be defined in traditional Jewish terms nor in terms of earthly kingship. He was not just "any king." He could walk on water, for heaven's sake! He was God's Son in a way no one else ever was or could be.

What Others are Saying:

William Barclay: Their minds were obtuse, that was the root problem—they were ding-a-lings by choice, not by nature.[6]

Something to Ponder

It is important to note that the understanding of Jesus Christ's deity was given only to those who were already committed to follow him. Faith opens spiritual eyes. Believers are able to see spiritual truths the general run of people can't be expected to grasp.

God "I Am"

☞ **GO TO:**

Exodus 3 (bush)

Isaiah 43:10–11, 25 (God's name)

John 1:14, 18 (Revealer of God)

Bible scholars attach special significance to the words Jesus said as he walked to his disciples on the water: *"It is I"* (John 6:20). The literal translation of his words from the original language (Greek) of the New Testament is, *"I am."* It echoes God's introduction of himself to Moses in the burning <u>bush</u> (see GWBI, page 26; GWMB, page 74). Moses asked for the identity of the One who was sending him back to Egypt to deliver Israel from slavery. The voice from the flaming bush replied, in Hebrew, *"YHWH"* (*Yahweh*)—*I Am.* Israel came to use *I Am* as <u>God's name</u>. Jesus, on a number of occasions (see chart, page 265), identified himself with that same phrase. His followers came to understand he was claiming to be the personal, human <u>Revealer of God</u>.

Jesus' "I Am" Claims

"**I am** the bread of life. He who comes to me will never go hungry" (John 6:35, 41, 48, 51).

"**I am** the light of the world. Whoever follows me will never walk in darkness" (John 8:12).

"Before Abraham was born, **I am**." (Christ, like God, always existed.) (John 8:58).

"**I am** the gate for the sheep. Whoever enters through me will be saved" (John 10:7, 9).

"**I am** the good shepherd. The good shepherd lays down his life for the sheep" (John 10:11, 14).

"**I am** the resurrection and the life. He who believes in me will live, even though he dies" (John 11:25).

"**I am** the way and the truth and the life. No man comes to the Father except through me" (John 14:6).

"**I am** the vine; you are the branches. If a man lives in me and I in him, he will bear much fruit" (John 15:1–5).

The King Chasers

The boat carrying Jesus and the 12 landed near the lakeshore town of Gennesaret (see illustration, page 259) on Galilee's western shore. When the townspeople recognized them, they immediately brought sick people to him from all over the neighboring countryside, believing if they could touch the tassels on his robe, they'd be cured.

> **John 6:26–27** Jesus answered, "I tell you the truth, you are looking for me, not because you saw miraculous signs but because you ate the loaves and had your fill. Do no work for food that spoils, but for food that endures to eternal life, which the Son of Man will give you. On him the Father has placed his seal of approval."

A Chicken In Every Pot

Meanwhile, boats arrived at Capernaum carrying some of the multitudes Jesus had fed near Bethsaida. The king-chasers saw in the feeding of the 5,000 the answer to their economic and nutritional crisis. Anyone who could promise "a chicken in every pot" could have their vote—and, if need be, their sword. But they failed to see Jesus as the *spiritual* nourisher Israel needed more desperately than it needed food.

Dig Deeper

GOSPEL QUARTET IN HARMONY

Matthew 14:34–36
Mark 6:53–56
John 6:22–27

Leonard I. Sweet: One of the most forgotten principles of the Christian life is that of the uselessness of God—that God is not to be used as some passport out of perdition, or some cosmic bell-hop, or some divine welfare state that gives unlimited benefits and never exacts taxes.[7]

Leon Morris: Instead of seeing in the bread a sign, they had seen in the sign only the bread.[8]

Bringing Home The Bacon—Jesus Style

There are two kinds of food people work for, Jesus insisted (John 6:27):

- *"Food that spoils"*—physical food
- *"Food that endures to eternal life"*—spiritual food

They were working hard to provide enough of the first sort of food for their families. Jesus urged them to work for the second sort of food. He had proven he could supply the food needed to keep body and soul together. Now he tells them he can also supply the <u>eternal food</u> needed to live forever . . . if they'll *"work"* for it!

☞ **GO TO:**

Isaiah 55:1–2 (eternal food)

> **Matthew 6:28** Then they asked him, "What must we do to do the works God requires?"

The Work Of Believing

These Jewish questioners were asking, "Which works of the Law are required to earn this food that won't spoil?" The question was based on two defective beliefs:

☞ **GO TO:**

Ephesians 2:8–9; Isaiah 64:6 (works)

1. That human beings must produce *"**works**"* that win God's favor
2. That human beings are capable of pleasing God by the works they do

works: *moral acts performed by people to win God's approval*

the one he has sent: *Jesus' reference to himself, used 60 times*

Jesus' answer is incredible good news to people who can accept it: *"The work of God is this: to believe in **the one he has sent**"* (John 6:29).

Jesus was getting too personal. It was okay for him to solve their economic, nutritional, and political problems, but the idea they should look to him to solve their problem of spiritual malnutrition cut too close for comfort. The kingmakers began to squirm.

The <u>only work</u> God requires is the "work" of faith—personal commitment to the truth that Jesus is the One sent from God and that what he has done for us in his life, death, and resurrection is enough to save us from the consequences of our sins. God's approval and eternal life cannot be earned by human moral and righteous acts (rule-keeping, self-denial, being religious, doing enough good deeds to outweigh our sins). But, at the same time, good works are the <u>fruit</u> of people who have been made right with God through faith in Jesus Christ. Faith includes a <u>willingness to follow</u> him into a lifestyle like his.

> **John 6:30–31** So they asked him, "What miraculous sign then will you give that we may see it and believe you? What will you do? Our forefathers ate the manna in the desert; as it is written: 'He gave them bread from heaven to eat.'"

"I'll Believe If I See It . . . Again . . . And Again!"

The rabbis taught when Messiah came he would bring **manna**, just as Moses did during Israel's 40 years in the wilderness (see GWHN, pages 179–180). Feeding over 5,000 with a boy's lunch was okay. (Ho hum.) "But let's see if you can duplicate the daily shower of miraculous food Moses gave us! Do that, and we'll believe!"

The gall of those guys! The sheer, ugly, see-through deceit of trying to manipulate Jesus! Do this, and we'll believe? Hogwash! They had no intention of admitting their spiritual poverty and looking to the young Nazarene for help.

As for Jesus, it was all so-o-o-o familiar; he'd been there, done that. It was another "summer rerun" of the devil's temptation in the desert: "Turn these <u>stones to bread</u> so we will know you are the Son of God!" (Luke 4:3). He counterattacked with the truth, as he had in the desert (John 6:32–33):

- In the first place, Moses wasn't the source of the manna—God was (verse 32).

- In the second place, God is the only source of *"the true bread"* needed for eternal life (verse 32).

- In the third place, even the manna wasn't "the bread of God." The bread of God is a person *"who comes down from heaven"* and *"gives life to the world"* (verse 33).

Remember This . . .

☞ **GO TO:**

John 3:16; 5:24; Romans 1:17; 10:9–11 (only work)

James 2:14–26; Ephesians 2:10; Galatians 5:22–23; John 15:5 (fruit)

John 8:31; 1 Peter 2:21 (willingness to follow)

manna: waferlike food appearing on the desert floor each morning but the Sabbath

☞ **GO TO:**

Exodus 16 (manna)

Matthew 4:1–4; Luke 4:1–4 (stones to bread)

John 6:34–36 "Sir," they said, "from now on give us this bread." Then Jesus declared, "I am the bread of life. He who comes to me will never go hungry, and he who believes in me will never be thirsty. But as I have told you, you have seen me and still you do not believe.

The Bread Of God

Jesus was no stranger to hunger. When he faced the temptation to go against God's will by turning stones to bread, he hadn't eaten for 40 days! He understands the desperation of people who go to bed hungry every night. He clearly teaches his disciples to care for the poor and <u>feed the hungry</u>. Certainly, a never-ending supply of bread would be a dream come true. (Read about the bread of Bible times in GWHN, pages 8–9.) But the king chasers had a gnawing spiritual need even more desperate than their need for food. Jesus had been sent by God to meet that need.

☞ **GO TO:**

Matthew 25:34–43;
  Luke 12:33; Romans
  15:25–28;
  2 Corinthians 8–9
  (feed the hungry)

John 6:37–40 All that the Father gives me will come to me, and whoever comes to me I will never drive away. For I have come down from heaven not to do my will but to do the will of him who sent me. And this is the will of him who sent me, that I shall lose none of all that he has given me, but raise them up at the last day. For my Father's will is that every one who looks to the Son and believes in him shall have eternal life, and I will raise him up at the last day."

The Politics Of Eternity

No more beating around the bush. He said it straight out, so clear they couldn't miss it unless they chose to. Jesus himself is the nourisher who can satisfy the deepest needs of people. Sent by God himself, he came down from heaven to earth, to be the life-giving food famished souls must have or die.

Remember
This . . .

Satisfaction of spiritual hunger depends on two things: (1) coming to Jesus to meet our true needs and be assured of eternal life and (2) believing in Jesus as the one who can link us to God in a personal relationship.

Bread for the Hungry from John 6

Jesus' Claims	Reference
He came down from heaven	verse 38
He was sent by God	verses 38–39
He does the Father's will, not his own	verse 38
He is able to safeguard everyone the Father gives him	verse 39
He can and will raise the dead at the **last day**	verses 39–40
The person who trusts in him is assured of eternal life	verse 40

last day: events prophesied to happen at the end of time

The choice to come or not to come to Jesus leads to one of two positions: (1) A person may remain unconvinced (John 6:36). They met him, heard him teach, saw him work miracles, but still did not believe he was what he claimed. Or (2) A person may want to belong to Christ (verses 37, 39). Nobody comes without God's help. Those who come are always welcomed.

Something to Ponder

> **John 6:41–42** At this the Jews began to grumble about him because he said, "I am the bread that came down from heaven." They said, "Is this not Jesus, the son of Joseph, whose father and mother we know? How can he now say, 'I came down from heaven'?"

KEY Outline:

Believers
Are gifts from God
Will not be turned away
Will not be lost
Will be raised at the last day
Will live forever

Gagging On Good Bread

Jesus' old enemies, members of the Jewish religious establishment, have now joined the discussion. At this point the discussion may have moved from the lakeshore to the synagogue at Capernaum (John 6:59).

They dismissed his claim to be from God, on intellectual grounds: How could Jesus be from God? Everybody knew he was Joe's kid! Jesus did not argue with them. He simply went on to tell them that only those whose spiritual ears were tuned to the Father's voice would be able to hear and learn and come to him (verses 44–45).

You can't argue people into believing if they don't want to believe. Nobody ever finds his way to God by reasoning alone. Faith makes sense. But ultimately the Spirit of God will have to instruct the hearts and minds of people you're trying to convince. Real faith is itself a miracle.

ACT OF THE HOLY SPIRIT

Real faith is a miracle from the Holy Spirit

Remember This . . .

Oswald Chambers: There is no delusion in Christian experience, it begins outside me by creating in me an enormous craving, akin to thirst or to hunger. This craving is created by the reality of the Redemption, not by my penetrating insight, but by what John calls "the drawing of the Father" (John 6:44).[9]

> **John 6:51–57** "I am the living bread that came down from heaven. If anyone eats of this bread, he will live forever. This bread is my flesh, which I will give for the life of the world." Then the Jews began to argue sharply among themselves, "How can this man give us his flesh to eat?" Jesus said to them, "I tell you the truth, unless you eat the flesh of the Son of Man and drink his blood, you have no life in you. Whoever eats my flesh and drinks my blood has eternal life, and I will raise him up at the last day. For my flesh is real food and my blood is real drink. Whoever eats my flesh and drinks my blood remains in me, and I in him. Just as the living Father sent me and I live because of the Father, so the one who feeds on me will live because of me."

KEY Outline:

Spiritual Health Food
Jesus' flesh
- personal
  relationship
Jesus' blood
- share his life

☞ **GO TO:**

Leviticus 17:10–14
(drinking blood)

Shock Diet For Malnourished Spirits

Jesus did not make it easy for people to follow him. Nothing as simple as, "Go to church, and pay your tithe." He spread before his opponents and friends alike a spiritual diet they were bound to choke on unless they were ready to chew on some tough meat and crusty bread and drink some bitter grog.

Here is the spiritual diet of those who live forever:

- The entre: Jesus' flesh.
- The drink: Jesus' blood.

The response among the Galileans listening to Jesus was shock and revulsion. The Old Testament taught clearly that <u>drinking blood</u> was absolutely forbidden. Obviously, Jesus' statements were never meant to be taken literally, but figuratively. But to the Jews, even the thought of drinking blood was repulsive. Even non-Jews often find these words offensive, always puzzling.

What did Jesus mean? These are explosive pictures of Christian faith, and they are shocking enough to emphasize the radical nature of what it means to live by faith in Jesus. "Eating his flesh" and "drinking his blood" are metaphors for the real spiritual processes involved in being a Christian.

Everything in the Christian life, as taught in the New Testament, begins and ends and revolves around a living, personal relationship with Christ, carried on by faith. Jesus Christ is the center of everything for the Christian. Without him, the Christian faith has no life and nothing to offer the hungry world.

Remember This . . .

Lawrence O. Richards: The relationship with Christ symbolized by eating his flesh is initiated and sustained by faith's participation in all that Jesus is and all he has done for us. . . . By faith we do participate in Jesus' death and resurrection. We have partaken of his body and blood, and received his gift of eternal life.[10]

What Others are Saying:

Leon Morris: This eating and drinking are absolutely necessary for eternal life. Those who do not eat and drink have no life. Eating and drinking thus appear to be a very graphic way of saying that men must take Christ into their innermost being. . . . a challenge to enter the closest and most intimate relation with him.[11]

Augustine: Believe and you have eaten.[12]

Eating Jesus' Flesh and Drinking Jesus' Blood

What It Means	Supporting Scriptures
Taking Jesus Christ into our lives	John 1:12; Colossians 1:27
Appropriating the benefits of Jesus' suffering and death as our own	Romans 6:4–5; Galatians 2:20
Personally participating in his sufferings	Romans 8:17; Colossians 1:24
Sharing in the divine nature of Jesus through his indwelling spirit	2 Peter 1:4
Drawing inspiration, hope, and strength from Jesus' humanness	Hebrews 2:6–9, 16–18
Unity with Christ: He becomes part of us, we become part of him	1 Corinthians 6:17; 12:12–13, 27
Sharing the richness and satisfaction of Christ's abundant life	John 10:10; 1 John 5:11–12
Continuous fellowship with Jesus	Matthew 28:20; 1 John 1:3,
Drawing from Jesus daily spiritual nourishment we need to survive	2 Timothy 4:17; Philippians 4:13
Symbolized in the bread and wine of the Lord's Supper	Luke 22:17–20; 1 Corinthians 11:23–26

Captured By Life

The synagogue in Capernaum seemed shaken to its foundations by these teachings (John 6:59). A bitter <u>argument</u> broke out, probably between Jesus' supporters and his ecclesiastical enemies (verse 52).

☞ **GO TO:**

Matthew 10:34; Luke 12:51 (argument)

disciples: *seekers not committed to the teacher or his beliefs*

☞ **Check It Out:**

John 6:59–71

The enemies of Jesus might be expected to misunderstand, but even his **disciples** struggled with this latest teaching. Many who called themselves "disciples" had accompanied him throughout Galilee but weren't ready to give him the place in their lives he was calling for. The idea of eating his flesh and drinking his blood was as revolting to them as to the religious leaders. They had no intention of giving him the depth of allegiance those word pictures suggested. Many deserted his ranks (verses 60–66). He made no attempt to stop them. And, true to himself, he never offered them cheap grace, "easy believism," or costless discipleship in order to get them to stay. The crowd melted like a snowball in July. Just a few were left. The 12 were standing nearby.

What Others are Saying:

Michael Card: Many of his disciples were offended and left. "This is a hard teaching," they said. "Who can accept it?" I wonder how many other hard sayings it had taken to bring them to this point. Once again, as they were leaving, you might have expected at least an explanation from Jesus, "No, you misunderstood. I know these things are hard to hear but just hang in there a little longer and it will all make sense." Instead Jesus turned to the Twelve. . . .[13]

> **John 6:67–69** "You do not want to leave too, do you?" Jesus asked. "Lord, to whom shall we go?" [Peter answered]. "You have the words of eternal life. We believe and know that you are the Holy One of God."

No Place I'd Rather Be

Peter's answer does not mean all his questions were answered. But it expresses a genuine conviction that gripped him and the others. And it glows as the brightest spot in this story.

While many others revealed the shallowness of their motives and slid shamefaced back into the dark from which they'd crawled to follow Jesus, these 12 were convinced they had made the right choice. There would be other moments of choice for them (verses 70–71). But at this point, weak as they were, they were heroes of the faith. And their fledgling faith warmed the heart of their Lord.

What Others are Saying:

Robert E. Coleman: To the great disappointment of the revolutionary Zealots, Jesus led no crusade to forcefully overthrow the civil authority. . . . His approach was far more radical—and realistic. He attacked the root of man's problem, not its symptoms. Without this basic conversion, any restructuring of society would be superficial. To be sure, just social systems promote the common good, and therefore should be sought. But all governments of men, however good, are still under God's judgment and will perish. So whatever the system, the self-serving sinners in it need to become a part of that Kingdom where love motivates every desire. This is the king of revolution Jesus came to lead.[14]

Study Questions

1. What food was available for Jesus to use in feeding the 5,000? With whom do you most identify in this story? (a) *The crowd:* waiting for a miracle, (b) *Philip:* crunching the numbers and overwhelmed, (c) *Andrew:* coming up short, or (d) *The boy with the lunch:* if Jesus wants it he can have it.

2. What is the significance of Jesus' use of "I Am" in reference to himself? Identify five of his "I am" statements and tell what they mean?

3. What two kinds of food do people work for? What is "the work of God"?

4. In John 6:38–40 what six claims does Jesus make concerning himself?

5. What did Jesus mean when he told his followers they must eat his flesh and drink his blood?

CHAPTER WRAP-UP

- Jesus fed a crowd of over 5,000 a satisfying meal using only a little boy's lunch—five barley loaves and two small fish. (Mark 6:30–44)

- Many in the crowd wanted to crown Jesus king, seeing in him the solution to their economic problems and a military-political deliverer from Roman rule. Politics was not on Jesus' kingdom agenda. He escaped to a mountain to pray. (John 6:14–15)

- Jesus' disciples got into a boat to return to Capernaum and got caught in a storm. As they struggled against the wind, Jesus came to them, walking on top of the water. (Matthew 14:22–34)

- The crowds Jesus fed found him in Capernaum. He told them he was not merely the supplier of physical food, but the spiritual bread they needed for eternal life. (John 6:22–51)

- When he used the metaphor of eating his flesh and drinking his blood to press their need to take him into their lives and depend on him for daily spiritual sustenance, many deserted him. The 12 reaffirmed their commitment to be with him. (John 6:52–69)

19 RELIGION VERSUS REALITY

CHAPTER HIGHLIGHTS

- Tradition versus Reality
- Clean Hands versus Clean Hearts
- Lost Sheep and Puppy Dogs
- Power for Life's Realities
- Religious Politics
- Seeing People

Let's Get Started

Jesus of Nazareth was always in trouble with the religious authorities. He taught that eternal life could not be found in dutiful rule keeping or spiritless observance of religious ceremonies. Eternal life was found only in a dynamic personal relationship with God. Such radical thinking threatened the system and institutions on which the teachers and clerics depended for their livelihood and influence.

In the discussions growing out of the feeding of the 5,000 (John 6), Jesus carried his radical ideas to still more disconcerting depths. He declared that he was the *living bread*, which provided spiritual sustenance for a life-giving relationship with God, and that to find eternal life, people needed to take him into their lives and feed on him. This bold claim added fuel to his enemies' fire. The chasm between Jesus and the authorities became a gaping canyon. Many rank-and-file Jews joined their leaders in opposing the brash young rabble-rouser. Even the enthusiasm of many of Jesus' friends cooled (John 6:66).

GOSPEL QUARTET IN HARMONY

Matthew 15:1–6;
15:10–16:12
Mark 7:1–8:26
John 7:1

> **Mark 7:5** So the Pharisees and teachers of the law asked Jesus, "Why don't your disciples live according to the tradition of the elders instead of eating their food with 'unclean' hands?"

Tradition Versus Reality

Pharisees and lawyers came from Jerusalem loaded for bear, intent on exposing Jesus and his followers as lawbreakers. Every-

☞ **Check It Out:**

Matthew 15:1–6

Mark 7:1–13

where he went these religious scalp hunters were there, watching. In a classic "Aha!" they saw the disciples eating without the elaborate handwashing ceremony observed by strict Jews. They confronted Jesus about this unthinkable breach of etiquette and religious correctness. It was not an issue of hygiene or of true spirituality, but of overscrupulous, legalistic, meaningless religious minutiae.

"*Tradition!*" What is referred to that way in this passage (Mark 7:3–5, 8, 9, 13) were customs and practices, based on rulings by earlier teachers of Old Testament Law. This so-called "oral law" came to be viewed by the Pharisees and lawyers as having as much authority as God's written Law in the **Pentateuch**.

Pentateuch: first five books of the Old Testament

Nothing angered Jesus like religious nitpicking, which served no true spiritual purpose. You can almost see him shaking his head in disgust.

hypocrites: Greek meaning: "actors in a play"; pretenders

> **Mark 7:6–9** He replied, "Isaiah was right when he prophesied about you **hypocrites**; as it is written: 'These people honor me with their lips, but their hearts are far from me. They worship me in vain; their teachings are but rules taught by men.' You have let go of the commands of God and are holding on to the traditions of men" And he said to them: "You have a fine way of setting aside the commands of God in order to observe your own traditions!"

The Love Ban

In a tone tinged with sarcasm, Jesus turned the spotlight of truth on a glaring hypocrisy practiced by these self-appointed religious "policemen." He quoted one of the Ten Commandments: "*Honor your father and your mother*" (Mark 7:10; Exodus 20:12). God considered the breaking of that particular mandate so serious, Jesus reminded them, that he prescribed the death penalty for "*anyone who curses his father or mother*" (Mark 7:10; Exodus 21:17).

curses: dishonors, disrespects, belittles

corban: "a gift devoted to God"; banned from all other uses

Jesus blew them out of the water with his exposé of a common practice that broke the commandment to honor one's parents all to smithereens. In spite of what the Law of God said, the *traditions* provided a completely legal way to avoid the expense of caring for one's father and mother. All you had to do was to announce to your parents that what you had been saving to help them was "*corban*." This meant it now belonged to God and was no longer available for nonreligious purposes!

A person might make a *corban* declaration in order to appear spiritual. If he later changed his mind, the ruling of the scribes declared he couldn't renege on his rash oath. He had to keep it, no matter the consequences.

The Rule of Corban was great for the Temple treasury, but it allowed or forced some people to break one of God's most precious commandments! Jesus called it by its real name—*hypocrisy*—and used it as an example of how religious people honor man-concocted traditions above God's Law!

"*You do many things like that,*" he added (verse 13). This was just one example.

KEY POINT

Christ despises hypocrisy. Hypocritical worship is useless.

Dan McCartney and Charles Clayton: Tradition was quite binding, even blinding, in the Judaism of Jesus' day. . . . Tradition can, if not continually challenged, lull people into a comfortable, dogmatic slumber from which they may never awake.[1]

What Others are Saying:

William Barclay: Jesus was attacking a system which put rules and regulations before the claim of human need. . . . Nothing that prevents us helping a fellow man can ever be a rule approved by God.[2]

Religious rules and practices based on the past easily become substitutes for true responsiveness, obedience, and love for God.

Something to Ponder

Clean Hands Versus Clean Hearts

As for the issue of ceremonial handwashing that started this discussion with the Jewish legal beagles, instruction concerning washing hands before eating was not found in the Scriptures. Handwashing in the Bible is

- prescribed for anyone who touches a dead body (Deuteronomy 21:6—not a bad idea!)
- a word picture of separation of God-worshipers from evildoers (Psalm 26:6)
- an attempt by a cowardly judge to absolve himself of responsibility in an unjust court decision (Matthew 27:24—it didn't work—he was still guilty!)
- a word picture of turning from sin and getting right with God (James 4:8–10)

☞ **Check It Out:**

Matthew 15:10–20

Mark 7:14–23

- a tradition practiced by Pharisees and other strict Jews (Mark 7:3–4—good for hygiene, perhaps, but spiritually useless!)

The truth is, God doesn't care if you wash your hands before you eat or not. I don't care what your mother told you—cleanliness is not, never has been, "close to godliness." That's not in the Bible either! But the religious leaders of Israel made a rule out of it. Jesus and his rugged backcountry disciples ignored it!

> **Mark 7:15** "Nothing outside a man can make him 'unclean' by going into him. Rather, it is what comes out of a man that makes him 'unclean.'"

KEY POINT

Spirituality and holiness are not ceremonial or religious matters, they are issues of the heart.

☞ **GO TO:**

Acts 10:9–16; Romans 14:14, 17–18, 20; 1 Corinthians 8:8 (all foods "clean")

Jeremiah 17:9; Romans 3:9–18; Galatians 5:19–21 (men's hearts)

Bless Your Dirty Heart!

So what's wrong with washing before you eat (and other outward matters of hygiene and appearance)? Nothing, unless you make a religion of it. If it honors your mother to wash your hands, scrub behind your ears, clean under your fingernails, or shave your scruffy face, do it—the Bible says "Honor your mother." None of that concerns Jesus here. His concern is that we know where outward cleanliness fits in the scheme of real spiritual issues.

Later, alone with his disciples, he said: *"Don't you see that nothing that enters a man from the outside can make him 'unclean.' For it doesn't go into his heart but into his stomach, and then out of his body"* (Mark 7:18–19). Mark, the author, comments: *"In saying this, Jesus declared <u>all foods "clean."</u>*

What Jesus was really concerned about was a person's heart, so he explained it more. *"What comes out of a man is what makes him 'unclean.' For from within, out of <u>men's hearts</u>, come evil thoughts, sexual immorality, theft, murder, adultery, greed, malice, deceit, lewdness, envy, slander, arrogance and folly. All these evils come from inside and make a man 'unclean'"* (Mark 7:20–23).

What Others are Saying:

William Barclay: In effect Jesus was saying that *things* cannot be either unclean or clean in any real religious sense of the term. Only *persons* can be really defiled; and what defiles a person is his own actions, which are the product of his own heart. With one sweeping pronouncement Jesus declared . . . that uncleanness has nothing to do with what a man takes into his body, and everything to do with what comes out of his heart.[3]

The Pretender

A hypocrite is a pretender, which is all well and good if you're on Broadway or Saturday night TV. But pretended Christianity is useless, meaningless, impotent, and downright destructive. It is hypocrisy for a person to make a show of keeping rules and religious traditions while his or her inner life is polluted with spiritual filth—motives, attitudes, and actions that foul the heart and spirit and soil the life. The hypocrite can change. But he/she must stop playing religious games and get <u>honest</u> with God!

Lost Sheep And Puppy Dogs

With pressure from his enemies increasing in Galilee, Jesus and the 12 crossed the border into the gentile district of Phoenicia, along the Mediterranean coast. He wanted no one to know where they were (Mark 7:24). Jewish people were unlikely to follow him there. But getting "away" was impossible. A Phoenician-born woman of mixed <u>Greek and Canaanite</u> heritage found him, got down on her knees, and begged him to deliver her daughter from the harassing evil spirit that had taken possession of her. At first Jesus ignored her pleas. But she kept shrieking her desperate request. The disciples urged him to send her away.

His conversation with this Gentile mother includes some intriguing lines.

"I was only sent to the lost sheep of Israel," he said (Matthew 15:24). The priority of his ministry was <u>his own</u> people, to whom the messianic promises had been given. With a few <u>notable exceptions</u>, he kept with that program. Jesus understood his human and time limitations—to get the job done he'd been sent to do, he could not afford to open the door wide to the Gentiles. His followers would do that after his <u>resurrection</u>.

"Lord, help me!" she answered (Matthew 15:25). With his basic nature of compassion toward people in need, Jesus could hardly walk away.

"First let the children eat all they want," he told her, *"for it is not right to take the children's bread and toss it to their dogs"* (Mark 7:27). The *"children"* are God's children, the Jews. It was not unusual for Jews to refer to Gentiles as *dogs*. The Greek word Jesus used for *dogs* was different from the one that would normally be used in an insult. It was a term that could be taken affectionately. Alternate translations include "pet dogs," "lap dogs," or "puppies." We can't see Jesus' face, but the needy woman could. It

Something to Ponder

☞ **GO TO:**

1 John 1:5–10 (honest)

☞ **Check It Out:**

Matthew 15:21–28

Mark 7:24–30

☞ **GO TO:**

Mark 7:26; Matthew 15:22 (Greek and Canaanite)

John 1:11–12 (his own)

John 4:4–42; Luke 7:1–10 (notable exceptions)

Acts 1:8; 10; 11; 13; 28:25–28; Romans 9:22–26; Ephesians 2:12 (resurrection)

KEY POINT

As a man, Jesus had to function within human limitations.

KEY Outline:

Effective Prayer
Confident in Christ's
*   power*
Persistent
Yields to God's priorities
Humble
Believing

Something
to Ponder

☞ **Check It Out:**

Matthew 15:29–38

Mark 7:31–8:9

GOSPEL QUARTET
IN HARMONY

Matthew 15:32–38
Mark 8:1–9

☞ **GO TO:**

Matthew 14:15–21;
Mark 6:35–44; Luke
9:12–17; John 6:4–
13 (the 5,000)

Mark 5:18–20; Luke
8:38–39 (madman)

makes all the difference in the world if the word was said with an angry scowl or a tender smile. I see Jesus smiling as he spoke.

"Yes, Lord," she replied, "but even the dogs under the table eat the children's crumbs" (Mark 7:28). She was acknowledging the rightness of Jesus' priorities. As a Gentile, she understood she was not one of the chosen. She wasn't demanding her "rights." She was pleading for what any pet housedog could expect: the scraps the children throw away.

Her combination of persistence, confidence in his authority and goodness, humility, and respect for the priorities to which he was committed made her faith *"great"* (Matthew 15:28). Her request was granted. Her daughter was healed.

Power For Life's Realities

On his return from the brief hiatus to Phoenicia, refreshed, he plunged back into the crowds that came to be healed. The lame walked away. The handicapped left without their handicaps. The blind went seeing. The "Hallelujahs" of the dumb rang in the air. The deaf heard the dumb shouting. There was apparently no human need or impairment for which his power was not adequate.

> **Matthew 15:35–37** He told the crowd to sit down on the ground. Then he took the seven loaves and the fish, and when he had given thanks, he broke them and gave them to the disciples, and they in turn to the people. They all ate and were satisfied.

Deja Vu All Over Again!

Two New Testament historians report a second incident in which Jesus fed a large crowd with a tiny amount of food. The differences between this miracle meal multiplication and the feeding of the 5,000 include the following:

- This time the crowd was 4,000 men, plus women and children (Matthew 15:38).
- The scene was a desolate area in Decapolis, east of Galilee (Mark 7:31), a province with a mixed Jewish-Gentile population. Some think the liberated madman whom Jesus healed helped bring this crowd together.
- This time the people had gone three days without food (Mark 8:2).

- The number of loaves to work with this time was *"seven, and a few small fish"* (Matthew 15:34).
- The leftovers filled seven baskets (Matthew 15:37). The word for *basket* is different this time. The baskets used to gather leftovers after the 5,000 were fed were long, narrow-necked baskets in which Jews carried food when they traveled. This time, the basket is the same as the one used to help Paul <u>escape</u> over the Damascus wall—large, open at the top, and used mainly by Gentiles.
- The motivation for both miracles was Christ's compassion for the hungry (Matthew 14:14; 15:32; Mark 6:34; 8:2).

EARLY CHURCH LIFE: It is possible this picnic in the desert included Gentiles and Jews together—a symbol that the time was coming when non-Jews would be included in the Gospel.

Lawrence O. Richards: The need for food is one of the most basic of human needs. Jesus was not only concerned about people's spiritual condition, he was moved by compassion for physical hunger as well. We cannot represent Jesus adequately if we are moved only by the need to win lost souls. To represent Jesus we must be as concerned for the hungry, the homeless, and the oppressed as our Lord was for the hungry multitudes.[4]

The Wacky World Of Religious Politics

After the 4,000 were well fed and sent home, Jesus and his men once again sailed across the lake, this time at its widest part, and landed near the lakeshore town of **Magdala** (see illustrations, pages 259 and 289), home of **Mary Magdalene**.

The Odd Couple

Jesus' perennial detractors, the Pharisees, were waiting for him. This time, they were joined by the Sadducees, evidence that a rather strange political alliance was being brought together to oppose him. Often the Pharisees appeared with their legalistic mentors, the lawyers (scribes). But to team up with the Sadducees would have required both a theological and practical stretch.

PHARISEES: (Hebrew: "separated ones.") They were theologically **orthodox**. They believed in angels, the immortality of the human soul, the resurrection of the righteous dead, the sovereignty of God, human free will, and that the Old

KEY POINT

Christ desires to meet our material needs.

☞ **GO TO:**

Acts 9:23–25 (escape)

☞ **Check It Out:**

Matthew 15:39–16:12

Mark 8:10–21

What Others are Saying:

☞ **GO TO:**

Luke 8:1–3 (Magdalene)

Magdala: Magadan (Matthew 15:39) or Dalmanutha (Mark 8:10)

Mary Magdalene: woman from whom Jesus cast seven devils

orthodox: conforming to established doctrine; conservative

Who's Who

Testament in its entirety was the Word of God, along with the oral traditions of the ancient rabbis who interpreted the Scriptures. They were committed (1) to strict observance of all the ordinances and purity rituals of Judaism and (2) to meticulously carry out religious duties including tithing and ceremonial washings.

Who's Who

providence: *God's personal guidance, care, and involvement*

SADDUCEES: (Hebrew: "righteous ones.") Both theologically and practically, they were the Pharisees' opposites. They did not believe in angels or spirits, life after death, or the resurrection. They believed humans had total free will, without any influence by fate or the **providence** of God. Only the first five books of the Old Testament were authoritative. They did not believe in or practice the oral traditions. They were the party of the well-to-do, the aristocratic priesthood, and fiercely protected the status quo, which kept them in official charge of Jewish religious life.

And Herodians Make Three

The fact that the Pharisees and Sadducees, two widely divergent groups, could join forces shows how determined they were to get rid of Jesus. In fact, as the conspiracy to silence Christ developed, this theological odd couple was joined by the <u>Herodians</u>—a political party with little concern for theology, except as it affected their political aims.

☞ **GO TO:**

Matthew 22:16–17;
  Mark 3:6; 8:15; 12:13
  (Herodians)

Who's Who

☞ **GO TO:**

Exodus 12:15–20;
  13:3–10; 34:25;
  2 Corinthians 5:6–8
  (yeast)

yeast: *biblical symbol of impurity*

HERODIANS: These were political supporters of Herod the Great, and then of his son and successor, Herod Antipas. Their agenda called for keeping Herod firmly established in power and maintaining friendship with Rome, which they saw as advantageous. They joined with the Pharisees and Sadducees to oppose Jesus, not primarily on religious grounds, but because they saw him and his movement as a political threat.

> **Mark 8:15** "Be careful," Jesus warned them. "Watch out for the **yeast** of the Pharisees and that of Herod."

☞ **Check It Out:**

Matthew 16:5–12

Mark 8:13–21

Warning: Pharisee, Sadducee, And Herodian Thinking May Be Dangerous To Your Health!

Back in the boat headed across Galilee, this time for Bethsaida on the north shore, Jesus reflected on the most recent confrontation with the developing conspiracy against him. He warned his disciples about the yeast of the three groups aligned against him.

The disciples, not known for deep reflection on the events taking place around them, but for saying the first thing that came into their heads no matter how dumb it was, responded by whispering among themselves, "It's because we forgot to bring bread."

Jesus knew what they were thinking. *"Why are you talking about having no bread? Do you still not see or understand? Are your hearts hardened? Do you have eyes but fail to see, and ears but fail to hear? And don't you remember?"* (Mark 8:17–18).

"Remember what?" the disciples thought.

Here's a very loose paraphrase of Jesus' response in Matthew 16:8–11 and Mark 8:17–21: "Don't you remember the feeding of the 5,000 with five barley buns, when you gathered 12 baskets of leftovers? And when the 4,000 were fed with seven barley buns, and you collected 7 baskets of leftovers? What do you think that was all about anyway? Do you think when you are with me you really have to worry about bread? Get off the bread already! Where's your faith?"

Matthew 16:12 says, *"Then they understood that he was not telling them to guard against the yeast used in bread, but against the teaching of the Pharisees and Sadducees."*

Jesus' concern was that his men guard against infection with the distorted ideas of the Pharisees, Sadducees, and Herodians concerning the kingdom of God.

- Pharisees wanted a kingdom shaped by the traditions of the elders, based on the same spiritually deadly legalism that made them the nitpicking, killjoys they were.

- Sadducees rationalized Old Testament messianic prophecies and denied the promise of the kingdom. Infection with their thinking would bury the kingdom dream.

- Herodians would have placed some member of Herod's family on the throne as the promised king, and built a political kingdom riddled with Herodian corruption.

The messianic kingdom Christ was sent to establish on earth runs counter to all these ideas. It is based on life in the Spirit and shaped by love, not rules, tradition, or political maneuvering.

KEY POINT

If we forget God can supply our needs, we open ourselves to corrupting spiritual influences.

KEY Outline:

Kingdom Dreams
Pharisees
- deadly legalism

Sadducees
- no dream

Herodians
- Herod on the throne

Jesus
- Spirit life
- love
- freedom
- grace

> **Mark 8:23–24** He took the blind man by the hand and led him outside the village. When he had spit on the man's eyes and put his hands on him, Jesus asked, "Do you see anything?" He looked up and said, "I see people; they look like trees walking around."

Seeing People As Walking Trees

When the boat arrived at Bethsaida, someone brought a blind man with the request that Jesus *"touch him."* Jesus brought him outside the village and *"spit on the man's eyes."* The New Testament historians report Jesus using spit in a healing process three times:

1. In taking away a speech impediment (Mark 7:33)
2. In restoring sight to a man born blind (John 9:6)
3. In restoring sight to this blind man (Mark 8:23)

People in the past thought human saliva had healing properties. (I guess we still do—whenever I burn my finger the first thing I do is stick it in my mouth!) We know that spit alone can't make a blind man see, but Jesus used it as a way to <u>encourage</u> the man's faith for healing.

This is the only miracle Jesus performed that happened in two stages. In the first stage (after Jesus' first touch), the man said, *"I see people; they look like trees walking around"* (Mark 8:24). In the second stage (after Jesus' second touch), the Bible reports, *"His eyes were opened, his sight was restored, and he saw everything clearly"* (verse 25).

Perhaps Jesus' choice to heal this man this way was related to the conversation he'd just had with his disciples on the boat (verses 14–21). After all they had seen they still doubted his ability to feed them, and they still were unaware of the danger of mixing legalistic traditionalism and worldly politics with pursuit of the kingdom dream. They saw more clearly than others—but not yet clearly enough to be entrusted with leadership of the kingdom community.

Robert L. Thomas and Stanley N. Gundry: This case in Bethsaida, occurring as it did in two stages, is the only instance of a gradual cure by Jesus. Perhaps the Twelve needed to learn that every miracle would not be instantaneous. In some cases the victory of divine power over sin and sickness would be gradual.[5]

KEY POINT

If we aren't seeing clearly, we need a second touch from Jesus.

☞ **GO TO:**

Mark 5:28; Acts 5:15; 19:12 (encourage)

Something to Ponder

What Others are Saying:

Seeing Clearly

Like the <u>blind man</u> at Bethsaida after Jesus' first touch who saw men like trees walking and then after the second touch was able to see everything clearly, Jesus' closest disciples gradually came to realize who it was they had linked up with.

- John the Baptist had introduced him to them as the Lamb of God (John 1:35).
- Andrew told his brother Peter, *"We have found the Messiah!"* (John 1:41).
- Philip described Jesus as the one Moses wrote about in the Law, and about whom the prophets also wrote (John 1:45).
- Nathanael (Bartholomew) said to Jesus, *"You are the Son of God; you are the king of Israel"* (John 1:49).

No doubt they believed the words they were saying. But full understanding of the real significance of the words would require the next three years in intimate contact with Jesus.

It is an experience repeated with each individual who makes his or her first **confession** that <u>Jesus is Lord</u> and begins to walk with him by faith. The confession is real. The walk of faith is often life-changing. But full understanding of what has been confessed and begun comes only through months and years of exposure to Christ's story and teachings and experience walking with him by faith in the realities of everyday life.

For the disciples the startling reality of Christ's cross would gradually grip them as the rest of his story unfolded. The cross and the resurrection would completely transform their perception of the man Jesus from Nazareth.

An unknown author: He was born in an obscure village, the child of a peasant woman. He grew up in still another village, where he worked in a carpenter shop until he was thirty. Then for three years he was an itinerant preacher.

He never wrote a book.
He never held an office.
He never had a family or owned a house.
He didn't go to college.
He never traveled 200 miles from the place where he was born.

 GO TO:

Mark 8:22–26
(blind man)

Remember This . . .

confession: *verbal agreement that Jesus is who he claims to be*

GO TO:

Romans 10:9–10
(Jesus is Lord)

Something to Ponder

He did none of the things one usually associates with greatness.

He had no credentials but himself.

He was only 33 when public opinion turned against him. His friends ran away. He was turned over to his enemies and went through the mockery of a trial. He was nailed to a cross between two thieves.

When he was dying, his executioners gambled for his clothing, the only property he had on earth. When he was dead, he was laid in a borrowed grave through the pity of a friend.

Nineteen centuries have come and gone, and today he is the central figure of the human race, the leader of mankind's progress.

All the armies that ever marched, all the navies that ever sailed, all the parliaments that ever sat, all the kings that ever reigned, put together, have not affected the life of man on earth as much as that One Solitary Life.

Study Questions

1. What was Jesus' chief objection to the traditions of the Pharisees and lawyers? What did he call them?
2. How does Jesus' idea of being "unclean" differ from that of the Pharisees?
3. What was there about the Phoenician woman's faith that made it so "great"?
4. What point was Jesus making by reminding his disciples of the feedings of the 5,000 and 4,000 and the leftovers from each event?
5. Why was Jesus concerned that his followers beware of the "yeast" (teachings) of the Pharisees, Sadducees, and Herodians?
6. List three times Jesus used spit in the performance of a healing miracle?

CHAPTER WRAP-UP

- Jesus' enemies accused Jesus of letting his disciples eat without the ceremonial hand-washings prescribed by traditions. He turned their accusations against them, showing how their man-made traditions were forcing people to break the Laws of God. (Mark 7:1–13)

- Food, Jesus declared, has nothing to do with a person's spiritual purity. What matters is what is in the person's heart. A heart full of sin can only express itself in outward sin. Food is not a spiritual issue. All foods are ceremonially clean. (Mark 7:14–23)

- On a visit to Phoenicia, Jesus answered the plea of a Greek woman to heal her daughter, in a sense, pronouncing Gentiles ceremonially clean and accepted by God if they have faith. (Mark 7:24–30)

- On return to Galilee from Phoenicia, Jesus did many healing miracles and, in a repeat performance of the feeding of the 5,000, satisfied the hunger of a crowd of 4,000 using a tiny amount of food. (Mark 7:31–8:10)

- The religious and political forces lining up against Jesus began to solidify, bringing together divergent groups whose only bond was refusal to accept him as Messiah. He warned his disciples to beware of letting their thinking become corrupted by theirs. (Mark 8:10–21)

APPENDIX A — MAP OF PALESTINE

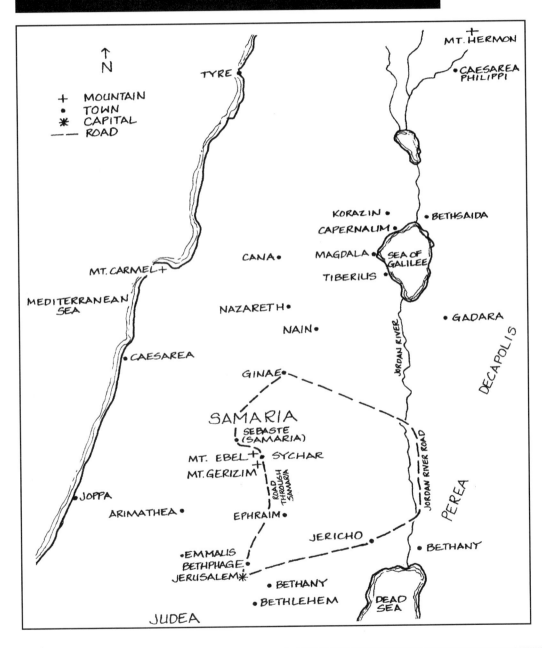

Parables of the Kingdom

Identified by "The kingdom of God is like . . ."

Category 1: The Kingdom Now

Structure, values, processes, attitudes under God's present reign

Parable	Illustrated Truth	Matthew	Mark	Luke	John
Capstone	Christ, kingdom foundation and head	21:42–44			
Growing seed	Natural process of kingdom growth		4:26–29		
Hidden treasure	The kingdom a priceless discovery	13:44			
Mustard seed	How the kingdom grows	13:31–32	4:31–32	13:18–19	
Old and new treasure	Sharing from experience	13:51–52			
Pearl of great price	Total commitment to gain the kingdom	13:45–46			
Sheep and goats	Jesus' oneness with people in trouble	25:31–46			
Sower, seed, soils	Listening, receiving the word	13:3–9, 18–23	4:3–20	8:4–15*	
Two sons	Words versus actions	21:28–32*			
Unmerciful servant	Forgiveness, torment of unforgiveness	18:23–35			
Weeds (tares)	Dealing with enemies in the church	13:24–30, 36–43			
Yeast (leaven)	Change, inner influence of the kingdom	13:33		13:20–21	

* Explained by Jesus

Parables of the Kingdom

Identified by "The kingdom of God is like . . ."

Category 2: The Kingdom Future

Last days, Christ's Second Coming, Judgment, Rewards

Parable	Illustrated Truth	Matthew	Mark	Luke	John
Alert servants	Readiness for Christ's return		13:32–37	12:35–40	
Capstone	Christ, kingdom foundation and head	21:42–44			
Fig tree, new leaves	Signs of the Christ's return	24:32–35*	13:28–31*	21:29*	
Fishing net	Separation of wicked from righteous		13:47–50*		
Great banquet	Accepting the Lord's invitation			14:16–24	
Laborers in vineyard	Fairness of God's grace, rewards	20:1–16			
Marriage (king's son)	Need to accept God's invitation	22:1–14			
Sheep and goats	Jesus' identification with people in trouble	25:31–46*			
Talents	Stewardship of gifts, opportunities	25:14–30			
Tenants	Rejection of Christ, loss of kingdom	21:33–41	12:1–9	20:9–16	
Ten minas	Wise and unwise handling of trust			19:12–27	
Ten virgins	Preparedness for Christ's coming	25:1–13			
Weeds (tares)	Dealing with enemies in the church	13:24–30, 36–43*			
Wise manager	Readiness for Christ's return			12:42–48	

* Explained by Jesus

Parables about Resources and Priorities

Parable	Illustrated Truth	Matthew	Mark	Luke	John
Rich fool	Foolish priorities, hoarding	16:19–31			
Rich man and Lazarus	Danger of indifference to the poor			12:16–21	
Sheep and goats	Jesus' identification with people in trouble	25:31–46*			
Shrewd manager	Creativity in use of worldly resources			16:1–15	
Talents	Stewardship of gifts, opportunities	25:14–30			
Ten minas	Wise and unwise handling of trust			19:12–27	
Ten virgins	Preparedness for Christ's coming	25:1–13			

* Explained by Jesus

Parables about Grace and Forgiveness

Parable	Illustrated Truth	Matthew	Mark	Luke	John
Fig tree, barren	God's patience, second chance			13: 6–9	
Laborers in vineyard	Fairness of God's grace, reward	20:1–16			
Lost coin	Joy over repentant sinners			15:8–10	
Lost sheep	God's unwillingness to lose people	18:12–14		15:3–7	
Pharisee and tax collector	Spiritual pride, humility and mercy			18:9–14	
Prodigal son	Repentance, God's forgiveness			15:11–32	
Two debtors	Forgiveness, worship			7:36–50	
Unmerciful servant	Forgiveness, torment of unforgiveness	18:23–35			
Weeds (tares)	Dealing with enemies in the church	13:24–30, 36–43*			

* Explained by Jesus

Parables about Prayer

Parable	Illustrated Truth	Matthew	Mark	Luke	John
Friend at midnight	Boldness in prayer			11:5–13*	
Persistent widow	Prayer as a battle for justice			18:1–8	
Pharisee and tax collector	Spiritual pride, humility and mercy			18:9–14	

* Explained by Jesus

Parables about Various Spiritual Issues

Parable	Illustrated Truth	Matthew	Mark	Luke	John
Good Samaritan	Neighbor loving			10:25–37	
Good Shepherd	Christ's relationship to his followers				10:1–16
House on the rock	Foundation for life	7:24–27		7:48–49	
Master and servant	Servanthood and unworthiness			17:7–10*	
New patch, old shirt	Difficulty combining old and new	9:16	2:21	5:36	
New wine, wineskins	Teachability, flexibility needed	9:17	2:22	5:37–38	
Tower, warring king	Counting the cost of following Christ			14:28–33	
Vine and branches	Oneness with Christ, fruitfulness				15:1–5

* Explained by Jesus

APPENDIX C — THE ANSWERS

CHAPTER 1

1. The Roman Empire was oppressing the Jews at the time of John's and Jesus' conception and birth.
2. Old Testament promises concerning Christ's birth include those found in Genesis 49:10; Deuteronomy 18:18; 2 Samuel 17:12–16; Isaiah 7:14; Isaiah 9:6–7; Isaiah 61:1–4; and Ezekiel 37:21–28.
3. The angel predicted the following about John the Baptist: (1) He will be great; (2) He will not drink wine; (3) He will be filled with the Spirit from birth; (4) He will bring people to the Lord; (5) He will reconcile families; (6) He will have the spirit and power of Elijah; and (7) He will prepare a people for the Lord. (Luke 1:14–17)
4. To keep Zechariah from expressing his doubts, his ability to speak was taken away. (Luke 1:20)
5. This question calls for your personal answer. Gabriel's five predictions concerning Mary's baby (Luke 1:31–35) were (1) He will be great; (2) He will be known as the Son of God; (3) He will rule on David's throne; (4) He will be king of Israel—house of Jacob; and (5) His kingdom will never end.
6. The three "revolutions" Christ accomplished are (1) spiritual, (2) social, and (3) economic. (Luke 1:46–55)

CHAPTER 2

1. Joseph thought Mary was pregnant by another man and considered divorcing her—breaking off the betrothal—(Matthew 1:18–19). An angel in a dream convinced him Mary's baby had been conceived by the Holy Spirit (Matthew 1:20–21).
2. God moved Caesar Augustus to decree a census, requiring all Jewish men to return to their ancestral towns to be registered (Luke 2:1–30). This forced Joseph to go to Bethlehem. Knowing God arranged world events according to his plans in Jesus' day may make you feel more secure about God's control over today's current events.

3. Shepherds were likely to be outside with their flocks in February and March—30 days prior to the Feast of Passover (though some might be there all winter). Their sheep were probably kept for sacrifices at the Temple.
4. When a first son was born, three ceremonies were required: (1) Circumcision, (2) Redemption of the firstborn, and (3) for the mother: Purification after childbirth. (Luke 2:21–24)
5. The Magi were scholars, scientists, astrologers, and priests in the countries from which they came. They were wise men who recognized who Jesus was and worshiped him. From them we might learn to seek Christ, to bring him spiritual gifts, and to worship him.
6. (a) *"Immanuel"* means Christ is "God with us." (b) *"You Bethlehem . . ."* predicts the birthplace of the Messiah.

CHAPTER 3

1. (a) *"Out of Egypt I called my son,"* was a prophecy that Joseph, Mary, and Jesus would return to Israel after their escape into Egypt. (b) *"He will be called a Nazarene"* expresses that Christ was despised like the little town where he grew up.
2. Jewish childhood religious education began with Psalms sung and stories told while the child was still nursing.
3. Bar mitzvah means "son of the commandment." It was celebrated at age 12 (Luke 2:42). It signified the beginning of manhood.
4. Possible explanations of differences between Matthew's and Luke's genealogies: (1) Matthew gives Jesus' royal descent, establishing his right to David's throne; (2) Matthew gives Joseph's genealogy; Luke gives Mary's; (3) Jewish men were often known by more than one name; (4) A brother might marry his brother's widow and raise children in his brother's name; and (5) Luke shows Christ's identification with all mankind; Matthew shows Jesus is Joseph's legal son.

5. The notorious women are examples of Christ's identification with sinners and how grace raises sinners to value and significance. One possible way such identification may make you feel is accepted or loved.
6. Christ came as a human being (1) to show what God is like, (2) to show how to live by faith, (3) to show what it means to be human, and (4) to fill his role as High Priest.

CHAPTER 4

1. Old Testament prophecies foretold the work of Messiah's advance man (Malachi 3:1; 4:5–6; Isaiah 40:3–5). Israel looked for one like Elijah (Malachi 4:5–6; 2 Kings 1:2–8).
2. The essence of John the Baptist's message was *repentance* (Luke 3:3). Repentance is willingness to turn from sin and be changed in lifestyle and values.
3. Pharisees and Sadducees were told to share what they had with others (Matthew 3:8–10). Tax collectors were told to stop cheating the public and collect only what the law demanded (Luke 3:12–13). Soldiers were told to stop accusing people falsely and extorting money by threat of violence (Luke 3:14).
4. John insisted people who thought they were "God's special people" should approach God like pagans needing to learn from the ground up how to walk with the Lord.
5. John's baptism signified preparedness to receive the Messiah and willingness to forsake sins (Matthew 3:6; Mark 1:5). Christian baptism signifies receiving and becoming one with the Lord, dying to one's old way of life, and being spiritually raised to new life in Christ (Acts 2:41; 8:35–39).
6. Christ's baptism is greater than John's because (1) Christ baptizes with the Holy Spirit; (2) Christ baptizes with fire; and (3) Christ cleanses the useless chaff from a person's life. (Luke 3:16–17)
7. Many people feel affirmed as a child of Christ in a variety of ways from a deep feeling of peace to a new ability to refrain from former sins.

CHAPTER 5

1. Bible names for the tempter include devil *"slanderer, accuser"* (Matthew 4:1); tempter (Matthew 4:3); Satan *"adversary, enemy"* (Matthew 4:10); serpent (2 Corinthians 11:3); dragon (Revelation 12:3); Abaddon *"ruin"* (Job 31:12); Apollyon (Revelation 9:11); Beelzebub *"prince of devils, lord of flies"* (Matthew 12:24); Belial *"worthlessness, lawlessness"* (Luke 4:2–6); Lucifer *"shining one, light being"* (Isaiah 14:12); enemy (Matthew 13:39).
2. Jesus' tactics were these: (d) He quoted Scripture (Matthew 4:4, 7, 10), and (f) he ordered Satan to leave (Matthew 4:10).

3. The devil tempted Jesus to (1) turn stones to bread, which would appeal to Jesus because he was hungry; (2) jump off the Temple, which would appeal to Jesus as a quick way to prove he was God's Son; and (3) worship the devil, which appeared to be a less costly way to win the world than going to the cross. (Matthew 4:1–11)
4. (1) Turning stones to bread would divert God's gifts to a selfish purpose. (2) Jumping off the Temple would manipulate God to fit Jesus' purpose rather than God's and violate the trust relationship between them. (3) Giving the devil respect would compromise God's plan of salvation and roadblock the kingdom of righteousness.
5. Many believers say they struggle with selfish desires and wanting to seek shortcuts to spiritual growth. Jesus' experience may teach us to act for the good of others, to put up with difficulties, and to rest knowing God has our best in mind.

CHAPTER 6

1. God has expressed himself (1) in creation (John 1:3); (2) in the existence of life (verse 4); (3) in human messengers (verses 6–8); (4) in the Old Testament Law (verse 17); and (5) in Jesus Christ (verses 14, 18).
2. John 1:1–5 says the Word existed in the beginning, was with God, was God, has existed as long as God has, was involved in creating everything, all life owes its existence to him, and the life he gives enlightens people.
3. These facts suggest the mystery of the Trinity—one God in three persons. (John 10:30; 9:38; 14:9; 20:28–29; Matthew 28:19)
4. Christ is the source of biological life (Colossians 1:16–17), eternal life (John 5:24–26), and spiritual life (Galatians 2:20; Romans 5:10; Philippians 4:13).
5. The Word (Christ) came into the world and lived among us. (John 1:9–10, 14)
6. A person becomes a child of God by receiving and believing in Christ (John 1:12).

CHAPTER 7

1. Priests, Levites, and Pharisees were sent to investigate John's identity. (John 1:19, 24)
2. John claimed to be *"the voice of one calling in the desert, 'Make straight the way for the Lord.'"* He got his authority from God. (John 1:23)
3. *Lamb of God* can mean (1) substitute sacrifice; (2) sacrifice to deliver you from sin's slavery; (3) sacrifice to take away sins and assure fellowship with God; (4) submissive servant giving his life for people's transgressions; (5) champion giving victory over sin; or (6) judge who takes your judgment on himself.

4. God gave John the sign of the Holy Spirit descending on Jesus like a dove. (John 1:32–34)

5. Peter and Nathanael were introduced to Jesus by a friend or relative. (John 1:41–42, 45)

6. Six titles for Jesus in John 1:29–51 are Lamb of God, Son of God, Rabbi, Messiah (Christ), King of Israel, and Son of Man. There is no one right answer to the second question. Many people today think of Jesus as Son of God or Son of Man because they emphasize either his divine qualities or his humanness.

CHAPTER 8

1. The miracle of water turned to wine demonstrates that (1) religious rules are replaced by Jesus' personal authority; (2) God's glory can be seen in everyday situations; (3) God joins human celebrations; (4) Jesus' authority extends to created things; and (5) miracles help people believe in Jesus. (John 2:11)

2. The Temple market angered Jesus because the merchants were misusing religious rules to make unfair profits from worshipers, especially the poor. (John 2:16)

3. The merchants were misusing the following rules. (1) The Temple tax rule: All money had to be exchanged for Temple currency at very high exchange rates. (2) The rule of unblemished sacrificial lambs: Temple inspectors tended to disapprove lambs purchased outside, and prices inside the Temple were inflated. (3) The rule of alternate sacrifices for the poor: Temple inspectors disapproved birds purchased outside, while high prices were charged inside.

4. Jesus said, *"Destroy this temple, and I will raise it again in three days."* He was telling them to watch for his resurrection from the dead. (John 1:19–22)

5. Nicodemus believed Jesus was a teacher, from God, and that God was with him. (John 3:2)

6. *Again* can mean "from the beginning," "for the second time," "anew," or "from above."

7. Personal answers will vary. People have been attracted to Jesus through the Christlike qualities in one of their friends, by reading about Christ in Scripture, and hearing about Jesus in sermons.

CHAPTER 9

1. Essentials to healing and salvation represented by looking to Moses' bronze snake are (1) acceptance of personal responsibility for sin, (2) trust in the reliability of God's instructions, (3) obedience, and (4) turning to God in faith.

2. Those who trust in Christ are saved, but those who refuse to believe choose condemnation by their unwillingness to accept God's offer of salvation. (John 3:18)

3. When people followed Jesus, John knew he had succeeded in what God sent him to do—just as the bridegroom's friend succeeds when the bride and groom are married. (John 3:27–30)

4. Jesus left for Galilee to postpone a confrontation with Herod and the Pharisees, and to meet a needy woman in Samaria. (John 4:1–4)

5. Animosity between Samaritans and Jews developed because (1) Samaritans were a mixed race (2 Kings 17:24); (2) practiced a corrupt religion (2 Kings 17:25–41; John 4:20, 22); and (3) had tried to stop the rebuilding of Jerusalem after the exile (Nehemiah 4).

6. In John 4:21–24 Jesus gave the following principles of worship: (1) physical location for worship is irrelevant; (2) God must be worshiped as he is not as we wish him to be; (3) Scripture reveals what God is like and how he wants to be worshiped; and (4) God wants worshipers who worship him in spirit and in truth.

CHAPTER 10

1. Jesus is looking for people who believe in him because of his character and his word, with or without visible proof. (John 4:48; 20:29)

2. Herod's official demonstrated his faith by taking Jesus at his word. (John 4:50)

3. The five things the Lord anointed Jesus to do (Luke 4:18–19) are (1) bring hope to the poor, (2) liberate prisoners, (3) restore sight to the blind, (4) release the oppressed, (5) proclaim God's grace (*"the year of the Lord's favor"*). Any one of these things may be what you need most.

4. The Nazarenes refused to believe because they knew Jesus' family and because he told them God loved Gentiles. (John 4:22, 25–27)

5. Symptoms of evil spirit activity include screaming, disruptive acts, fear, antisocial behavior, super strength, terror of God, muteness, blindness, suffering, deafness, convulsions, rigidity, self-destructiveness, shouting, religious speech, torment, and clairvoyance. (Luke 4:33–35; Mark 5:1–17; Matthew 9:32–34; 12:22–23; 15:21–28; Mark 9:14–29; Luke 4:41; 13:11–13; Acts 5:16–18; 16:16–24)

6. Jesus' authority over evil spirits tells us we should listen to whatever he says. (Luke 4:32, 36)

7. Jesus' authority may affect many areas of your life and include comfort or freedom from worry about enemies, evil, and illness.

CHAPTER 11

1. When success threatened to deter Jesus he got alone and prayed. (Luke 4:42)

2. The Jews believed (1) the universe is God's kingdom, (2) Christ came to govern as king, and (3) Christ will

set up a political kingdom and rule the world from Jerusalem. They failed to understand the necessity for Christ to suffer and die as a sacrifice to atone for human sin (Isaiah 53).

3. The church is the advance contingent of the kingdom of God. (Matthew 16:16–19)
4. When he saw Christ's power, Simon confessed he was a sinful man. (John 5:8)
5. Believing only God can forgive was a cover-up for unwillingness to forgive others. (Luke 5:22–23; Luke 7:47–50)
6. Jesus restored the paralyzed man's ability to walk. (Luke 5:23–25)

CHAPTER 12

1. Rules added to Sabbath restrictions included (1) carry nothing heavier than a teaspoon; (2) travel no farther than the synagogue; (3) untie no knots; (4) tailors who accidentally carry a needle on the Sabbath have committed a crime; and (5) wearing false teeth on the Sabbath is wrong. A man could be stoned to death for carrying his bed on the Sabbath.
2. The healed man defended himself by saying, "The man who healed me told me to do it" (John 5:11). Jesus defended his actions by saying, "God works on the Sabbath" (John 5:17).
3. Christ is equal to his Father in heaven in that (1) Christ and his Father both work on the Sabbath; (2) Christ's actions mirror God's; (3) the Father reveals to Jesus everything he is doing; (4) both can raise the dead; (5) to honor one is to honor the other; (6) both can give eternal life; and (7) both are self-existent and not dependent on anyone else for life. (John 5:17–27)
4. The four witnesses who verify Christ's claims are (1) John the Baptist, (2) Christ's saving mission, (3) the Father's voice, (4) Old Testament Scripture. (John 5:35–39)
5. The scribes and Pharisees neglected God's desire for *"mercy, not sacrifice"* by condemning the disciples for plucking grain on the Sabbath. (Matthew 12:1, 2)
6. By healing the withered hand Jesus demonstrated that *"it is lawful to do good on the Sabbath"* and that a person is more valuable than a sheep! (Matthew 12:12)
7. Examples of offering sacrifice while neglecting mercy could include giving a tithe to the church while being angry about doing so or denying yourself some comfort while failing to forgive someone who has hurt you.

CHAPTER 13

1. Jesus chose 12 disciples to be apostles (Luke 6:13). The names of the 12 chosen are Peter (Simon) and Andrew, fishermen and brothers; James and John, fishermen and brothers; Philip and Bartholomew (Nathanael), possibly brothers; Matthew (Levi the tax collector) and James, possibly brothers; Thomas; Simon the Zealot (the Cananaean), political radical; Thaddaeus (Judas son of James); and Judas Iscariot.
2. A kingdom may be defined as (1) a king's domain; (2) government under a king; (3) people ruled by a king; (4) society or culture under a king's rule; and (5) nation, city, or community where a king's subjects live.
3. Jesus' Sermon on the Mount teachings were for his disciples (Matthew 5:1; Luke 6:17), people who are "born again" (John 3:3, 5).
4. The situation and future of the rich are described with the word *woe* (Luke 6:24). Jesus states the dangers of material possessions because his disciples are to be known for generosity; if they cling tightly to worldly things, they won't have a liberal spirit.
5. Jesus fulfills the Law by giving his disciples a fuller understanding of sinful motives and attitudes as well as outward actions condemned by the Ten Commandments. (Matthew 5:17, 20)
6. We love our enemies by (1) doing them good, (2) blessing them, and (3) praying for them.
7. Possible answers may include the need to forgive someone, to stop judging others, or to be honest about your faults.

CHAPTER 14

1. The centurion recognized Jesus' authority (1) is similar to earthly authority, (2) extends over people and created things (i.e., disease), and (3) transcends space and distance. (Luke 7:7–10)
2. God feels people's pain; his compassion moves him to help. (Luke 7:13–16)
3. John ate simple food, drank no wine, and dressed in rough clothing; Jesus went to parties and dinners, ate normal food, drank wine, and spent time with sinners (Luke 7:33–34). Because the religious leaders rejected God's purposes for their lives they rejected both John and Jesus (Luke 7:30).
4. Unlike the Pharisee, the woman washed Jesus' feet, wiped them, kissed him, and anointed him with oil (Luke 7:44–46). She did it because she knew she was forgiven; the Pharisee had not experienced forgiveness (Luke 7:47).
5. Just as Jonah spent three days in the belly of the big fish and came out alive (Jonah 1:17), Jesus would be buried and rise from the dead the third day. (Matthew 12:40)
6. If you are doing God's will by obeying Scripture in your daily life, those around you will probably view you as a close relative of Jesus.

CHAPTER 15

1. A parable is a saying, story, or metaphor that communicates truth by comparison. "An earthly story with a heavenly meaning."
2. The seed is the word of God, Christ's kingdom teaching (Matthew 13:19). Rocky places are listeners with prejudices, stubbornness, or fear that keep the word from taking root in their lives.
3. Teaching with parables (1) grabs the listener's attention, (2) turns abstract truth into pictures, (3) starts where the listener is and leads him to what he should know, (4) disarms listeners' defenses, (5) gives listeners room to do their own thinking, and (6) makes it easy to remember the point.
4. Jesus' goal in teaching was to help his disciples become like their teacher.
5. When interpreting Jesus' parables: (1) note the context, (2) focus on the main point, and (3) consider the culture and customs of Jesus' time.
6. Depending on your circumstances, to get tuned in on Jesus' voice you might read Psalm 46 or 51, or Job 38–40:2.

CHAPTER 16

1. When the storm hit the boat Jesus was asleep in the stern (Mark 4:38). Trials or losses can make us feel that God does not care about us, although we are wrong when we believe that.
2. The disciples asked, "Who is this?" (Mark 4:41). His ability to command the storm tells us Jesus is Lord—his word has authority over the elements.
3. The people of Gadara clamped the demon-possessed man in chains (Luke 8:29). We use drugs and confinement in hospitals to control the mentally ill, avoid them, and fear them.
4. The evil spirits were terrified, recognized who Jesus was, and begged him not to send them to the place of the dead (Mark 5:7; Luke 8:31). Jesus is more powerful than evil spirits, and they fear him (1 John 4:4).
5. The townspeople were afraid and asked Jesus to leave (Luke 8:37). They valued pigs and profits more than people and rejected any solution that was costly to them.
6. Religious leaders saw Jesus touch a woman with a menstrual problem, but failed to appreciate the end of her 12-year ordeal. They saw Jesus touch a dead body, but failed to appreciate the relief of the parents and the girl whose life was given back to her.

CHAPTER 17

1. Jesus saw that the crowds were harassed and helpless (Matthew 9:36). He felt compassion. He asked his disciples to pray for spiritual harvesters (verse 38).
2. Jesus told his disciples to expect persecution when he sent them out.
3. Families may be united or divided when one member believes Jesus' claims. One believer could tell others in the family and bring them to Christ. Unbelieving family members may reject Jesus' claims, feel guilty or threatened, and cut off communication with the believer.
4. Christian witnesses and workers work best in teams (Ecclesiastes 4:9–12). Jesus sent his disciples out in teams of two (Matthew 10; Luke 10).
5. Herod thought John the Baptist had returned from the dead (Mark 6:16). He had beheaded John to please his illegitimate wife (Matthew 14:6–11).

CHAPTER 18

1. The only available food for feeding the 5,000 was five barley loaves and two small fish. (John 6:9)
2. "I Am" is Jesus' way of identifying himself with God, as God's Son. His "I am" statements and their meanings include I am (1) the bread of life (John 6:35, 41, 48, 51)—spiritual nourishment; (2) the light of the world (John 8:12)—no darkness if you're following Jesus; (3) before Abraham (John 8:58)—Christ's pre-existence; (4) the gate for the sheep (John 10:7, 9)—gateway to spiritual safety, salvation; (5) the good shepherd (John 10:11, 14)—lays down his life for the flock; (6) the resurrection and the life (John 11:25)—spiritual and eternal life, resurrection from the dead; (7) the way, the truth, the life (John 14:6)—the way to the Father; and (8) the vine (John 15:1–5)—fruitful relationship with Christ.
3. People work either for (1) food that spoils or (2) eternal food (John 6:27). The work of God is to believe on Jesus, *"the one God has sent"* (verse 29).
4. Jesus claims (1) he came down from heaven (verse 38); (2) he was sent by God (verses 38–39); (3) he does the Father's will, not his own (verse 38); (4) he safeguards those the Father gives him (verse 39); (5) he will raise the dead (verses 39–40); and (6) trust in him assures eternal life (verse 40).
5. To eat Jesus' flesh and drink his blood means to take him into our lives and maintain an intimate, daily, dependent, personal spiritual relationship with him.

CHAPTER 19

1. The Pharisees and lawyers nullified the authority of God's word (Mark 7:13). Jesus called them hypocrites (verse 6).
2. Jesus demands that people deal with their dirty hearts (the sin inside). The Pharisees settled for "ceremonial" (external, religious, ritual) cleansing. (Mark 7:15–23)

3. The Phoenician woman's faith was great because of her persistence, confidence in Jesus' authority and goodness, humility, and respect for his plans and priorities. (Matthew 15:21–28; Mark 7:24–30)

4. Jesus was reminding his disciples they did not need to worry about bread when he was with them. He would supply what they needed. (Mark 8:19–20)

5. Thinking like Pharisees, Sadducees, or Herodians would undermine Jesus' followers' perception and experience of the kingdom of God.

6. Jesus used spit in three healing miracles: healing a speech impediment (Mark 7:33) and healing blind men on two different occasions (John 9:6; Mark 8:23).

APPENDIX D — THE EXPERTS

Henry Alford—Dean of Canterbury, England; author of *The New Testament for English Readers* Bible commentary.

Ronald B. Allen—Professor of Bible Exposition at Dallas Theological Seminary.

Neil T. Anderson—Chairman of the Practical Theology Department at Talbot School of Theology of Biola University.

Athanasius—Fourth century bishop of Alexandria; author; called "Father of Orthodoxy." The Athanasian Creed was named after him.

Augustine of Hippo—Fourth century bishop of Hippo, North Africa; a major influence on Christianity; he made the grace of God the theme of Western Christian theology.

William Barclay—New Testament scholar and writer; professor of Divinity and Biblical Criticism at the University of Glasgow; author of many books, including the multivolume *Daily Study Bible* commentary on all the New Testament books.

Albert Barnes—Pastor, First Presbyterian Church in Philadelphia for 35 years; his multivolume *Barnes' Notes* Bible commentary series has sold two million copies.

Donald Grey Barnhouse—Founder of *Eternity* magazine and *The Bible Study Hour* radio program; pastor.

Ray E. Baughman—Director of Correspondence School, Dallas Bible College; author.

Dietrich Bonhoeffer—German theologian, cofounder of the Confessing Church in Germany, martyred by the Nazis for resistance against Nazi persecution of Jews.

Leslie F. Brandt—Lutheran minister, evangelist, and retreat leader; author.

Stuart and Jill Briscoe—Pastor and wife, Elmbrook Church, Wisconsin; Capernwray Missionary Fellowship of Torchbearers, England.

Harold O. J. Brown—Ph.D. from Harvard; professor of Biblical and Systematic Theology at Trinity Evangelical University.

John Bunyan—Scotsman, author of the classic Christian allegory, *Pilgrim's Progress*.

Michael Card—Contemporary Christian author, composer, performer, and recording artist who lives in Nashville, Tennessee.

Lewis Sperry Chafer—Founder of Dallas Theological Seminary.

Oswald Chambers—Principal of Bible Training School, London; founder of two YMCA desert camps in Egypt during World War 1 where he ministered to British soldiers.

Charles Clayton—Executive Director of World Vision in Great Britain.

Clement of Alexandria—Second century theologian; head of Christian School in Alexandria, Egypt; mentor of Origen who greatly influenced Christian theology.

Robert E. Coleman—Professor of Evangelism at Trinity Evangelical Divinity School, Deerfield/Chicago.

Bill Comeau—Published poet, playwright, author, songwriter, and educational consultant.

W. Robert Cook—Professor of Biblical Theology, Western Conservative Baptist Seminary, Portland.

Gordon Cosby—Founder and pastor of Church of the Saviour, Washington, D.C.

John Chrysostom—Fourth century Christian Bible expositor-preacher (his name means "golden-mouth"); exiled for attacks against church and civil government vices.

Alfred Edersheim—Scholar of Jewish history and society during Bible times.

Ephrem the Syrian—Distinguished orator, poet, hymn writer, and teacher of the fourth century Syrian Church; called "the guitar of the Holy Spirit."

Harry Emerson Fosdick—Pastor of Riverside Church, New York City; professor of Practical Theology at Union Theological Seminary; popular radio preacher; author.

Richard J. Foster—Professor of Spiritual Formation, Azusa Pacific University, Azusa, California; founder of Renovarré renewal ministry; author.

R. T. France—Principal of Wycliffe Hall in the University of Oxford; lecturer in Biblical Studies at the University of Ife, Nigeria.

Audrey I. Girard—Elementary teacher and intervention specialist; published Christian songwriter; assistant to author.

Billy Graham—International crusade, radio, and TV evangelist; he has presented the Gospel face-to-face to more people than any man in history; author of many inspirational classics read by millions; founder of *Christianity Today* and *Decision* magazines.

Henry H. Halley—Author of the well-known and widely used *Halley's Bible Handbook*, which has sold nearly two million copies.

Matthew Henry—Seventeenth century Biblical expositor, expelled from the Church of England in 1662; Presbyterian pastor; authored multivolume Bible commentary still popular today.

Thomas á Kempis—Fifteenth century German mystic; copyist (copied the entire Bible four times); author of devotional writings, including *The Imitation of Christ*.

Madeleine L'Engle—Prolific author; winner of the Newberry Award for *A Wrinkle in Time*; poet; lecturer; Christian retreat leader.

C. S. Lewis—Fellow of Magdalen College, Oxford University; author of books on theology and fantasy: i.e., *The Chronicles of Narnia*.

Martin Luther—Father of the Protestant Reformation.

John F. MacArthur Jr.—Pastor/teacher of Grace Community Church, Sun Valley, California; president of The Master's College and Seminary; speaker on the daily *Grace To You* radio broadcast.

I. Howard Marshall—Senior lecturer in New Testament Exegesis, University of Aberdeen, Scotland.

Dan McCartney—Associate professor of New Testament at Westminster Theological Seminary.

Stephen M. Miller—Editorial adviser for *Christian History* magazine; freelance writer.

Leon Morris—Anglican priest; principal of Ridley College, Melbourne, Australia; author of many books, including commentaries on Luke, John, 1 Corinthians, Thessalonians, and Revelation.

Henri J. M. Nouwen—Taught at University of Notre Dame, Yale, and Harvard; from 1986 till his death in 1996 associated with L'Arche Community in France and Toronto.

Ted Olsen—Assistant editor of *Christian History* magazine.

J. I. Packer—Theologian; professor at Regent College, Vancouver, British Columbia; former associate principal of Trinity College, Bristol, England.

Papias—A disciple of the apostle John; second century Bible scholar, author, and martyr.

Blaise Pascal—Seventeenth century French physicist; formulator of the mathematical theory of probability, a fundamental element of modern theoretical physics, member of the Roman Catholic reform movement known as Jansenism.

Eugene H. Peterson—Professor of Spiritual Theology at Regent College in Vancouver, British Columbia; author of many books; contributing editor to *Leadership Journal*.

Frank Peretti—Christian novelist and storyteller; author of *This Present Darkness*.

John Pollock—Cambridge-educated English clergyman; biographer of Billy Graham, Jesus Christ (*Master: A Life of Jesus*), and Paul (*Apostle: A Life of Paul*).

Lawrence O. (Larry) Richards—Theologian, Bible scholar, ecclesiologist, prolific author of more than 175 books, including Bible commentaries and reference works for pastors, church leaders, teachers, laymen, and youth.

Don Richardson—Missionary among the Asmat people (headhunters and cannibals) of New Guinea; anthropologist.

John Charles Ryle—Nineteenth century bishop of Liverpool, England.

Francis Schaeffer—Founder, with his wife Edith, of L'Abri, an international study and ministry community in the Swiss Alps; author of 23 books.

Howard A. Snyder—Formerly dean of Free Methodist Seminary in San Paulo, Brazil; Director of Light and Life Men International; author of books on church renewal.

John G. Stackhouse Jr.—Sanwoo Youtong Chee Professor of Theology at Regent College, Vancouver, British Columbia.

Tim Stafford—Editor of Campus Life Books; senior writer for *Christianity Today*.

Robert H. Stein—Professor of New Testament at Bethel College, St. Paul, Minnesota.

Leonard I. Sweet—Dean of the Theological School, vice president, and professor of Post-Modern Christianity at Drew University, Madison, New Jersey.

Charles R. Swindoll—President of Dallas Theological Seminary; popular Bible expositor and author; heard daily on *Insight for Living* radio broadcast.

Joni Eareckson Tada—Author of over 20 books; founder and president of Joni and Friends, a ministry to the disabled.

A. W. Tozer—Editor of *The Alliance Witness*; pastor, conference speaker, author; described as "a twentieth century prophet."

Merril F. Unger—Biblical scholar and researcher; author of *Unger's Bible Dictionary.*

Walter Wangerin Jr.—Award-winning author; holder of the Jochum Chair at Valparaiso University in Indiana where he is a writer-in-residence.

Robert Webber—Editor of the eight-volume *Complete Library of Christian Worship*; author of contemporary books on worship.

Stu Weber—Founder of Good Shepherd Community Church in Portland, Oregon; speaker at Family Life marriage and parenting conferences.

Thomas B. White—Director of Frontline Ministries in Corvallis, Oregon; international speaker at seminars on spiritual warfare.

Dallas Willard—Professor at the University of Southern California's School of Philosophy; visiting professor at the University of Colorado.

Note: To the best of our knowledge, all of the above information is accurate and up to date. In some cases we were unable to obtain biographical information.

—THE STARBURST EDITORS

ENDNOTES

Introduction

1. Madeleine L'Engle, *Walking on Water: Reflections on Faith and Art* (Wheaton, IL: Shaw, 1980), 60.
2. Henry H. Halley, *Halley's Bible Handbook,* 23rd ed. (Grand Rapids, MI: Zondervan, 1962), 10.
3. John G. Stackhouse Jr., "The Jesus I'd Prefer to Know," *Christianity Today,* December 7, 1998, 69.
4. Ibid.
5. Papias, an early church leader, quoted in William Barclay, *Matthew* (Philadelphia: Westminster, 1975), 5.
6. Papias, quoted in Eusebius and in Thomas C. Oden and Christopher A. Hall, eds., *Ancient Christian Commentary on Scripture: New Testament II—Mark* (Downers Grove, IL.: InterVarsity, 1998), xxi.
7. William Barclay, *The Gospel of Luke* (Philadelphia: Westminster, 1975), 1.
8. Clement of Alexandria, about 180 A.D., quoted in Robert C. Girard, *Adult Living Today* (Wheaton, IL.: Scripture Press, 1995), 3.

Chapter 1

1. Oswald Chambers, *Christian Discipline, vol.* 2 (Fort Washington, PA: Christian Literature Crusade, 1936), 152.
2. Francis Schaeffer, *How Shall We Then Live?* (Old Tappan, NJ: Revell, 1976), 71.
3. William Barclay, *The Gospel of John* (Philadelphia: Westminster, 1975), 13.
4. Eugene H. Peterson, "This Profound Mystery" (an interview with Eugene H. Peterson), *Cross Point* (winter 1998), 2.
5. John F. MacArthur Jr., *God With Us* (Grand Rapids, MI: Zondervan, 1989), 46.
6. J. I. Packer, *Knowing God* (Downers Grove, IL: InterVarsity, 1973), 50–51.
7. Leon Morris, *Luke* (Grand Rapids, MI: Eerdmans, 1988), 85.

Chapter 2

1. Charles R. Swindoll, *Growing Strong in the Seasons of Life* (Portland, OR: Multnomah, 1983), 35.
2. Ronald B. Allen, *The Majesty of Man* (Portland, OR: Multnomah, 1984), 121.
3. Michael Card, *Immanuel: Reflections on the Life of Christ* (Nashville: Thomas Nelson, 1990), 63.
4. Albert Barnes, *Barnes Notes* (Grand Rapids, MI: Baker, 1979), 18.

5. Card, *Immanuel*, 62.
6. Alfred Edersheim, *Sketches of Jewish Social Life* (Grand Rapids, MI: Eerdmans, 1990), 81–82.
7. Stuart and Jill Briscoe, *Meet Him at the Manger,* quoted in *Christianity Today,* December 7, 1998, 48.
8. Barclay, *Luke,* 22.
9. Ibid., 25.
10. Matthew Henry, *Commentary on the Whole Bible,* one volume ed. (Grand Rapids, MI: Zondervan, 1961), 1418.
11. William Barclay, *Luke,* 25.
12. Audrey I. Girard, personal journals.
13. Barclay, *Luke,* 26.
14. Lawrence O. Richards, *The Victor Bible Background Commentary* (Wheaton, IL: Victor, 1985), 16.
15. MacArthur, *God With Us,* 114.

Chapter 3

1. Audrey I. Girard, personal journals.
2. Robert L. Thomas and Stanley N. Gundry, *A Harmony of the Gospels* (San Francisco, CA: HarperCollins, 1978), 32.
3. *Revell Bible Encyclopedia* (Old Tappan, NJ: Revell, 1990), 425.
4. Ronald B. Allen, *The Majesty of Man* (Portland, OR: Multnomah, 1984), 118.
5. Robert E. Coleman, *The Mind of the Master* (Old Tappan, NJ: Revell, 1977), 21.
6. Allen, *The Majesty of Man,* 125.

Chapter 4

1. Barclay, *Luke,* 32.
2. Halley, *Halley's Bible Handbook,* 398.
3. Stephen M. Miller, "Select Circle," *Christian History,* issue 59, p. 33.
4. Albert Barnes, *Barnes Notes: Matthew and Mark* (Grand Rapids, MI: Baker, 1949), 22.
5. John Killinger, *A Devotional Guide to Luke: The Gospel of Contagious Joy* (Waco, TX: Word, 1980), 27.
6. Richard J. Foster, *Prayer: Finding the Heart's True Home* (San Francisco, CA: Harper, 1992), 42.
7. Morris, *Luke,* 107.
8. *Expository Dictionary of Bible Words* (Grand Rapids, MI: Zondervan, 1985), 101.
9. Clark Peddicord, *Jesus, The Powerful Servant* (San Bernardino, CA: Here's Life, 1984), 39.

10. Henry Alford, *The New Testament for English Readers* (Chicago: Moody, n.d.), 17.
11. Audrey I. Girard, personal journals.

Chapter 5

1. William Barclay, *The Gospel of Matthew, vol. 1* (Philadelphia, PA: Westminster, 1975), 63.
2. *Revell Bible Dictionary*, 971.
3. George Adam Smith, quoted in William Barclay, *Matthew*, 63.
4. Merilyn Hargis, "On the Road," *Christian History* 17, issue 59 (no. 3), 31.
5. Ted Olsen, "Getting Physical," *Christian History* 17, issue 59 (no. 3), 27.
6. Chrysostom, *The Gospel of St. Matthew, Homily 13.1,* quoted in Oden and Hall, *Ancient Christian Commentary on Scripture, vol. 2: Mark* (Downers Grove, IL: InterVarsity, 1998), 17.
7. Quoted in Donald Grey Barnhouse, *The Invisible War* (Grand Rapids, MI: Zondervan, 1965), 156.
8. Denis de Rougemont, *La Part du Diable,* quoted in Barnhouse, *The Invisible War,* 156.
9. Charles C. Ryrie, *Basic Theology* (Wheaton, IL: Victor, 1986), 137.
10. W. Robert Cook, *The Christian Faith: Systematic Theology in Outline Form* (W. Robert Cook, 1981), 235–236.
11. Thomas á Kempis, *Á Kempis,* 32.
12. Roger Elwood, quoted in *The Believer's Guide to Spiritual Warfare* (Ann Arbor, MI: Servant, 1990), 31.
13. Quoted in Oden and Hall, *Ancient Christian Commentary on Scripture: Mark,* 17.
14. *Revell Bible Dictionary,* 971.
15. *Adult Teaching Guide* (Wheaton, IL: Scripture Press, September-November 1994), 44.
16. Walter Wangerin Jr., *The Book of God* (Grand Rapids, MI: Zondervan, 1996), 624.
17. Albert Barnes, *Barnes Notes: Matthew and Mark*, 12.
18. Wangerin, *The Book of God,* 624.
19. Barclay, *Matthew*, 70.
20. Larry Richards, *The Servant King* (Elgin, IL: Cook, 1976), 43–44.

Chapter 6

1. Raymond E. Brown, *The Gospel According to John* (New York: Anchor Bible, 1966), 1.
2. Card, *Immanuel*, 36.
3. Packer, *Knowing God*, 58.
4. Lawrence O. Richards, *The Victor Bible Background Commentary: New Testament* (Wheaton, IL: Victor, 1994), 212.
5. Coleman, *The Mind of the Master*, 119.
6. C. S. Lewis, quoted in J. I. Packer, "Can the Dead Be Converted?" *Christianity Today,* January 11, 1999, 82.
7. R. Bultmann, *The Gospel of John* (Oxford: Blackwell, 1971), 35.
8. Halley, *Halley's Bible Handbook*, 12.
9. Richards, *Background Commentary,* 215.
10. Eugene Peterson, *The Message: The New Testament In Contemporary Language* (Colorado Springs, CO: NavPress, 1993), 162.
11. Candy Paull, *The Art of Abundance* (Tulsa, OK: Honor Books, 1998), 41.
12. Richards, *Background Commentary*, 216.
13. Don Richardson, *Eternity in Their Hearts* (Ventura, CA: Regal, 1981), 54.
14. Richards, *Background Commentary,* 214–215.

15. From the hymn, "Holy, Holy, Holy," by Reginald Heber.
16. *Revell Bible Dictionary*, 995.
17. Coleman, *The Mind of the Master,* 22.
18. John Bunyan (source unknown).
19. *The Amplified New Testament* (Grand Rapids, MI: Zondervan, 1958).
20. Billy Graham, *How to Be Born Again* (Waco, TX: Word, 1977), 183.
21. Coleman, *The Mind of the Master,* 21.
22. Leon Morris, *The Gospel According to John* (Grand Rapids, MI: Eerdmans, 1971), 117.
23. Barclay, *John,* vol. 1, 75.

Chapter 7

1. Richards, *Background Commentary,* 219.
2. Lewis Sperry Chafer, *Grace* (Grand Rapids, MI: Zondervan, 1922), 163.
3. Morris, *John*, 140–141.
4. Dom J. Howton, quoted in Morris, *John,* 153.
5. George R. Beasley-Murray, *Word Biblical Commentary* (Waco, TX: Word, 1987).
6. Richards, *Background Commentary,* 220.
7. Morris, *John,* 168.
8. Richards, *Background Commentary*, 220.

Chapter 8

1. Card, *Immanuel*, 103.
2. Alfred Edersheim, *Sketches of Jewish Life.*
3. Barclay, *John,* vol. 1, 95.
4. Leonard I. Sweet, *Quantum Spirituality* (Dayton, OH: Whaleprints, 1991, 1994), 85.
5. Robert H. Stein, "Wine-Drinking in New Testament Times," *Christianity Today,* June 20, 1975, 9–11.
6. Barclay, *John,* vol. 1, 100.
7. Halley, *Halley's Bible Handbook,* 434.
8. I. Howard Marshall, "The New Testament Miracles," *Eerdmans' Handbook to the Bible* (Grand Rapids, MI: Eerdmans, 1973), 519.
9. Billy Graham, *Just As I Am* (New York: Harper, 1997), 34.
10. Josephus, *Antiquities of the Jews.*
11. Richardson, *Eternity in Their Hearts,* 111–112.
12. Blaise Pascal, noted physicist, source unknown.
13. Oswald Chambers, *My Utmost for His Highest* (New York: Dodd Mead, 1946), 10.
14. Johnny Cash, quoted in Billy Graham, *How to Be Born Again* (Waco, TX: Word, 1977), 153.

Chapter 9

1. George Beasley-Murray, *Word Biblical Commentary,* vol. 36: *John* (Waco, TX: Word, 1987), 51.
2. Morris, *John,* 229.
3. Augustine, quoted in Barclay, *John,* vol. 1, 138.
4. Lewis Sperry Chafer, *Grace: The Glorious Theme* (Grand Rapids, MI: Zondervan, 1950), 41.
5. Morris, *John,* 231.
6. Barclay, *John,* vol. 1, 139–140.
7. Richards, *Background Commentary*, 222.
8. Thomas and Gundry, *Harmony,* 44 (footnote).
9. Cook, *The Christian Faith in Outline Form,* 331.
10. Harold O. J. Brown, *Heresies: The Image of Christ in the Mirror of Heresy And Orthodoxy from the Apostles to the Present* (Garden City, NY: Doubleday, 1984), 59.

11. Allen, *The Majesty of Man*, 111, 118.
12. Barclay, *John*, 150.
13. Packer, *Knowing God*, 109.
14. Tim Stafford, *Knowing the Face of God* (Grand Rapids, MI: Zondervan, 1986), 102.

Chapter 10

1. Josephus, *Antiquities of the Jews*, quoted in Barclay, *John*, 41.
2. Barclay, *John*, 174–175.
3. Richards, *Background Commentary*, 228.
4. Coleman, *The Mind of the Master*, 54.
5. Richards, *Background Commentary*, 157.
6. Leslie F. Brandt, *Jesus/Now* (St. Louis: Concordia, 1978), 113.
7. Mark 1:17, NRSV.
8. Barclay, *Matthew*, 77.
9. Ibid., 77–78.
10. Jerome, quoted in Oden and Hall, *Ancient Christian Commentary on Scripture: Mark*, 20.
11. D. Stuart Briscoe, *The Fullness of Christ* (Grand Rapids, MI: Zondervan, 1965), 145.
12. Coleman, *Mind of the Master*, 65.
13. Albert Barnes, *Notes on the New Testament* (Grand Rapids, MI: Baker, 1949), 81.
14. Richards, *Bible Handbook*, 480.
15. Neil T. Anderson, *The Bondage Breaker* (Eugene, OR: Harvest House, 1990), 25–26.

Chapter 11

1. Elizabeth O'Conner, *Call to Commitment*, quoted in *World Vision*, June-July 1990, 15.
2. Howard A. Snyder, *The Community of the King* (Downers Grove, IL: InterVarsity, 1977), 40–41.
3. Audrey I. Girard, personal journals.
4. Gordon Cosby, "New Servnt Leadership School," *Faith At Work*, January-February 1990, 8.
5. Joni Eareckson Tada, "The World's Weakest—516 Million Strong," *World Vision*, June-July 1990, 7–8.
6. Cosby, "New Servant Leadership School," 8.
7. Quoted in Ted Olson, "Getting Physical," *Christian History*, issue 59, 27.
8. Barclay, *Luke*, 296.
9. Edersheim, *Sketches of Jewish Life*, 57.

Chapter 12

1. John 5:4, missing from the best manuscripts of the Gospel of John (see NIV margin).
2. Quoted in Barclay, *John*, 182.
3. Bill Comeau, *Doubters and Dreamers* (Nashville: The Upper Room, 1973).
4. Richards, *The Bible*, 154.
5. John Pollock, *Master: A Life of Jesus* (Wheaton, IL: Victor, 1985), 85.
6. Richards, *Background Commentary*, 232.
7. Dallas Willard, *The Divine Conspiracy: Rediscovering Our Hidden Life in God* (San Francisco: Harper, 1998), 81.
8. Packer, *Knowing God*, 131.
9. C. S. Lewis, *The Case for Christianity* (New York: Macmillan, 1965), 45.
10. John Masefield, *The Everlasting Mercy*, quoted in Morris, *John*, 333.
11. John Charles Ryle, *Expository Thoughts on the Gospels: John*, 3 vols. (London, 1957), quoted in Morris, 334.

12. Barclay, *Luke*, 73.
13. Athanasius, *Homilia de Semente*, 28, quoted in Oden and Hall, *Ancient Christian Commentary on Scripture: N.T. II*, 37.
14. Philip Lloyd, *The Life According to St. John* (London and Oxford, 1936), quoted in Morris, *John*, 335.

Chapter 13

1. Barclay, *Mark*, 69.
2. Stu Weber, *All the King's Men* (Sisters, OR: Multnomah, 1998), 33–34.
3. F. R. Maltby, quoted in Barclay, *Luke*, 75.
4. Dietrich Bonhoeffer, *The Cost of Discipleship* (New York: Macmillan, 1963), 125.
5. Larry Richards, *The Servant King* (Colorado Springs, CO: Cook, 1976), 58–60.
6. Polycarp, quoted in Barclay, *Matthew*, 115.
7. Barclay, *Matthew*, 121.
8. Robert Weber, "Conservative Radicalism," *Eternity*, June, 1974.
9. Harry Emerson Fosdick, *The Man from Nazareth* (New York: Pocket Books, 1953; first published by Harper and Brothers, 1949), 126.
10. R. T. France, *Matthew, Evangelist and Teacher* (Grand Rapids, MI: Zondervan, 1989), 196–197.
11. Richards, *Background Commentary*, 29.
12. Henri J. M. Nouwen, *Seeds of Hope* (New York: Doubleday, 1989), 238.
13. Adapted from Lawrence O. Richards, *Handbook*, 474.
14. Barclay, *Matthew*, 182.
15. Foster, *Prayer*, 8.
16. *Classics Devotional Bible* (Grand Rapids, MI: Zondervan, 1996), 1118.
17. Sweet, *Quantum Spirituality*, 89.
18. Chambers, *My Utmost for His Highest*, 180.
19. Ibid., 183.
20. C. S. Lewis, *Mere Christianity*, bk. 4 (New York: Macmillan, 1952), 163.

Chapter 14

1. Barclay, *Mark*, 150.
2. Sweet, *Quantum Spirituality*, 90.
3. Barclay, *Luke*, 93.
4. Dan McCartney and Charles Clayton, *Let the Reader Understand* (Wheaton, IL: Victor, 1994), 192.
5. John Charles Ryle, quoted in Richards, *Background Commentary*, 115.

Chapter 15

1. Kaari Ward, ed., *Jesus and His Times* (Pleasantville, NY: Reader's Digest Association, 1987), 237.
2. Emily Dickenson, quoted in Andrew G. Hodges, *Jesus: An Interview across Time* (Birmingham: Village House, 1986), 196.
3. J. R. Dummelow, *A Commentary on the Holy Bible* (New York: Macmillan, 1923), 1056.
4. A. W. Tozer, *The Pursuit of God* (Harrisburg, PA: Christian Publications, 1948), 83.
5. Willard, *The Divine Conspiracy*, 107.
6. Frank Peretti, *Fiction Sampler* (Waco, TX: Word, 1998), inside front cover.
7. Willard, *The Divine Conspiracy*, 114.
8. Barclay, *Matthew, vol. 2*, 62.
9. Halley, *Halley's Bible Handbook*, 348.

10. Merril F. Unger, *Unger's Bible Dictionary* (Chicago: Moody, 1957), 824.
11. Halley, *Halley's Bible Handbook*, 348.
12. Dietrich Bonhoeffer, quoted in *NRSV Classics Devotional Bible* (Grand Rapids, MI: Zondervan, 1996), 1129.

Chapter 16

1. Thomas and Gundry, *A Harmony*, 87.
2. Sweet, *Quantum Spirituality*, 165.
3. Ephrem the Syrian, quoted in *Ancient Christian Commentary on Scripture, II, Mark*, 64.
4. Halley, *Halley's Bible Handbook*, 373.
5. Richards, *Background Commentary*, 480.
6. Edersheim, *Sketches of Jewish Social Life*, 282.

Chapter 17

1. Barclay, *Matthew*, 356.
2. Robert E. Coleman, *The Master Plan of Evangelism* (Grand Rapids, MI: Revell, 1964), 84.
3. Dietrich Bonhoeffer, quoted in *NRSV Classics Devotional Bible*, 1122.
4. Ibid.
5. Packer, *Knowing God*, 218.
6. Barclay, *Matthew*, 395.
7. Girard, personal journals.
8. Coleman, *Master Plan*, 87.
9. Chrysostom, *Ancient Christian Writers: The Works of the Fathers in Translation*, vol. 31, J. Quasten, ed. (New York: Newman, 1946), 311.

Chapter 18

1. John Pollock, *The Master* (Wheaton, II · Victor, 1985), 93.
2. Morris, *John*, 345.
3. Ray E. Baughman, *The Life of Christ Visualized* (Chicago: Moody, 1968), 84.
4. Augustine of Hippo, quoted in Morris, *John*, 339.
5. Coleman, *The Mind of the Master*, 91–92.
6. Barclay, quoted in Charles Swindoll, *Growing Strong in the Seasons of Life* (Portland, OR: Multnomah, 1983), 229.
7. Sweet, *Quantum Spirituality*, 204.
8. Morris, *John*, 358.
9. Oswald Chambers, *Still Higher for His Highest* (Grand Rapids, MI: Zondervan, 1970), 86.
10. Richards, *Background Commentary*, 234–235.
11. Morris, *John*, 378–379.
12. Augustine of Hippo, quoted in Richards, *Background Commentary*, 234.
13. Card, *Immanuel*, 83.
14. Coleman, *The Mind of the Master*, 89–90.

Chapter 19

1. Dan McCartney and Charles Clayton, *Let the Reader Understand* (Wheaton, IL: Victor, 1994), 73.
2. Barclay, *Mark*, 174.
3. Ibid., 176.
4. Richards, *Background Commentary*, 124.
5. Thomas and Gundry, *A Harmony of the Gospels*, 115.

INDEX

Boldface numbers refer to defined (What?) terms in the sidebar.

A

Aaron:
  John the Baptist as from clan of,
    3
  priests as descendants of, 3, 92
Abaddon, Satan as, 68
Abijah, 6
Abilene, 52–53
Abraham:
  as God's friend, 44
  Jesus as descendant of, 43
Abyss, **235**
Accuser, Satan as, 68
A.D., **xii**
Adam, 81
  Jesus traced back to, 43, 47
Adultery, 12, 45
  Jesus on, 195
Adversary, Satan as, 68
Aenon, **124**
Agnostic, **80**
Alexander the Great, xvii, 4
Alexander (son of Herod), 40
Alexandria, 79
  Jews in, 38
Alford, Henry, on Spirit of God in
  dove form, 63
Allen, Ronald B:
  on Jesus as a baby, 25–26
  on Jesus as born to die, 45
  on Jesus as both God and man,
    129
  on Jesus, humanity of, 46
Alphaeus, 187
Altar of incense, **8**
Amazed, **207**

Among you, **94**
Amplified Bible, the, 190
Anderson, Neil T., on Satan, being
  harassed by, 150
Andrew, 96–97, 147–148, 159–160,
  185–186
  on Jesus, 99, 285
    (*See also* Apostles,
    Disciples)
Angel(s):
Annunciation, 10–12
  birth of Jesus, announcing, 21,
    27
  birth of John the Baptist,
    announcing, 8–9
  devil as, 67
  Gabriel (*see* Gabriel)
  Jesus, ministering to after
    temptation, 75
  Joseph as guided by, 37, 40
  and Mary, (the Annunciation),
    10–12
  shepherds, appearing to, 27–28
  Zechariah, appearing to, 8
Animals:
  sacrificial, 27, 107
    (*See also* individual animals)
Anna, 21, 30–31
Annas, 52–53
Annunciation, 10–12
Anointed, **5, 144**
Anointing, **63**
Antioch church 144
Antipas, Herod (*see* Herod Antipas)
Antipater, 38
Apollyon, Satan as, 68

Apostle(s), **xiv, 78** 186–188
  (*See also* Disciples and indi-
    vidual names)
Apostleship, **147**
Apostolic, **97**
Aramaic, xvii, 140, **144**, 195
Archaeological, **xiii**
Archelaus, 39–40
Aristobulus, 40
Ark of the Covenant, 8
Ascension, **120**
Asher, 31
Asmat people of New Guinea, 113–
  114
Assyria, 4
Assyrian conquest, 127
Assyrians, beliefs of, 79
Astrologers (*see* Magi)
Athanasian Creed, on Jesus as God
  and man, 14
Athanasius, on Jesus healing man
  with withered hand, 179
Atone, **157**
Atonement, **42**
Atonement, Festival of, 6
Augustine of Hippo:
  on belief, 271
  on feeding the five thousand,
    260
  on God's love, 120
Aurelius, Marcus, on Reason, 70
Authority, **245**

B

Babylon, Jewish population in, 31
Babylonian Empire, 4

Babylonian exile, **31**, **127**
Babylonian Talmud, 31
Babylonians, beliefs of, 79
Bag, **247**
Baptism, 58–63
ritual bath, illustration of, 59
  by Jesus, 60
  of Jesus, 61–63, 94
  John the Baptist and, 53, 58,
    93–94
  meaning of, 59
  (*See also* John the Baptist)
Baptismal pool, illustration of, 59
Baptist, John the (*see* John the
  Baptist)
Baptize with, **82**
Baptized, **210**
Baptizes, **60**
Bar mitzvah, 41, 43
Barclay, William:
  on a child as being a gift, 29
  on Christians in the world, 193
  on cleanliness and godliness,
    278
  on the disciples, 186
  on God in Jesus, 88
  on God, loyalty to, 250
  on Jesus, acceptance or rejection
    of, 124
  on Jesus, healing official's son,
    142
  on Jesus, regarding rules and
    regulations, 277
  on Jesus, temptation of, 74
  on John the Baptist and Jesus,
    54
  on loyalty to God, 250
  on Luke, gospel of, xvi
  on Mary's faith and trust, 12
  on official's son, Jesus healing,
    142
  on parables, 225
  on rules and regulations, Jesus
    regarding, 277
  on seeking, attitude of, 198
  on shepherds, 28
  on spiritual dullness, 264
  on temptation, 66
  on temptation of Jesus, 74

Barley loaves, **260**
Barnabas, Mark and, xv
Barnes, Albert:
  on Jesus' birth, time of year of,
    26
  on Jesus' teaching, 149
Barren, barrenness, 9
Bartholomew (possibly Nathanael),
  187, 285
  (*See also* Apostles, Disciples,
    Nathanael)
Basiliko, 142
Baskets, **260**
Bath, ritual, illustration of, 59
Bathsheba, 45
Baudelaire, on the devil, 68
Baughman, Ray E., on feeding the
  five thousand, 260
B.C., **xii**
Beasley-Murray, George R., on
  Jesus from Nazareth, 98
Beatitudes, **189**–192, 204
Beelzebub, **214**
  Satan as, 68
Begged, **142**
Beginning, the, **80**
Belial, Satan as, 68
Believe, meaning of, 86
Believers, **xix,** 269
Belts, **246**
Benedictus, 16
Bethany, 23, **91**
Bethesda, Pool of, 169–171, 183
Bethlehem:
  David, as hometown of, 21, 23
  flight from to Egypt, map of, 39
  Jesus as born in, 25–35
  Micah's prophecy and, 21
Bethsaida, 23, **97**, 258, 282–285
Betrothal, customs, 20
Bible:
  Amplified Bible, the, 190
  books in, xii
  as God revealing self, 80
  man-made additions to,
    171–172
  New International Version (NIV),
    xvii
  purpose of, xix

  reading of, xvii–xix
  setup of, xii
  young Jesus' knowledge of, 41
  (*See also* New Testament, Old
    Testament)
Bima, **144**
Birth:
  of Jesus (*see* Jesus' birth)
  new (*see* Born again)
Blasphemous, **173**
Blasphemy, **163,** 216
Bleeding, **238**
Bleeding woman, Jesus healing,
  237–239
Blessed, meanings of, 190
Blessing, **197**
Blind man, Jesus healing, 106, 284
Body and blood of Jesus, in
  "spiritual diet," 270–271
Bonhoeffer, Dietrich:
  on following Christ, 249
  on grace, 228
  on Jesus and disciples, 245
Born again, 86–87, **190**
  Cash, Johnny, on being, 116
  Chambers, Oswald, on being,
    116
  childlike approach to being, 115
  description of, 115
  Graham, Billy, on being, 87, 110
  implications of, 113–116
  Jesus defining, 112
  meaning of, 113–116
  stages of being, 116
  (*See also* Christians, Christian-
    ity, Nicodemus)
Brandt, Leslie F., on Jesus,
  Nazareth's rejection of, 146
Bread, 260
  consecrated, 178
  living, Jesus as, 275
  physical and spiritual, 265–271,
    273
  (*See also* Feeding the multi-
    tudes, Loaves and fishes)
Bread of Life, Jesus as, 261
Brethren, **217**
Bridal dress, illustration of, 102
Bridegroom's friend, **125**

Briscoe, Stuart, on fish as metaphor, 148

Briscoe, Stuart and Jill, on Christmas, 27

Bronze snake, **121**

Brown, Harold O. J., on Jesus as God and man, 129

Bultmann, R., on God as self-revealing, 80

Bunyan, John, on becoming a Christian, 86

Burnt offering, **29**

C

Caesar, Julius, 4

Caesar, Tiberius, 52

Caesar, as title of Roman emperors, 52

Caesar Augustus, **7**, 21–22

Caesarea, Paul jailed in, xv–xvi

Caesarea Philippi, 23

Caiaphas, 52–53

Cana, 23

    wedding at, 101–107, 116

Canaanite, 279

Cananaean, **187**

Capernaum, 23, 107

    Jesus, as home of, 159, 163

    Jesus' ministry in, 147–153, 155, 271

Caravansary, 24

Card, Michael:

    on disciples, larger group leaving, 272

    on Jesus' birth, time of year of, 26

    on Jesus enjoying parties, 102

    on Jesus and tears, 26

    on John 1, first sentences of, 77

Carpenter:

    Jesus as, 41, 285

    Joseph as, 41

Cash, Johnny, on being born again, 116

Casting net, **148**

Caves, as used for animal shelters, 24

Cemetery, **208**

Census, 21

Centurion, **206**

Centurion's servant, Jesus healing, 206–207

Centurions as "good guys," examples, 207

Cephas (Peter), 97

Ceremonial laws, **149**

Ceremonially clean, **29**

Chafer, Lewis Sperry:

    on Jesus, rejection of, 123

    on John the Baptist, preaching of, 94

Chambers, Oswald:

    on being born again, 116

    on Christian experience of hunger, 270

    on Christian witness, 201

    on hope, 6

    on Jesus' messages as for heart, not head, 202

Charity, 196

Chazzan, **144**

Childbearing, significance in Bible time of, 9

Childbirth, first-century customs regarding, 29

Childlessness, stigma of, 9

Children of God, 85–86

    Jews as, 279

Children:

    education of in Jesus' time, 41

    as gifts from God, 30

    Jesus' advice to be like, 115

Children of God, 85–86

    Jews as, 279

Christ, **83**

    Jesus, title of, 83

    (*See also* Jesus Christ, Savior, Messiah)

Christ's birth, illustration of historical events surrounding, 22

Christ's revolution, three types of, 15–16

Christian leaders, task of, 96

Christian witness, 201

    effective, 247

    power and, 28

    pride and, 28

    rejection of, 146

    wealth and, 28

Christian, becoming, 86

    (*See also* Born again)

Christianese, **202**

Christianity:

    cost of, 249–250

    flesh and blood of Jesus as spiritual "diet" of, 270–271, 273

    (*See also* Born again)

Christians:

    baptism of, 59

    believers, 269

    early, challenging established authorities, 93

    furthering own vs. Christ's plans, 261

    getting along with other, 201

    ideal lifestyle of, 196–197

    pagans, spreading word to, 79

    persecution of, 248–251

    testing of, 66

    in the world, 193

    (*See also* Born again)

Christmas, 27

Chrysostom:

    on Jesus, temptation of, 67

    on Salome's dance, 254

Church, **157, 189**

    early, 133, 159, 181

    Gentile, 180

    as Temple, 109

Chuza, 144

Circumcision, 28–29

City on a hill, metaphor of, 193

Clayton, Charles (*see* McCartney, Dan, and Charles Clayton)

Cleanliness and godliness, 278, 287

Clement of Alexandria, on John, gospel of, xvi

Cleopatra, 40

Coleman, Robert E.:

    on disciples, Jesus training, 245

    on evangelism, 79

    on God as man, 46

    on the incarnation of Christ, 87

    on the Old Testament, Jesus and, 144

Evil spirits, 149–152
  (*See also* Demon-possession)
Exile, **31**, **127**
Expatriates, **38**
Expression, **208**
Extrabiblical, **171**

F

Faith, 266–269
  of centurion(s), 206–207
  community, as best expressed
    in, 213
  in God vs. in a person, 203
  in Jesus, 86
  living, 224
  of Mary, 12
  meaning of, true, 73
  as miracle, 269–270
  of Peter, 272
  of Phoenician woman, 279–280
  reasons for, 143
  as only "work" God requires,
    267
  of Zachariah, 9, 11
Fasting, **31**
  of Jesus, 65–67, 268
  hypocritical piety and, 197
Favor, **5**
Feast (*see* individual feasts)
Feast of Tabernacles, **169**
Feeding of the five thousand, 106,
  258–261, 273
Festivals, major, **6**
Fever, **152**
Fishing net, parable of, 227
Finger of God, **215**
First day, **180**
Firstborn, redemption of, 29
Fish, 260
  metaphor of, 148, 160
  loaves and fishes, miracle of,
    106, 280–281
Fishermen, disciples as, 147–148,
  159–160
5 B.C., **3**
Five shekels, **29**
Five thousand, feeding of, 106,
  258–261, 273
Flesh, **87**

Flesh and blood of Jesus, as
  "spiritual diet," 270–271
Flight to Egypt, map of, 39
Follow me, **97**
Food, physical and spiritual, 265–
  271, 287
Foolishness, nature of, 203
Foot-washing, ritual of, 104
  and the forgiven prostitute,
    211–212
Forerunner, **14**, 56, **125**
Forgive, **201**
Forgiveness, 163–165, 200
Forty days and 40 nights, 66–67
Fosdick, Harry Emerson, on Jesus'
  faith in his disciples, 193
Foster, Richard J.:
  on children's prayers, 198
  on repentance, the need for, 58
Fourth watch, **263**
France, R. T., on Old Testament,
  Jesus as key to interpreting,
  194
From birth, **9**
Fruit of the spirit, 202

G

Gabriel, the angel, 8
  Annunciation, 10–12
  Elizabeth and, 14
  Joseph, appearance to, 20
  Mary, visit to, 10–12, 14
  Zechariah and, 9
Gadara, 234, 241
Galilean basin, 263
Galileans, description of, 140
Galilee, 139, **158**, 282
  Asher, tribe of in, 31
  description of, 140
  disciples' ministry in, 246–249
  Herod Antipas as ruler of, 53,
    126
  holy family's return to, 38
  Jesus as from, 98, 139–140
  Jesus' ministry in, 139–140
  Lake or Sea of, 231–123
  Mary as from, 10
  Mary and Joseph, home of, 21
  Nathanael as from, 98

people of, reputation, 98
rulers of, 39–40
trade routes through, map of,
  141
Galilee, Sea or Lake of, xvi, 97,
  159, 231–233,
  illustration of, 259
Gamaliel, 31
Genealogies, importance of, 43
Generosity, 196, 199–200
Gennesaret, 265
  Lake or Sea of, 159
  (*See also* Galilee, Sea of)
Gentile(s):
  born again, 113
  dogs, as called, 279–280
  Jesus and, 182
  Jesus and Phoenician woman,
    279–280
  Jesus on, 146, 153
Gentile church, 180
Gentile houses, **206**
Gerazim, Mount, 131
Gergesa, 23
Gifts of the Magi, usefulness of, 38
Girard, Audrey I.:
  on denial of self–interests, 251
  on dove, Spirit of God appear-
    ing as, 63
  on Jesus and children, signifi-
    cance in our lives of, 30
  on Jesus at age 12, 42
  on the kingdom of God, 158
Glory, **106**
Goatskin wine bottle, illustration
  of, 166
God:
  Abraham as friend of, 44
  Bible as revealing self, 80
  children of, 85–86, 279
  Elyon, 11
  faith in, 121
  finger of, 215
  as "I am," 264
  and Jesus (*see* God (Jesus))
  kingdom of, 112, 156–159, 167,
    200
  knowing, as key to full life, 80
  love of, for all people, 119–120

nature of, 87–88, 109
nothing as impossible with, 11–13
obeying, 121
as person, 133–134
plural references to, 83–84
reign of, 158
self-expression of, 82
as spirit, 132
testing, wrongness of, 72–73
Trinity of, 83–85
as wanting people to know him, 80
Word of (*see* Bible)
Word of (Living Word), 78–83
worship of, 74
wrath of, 125
Yahweh as, xix, 20, 59
(*See also* individual topics)
God (Jesus):
  Jesus, access to through, 83, 100
  Jesus, oneness with, 84
  Jesus as, 87–88, 100
  Jesus as clearest expression of, 89
  Jesus as son of, 42, 120
  in Jesus, 12–13
God's Word (*see* Bible)
God's wrath, **125**
Godliness, cleanliness and, 278, 287
God-provided Ram, the, 95
Gold, 34
Good news, **52**
Gorion, 111
Gospel, **77**
  (*See also* Bible, New Testament)
Gospels, **xiv**
  four, xiv–xvii
  synoptic, xvi
  (*See also* individual gospels John, Luke, Mark, Matthew)
Grace, **87, 129, 207**
  giving, 201
Graham, Billy, on being born again, 87, 110
Greatness, meaning of, 158
Greek (language), xvii, 140, 279
  as Roman Empire's universal language, 78

Greek Empire, 4
Greeks (Plato's disciples), beliefs of, 79
Greeks (Stoics), beliefs of, 79
Greeting, **246**
Gundry, Stanley (*see* Thomas, Robert L., and Stanley N. Gundry)

H
Halley, Henry H.:
  on Bible as God revealing self, 80
  on demon possession, 234
  on John the Baptist and Elijah, 55
  on kingdom of Jesus, nature of, 225
  on Old and New Testaments, xii
  on water changed to wine, miracle of, 106
Hand-washing:
  the Bible on, 277–278
  ritual of, 104
Hanukkah, 6
Healing:
  essentials to, 122
  Jesus' ministry of, 152
Healing miracles, Jesus performing, 106
  (*See also* Jesus, miracles by (healing))
Heaven, 120, 189
  kingdom of, 156–159, 189
  (*See also* Kingdom of God)
Hebrew (language), xvii, 140, 144
Hebrew (people) (*see* Israelites, Jews)
Hellenization, **4**
Henry, Matthew, on Mary's sin offering, 29
Hermon, Mount, 52
Herod (the Great), **7–8, 22, 52**
  Antipater as son of, crucifying, 38
  characteristics of, 7
  death of, 38
  family's faith in Jesus, 143–144
  illness of, 38

jealousy of, 37
Jerusalem, controlling, 7
Jews and, 7
Magi disobeying, 33–34
male infants, killing of, 37–40
paranoia of, 33
supporters of (Herodians), 282
wickedness of, 38
Herod Agrippa, 40
Herod Antipas, 39–40, 52, 126, **253**
  family's faith in Jesus, 143–144
Herodians and, 282
  Jesus and, 252–253
  John the Baptist and, 209, 253–254
  Machaerus Castle, 209
  supporters of (Herodians), 282
Herod Philip, son of Cleopatra, 40
Herod Philip, son of Herod, 39–40
Herod the Tetrarch (*see* Herod Antipas)
Herod's family tree, illustration of, 40
Herod's Temple, 7
Herodians, **181**, 282–283
Herodias, 40, 126, 253–254
Hidden treasure, parable of, 227
High noon, **127**
Highly favored, **10**
Hillel, **31**
His home, **163**
Holy Land (*see* Israel)
Holy of Holies, **8**
Holy place, **8**
Holy Scriptures (*see* Bible)
Holy Spirit:
  as dove, appearing, 96
  and Mary, 12
  Mary and Elizabeth, and, 14
  in Trinity, 83–84
Homo sapien, **76**
Honey, 55–56
Hope, 6
Horned Lamb, 95
Hospitality, customs of, 211–213
House, **42**
Houses, built on rock or sand, parable of, 203

Howton, Dom J., on Christ representing God, 96
Hunger, physical and spiritual, 265–271, 273
Hymn, John 1 opening as early Christian, 77–78
Hypocrisy, **197**, 204, 279
Hypocrites, **276**

I

"I am," God and Jesus as, 264–265
Idumean, **7**
  Herod as, 38
Immanuel, 5, 20
Incarnate Word, 76
Incarnation, 120
Incense, 8, 34
Incest, 45
Inn, 24–25
Innocent, 248
Instinctively knew, 61
Isaiah, prophecy of, 53–54, 93, 145, 153, 182
Israel, **4**
  freedom, as yearning for, 4
  as "house of Jacob," 11
  Jesus, at time of, 3–4
  occupation of, chart, 4
  Old Testament, significance in, xii
  Roman occupation of, 4, 261
    (*See also* Palestine, Promised Land)
Israelites, **5**
  (*See also* Jews)
Iturea, 39–40, 52

J

Jacob, 5
  Jesus as of house of, 11
  "star out of," 32
Jacob's well, **127,** 130
Jairus, and daughter's resurrection, 236–241
James (brother of John), xvi, 147–148, 159–160, 185–187
  (*See also* Apostles, Disciples)
James ("the Younger"), 187
  (*See also* Apostles, Disciples)
Jericho, 23

Jerome, on following Jesus, 148
Jerusalem, 23
  Herod controlling, 7
  map of, 170
  redemption of, 20
  Temple in, 27
Jeshimmon, 66
Jesus Christ, xiii, **20,** 206, 285–286
  Abraham in genealogy of, 43
  Adam in genealogy of, 43, 63
  angels ministering to after temptation, 75
  anger of, 107
  authority of, 207
  baptism of, 61–63, 94, 96
  baptism by, 60
  belief in, 110, 175, 266–269
  birth of, 25–35
    (*See also* Jesus' birth)
  as Bread of Life, 261
  brothers and sisters of, 41, 217
  as carpenter, 41, 285
  challenging authorities, 93
  characteristics of, 11
  Christ as title of, 83
  claims of, 128, 173–175, 269
  compassion of, 243–244, 254, 257, 279
  David as ancestor of, 11, 214
  as Deliverer, 31
  demons, exorcism of, 150
    (*See also* Demon-possession)
  devil and, 65
  disciples of (*see* Jesus and his disciples)
  Egypt, escape from Herod to, 37–38
  enemies of (*see* Enemies, of Jesus)
  evil spirits, ten confrontations with, 150
  family of, 41, 217
  family heritage of, 43–45, 47, 63
  fasting of, 65–67
  feeding the five thousand, 106
  flesh and blood of as spiritual "diet," 270–271, 273
  followers of (*see* Disciples)

Galilee, as from, 98, 139–140
  genealogy of, 43–45, 47, 63
  and Gentiles, 146, 153, 182, 279–280
  gospels as recording life of, xiv–xvii
    (*See also* John, Luke, Mark, Matthew)
  hatred of (*see* Enemies of Jesus)
  as healer, 182, 265, 284, 287
  healing ministry of, 152
  healing miracles by (*see* Jesus, miracles by (healing))
  Herod and, 33–34, 37–40
  humanness of, 13–14, 42, 46, 62–63, 127–128, 232–233, 279
  as "I am," 265
  Israel at time of, 3–4
  Jews and, 246–247
  John the Baptist (*see* Jesus and John the Baptist)
  Judea, reasons for leaving, 126
  judgment by, 176
  as King, 61, 182
  as Lamb of God, 27, 94–95, 285
  Lazarus raised from dead by, 106
  and leper, 161–62, 167
  as Liberator, 112
  life, as source of, 81
  life of, xiii, 206, 285–286
  lifestyle taught by, 196–197
  as light, 123
  light of, accepting, 86
  loaves and fishes, miracle of, 106, 280–281
  as Lord, xix, 190, 202, 285
  man, reasons for being, 46
  Mary as mother of, 10–14, 104–107, 217
  message of, 141
  as Messiah, 91, 134, 182
    (*See also* Messiah)
  ministry of (*see* (below) Jesus, ministry and teaching of)
  miracles by, 72, 106, 142
    (*See also* (below) Jesus, miracles by (healing, nature, resurrection))

the blind man, 106, 284
the centurion's servant, 206–207
the leper, 161–62, 167
the official's son, 106, 142–143
speech impediment, the man
with, 284
the paralyzed man, 106, 163,
167
Peter's mother-in-law, 152
the Phoenician woman's
daughter, 287, 279–280
at the Pool of Bethesda, 169–
171, 183
withered hand, the man with,
179
Jesus, miracles by (nature):
feeding the multitudes, 287
feeding the five thousand, 106,
258–261, 273
loaves and fishes, 106, 280–281
calming the storm, 231–233,
241
casting the nets, 160
walking on water, 106, 263, 273
water, changing to wine, 104–
107, 116
Jesus, miracles by (resurrection):
daughter of Jairus, 236–241
Lazarus, 106
the widow's son, 208–209
Jesus and the Old Testament:
Bible knowledge as child, of, 41
as key to interpreting, 144, 194,
204
messianic promises/prophecy
in, 5, 31–32, 54, 130, 209
on Old Testament command-
ments, 195
Old Testament as witness for,
177
Jesus is Lord, **190**
Jewish education, 41
Jews, **xvii**
in Alexandria, 38
beliefs of, Old Testament, 79
as children of God, 279
Herod and, 7
Israelites, 5
Jesus and, 246–247

Jesus as, 91
New Testament, as writers of,
91
Sabbath and first-century, 171–
174
as trilingual, xvii
Jews (religious leaders), **173**
Joanna, 144
John (apostle), xvi, 97, 147–148,
159–160, 185–187
as "disciple whom Jesus loved,"
xvi
(*See also* Apostles, Disciples)
John the Baptist, 8
actions of, 54
Aaron, as from clan of, 3
birth of, 8–9, 16
characteristics of, 8, 55
courage of, 253
death of, 126, 252–255
diet of, 55
disciples of, 96, 100, 135
disciplined life of, 211
doubting Jesus, 209
Elijah, similarities to, 55, 92,
210
as evangelist, 8
as forerunner of Jesus, 56–60
as great in God's eyes, 8
as greatest prophet, 3
as guide, 9
and Jesus (*see* John the Baptist
and Jesus)
and locusts and honey, 55
Messiah, considered by some to
be, 91–92
naming of, 16
as peacemaker, 8
preaching of, 52–61, 89, 91
as prophet, 3, 9, 55, 96, 210
as River Prophet, 92
role of, 100
significance of, 93, 210
as spiritual, 8
strict life of, 211
as teetotaler, **8**
vision of, at Jesus' baptism, 96
John the Baptist and Jesus, 14, 51,
60, 99, 285

baptizing Jesus, 61–62, 96
compared to, 82, 124–125, 252–
253, 255
Jesus complimenting, 209–210
as cousin (or relative) of, 16–17,
124
as friend of, 124
questioning if Jesus was really
Messiah, 157, 209
relationship with, 124
significance to Jesus, 53–54
as witness for Jesus, 176
John Mark (*see* Mark)
John, gospel of, xiv, xvi, 77–78
John's Life of Christ, seven signs
proving claims of, 105–106,
169
Jonah, 216–218
Jordan River, 124, 159
Jesus' baptism in, 62
Jews' baptism in, 59
John the Baptist preaching near,
54
Jordan Valley, 23
Joseph, father of Jesus:
poverty of, 29
angel in dream of, 37
angels guiding, 40
as carpenter, 41
David as ancestor of, 23–24
death of, 103
Gabriel's appearance to, 20
Jesus as adopted son of, 13
Mary and, 19–21
poverty of, 29
qualities of, 20
Josephus, 56
on Galileans, 140
Joshua, Jesus as Greek for, 20
Josiah, King, 44
Jubilee, Year of, 144
Judah (person), 5
Judah (territory), 4
Herod as king of, 7
Judaism, baptism at conversion to,
58–59
Judas (of Galilee), 250
Judas (Iscariot), 188
(*See also* Apostles, Disciples)

Prayer, 198
  children and, 198
  effective, 280
  the Lord's, 197
  show-off piety and, 196
Prejudice, Jesus and, 129
Presentation, the (of Jesus to God
    in the Temple), 27–31
Priest(s), 5, **42**, 92
  Zechariah as, 6
Priestly clan, Aaron as ancestor of,
    6
Prince of devils, Satan as, 68
Proboscis, 152
Prodigal son, parable of, 293
Promised Land, **121**
Prophecies, prophecy, **156**
  ancient, as given to Jews, 246
  messianic, 31, 40, 54
  (*See also* Old Testament,
      Prophet(s))
Prophet, the, **261**
Prophet(s), 92–93
  Daniel as, 31–32
  Elijah as, 55
  Elijah and John the Baptist,
      compared, 55
  Elisha, 208
  false, 202
  having no honor in own
      country, 139, 146
  Isaiah as (*see* Isaiah's prophecy)
  Jesus, regarding, 98
  Jesus as, 93, 98–99, 131, 205
  John the Baptist as greatest ever
      born, 3, 55, 210
  Malachi as, 54
  Micah as, 21, 33
  Moses as, 93, 131
  as scorned in hometown, 139,
      146
  Simeon as (*see* Simeon)
Prophetess, Anna as, 31
Prostitute, prostitution, 45
  the forgiven, 211–213, 218
Providence, 282
Publicans, 165
Purification, after childbirth, 29
Purim, 6

Pure in heart, as blessed, 191
Purity, sexual, 196

Q
Quest of the Historical Jesus, The,
    xiii
Quiet in the Land, 30
Quirinius, 21–22
Qumran, 55

R
Rabbi, **96**
  Jesus as, 99
Rabbinic, 60
Rabbinical teaching, 156
Raca, 195
Rahab, 45
Rebirth, spiritual (*see* Born again)
Red Sea, 59
Redemption of Jerusalem, 30
Redemption price, 29
Religion:
  hypocrisy and, 204, 279
  as private, invalidity of, 193
  problem with rigidity in, 173
  (*See also* Christianity)
Religions:
  first-century beliefs, 79
  world, 82
Religious leaders, Jesus confront-
    ing, 214–215
Renewal, spiritual, 119
Repentance, **124**
Resurrection, 175
  last day, 269
Resurrection miracles:
  by Elisha, 208
  by Jesus, 208–209, 236–241
Revell Bible Dictionary:
  on Jesus' family tree, women in,
      45
  on Jesus, temptation of, 66, 70
Revenge, Jesus on, 195–196
Richards, Larry (Lawrence O.):
  on the beatitudes, 191
  on demon-possession, 236
  on faith and miracles, 143
  on family "trade secrets," 174
  on the feeding of the multi-

tudes, 281
  on flesh and blood of Jesus as
      symbol, 271
  on Jesus' living presence with
      us, 99
  on John the Baptist, about Jesus,
      83
  on John the Baptist, significance
      of, 93
  on light shed by Christ, 82
  on miracles, faith and, 143
  on religious leaders, Jesus and,
      173
  on stars, reliance on for
      directions, 32
  on temptation of Christ, 75
  on witnessing, angry rejection
      of, 146
  on "the Word of God," 79
Richardson, Don:
  on the Asmat people of New
      Guinea, 113
  on religion, 82
Riches, worldly vs. heavenly, 198–
    199, 204
Righteousness, **194**
  those who are persecuted for as
      blessed, 191
  those who thirst for as blessed,
      191
River Prophet, John the Baptist as,
    92
Rock,
  house on, parable of, 203
  Peter as meaning, 97
Roman(s):
  beliefs of, 79
  centurion as, 206
  Israel, occupation by, 4, 261
  persecution by, 250
Roman Empire, **xvii**
  Caesar Augustus as ruler of, 22
  Quirinius as governor of, 22
Roman Imperial government, 21
Rome, 126
  Paul in, xvi
Rosh Hashanah, 6
Ruin, Satan as, 68
Ruth, 45

Well along in years, **6**
Widow's son, Jesus resurrecting,
208–209
Willard, Dallas:
    on God's character, 175
    on living one's faith, 224
    on parables, 223
Wine:
    water changed to, 103–107
    facts regarding, 105
    goatskin wine bottle, illustration
        of, 166
    and wedding at Cana, 103–107
    and wineskins, metaphor of,
        165–168
Wisdom, nature of, 203
Wise men, the three (Magi), 31–32
    gifts to Jesus, 38
    Herod and, 33–34
    Jesus, time of visit to, 33
    star, following, 32
Withdrew, **262**
Without limit, **125**
Witness, Christian, 201

effective, 247
power and, 28
pride and, 28
rejection of, 146
wealth and, 28
Witnesses, testifying for Jesus,
    176–177
Woe, **192**
Wolves, metaphor, 248
Woman at the well, the, 126–135
Women, in Jesus' family tree, 45
Wonders, **142**
Word, living, 78–83
Word of God, **54**
Words, power of Jesus', 240
Works, **266**
World, **221**
World order, **66**
Worship, **132**
    Jesus on, 132
    principles of effective, 133–134
Worthlessness, Satan as, 68
Worthy, **246**
Wrongdoing (*see* Sin)

Y
Yahweh, xix, 20, 59
Year of the Lord's favor (Year of
    Jubilee), **144**
Yeast, **282–283**
parable of, 227
Yom Kippur, 6

Z
Zeal, **109**
Zealot, **5**
Zealot, Simon the, 187
Zebedee, 187
Zechariah, 6, 8–9, 14
    birth of son John, 16
    faith and doubt of, 9, 11
    John the Baptist as son of, 53
    as priest, 92
    song of, 16
    speechlessness of, 9
Zion, Mount, **132**
    (*See also* Temple Mount)

Books by Starburst Publishers®

(Partial listing—full list available on request)

The *God's Word for the Biblically-Inept*™ series is already a best-seller with over 100,000 books sold! Designed to make reading the Bible easy, educational, and fun! This series of verse-by-verse Bible studies, topical studies, and overviews mixes scholarly information from experts with helpful icons, illustrations, sidebars, and time lines. It's the Bible made easy!

Life of Christ, Volume 1—God's Word for the Biblically-Inept™
Robert C. Girard

Girard takes the reader on an easy-to-understand journey through the gospels of Matthew, Mark, Luke, and John, tracing the story of Jesus from his virgin birth to his revolutionary ministry. Learn about Jesus' baptism, the Sermon on the Mount, and his miracles and parables.
(trade paper)   ISBN 1892016230 $16.95

The Bible—God's Word for the Biblically-Inept™
Larry Richards

An excellent book to start learning the entire Bible. Get the basics or the in-depth information you are seeking with this user-friendly overview. From Creation to Christ to the Millennium, learning the Bible has never been easier.
(trade paper)   ISBN 0914984551 $16.95

Revelation—God's Word for the Biblically-Inept™
Daymond R. Duck

End-Time Bible prophecy expert Daymond R. Duck leads us verse by verse through one of the Bible's most confusing books. Follow the experts as they forge their way through the captivating prophecies of Revelation!
(trade paper)   ISBN 0914984985 $16.95

Daniel—God's Word for the Biblically-Inept™
Daymond R. Duck

Daniel is a book of prophecy and the key to understanding the mysteries of the Tribulation and End-Time events. This verse-by-verse commentary combines humor and scholarship to get at the essentials of Scripture. Perfect for those who want to know the truth about the Antichrist.
(trade paper)   ISBN 0914984489 $16.95

Health & Nutrition—God's Word for the Biblically-Inept™
Kathleen O'Bannon Baldinger

The Bible is full of God's rules for good health! Baldinger reveals scientific evidence that proves the diet and health principles outlined in the Bible are the best for total health. Learn about the Bible Diet, the food pyramid, and fruits and vegetables from the Bible! Experts include Pamela Smith, Julian Whitaker, Kenneth Cooper, and T. D. Jakes.
(trade paper)   ISBN 0914984055 $16.95

Men of the Bible—God's Word for the Biblically-Inept™
D. Larry Miller

Benefit from the life experiences of the powerful men of the Bible! Learn how the inspirational struggles of men such as Moses, Daniel, Paul, and David parallel the struggles of men today. It will inspire and build Christian character for any reader.
(trade paper)   ISBN 1892016079 $16.95

Women of the Bible—God's Word for the Biblically-Inept™
Kathy Collard Miller

Finally, a Bible perspective just for women! Gain valuable insight from the successes and struggles of such women as Eve, Esther, Mary, Sarah, and Rebekah. Interesting icons like "Get Close to God," "Build Your Spirit," and "Grow Your Marriage" will make it easy to incorporate God's Word into your daily life.
(trade paper)   ISBN 0914984063 $16.95

Genesis—God's Word for the Biblically-Inept™
Joyce L. Gibson

Genesis is written to make understanding and learning the Word of God simple and fun! Like the other books in this series, the author breaks the Bible down into bite-sized pieces making it easy to understand and incorporate into your life. Readers will learn about Creation, Adam and Eve, the Flood, Abraham and Isaac, and more.
(trade paper)   ISBN 1892016125 $16.95

Prophecies of the Bible—God's Word for the Biblically-Inept™
Daymond R. Duck

God has a plan for this crazy planet, and now understanding it is easier than ever! Best-selling author and End-Time

prophecy expert Daymond R. Duck explains the complicated prophecies of the Bible in plain English. Duck shows you all there is to know about the end of the age, the New World Order, the Second Coming, and the coming world government. Find out what prophecies have already been fulfilled and what's in store for the future!
(trade paper)   ISBN 1892016222 $16.95

Romans—God's Word for the Biblically-Inept™
Gib Martin

The best-selling *God's Word for Biblically-Inept™* series continues to grow! Learn about the apostle Paul, living a righteous life, and more with help from graphics, icons, and chapter summaries. (Available Summer 2000.)
(trade paper)   ISBN 1892016273 $16.95

The **What's in the Bible for . . .™** series focuses its attention on making the Bible applicable to everyday life. Whether you're a teenager or senior citizen, this series has the book for you! Each title is equipped with the same reader-friendly icons, call-outs, tables, illustrations, questions, and chapter summaries that are used in the **God's Word for the Biblically-Inept™** series. It's another easy way to access God's Word!

What's in the Bible for . . .™ Women
Georgia Curtis Ling

What does the Bible have to say to women? Women of all ages will find biblical insight on topics that are meaningful to them in four sections: Wisdom for the Journey; Family Ties; Bread, Breadwinners, and Bread Makers; and Fellowship and Community Involvement. This book uses illustrations, bullet points, chapter summaries, and icons to make understanding God's Word easier than ever!
(trade paper)   ISBN 1892016109 $16.95

What's in the Bible for . . .™ Teens
Mark and Jeanette Littleton

This is a book that teens will love! *What's in the Bible for . . . Teens* contains topical Bible themes that parallel the challenges and pressures of today's adolescents. Learn about Bible prophecy, God's plan for relationships, and peer pressure in a conversational and fun tone. Helpful and eye-catching "WWJD?" icons, illustrations and sidebars included. (Available Fall 2000.)
(trade paper)   ISBN 1892016052 $16.95

What's in the Bible for . . .™ Mothers
Judy Bodmer

Is home schooling a good idea? Is it okay to work? At what age should I start treating my children like responsible adults? What is the most important thing I can teach my children? If you are asking these questions and need help answering them, *What's in the Bible for . . . Mothers* is especially for you! Simple and user-friendly, this motherhood manual offers hope and instruction for today's mothers by jumping into the lives of mothers in the Bible (e.g., Naomi, Elizabeth, and Mary) and by exploring biblical principles that are essential to being a nurturing mother.
(trade paper)   ISBN 1892016265 $16.95

(see page v for purchasing information)

•   **Learn more at www.biblicallyinept.com**   •

The **God's Vitamin "C" for the Spirit™** series has already sold over 250,000 copies! Jam-packed with stories from well-known Christian writers that will lighten your spirit and enrich you life!

God's Vitamin "C" for the Spirit™
by Kathy Collard Miller & D. Larry Miller
(trade paper) ISBN 0914984837 $12.95

God's Vitamin "C" for the Spirit™ of Women
by Kathy Collard Miller
(trade paper) ISBN 0914984934 $12.95

God's Chewable Vitamin "C" for the Spirit™ of Moms
(trade paper) ISBN 0914984-942 $6.95

God's Vitamin "C" for the Hurting Spirit™
by Kathy Collard Miller & D. Larry Miller
(trade paper) ISBN 0914984691 $12.95

God's Chewable Vitamin "C" for the Spirit™
(trade paper) ISBN 0914984-845 $6.95

God's Vitamin "C" for the Spirit™ of Men
by D. Larry Miller
(trade paper) ISBN 0914984810 $12.95

God's Chewable Vitamin "C" for the Spirit™ of Dads
(trade paper) ISBN 0914984-829 $6.95

God's Vitamin "C" for the Christmas Spirit™
by Kathy Collard Miller & D. Larry Miller
(cloth) ISBN 0914984853 $14.95

The Weekly Feeder: A Revolutionary Shopping, Cooking, and Meal-Planning System

Cori Kirkpatrick

A revolutionary meal-planning system, here is a way to make preparing home-cooked dinners more convenient than ever. At the beginning of each week, simply choose one of the eight preplanned menus, tear out the corresponding grocery list, do your shopping, and whip up each fantastic meal in less than 45 minutes! The author's household management tips, equipment checklists, and nutrition information make this system a must for any busy family. Included with every recipe is a personal anecdote from the author emphasizing the importance of good food, a healthy family, and a well-balanced life.

(trade paper)   ISBN 1892016095 $16.95

God Stories: They're So Amazing, Only God Could Make Them Happen

Donna I. Douglas

Famous individuals share their personal, true-life experiences with God in this beautiful new book! Find out how God has touched the lives of top recording artists, professional athletes, and other newsmakers like Jessi Colter, Deana Carter, Ben Vereen, Stephanie Zimbalist, Cindy Morgan, Sheila E., Joe Jacoby, Cheryl Landon, Brett Butler, Clifton Taulbert, Babbie Mason, Michael Medved, Sandi Patty, Charlie Daniels, and more! Their stories are intimate, poignant, and sure to inspire and motivate you as you listen for God's message in your own life!

(cloth)   ISBN 1892016117 $18.95

Since Life Isn't a Game, These Are God's Rules: Finding Joy & Fulfillment in God's Ten Commandments

Kathy Collard Miller

Life is often referred to as a game, but God didn't create us because he was short on game pieces. To succeed in life, you'll need to know God's rules. In this book, Kathy Collard Miller explains the meaning of each of the Ten Commandments with fresh application for today. Each chapter includes Scripture and quotes from some of our most beloved Christian authors including Billy Graham, Patsy Clairmont, Liz Curtis Higgs, and more! Sure to renew your understanding of God's rules.

(cloth)   ISBN 189201615X $16.95

God's Little Rule Book: Simple Rules to Bring Joy & Happiness to Your Life

Starburst Publishers

Let this little book of God's rules be your personal guide to a more joyful life. Brimming with easily applicable rules, this book is sure to inspire and motivate you! Each rule includes corresponding Scripture and a practical tip that will help to incorporate God's rules into everyday life. Simple enough to fit into a busy schedule, yet powerful enough to be life changing!

(trade paper)   ISBN 1892016168 $6.95

Life's Little Rule Book: Simple Rules to Bring Joy & Happiness to Your Life

Starburst Publishers

Let this little book inspire you to live a happier life! The pages are filled with timeless rules such as, "Learn to cook, you'll always be in demand!" and "Help something grow." Each rule is combined with a reflective quote and a simple suggestion to help the reader incorporate the rule into everyday life.

(trade paper)   ISBN 1892016176 $6.95

God's Abundance

Edited by Kathy Collard Miller

Over 100,000 sold! This day-by-day inspirational is a collection of thoughts by leading Christian writers such as Patsy Clairmont, Jill Briscoe, Liz Curtis Higgs, and Naomi Rhode. *God's Abundance* is based on God's Word for a simpler, yet more abundant life. Learn to make all aspects of your life—personal, business, financial, relationships, even housework a "spiritual abundance of simplicity."

(cloth)   ISBN 0914984977 $19.95

Promises of God's Abundance

Edited by Kathy Collard Miller

Subtitled: *For a More Meaningful Life*. The Bible is filled with God's promises for an abundant life. *Promises of God's Abundance* is written in the same way as the best-selling *God's Abundance*. It will help you discover these promises and show you how simple obedience is the key to an abundant life. Scripture, questions for growth, and a simple thought for the day will guide you to a more meaningful life.

(trade paper)   ISBN 0914984098 $9.95

Stories of God's Abundance for a More Joyful Life

Compiled by Kathy Collard Miller

Like its successful predecessor, *God's Abundance* (100,000 sold), this book is filled with beautiful, inspirational, real life stories. Those telling their stories of God share scriptures and insights that readers can apply to their daily lives. Renew your faith in life's small miracles and challenge yourself to allow God to lead the way as you find the source of abundant living for all your relationships.

(trade paper)   ISBN 1892016060 $12.95

More of Him, Less of Me

Jan Christiansen

Subtitled: *A Daybook of My Personal Insights, Inspirations & Meditations on the Weigh Down™ Diet*. The insight shared in this year long daybook of inspiration will encourage you on your weight-loss journey, bring you to a deeper relationship with God, and help you improve any facet of your life. Each page includes an essay, Scripture, and a tip-of-the-day that will encourage and uplift you as you trust God to help you achieve your proper weight. Perfect companion guide for anyone on the Weigh Down™ diet!
(cloth) ISBN 1892016001 $17.95

Desert Morsels: A Journal with Encouraging Tidbits from My Journey on the Weigh Down™ Diet

Jan Christiansen

When Jan Christiansen set out to lose weight on the Weigh Down™ diet she got more than she bargained for! In addition to *losing* over 35 pounds and *gaining* a closer relationship with God, Jan discovered a gift—her ability to entertain and comfort fellow dieters! Jan's inspiring website led to the release of her best-selling first book, *More of Him, Less of Me*. Now, Jan serves another helping of *her* wit and *His* wisdom in this lovely companion journal. Includes inspiring Scripture, insightful comments, stories from readers, room for the reader's personal reflection, and *Plenty of Attitude* (p-attitude).
(cloth) ISBN 1892016214 $16.95

On the Brink

Daymond R. Duck

Subtitled: *Easy-to-Understand End-Time Bible Prophecy*. From the author of *Revelation* and *Daniel—God's Word for the Biblically-Inept™*, *On the Brink* is organized in biblical sequence and written with simplicity so that any reader will easily understand end-time prophecy. Ideal for use as a handy reference book.
(trade paper) ISBN 0914984586 $11.95

Purchasing Information

www.starburstpublishers.com

Books are available from your favorite bookstore, either from current stock or special order. To assist bookstores in locating your selection, be sure to give title, author, and ISBN. If unable to purchase from a bookstore, you may order direct from STARBURST PUBLISHERS. When ordering please enclose full payment plus shipping and handling as follows:

Post Office (4th class)
$3.00 with a purchase of up to $20.00
$4.00 ($20.01–$50.00)
5% of purchase price for purchases of $50.01 and up

United Parcel Service (UPS)
$4.50 (up to $20.00)
$6.00 ($20.01–$50.00)
7% ($50.01 and up)

Canada
$5.00 (up to $35.00)
15% ($35.01 and up)

Overseas
$5.00 (up to $25.00)
20% ($25.01 and up)

Payment in U.S. funds only. Please allow two to three weeks minimum (longer overseas) for delivery. Make checks payable to and mail to:

Starburst Publishers® • P.O. Box 4123 • Lancaster, PA 17604

Credit card orders may be placed by calling 1-800-441-1456, Mon–Fri, 8:30 A.M. to 5:30 P.M. Eastern Standard Time. Prices are subject to change without notice. Catalogs are available for a 9 x 12 self-addressed envelope with four first-class stamps.

NOTES

NOTES